DAILY PRAYER 2021

Sunday Year B ◆ Weekday Year I

*A book of prayer for each
day of the liturgical year.*

Edrianne Ezell
Deacon Kurt Heinrich
Mary Heinrich
Timothy A. Johnston

LTP
LITURGY
TRAINING
PUBLICATIONS

Nihil Obstat
Rev. Mr. Daniel G. Welter, JD
Chancellor
Archdiocese of Chicago
March 13, 2020

Imprimatur
Most Rev. Ronald A. Hicks
Vicar General
Archdiocese of Chicago
March 13, 2020

The *Nihil Obstat* and *Imprimatur* are declarations that the material is free from doctrinal or moral error, and thus is granted permission to publish in accordance with c. 827. No legal responsibility is assumed by the grant of this permission. No implications is contained herein that those who have granted the *Nihil Obstat* and *Imprimatur* agree with the content, opinions, or statements expressed.

DAILY PRAYER 2021 © 2020 Archdiocese of Chicago: Liturgy Training Publications, 3949 South Racine Avenue, Chicago, IL 60609; 800-933-1800; fax: 800-933-7094; email: orders@ltp.org; website: www.LTP.org. All rights reserved.

Daily Prayer is based in part on the pattern established in *Children's Daily Prayer*, by Elizabeth McMahon Jeep. This book was edited by Timothy A. Johnston. Michael A. Dodd was the production editor, and Kari Nicholls was the designer and production artist.

Printed in the United States of America

ISBN: 978-1-61671-542-7

DP21

Table of Contents

Introduction

Rejoice always.
Pray without ceasing.
In all circumstances give thanks,
for this is the will of God for
you in Christ Jesus.

1 Thessalonians 5:16–18

Welcome to Daily Prayer 2021, Sunday Year B and Weekday Year I. This edition of the well-loved prayer book provides a familiar order of prayer for each day of the liturgical year, from the First Sunday of Advent, November 29, 2020, through December 31, 2021. Readings from the daily Mass are provided, and the prayer texts and reflections are connected to the liturgical time, solemnities, feasts of the Lord, and the memorials of the saints. The prayers on these pages will inspire and bring you to a deeper appreciation for the Word that is proclaimed and for the Eucharist that is shared in the liturgical life of the Church.

The Order of Prayer

Daily Prayer 2021 follows a simple order of prayer:

- Sign of the Cross and Opening Verse
- Psalm
- Scripture Reading
- Reflection
- Prayer of the Faithful
- Lord's Prayer
- Closing Prayer
- Sign of the Cross and Closing Verse

This order remains consistent for each day of the liturgical year, allowing its repetition to become part of your daily rhythm and routine.

Daily Prayer 2021 is organized by liturgical time, and the Psalter is located in the back of the book (pages 400–422). Everything you need is conveniently contained in this resource. Refer to the table of contents for easy reference.

DAILY HEADING

Daily Prayer 2021 is easy to use. A heading is provided for each day of prayer so you will always know where you are and what you should pray. The heading includes the date and the name of the liturgical observance. Typically, optional memorials are not celebrated in *Daily Prayer 2021*; however, when celebrated, the optional memorial will be noted in the heading. The liturgical observances are those according to the norms prescribed by the Secretariat of Divine Worship.

OPENING AND CLOSING VERSICLE WITH SIGN OF THE CROSS

The order of prayer begins each day with the Sign of the Cross and a versicle, or opening verse. The versicles are taken from the refrains proper to the Responsorial Psalms from the Mass; antiphons from *The Liturgy of the Hours* and *The Roman Missal*; verses from the Acclamation before the Gospel (*Lectionary for Mass*); and lines from Scripture, especially the psalms.

PSALMODY

The psalms are an important part of Catholic prayer. As poetic readings from Sacred Scripture, the psalms reflect upon God's saving work in various ways—praise, thanksgiving, and lamentation. The psalms in *Daily Prayer 2021* have been selected for their liturgical significance.

READING

Each day of prayer includes a reading from the daily Mass. This enables further reflection upon the Word of God proclaimed during the Eucharistic celebration (Mass)—the source and summit of our faith. On some days, excerpts, not the full text, from the Scripture passage have been selected. The Gospel is used for each Sunday, solemnity, and feast of the Lord. When the Scripture reading is taken from the observed Memorial or Commons, it is noted.

REFLECTION

The authors for this year have provided insights for meditation and reflection. These reflections guide the reader to a deeper relationship with God, neighbor, and self.

UNIVERSAL PRAYER

The Universal Prayer, sometimes referred to as the Prayer of the Faithful, is a prayer of the baptized who, through Christ, voice their concerns to God regarding the Church, the world, the oppressed, local needs, and other concerns. Thus, the prayers in this book connect the individual and small faith groups to the universal Church and those in most need of God's love and mercy. Although specific prayers are provided in this resource, others may be added.

THE LORD'S PRAYER

Jesus taught us how to pray. It is fitting to follow the Universal Prayer with the Lord's Prayer, for it encapsulates the humility and reverence we give to our God—and neighbor—while asking for his mercy and forgiveness.

When praying in a group, the leader may introduce the Lord's Prayer after the intercessions in these or similar words:

◆ Gathering these and all our unspoken prayers, we pray as Jesus taught us.

◆ Now let us offer together the prayer Jesus taught us.

◆ Now, let us raise our voices in prayer as we say: Our Father . . .

CLOSING PRAYER

The closing prayer follows the form of the traditional Collect. This prayer "is usually addressed to God the Father, through Christ, in the Holy Spirit" (*General Instruction of the Roman Missal*, 54). Essentially, this prayer "collects" our daily prayer, the prayers found in this book, and those of our hearts and minds, those as individuals or groups, into one Trinitarian prayer, concluding with our assent of faith in the response "Amen."

Using the Book

This resource may be used by individuals, families, or prayer groups; on retreats; to begin meetings or catechetical sessions, formational and youth ministry events; or as prayer with the aged, sick, and homebound. The prayers may be used at any time during the day, and given this book's convenient size, it is easily transported to meet various prayer needs and situations.

The order of prayer may be prayed silently or, especially for group prayer, prayed aloud. If used for prayer gatherings, it might be helpful to designate someone to open the prayer, to lead the Universal Prayer, to begin the Lord's Prayer, and to conclude the prayer. Select an additional volunteer to proclaim the reading. Allow the faithful to read the psalm together either as an entire group, or divide the stanzas among the faithful with alternating recitation.

Feel free to adapt these prayers for specific needs—intercessions (or petitions) may be added, music may begin and conclude the service, and the psalm response to the Universal Prayer and the Lord's Prayer may be chanted or sung.

Other Uses for Daily Prayer

Daily Prayer 2021 also may be used in other situations or for various needs.

◆ Use the Prayer of the Faithful during Mass. Since this book contains prayers for each day of the liturgical year, there are intercessions for every day of the year for Mass.

◆ Use the included reflections as homily sparkers and catechetical tools.

Customer Feedback

Daily Prayer 2021 is the twentieth edition of an annual publication; *Daily Prayer 2022* is already being prepared. Because it is an annual, it can be changed from year to year to become a better tool for your daily prayer. As you use this book and adapt it for yourself, you may have ideas about how it can be made more useful for your prayer. Feel free to email us at DailyPrayer@LTP.org.

About the Authors

EDRIANNE EZELL holds an MDIV from the Weston Jesuit School of Theology and a bachelor's degree in English literature and studies in religion from the University of Michigan. Unless otherwise noted, Ms. Ezell authored the texts for November 29–December 31, 2020 and January 1–May 1, 2021.

KURT HEINRICH, a deacon of the Diocese of Des Moines, holds a bachelor's degree in religious studies from Loras College. He has taught high school religion at Dowling Catholic High School for twenty-seven years. Unless otherwise noted, Deacon Heinrich authored the texts for September 23–December 31, 2021.

MARY HEINRICH holds an MA in pastoral ministry from the Aquinas Institute of Theology and a bachelor's degree in religious studies from Mount Mercy College. Unless otherwise noted, Ms. Heinrich authored the texts for June 16–September 22, 2021.

TIMOTHY A. JOHNSTON holds an MA in liturgical studies from St. John's School of Theology and Seminary, an MA in Catholic doctrine from Marquette University, and a bachelor's degree in music education from Quincy University. Mr. Johnston is currently an editor and liturgical training consultant with Liturgy Training Publications. As editor of this resource, Mr. Johnston contributed significantly to the Universal Prayer and final Collects throughout the resource.

✝ Let your face shine on us, that we may be saved.

Psalm 80 *page 412*

Reading *Mark 13:33–37*

Jesus said to his disciples: "Be watchful! Be alert! You do not know when the time will come. It is like a man traveling abroad. He leaves home and places his servants in charge, each with his own work, and orders the gatekeeper to be on the watch. Watch, therefore; you do not know when the lord of the house is coming, whether in the evening, or at midnight, or at cockcrow, or in the morning. May he not come suddenly and find you sleeping. What I say to you, I say to all: 'Watch!'"

Reflection

Our Gospel for this new liturgical year is a reminder that Jesus will come again. As we watch and wait, hope and pray, we also set about fulfilling our own particular tasks, the work that we must continue doing until the end. During this season of watchful preparedness we pause to ask ourselves what work Christ has entrusted to us and how well we are fulfilling our obligations in the household of faith.

Prayers *others may be added*

Mindful of our Lord's coming,
we pray:

♦ Keep us ever watchful, O Lord.

For your holy Church entering this Advent season, we pray: ♦ For leaders of nations, we pray: ♦ For those searching to know God's will, we pray: ♦ For friends and family who have lost hope, we pray: ♦

Our Father . . .

God our Father,
we are your servants,
the work of your hands.
Renew your spirit of holiness in us this
   Advent season.
Make us attentive to your presence,
and keep us faithful
   in our service to you.
Through Christ our Lord.
Amen.

✝ Let your face shine on us, that we may be saved.

✝ Let your face shine on us, that we may be saved.

Psalm 80 *page 412*

Reading *Romans 10:9–10*

Brothers and sisters: If you confess with your mouth that Jesus is Lord and believe in your heart that God raised him from the dead, you will be saved. For one believes with the heart and so is justified, and one confesses with the mouth and so is saved.

Reflection

A wonderful thing about our salvation is that we don't have to earn it. We can't save ourselves. Salvation is a gift from our infinitely loving God. St. Andrew and the other disciples told people about Jesus because they themselves had experienced freedom not only from sin and death but also from the terror of not being worthy of entering God's love. Today people still need to hear this good news, and they need to hear it from us.

Prayers *others may be added*

Mindful of our Lord's coming, we pray:

◆ Keep us ever watchful, O Lord.

For the Church as it brings light and hope to those in the shadows, we pray: ◆ For missionaries whom God sends to share the story of salvation, we pray: ◆ For those suffering from clinical depression, we pray: ◆ For those called to evangelize, we pray: ◆

Our Father . . .

Lord of all,
without you there is only sorrow
    and emptiness.
Enrich all who call upon you
    until there is no one left
    who does not know of your love
    and mercy.
Through Christ our Lord.
Amen.

✝ Let your face shine on us, that we may be saved.

✝ Let your face shine on us, that we may be saved.

Psalm 80 — page 412

Reading — Isaiah 11:1–3, 6–9

On that day, / A shoot shall sprout from the stump of Jesse, / and from his roots a bud shall blossom. / The Spirit of the LORD shall rest upon him: / a Spirit of wisdom and of understanding, / A Spirit of counsel and of strength, / a spirit of knowledge and fear of the LORD, / and his delight shall be the fear of the LORD. / Not by appearance shall he judge, / nor by hearsay shall he decide . . .

Then the wolf shall be a guest of the lamb, / and the leopard shall lie down with the kid; / The calf and the young lion shall browse together, / with a little child to guide them. / The cow and the bear shall be neighbors, / together their young shall rest; / the lion shall eat hay like the ox. / The baby shall play by the cobra's den, / and the child lay his hand on the adder's lair. / There shall be no harm or ruin on all my holy mountain; / for the earth shall be filled with knowledge of the LORD, / as water covers the sea.

Reflection

"Fear of the LORD*"* doesn't mean that people are afraid of God. It means they put God first in all that they do. God's spirit fills people who act with such a perfect reverence. When God's Kingdom comes in its fullness, even nature itself will fear God: predators will stop hunting and will eat hay peaceably with their prey. Violence and predation will end. Advent invites us to ask ourselves if we truly long for such a kingdom. Are we striving to be peaceful people who put God first in our lives?

Prayers — others may be added

Mindful of our Lord's coming, we pray:

◆ Keep us ever watchful, O Lord.

For the Church as she strives to be a model of wisdom, justice, and peace, we pray: ◆ For leaders striving to end corruption and inequality in their homelands, we pray: ◆ For those fleeing war and those trapped in conflict zones, we pray: ◆ For a deep reverence for all of God's creation, we pray: ◆

Our Father . . .

God of all creation,
the world awaits the transforming power
    of your grace.
As we watch for your Son's return,
fill us with the gifts of your Spirit.
Help us to put you first
    in all that we do.
Through our Lord Jesus Christ, your Son,
who lives and reigns with you
    in the unity of the Holy Spirit,
one God, forever and ever.
Amen.

✝ Let your face shine on us, that we may be saved.

✝ Let your face shine on us, that we may be saved.

Psalm 80
page 412

Reading
Isaiah 25:6–9

On this mountain the LORD of hosts / will provide for all peoples / A feast of rich food and choice wines. / On this mountain he will destroy / the veil that veils all peoples. / The web that is woven over all nations; / he will destroy death forever. / The LORD God will wipe away / the tears from every face; / The reproach of his people he will remove / from the whole earth; for the LORD has spoken.

On that day it will be said: / "Behold our God, to whom we looked to save us!"

Reflection

One of the great images of salvation in the Old Testament is the feast, a banquet of delicious and endless food. Given the absence of grocery stores and the unpredictability of crop yields, this description of God's promised future would have been deeply consoling. Although it is centuries later and some of us enjoy too much food, the prophet's words still remind us that God alone can satisfy our truest and deepest hungers.

Prayers
others may be added

Mindful of our Lord's coming, we pray:

◆ Keep us ever watchful, O Lord.

For the Church as it advocates for the least among us, we pray: ◆ For leaders of nations as they advocate to alleviate poverty and disease, we pray: ◆ For those struggling to provide for their families, we pray: ◆ For all who have died and for those who mourn them, we pray: ◆

Our Father . . .

Lord of Hosts,
your Son has given us a foretaste of life
  in your kingdom by sustaining us with
  his body and blood.
Draw all people to his truth and goodness.
Keep us from filling ourselves with
  things that will leave us feeling empty.
Help us bring our real needs to you
and to accept all that you offer us.
Through Christ our Lord.
Amen.

✝ Let your face shine on us, that we may be saved.

Thursday, December 3, 2020
Memorial of St. Francis Xavier, Priest

☩ Let your face shine on us, that we may be saved.

Psalm 80
page 412

Reading
Matthew 7:21, 24–27

Jesus said to his disciples: "Not everyone who says to me, 'Lord, Lord,' will enter the Kingdom of heaven, but only the one who does the will of my Father in heaven.

"Everyone who listens to these words of mine and acts on them will be like a wise man who built his house on rock. The rain fell, the floods came, and the winds blew and buffeted the house. But it did not collapse; it had been set solidly on rock. And everyone who listens to these words of mine but does not act on them will be like a fool who built his house on sand. The rain fell, the floods came, and the winds blew and buffeted the house. And it collapsed and was completely ruined."

Reflection

It is easy to say that Jesus is Lord. It is much harder to build our lives on his word and example. St. Francis Xavier allowed God to rebuild his life. He left a life of privilege to become a Jesuit and then a missionary in Asia. The changes in our own lives might not be so dramatic, but we must still show that Christ is the foundation of our lives. If we merely claim to believe in Jesus, then our lives and all we have built will eventually crumble and fall apart.

Prayers
others may be added

Mindful of our Lord's coming, we pray:

◆ Keep us ever watchful, O Lord.

May the Church constantly inspect its foundation to ensure that it stands solidly on Christ, we pray: ◆ May public officials strive to live and serve with integrity, we pray: ◆ May the Church of Christ in Asia be filled with the life of the Holy Spirit, we pray: ◆ May those who work in construction and manual labor remain safe from all harm, we pray: ◆

Our Father . . .

Lord Jesus,
you are the foundation that endures
    forever.
Keep us true to the faith we profess.
Whatever challenges come our way,
whatever hardships and dangers we face,
keep us standing solidly upon you,
who live and reign with God the Father
in the unity of the Holy Spirit,
one God, forever and ever.
Amen.

☩ Let your face shine on us, that we may be saved.

✝ Let your face shine on us, that we may be saved.

Psalm 80 *page 412*

Reading *Matthew 9:27–31*

As Jesus passed by, two blind men followed him, crying out, "Son of David, have pity on us!" When he entered the house, the blind men approached him and Jesus said to them, "Do you believe that I can do this?" "Yes, Lord," they said to him. Then he touched their eyes and said, "Let it be done for you according to your faith." And their eyes were opened. Jesus warned them sternly, "See that no one knows about this." But they went out and spread word of him through all that land.

Reflection

Although physically blind, the two men realize that Jesus is the descendant of David, the Messiah their people have long awaited. Their faith that Jesus will bring about God's Kingdom makes them persistent. First, they call out to Jesus. Then, when he seems to ignore them, they follow him right into the house and declare with utter conviction that he can heal them. And so he does. How do you need to be healed?

Prayers *others may be added*

Mindful of our Lord's coming,
we pray:

◆ Keep us ever watchful, O Lord.

May the faith of the Church persist in the face of disbelief, pain, and sin, we pray: ◆ May those who seek deeper meaning in their lives find their salvation in Christ, we pray: ◆ May medical professionals, especially those who specialize in eye diseases, grow in knowledge we pray: ◆ May those with physical disabilities, especially the visually impaired, know Christ's healing power, we pray: ◆

Our Father . . .

Heavenly Father,
we cry out for you
    to put an end to suffering.
Strengthen our faith when we are in pain.
Fill our minds with the vision
    of your coming kingdom,
and keep our eyes and our hearts
fixed on your Son,
    Jesus Christ, our healer,
who lives and reigns with you
in the unity of the Holy Spirit,
one God, forever and ever.
Amen.

✝ Let your face shine on us, that we may be saved.

✝ Let your face shine on us, that we may be saved.

Psalm 80 *page 412*

Reading *Isaiah 30:23–26*

[Thus says the Lord GOD:] / He will give rain for the seed / that you sow in the ground, / And the wheat that the soil produces / will be rich and abundant. / On that day your flock will be given pasture / and the lamb will graze in spacious meadows; / The oxen and the asses that till the ground / will eat silage tossed to them / with shovel and pitchfork. / Upon every high mountain and lofty hill / there will be streams of running water. / On the day of the great slaughter, / when the towers fall, / The light of the moon will be like that of the sun / and the light of the sun / will be seven times greater / like the light of seven days. / On the day the LORD binds up the wounds of his people, / he will heal the bruises left by his blows.

Reflection

Passages like these shape our vision of God's Kingdom. Abundance, prosperity, comfort, wisdom, righteousness, healing —all of which shape our hope in what is to come. Our prayers this Advent are for our Lord Jesus, the Good Shepherd, to gather us all into this new world, a world transformed and perfected by God.

Prayers *others may be added*

Mindful of our Lord's coming,
we pray:

◆ Keep us ever watchful, O Lord.

May the Church boldly proclaim the beauty and consolation of God's kingdom, we pray: ◆ May leaders of developing nations ensure that basic needs are provided for their people, we pray: ◆ May those who work in agriculture or with livestock, be blessed with abundance, we pray: ◆ May those who have died be welcomed at the heavenly banquet, we pray:

Our Father . . .

Holy Lord, our true Teacher,
our wants and desires
make it hard to see the goodness you
    offer us.
Direct our gaze to the path you would
    have us walk.
Keep us striding down the right path,
confident that we will come fully
    into your presence in the end.
We ask this through our Lord Jesus
    Christ, your Son,
who lives and reigns with you
in the unity of the Holy Spirit,
one God, forever and ever.
Amen.

✝ Let your face shine on us, that we may be saved.

✝ Prepare the way of the Lord!

Psalm 85 *page 413*

Reading *Mark 1:1–5, 7–8*

The beginning of the gospel of Jesus Christ the Son of God.

As it is written in Isaiah the prophet: / *Behold, I am sending my messenger ahead of you; / he will prepare your way. / A voice of one crying out in the desert: / "Prepare the way of the Lord, / make straight his paths."* / John the Baptist appeared in the desert proclaiming a baptism of repentance for the forgiveness of sins. People of the whole Judean countryside and all the inhabitants of Jerusalem were going out to him and were being baptized by him in the Jordan River as they acknowledged their sins. . . . And this is what he proclaimed: "One mightier than I is coming after me. I am not worthy to stoop and loosen the thongs of his sandals. I have baptized you with water; he will baptize you with the Holy Spirit."

Reflection

Waves of people go out to be baptized by John, but some people must have hesitated. As eager as they were for God to change their world, they must also have wondered what the changes would mean for them. Change makes us uncomfortable, even when we yearn for it. This season of preparation invites us to consider not only how our lives could keep changing, but also how willing we are to let God make such changes.

Prayers *others may be added*

Trusting in the God of our salvation, we pray:

♦ Draw near to us, O Lord.

For the Church as she listens to the transforming call of the Holy Spirit, we pray: ♦ For those seeking to reform government institutions for the betterment of those they serve, we pray: ♦ For those whose lives are in transition, we pray: ♦ For those who seek the stability of love in a world of change and upheaval, we pray: ♦

Our Father . . .

Gracious Father,
you are unchanging in your love for us.
Help us to answer your call to grow
    in holiness
and to mirror your love to others.
May each day bring us closer to the
    perfection of your love within us.
We ask this through our Lord Jesus
    Christ, your Son,
who lives and reigns with you
in the unity of the Holy Spirit,
one God, forever and ever.
Amen.

✝ Prepare the way of the Lord!

✝ Prepare the way of the Lord!

Psalm 85   *page 413*

Reading   *Luke 5:18–24*

And some men brought on a stretcher a man who was paralyzed; they were trying to bring him in and set him in his presence. But not finding a way to bring him in because of the crowd, they went up on the roof and lowered him on the stretcher through the tiles into the middle in front of Jesus. When Jesus saw their faith, he said, "As for you, your sins are forgiven."

Then the scribes and Pharisees began to ask themselves, "Who is this who speaks blasphemies? Who but God alone can forgive sins?" Jesus knew their thoughts and said to them in reply, "What are you thinking in your hearts? Which is easier, to say, 'Your sins are forgiven,' or to say, 'Rise and walk'? But that you may know that the Son of Man has authority on earth to forgive sins" — he said to the man who was paralyzed, "I say to you, rise, pick up your stretcher, and go home."

Reflection

It's easy to tell someone that his sins are forgiven because no one can prove or disprove the forgiveness. In the face of skepticism, Jesus verifies the forgiveness by healing the man. There is now no mistaking the truth: God extends mercy through Jesus. Yet people were so uncomfortable by this gift of forgiveness that they could not accept it. We, too, may react with astonishment and even skepticism at the offer of a gift we have done nothing to earn.

Prayers   *others may be added*

Trusting in the God of our salvation, we pray:

◆ **Draw near to us, O Lord.**

May the Church model both the giving and receiving of forgiveness, we pray: ◆ May national leaders strive for reconciliation, especially when they serve people devastated by violence, we pray: ◆ May each of us strive for reconciliation, we pray: ◆ May those seeking the salvation of Christ, grow in holiness and peace, we pray:

Our Father . . .

Father of Mercy,
we are preparing to celebrate
   the incarnation,
      the gift of your mercy come among us
      in the flesh.
Help us to welcome this tremendous gift.
Keep us from ever taking your
   forgiveness for granted.
Through Christ our Lord.
Amen.

✝ Prepare the way of the Lord!

Tuesday, December 8, 2020
Solemnity of the Immaculate Conception
of the Blessed Virgin Mary

✝ May it be done to me according to your word.

Canticle of Mary *page 421*

Reading *Luke 1:26–30a, 35b–38*

The angel Gabriel was sent from God to a town of Galilee called Nazareth, to a virgin betrothed to a man named Joseph, of the house of David, and the virgin's name was Mary. And coming to her, he said, "Hail, full of grace! The Lord is with you." But she was greatly troubled at what was said and pondered what sort of greeting this might be. Then the angel said to her, "Do not be afraid, Mary, . . . the Holy Spirit will come upon you, and the power of the Most High will overshadow you. Therefore the child to be born will be called holy, the Son of God. And behold, Elizabeth, your relative, has also conceived a son in her old age, and this is the sixth month for her who was called barren; for nothing will be impossible for God." Mary said, "Behold, I am the handmaid of the Lord. May it be done to me according to your word."

Reflection

The angel Gabriel came to a young, poor woman who lived in a small, insignificant village. He assured her that she would bear a child who would bring about a new era for her people. The woman is startled and hesitant, yet she offers herself up to God's will. No matter how insignificant we might think we are, we can also do significant things by saying *yes* to God and bearing the divine within us.

Prayers *others may be added*

Trusting in the God of our salvation, we pray:

♦ Draw near to us, O Lord.

For the Church's ordained and lay ministers, we pray: ♦ For governments and all political leaders, we pray: ♦ For single parents and those who are alone, we pray: ♦ For children and teens in foster care, we pray:

Our Father . . .

Lord of heaven and earth,
you sent your Son into the care of a
    woman both humble and courageous.
Grant us such faith so that we, too,
may be bravely obedient to your will.
We ask this through our Lord Jesus
    Christ, your Son,
who lives and reigns with you
in the unity of the Holy Spirit,
one God, forever and ever.
Amen.

✝ May it be done to me according to your word.

Wednesday, December 9, 2020
Advent Weekday

✝ Prepare the way of the Lord!

Psalm 85   *page 413*

Reading   *Isaiah 40:25–31*

To whom can you liken me as an equal? / says the Holy One. / Lift up your eyes on high / and see who has created these things: / He leads out their army and numbers them, / calling them all by name. / By his great might and the strength of his power / not one of them is missing! / Why, O Jacob, do you say / and declare, O Israel, / "My way is hidden from the Lord, / and my right is disregarded by my God"?

Do you not know / or have you not heard? / The Lord is the eternal God, / creator of the ends of the earth. / He does not faint nor grow weary, / and his knowledge is beyond scrutiny. / He gives strength to the fainting; / for the weak he makes vigor abound. / Though young men faint and grow weary, / and youths stagger and fall, / They that hope in the Lord will renew their strength, / they will soar as with eagles' wings; / They will run and not grow weary, / walk and not grow faint.

Reflection

God tells his people to look up at the stars, for it is by his power alone that they hang in the sky. God gives this very same strength to his people. What sustains the heavens, sustains us. When we feel weak, overwhelmed, or inconsolable, God offers us his tireless strength. That strength doesn't only enable us to move forward, it also enables us to walk with ever-greater confidence, endurance, and joy.

Prayers   *others may be added*

Trusting in the God of our salvation, we pray:

◆ Draw near to us, O Lord.

For the Church of Christ, we pray: ◆ For civil servants, we pray: ◆ For those who struggle to turn to others for help, we pray: ◆ For those rebuilding their lives after war, disease, or natural disasters, we pray: ◆

Our Father . . .

God, our strength,
when events in our world burden and
 sadden us,
remind us of your Son's wondrous advent
 in our lives.
Lift all worry from us until our hearts
 again soar with hope.
We ask this through our Lord Jesus
 Christ, your Son,
who lives and reigns with you
in the unity of the Holy Spirit,
one God, forever and ever.
Amen.

✝ Prepare the way of the Lord!

✝ Prepare the way of the Lord!

Psalm 85   *page 413*

Reading   *Isaiah 41:13, 17–20*

I am the LORD, your God, / who grasp your right hand; / It is I who say to you, "Fear not, / I will help you." . . . /

The afflicted and the needy seek water in vain, / their tongues are parched with thirst. / I, the LORD, will answer them; / I, the God of Israel, will not forsake them. / I will open up rivers on the bare heights, / and fountains in the broad valleys; / I will turn the desert into a marshland, / and the dry ground into springs of water. / I will plant in the desert the cedar, / acacia, myrtle, and olive; / I will set in the wasteland the cypress, / together with the plane tree and the pine, / That all may see and know, / observe and understand, / That the hand of the LORD has done this, / the Holy One of Israel has created it.

Reflection

The texts of Isaiah chapters 40–55 aim to inspire the displaced Israelites who longed for their homeland. God promises to help them; God promises to provide water and shade for those who undertook the journey home. Centuries later, God provided himself, love incarnate, for people lost in sin. This is love for which we thirst, and it leads to the one homeland for which we long.

Prayers   *others may be added*

Trusting in the God of our salvation, we pray:

◆ Draw near to us, O Lord.

May the baptized faithfully incarnate God's love, we pray: ◆ May governments craft policies that welcome and integrate immigrants and refugees, we pray: ◆ May all people advocate for better stewardship of our planet and its resources, we pray: ◆ May those who live apart from their family and friends live in hope, we pray: ◆

Our Father . . .

Lord, our God,
you accompany us on every step of
    our journey,
no matter how often we wander off.
Guide us when we encounter
    difficult terrain.
Nudge us forward when we want to
    turn back.
Give us strength to reach our true home.
We ask this through our Lord Jesus
    Christ, your Son,
who lives and reigns with you
in the unity of the Holy Spirit,
one God, forever and ever.
Amen.

✝ Prepare the way of the Lord!

✝ Prepare the way of the Lord!

Psalm 85 *page 413*

Reading *Isaiah 48:17–19*

Thus says the LORD, your redeemer, / the Holy One of Israel: / I, the LORD, your God, / teach you what is for your good, / and lead you on the way you should go. / If you would hearken to my commandments, / your prosperity would be like a river, / and your vindication like the waves of the sea; / Your descendants would be like the sand, / and those born of your stock like its grains, / their name never cut off / or blotted out from my presence.

Reflection

God urges us to obey him because he has a broader and much clearer vision of who we are and of what we and our world need. We are too small to take in the whole picture. God's commandments set us on a path that meets those needs. By following God's lead, we gain more than we could have imagined; even more than we could have measured or calculated.

Prayers *others may be added*

Trusting in the God of our salvation, we pray:

◆ Draw near to us, O Lord.

May the Church be guided by the Holy Spirit and obey her commands, we pray: ◆ May world leaders enact laws that ensure the betterment of all nations, we pray: ◆ May visionaries and mystics listen with the ear of their heart, we pray: ◆ May each of us come to know our limitations and trust in God, we pray: ◆

Our Father . . .

Holy One of Israel,
your Son is a gift of unimaginable and
     immeasurable love.
Prepare us to celebrate this gift anew.
Share with us your vision of a world
     overflowing with your divine presence.
Through Christ our Lord.
Amen.

✝ Prepare the way of the Lord!

✝ Prepare the way of the Lord!

Psalm 85
page 413

Reading
Revelation 12:1–6a

A great sign appeared in the sky, a woman clothed with the sun, with the moon under her feet, and on her head a crown of twelve stars. She was with child and wailed aloud in pain as she labored to give birth. Then another sign appeared in the sky; it was a huge red dragon, with seven heads and ten horns, and on its heads were seven diadems. Its tail swept away a third of the stars in the sky and hurled them down to the earth. Then the dragon stood before the woman about to give birth, to devour her child when she gave birth. She gave birth to a son, a male child, destined to rule all the nations with an iron rod. Her child was caught up to God and his throne. The woman herself fled into the desert where she had a place prepared by God.

Reflection

We might not understand all the symbolism of this passage, but the danger is clear. The woman is stalked by an evil so powerful it knocks stars from the sky. Yet God's power is greater. The male child (Jesus) defeats the dragon by his death and resurrection. The woman (the Church and, later, Mary) remains in danger on earth and finds sanctuary in God. Today we honor Mary's particular concern for those who are stalked by the evils of poverty, violence, and corruption.

Prayers
others may be added

Trusting in the God of our salvation, we pray:

◆ Draw near to us, O Lord.

For the Church as she accompanies the poor, refugees, and all those who seek God, we pray: ◆ For world leaders as they strive to promote peace and justice, we pray: ◆ For those who seek the living God in times of trouble, we pray: ◆ For nations and faith communities under Our Lady's patronage, we pray:

Our Father . . .

Almighty Father,
you have shared your Son's triumph over
   evil with us.
Protect us from sin and death,
and give us the courage to confront evil
   in all its forms.
We ask this through our Lord Jesus
   Christ, your Son
who lives and reigns with you
in the unity of the Holy Spirit,
 one God, forever and ever.
Amen.

✝ Prepare the way of the Lord!

✝ In my God is the joy of my soul.

Psalm 34 *page 406*

Reading *John 1:6–8, 19–23*

A man named John was sent from God. He came for testimony, to testify to the light, so that all might believe through him. He was not the light, but came to testify to the light.

And this is the testimony of John. When the Jews from Jerusalem sent priests and Levites to him to ask him, "Who are you?" he admitted and did not deny it, but admitted, "I am not the Christ." So they asked him, "What are you then? Are you Elijah?" And he said, "I am not." "Are you the Prophet?" He answered, "No." So they said to him, "Who are you, so we can give an answer to those who sent us? What do you have to say for yourself?" He said: "I am *the voice of one crying out in the desert, / 'make straight the way of the Lord,' /* as Isaiah the prophet said."

Reflection

John the Baptist gained attention because of his ministry, but he was quick to redirect attention to Jesus. When asked if he was the one for whom the Jewish people had long been waiting, John answered negatively. Even his statement about who he was pointed to Jesus. As Christmas draws closer, we might need to draw our own attention away from secular matters and back to Christ.

Prayers *others may be added*

To the God of peace, we pray:

◆ Accomplish your will, Lord Jesus.

May the Church's many ministries continually direct people's attention to Christ, we pray: ◆ May local and national leaders put the needs of their people first, we pray: ◆ May we reflect the joy of our Lord's coming to those around us, we pray: ◆ May we welcome the grace to set our own egos aside and respond to the needs of others, we pray: ◆

Our Father . . .

Lord of Light,
as we anticipate the Christmas season,
keep us steadfast in prayer and hope.
When our hearts wander,
    draw us gently back to you.
Through Christ our Lord.
Amen.

✝ In my God is the joy of my soul.

Monday, December 14, 2020
Memorial of St. John of the Cross,
Priest and Doctor of the Church

✝ In my God is the joy of my soul.

Psalm 34 *page 406*

Reading *Matthew 21:23–27*

When Jesus had come into the temple area, the chief priests and the elders of the people approached him as he was teaching and said, "By what authority are you doing these things? And who gave you this authority?" Jesus said to them in reply, "I shall ask you one question, and if you answer it for me, then I shall tell you by what authority I do these things. Where was John's baptism from? Was it of heavenly or of human origin?" They discussed this among themselves and said, "If we say 'Of heavenly origin,' he will say to us, 'Then why did you not believe him?' But if we say, 'Of human origin,' we fear the crowd, for they all regard John as a prophet." So they said to Jesus in reply, "We do not know." He himself said to them, "Neither shall I tell you by what authority I do these things."

Reflection

The leaders who question Jesus undermine their own authority by refusing to make a judgment about John the Baptist. At issue is the question of who truly acts for God. Jesus repeatedly demonstrated that he did God's will. Centuries later, John of the Cross was scrutinized and even imprisoned by people who questioned his actions; yet he persisted, and his writings inspire people to this day.

Prayers *others may be added*

To the God of peace, we pray:

◆ Accomplish your will, Lord Jesus.

That the Church follow God unswervingly as it exercises its authority, we pray: ◆ That public officials use their authority for the betterment of those they serve, we pray: ◆ That poets, writers, and artists may find inspiration in Christ, we pray: ◆ For contemplatives who teach us to be still and to deepen our union with God, we pray: ◆

Our Father . . .

Holy Lord,
free us from the fears and distractions
    that lead away from you.
Teach us how to work gracefully through
    the conflicts that arise
    as we strive to follow your Son,
who lives and reigns with you
in the unity of the Holy Spirit,
one God, forever and ever.
Amen.

✝ In my God is the joy of my soul.

✝ In my God is the joy of my soul.

Psalm 34   *page 406*

Reading   *Zephaniah 3:11–13*

On that day / You need not be ashamed / of all your deeds, / your rebellious actions against me; / For then will I remove from your midst / the proud braggarts, / And you shall no longer exalt yourself / on my holy mountain. / But I will leave as a remnant in your midst / a people humble and lowly, / Who shall take refuge in the name of the LORD: / the remnant of Israel. / They shall do no wrong / and speak no lies; / Nor shall there be found in their mouths / a deceitful tongue; / They shall pasture and couch their flocks / with none to disturb them.

Reflection

Zephaniah speaks about a remnant, a small number of people who will obey God in everything. In this remnant, those whom God punishes for turning away from him will see how to live as God intends and that God protects and nurtures those who live uprightly. As we prepare to celebrate the birth of Christ, and as our world awaits the fullness of his kingdom, we must be that remnant.

Prayers   *others may be added*

To the God of peace, we pray:

◆ **Accomplish your will, Lord Jesus.**

May the Church model humility, honesty, and morality, we pray: ◆ May the world welcome the witness of those who live as God intends, we pray: ◆ For those who sincerely seek to understand themselves and others, we pray: ◆ For those who are endangered by their pursuit of justice, we pray: ◆

Our Father . . .

Lord, you alone can turn us away from
    ourselves and back to you.
Forgive our sins.
Purify us.
Help us to call upon your name
    in everything we do.
We ask this through our Lord Jesus
    Christ, your Son,
who lives and reigns with you
in the unity of the Holy Spirit,
one God, forever and ever.
Amen.

✝ In my God is the joy of my soul.

✝ In my God is the joy of my soul.

Psalm 34 *page 406*

Reading *Isaiah 45:18, 21c–24*

For thus says the LORD, / The creator of the heavens, / who is God, / The designer and maker of the earth / who established it, / Not creating it to be a waste, / but designing it to be lived in: / I am the LORD, and there is no other. /

Who announced this from the beginning, / foretold it from of old? / Was it not I, the LORD, / besides whom there is no other God? / There is no just and saving God but me. / Turn to me and be safe, / all you ends of the earth, / for I am God; there is no other! / By myself I swear, / uttering my just decree, / and my unalterable word: / To me every knee shall bend; / by me every tongue shall swear, / Saying, "Only in the LORD / are just deeds and power. / Before him in shame shall come / all who vent their anger against him."

Reflection

Although for centuries God's chosen people had practiced monotheism, they believed in the existence of other gods. In passages like this one, God declares that he alone created all that is and he alone directs history. Those who entrust their lives to him will find salvation. Despite God's revelations of his saving power, most especially in his Son, we too often look for salvation where we won't find it. Advent is a time to set our sights on our true savior.

Prayers *others may be added*

To the God of peace, we pray:

◆ Accomplish your will, Lord Jesus.

For the Church engaged in ecumenical and interreligious dialogue, we pray: ◆ For leaders as they govern, we pray: ◆ For those struggling with addictions, we pray: ◆ For those who entrust themselves to their wealth or power, we pray: ◆

Our Father . . .

Lord of heaven and earth,
the world depends upon you for its
very existence,
yet we often take our lives into our
own hands.
When we forget you,
draw our eyes and hearts
back to your Son,
the perfect revelation
of your eternal and all-powerful love.
Through Christ our Lord.
Amen.

✝ In my God is the joy of my soul.

✝ Come teach us the path of knowledge.

Psalm 72 *page 412*

Reading *Genesis 49:2, 8, 10*

Jacob called his sons and said to them: / "Assemble and listen, sons of Jacob, / listen to Israel, your father. /

"You, Judah, shall your brothers praise / —your hand on the neck of your enemies; / the sons of your father shall bow down to you. . . . / The scepter shall never depart from Judah, / or the mace from between his legs, / While tribute is brought to him, / and he receives the people's homage."

Reflection

In the reign of King David, it was apparent that the tribe of Judah was indeed strong and elevated above the other tribes. David defeated Israel's enemies and inaugurated an era of relative peace. Centuries later, at the time of Jesus' birth, many Jews expected their Messiah to exhibit the same military and political prowess. Although Jesus was born into the tribe of Judah, his strength would manifest itself very differently.

Prayers *others may be added*

With hope and longing, we pray:

◆ Hear us, Wisdom of God Most High.

For those who exercise authority in the Church, we pray: ◆ For those who work tirelessly to resolve conflicts in different parts of the world, we pray: ◆ For soldiers who struggle with the repercussions of war, we pray: ◆ For the Jewish people, our spiritual ancestors, we pray: ◆

Our Father . . .

God Most High,
all power and glory belong to you alone,
yet you force no one to worship you.
As we celebrate the birth of your Son,
may we and all people be inspired
to humble ourselves before you
and to embrace the way of mercy
    and peace.
We ask this through our Lord Jesus
    Christ, your Son,
who lives and reigns with you
in the unity of the Holy Spirit,
one God, forever and ever.
Amen.

✝ Come teach us the path of knowledge.

✝ Come rescue us with your mighty power!

Psalm 72 *page 412*

Reading *Matthew 1:18–21*

This is how the birth of Jesus Christ came about. When his mother Mary was betrothed to Joseph, but before they lived together, she was found with child through the Holy Spirit. Joseph her husband, since he was a righteous man, yet unwilling to expose her to shame, decided to divorce her quietly. Such was his intention when, behold, the angel of the Lord appeared to him in a dream and said, "Joseph, son of David, do not be afraid to take Mary your wife into your home. For it is through the Holy Spirit that this child has been conceived in her. She will bear a son and you are to name him Jesus, because he will save his people from their sins."

Reflection

Joseph has a dream that seems to explain everything, but how could he understand what was happening? No woman in the history of his people had become pregnant through the power of God's Holy Spirit. Yet when Joseph awakens, he does exactly what he was told to do. He must have prayed often and deeply to accept what was happening. If we wish to participate in God's wondrous work in our world, we will also have to spend time listening for God.

Prayers *others may be added*

With hope and longing, we pray:

◆ Hear us, Lord.

For the Church's lay and ordained ministers, we pray: ◆ For all people of the world, we pray: ◆ For spiritual directors, we pray: ◆ For those who fear the voice of God during their prayer, we pray: ◆

Our Father . . .

Jesus, you are Emmanuel.
When you come to carry out your will
   in us,
give us the courage and trust
to do what you command.
As you came to dwell with us,
so may we dwell with you,
who live and reign
   with God the Father
in the unity of the Holy Spirit,
one God, forever and ever.
Amen.

✝ Come rescue us with your mighty power!

✝ Come save us without delay!

Psalm 72 *page 412*

Reading *Judges 13:2–7, 24–25a*

There was a certain man from Zorah, of the clan of the Danites, whose name was Manoah. His wife was barren and had borne no children. An angel of the LORD appeared to the woman and said to her, "Though you are barren and have had no children, yet you will conceive and bear a son. Now, then, be careful to take no wine or strong drink and to eat nothing unclean. As for the son you will conceive and bear, no razor shall touch his head, for this boy is to be consecrated to God from the womb. It is he who will begin the deliverance of Israel from the power of the Philistines."

The woman went and told her husband, "A man of God came to me; he had the appearance of an angel of God, terrible indeed. I did not ask him where he came from, nor did he tell me his name. But he said to me, 'You will be with child and will bear a son. So take neither wine nor strong drink, and eat nothing unclean. For the boy shall be consecrated to God from the womb, until the day of his death.'"

The woman bore a son and named him Samson. The boy grew up and the LORD blessed him; the Spirit of the LORD stirred him.

Reflection

God startles Manoah's wife with the news that she will bear a son who will begin the process of defeating an enemy of her people. God will act on behalf of Israel through her. In response, she and her husband ask how God wants them to raise this new child. As God intervenes in our own lives in ways big and small, we, too, should ask how God wants us to participate in his plan of salvation.

Prayers *others may be added*

With hope and longing, we pray:

◆ Hear us, Root of Jesse's Stem.

For the Church who bears witness to God's grace, we pray: ◆ For community leaders who promote the physical and emotional health of children, we pray: ◆ For couples unable to bear children, we pray: ◆ For people struggling to discern how God is acting in their lives, we pray: ◆

Our Father . . .

God of our salvation,
keep us ever watchful of the ways you are
    acting in our midst.
Make us quick to celebrate your
    movement among us,
and teach us how to participate in your
    saving work.
We ask this through our Lord Jesus
    Christ, your Son,
who lives and reigns with you
in the unity of the Holy Spirit,
one God, forever and ever.
Amen.

✝ Come save us without delay!

✝ Come and free the prisoners
of darkness!

Psalm 72 page 412

Reading Luke 1:26–30a, 35b–38

The angel Gabriel was sent from God to a town of Galilee called Nazareth, to a virgin betrothed to a man named Joseph, of the house of David, and the virgin's name was Mary. And coming to her, he said, "Hail, full of grace! The Lord is with you." But she was greatly troubled at what was said and pondered what sort of greeting this might be. Then the angel said to her, "Do not be afraid, Mary. . . . The Holy Spirit will come upon you, and the power of the Most High will overshadow you. Therefore the child to be born will be called holy, the Son of God. And behold, Elizabeth, your relative, has also conceived a son in her old age, and this is the sixth month for her who was called barren; for nothing will be impossible for God." Mary said, "Behold, I am the handmaid of the Lord. May it be done to me according to your word."

Reflection

Mary, who hasn't moved into the home of her future husband, doesn't understand how she'll become pregnant. The angel explains that she won't conceive in the usual way. Instead, her child will be conceived through the power of God alone. Human beings can participate in salvation, but we cannot initiate it. The story of the virginal conception reminds us that salvation is a gift.

Prayers others may be added

With hope and longing, we pray:

◆ Hear us, Key of David.

May the Church grow in humility as she prepares to celebrate the incarnation, we pray: ◆ May local and national leaders use their resources to strengthen their communities, we pray: ◆ May doctors, especially obstetricians and pediatricians, be filled with wisdom and compassion, we pray: ◆ May engaged couples find strength in Christ, we pray: ◆

Our Father . . .

Gracious Lord,
we are startled by the ways you visit us
    and invite us to participate
    in salvation.
May we be as ready to assent to your will
    as Mary was.
We ask this through our Lord Jesus
    Christ, your Son,
who lives and reigns with you
in the unity of the Holy Spirit,
one God, forever and ever.
Amen.

✝ Come and free the prisoners
of darkness!

✟ Shine on those who dwell in the shadow of death.

Psalm 72 *page 412*

Reading *Luke 1:39–45*

Mary set out in those days and traveled to the hill country in haste to a town of Judah, where she entered the house of Zechariah and greeted Elizabeth. When Elizabeth heard Mary's greeting, the infant leaped in her womb, and Elizabeth, filled with the Holy Spirit, cried out in a loud voice and said, "Most blessed are you among women, and blessed is the fruit of your womb. And how does this happen to me, that the mother of my Lord should come to me? For at the moment the sound of your greeting reached my ears, the infant in my womb leaped for joy. Blessed are you who believed that what was spoken to you by the Lord would be fulfilled."

Reflection

In the midst of affirming her young cousin's faith in God, Elizabeth makes another noteworthy remark. She exclaims with wonder that the mother of her Lord has come to visit her. Such a visit is an occasion of wonder, joy, and celebration. We do not have to try to find God. God comes to us; God is present in our daily living.

Prayers *others may be added*

With hope and longing, we pray:

◆ Hear us, Radiant Dawn.

May joy permeate the Church and inspire others to believe the Gospel, we pray: ◆ May God's blessing come upon all peoples, we pray: ◆ May safety and comfort be with all those who travel, we pray: ◆ May love and friendship fill all those who are alone or apart from family, we pray: ◆

Our Father . . .

Lord of light,
the world awaits the return of your Son.
Vanquish the darkness within us,
and sustain us with joy and hope
 until Christ comes again,
who lives and reigns with you
in the unity of the Holy Spirit,
one God, forever and ever.
Amen.

✟ Shine on those who dwell in the shadow of death.

Tuesday, December 22, 2020
Advent Weekday

✝ Come and save us, whom you formed from the dust!

Psalm 72
page 412

Reading
1 Samuel 1:24–28

In those days, Hannah brought Samuel with her, along with a three-year-old bull, an ephah of flour, and a skin of wine, and presented him at the temple of the LORD in Shiloh. After the boy's father had sacrificed the young bull, Hannah, his mother, approached Eli and said: "Pardon, my lord! As you live, my lord, I am the woman who stood near you here, praying to the LORD. I prayed for this child, and the LORD granted my request. Now I, in turn, give him to the LORD; as long as he lives, he shall be dedicated to the LORD." She left Samuel there.

Reflection

It seems odd that Hannah, after desperately wanting a child, gives him up. In an era of high infant mortality, women played a vital role for their tribe or nation by having children. Mothers ensured the survival of their people. Hannah does not know it, but her act of gratitude has even greater repercussions: her son will become one of Israel's great leaders. Sometimes our gestures of gratitude extend farther than we could have imagined.

Prayers
others may be added

With hope and longing, we pray:

◆ Hear us, King of All Nations.

May those who have dedicated themselves to ministry in the Church find joy and consolation in their work, we pray: ◆ May those in public office administer the financial resources of their people justly and transparently, we pray: ◆ May those who hoard resources, learn to open their hands, we pray: ◆ May we be quick to offer to others what we ourselves have received, we pray: ◆

Our Father . . .

Giver of life,
you answer the deepest prayers of
    our heart.
Help us to dedicate ourselves to you
as you have dedicated yourself to us.
We ask this through our Lord Jesus
    Christ, your Son,
who lives and reigns with you
in the unity of the Holy Spirit,
one God, forever and ever.
Amen.

✝ Come and save us, whom you formed from the dust!

Wednesday, December 23, 2020
Advent Weekday

✟ Come to save us, Lord our God!

Psalm 72 page 412

Reading Malachi 3:1–4, 23–24

Thus says the Lord GOD: / Lo, I am sending my messenger / to prepare the way before me; / And suddenly there will come to the temple / the LORD whom you seek, / And the messenger of the covenant whom you desire. / Yes, he is coming, says the LORD of hosts. / But who will endure the day of his coming? / And who can stand when he appears? / For he is like the refiner's fire, / or like the fuller's lye. / He will sit refining and purifying silver, / and he will purify the sons of Levi, / Refining them like gold or like silver / that they may offer due sacrifice to the LORD. / Then the sacrifice of Judah and Jerusalem / will please the LORD, / as in the days of old, as in years gone by.

Lo, I will send you / Elijah, the prophet, / Before the day of the LORD comes, / the great and terrible day, / To turn the hearts of the fathers to their children, / and the hearts of the children to their fathers, / Lest I come and strike / the land with doom.

Reflection

Christmas is almost here! Yet in the midst of the excitement all around us, we hear these stark prophetic words from Malachi. Our Lord is coming, but we might not want him to. He will scrutinize and purify people, and his judgment could be painful. As Advent ends and we enter our celebration of the birth of Jesus, we ask what more we should do to prepare for his return in glory.

Prayers *others may be added*

With hope and longing, we pray:

◆ Hear us, King and Giver of Law.

May we, the baptized, continually subject ourselves to God's scrutiny and purification, we pray: ◆ May prophets in our midst herald the reign of God, we pray: ◆ May those working in manufacturing industries find dignity in their work, we pray: ◆ May God purify those who have died and bring them into his kingdom, we pray: ◆

Our Father . . .

Jesus, our Emmanuel,
we are sometimes frightened by what
    your advent means for us.
Assure us of your love.
Give us the courage to welcome the ways
    you would have us change,
for we long to be with you,
who live and reign with God the Father
in the unity of the Holy Spirit,
one God, forever and ever.
Amen.

✟ Come to save us, Lord our God!

✝ The promises of the Lord I will sing forever!

Psalm 72 *page 412*

Reading *2 Samuel 7:1–5, 8b–12, 14a, 16*

When King David was settled in his palace, and the LORD had given him rest from his enemies on every side, he said to Nathan the prophet, "Here I am living in a house of cedar, while the ark of God dwells in a tent!" Nathan answered the king, "Go, do whatever you have in mind, for the LORD is with you." But that night the LORD spoke to Nathan and said: "Go, tell my servant David, 'Thus says the LORD: Should you build me a house to dwell in?'

"'It was I who took you from the pasture and from the care of the flock to be commander of my people Israel. I have been with you wherever you went, and I have destroyed all your enemies before you. And I will make you famous like the great ones of the earth. I will fix a place for my people Israel; I will plant them so that they may dwell in their place without further disturbance. Neither shall the wicked continue to afflict them as they did of old, since the time I first appointed judges over my people Israel. I will give you rest from all your enemies. The LORD also reveals to you that he will establish a house for you. And when your time comes and you rest with your ancestors, I will raise up your heir. . . . I will be a father to him, and he shall be a son to me. Your house and your Kingdom shall endure forever before me; your throne shall stand firm forever.'"

Reflection

When King David wishes to build a temple, God replies that he will make a dynasty, of the king. God promises to make David's hereditary line permanent. Only God can ensure permanence, stability, and peace. By calling Jesus "the son of David," we affirm not merely that he descends from David, but that he is the heir whose kingdom God makes firm forever.

Prayers *others may be added*

With hope and longing, we pray:

◆ Hear us, Son of David.

For Christians who gather to celebrate the incarnation, we pray: ◆ For those struggling to ensure stability in nations weakened by years of war, we pray: ◆ For those who have lost their homes, we pray: ◆ For builders, architects, and engineers, we pray: ◆

Our Father . . .

Lord of Hosts,
you vanquish sin and death
and invite us to rest forever in the
    permanence of your kingdom.
In all that we do, keep our eyes fixed on
    that which is eternal.
Through Christ our Lord.
Amen.

✝ The promises of the Lord I will sing forever!

✝ Glory to God in the highest!

Canticle of Zechariah   *page 422*

Reading   *Luke 2:8–14*

Now there were shepherds in that region living in the fields and keeping the night watch over their flock. The angel of the Lord appeared to them and the glory of the Lord shone around them, and they were struck with great fear. The angel said to them, "Do not be afraid; for behold, I proclaim to you good news of great joy that will be for all the people. For today in the city of David a savior has been born for you who is Christ and Lord. And this will be a sign for you: you will find an infant wrapped in swaddling clothes and lying in a manger." And suddenly there was a multitude of the heavenly host with the angel, praising God and saying: / "Glory to God in the highest / and on earth peace to those on whom his favor rests." /

Reflection

Every time we sing the Glory to God, we echo the angels' jubilant proclamation that God has brought us peace. At times, though, events in our lives and in the world seem to contradict God's peace and it becomes as hidden as the King, Savior, Messiah, and Lord who once slept in a manger. In such moments, we listen to the angels, and we join our voices to theirs in a prayerful proclamation.

Prayers   *others may be added*

To God who has visited his people, we pray:

♦ Daybreak from on high, hear our prayer.

May the grace of Christ fill us with unwavering peace, we pray: ♦ May the peace of Christ fill those affected by violence, we pray: ♦ May the abundance of Christ be shown to those who lack the necessities of life, we pray: ♦ May love and healing be with those who are estranged from friends and family, we pray: ♦

Our Father . . .

Prince of Peace,
come fill our world with what only you
    can give:
comfort, healing, joy, wisdom,
    compassion, peace.
We celebrate your light and your glory.
All our hope is in you,
who live and reign with God the Father,
in the unity of the Holy Spirit,
one God, forever and ever.
Amen.

✝ Glory to God in the highest!

✝ Glory to God in the highest!

Canticle of Zechariah *page 422*

Reading *Acts 6:8–10; 7:54–59*

Stephen, filled with grace and power, was working great wonders and signs among the people. Certain members of the so-called Synagogue of Freedmen, Cyrenians, and Alexandrians, and people from Cilicia and Asia, came forward and debated with Stephen, but they could not withstand the wisdom and the spirit with which he spoke.

When they heard this, they were infuriated, and they ground their teeth at him. But he, filled with the Holy Spirit, looked up intently to heaven and saw the glory of God and Jesus standing at the right hand of God, and he said, "Behold, I see the heavens opened and the Son of Man standing at the right hand of God." But they cried out in a loud voice, covered their ears, and rushed upon him together. They threw him out of the city, and began to stone him. . . . As they were stoning Stephen, he called out "Lord Jesus, receive my spirit."

Reflection

Stephen's vision revealed to him the truth of his faith, but holding fast to that faith cost him his life. He died as honorably, but as horrifically as Jesus did. We might not have such courage ourselves. That is okay. Instead, we ask God for the grace to make us courageous in smaller matters. In time, we may even gain the strength to be a bit bolder in our own profession of faith.

Prayers *others may be added*

To God who has visited his people, we pray:

◆ **Daybreak from on high, hear our prayer.**

May we stand in solidarity with those who suffer for their faith in Christ, we pray: ◆ May local and national leaders pursue policies that permit the freedom of religion, we pray: ◆ May God's strength fill those who are attacked because of their faith, we pray: ◆ May St. Stephen watch over those churches and individuals who bear his name, we pray: ◆

Our Father . . .

Heavenly Father,
your Spirit empowered St. Stephen
   to give witness to your Son
   despite the danger.
May we, too, persevere in faith
despite the obstacles we face.
Through Christ our Lord.
Amen.

✝ Glory to God in the highest!

✟ Glory to God in the highest!

Canticle of Zechariah   *page 422*

Reading   *Luke 2:22, 39–40*

When the days were completed for their purification according to the law of Moses, they took [Jesus] up to Jerusalem to present him to the Lord.

When they had fulfilled all the prescriptions of the law of the Lord, they returned to Galilee, to their own town of Nazareth. The child grew and became strong, filled with wisdom; and the favor of God was upon him.

Reflection

Getting to Jerusalem was no easy task for poor Galilean villagers. That they made the journey shows how devout Mary and Joseph were. They were committed to raising their son well, and under their guidance, Jesus flourished. As parents, Mary and Joseph had a vital role to play in forming their son, but their whole village would have helped. Even if we are not parents ourselves, we must still help children to grow and learn.

Prayers   *others may be added*

To God who has visited his people, we pray:

♦ **Daybreak from on high, hear our prayer.**

For families and parishes entrusted with the religious formation of children, we pray: ♦ For families forced apart by economic need, we pray: ♦ For Catholic schools and educators, we pray: ♦ For those who were not raised in loving homes, we pray: ♦

Our Father . . .

God of Israel,
your Son thrived in the care of parents
who were obedient to your word.
Give us the wisdom to aid in the
    formation of children
    in what we say and how we act.
We ask this through our Lord Jesus
    Christ, your Son,
who lives and reigns with you
in the unity of the Holy Spirit,
one God, forever and ever.
Amen.

✟ Glory to God in the highest!

✝ Glory to God in the highest!

Canticle of Zechariah   *page 422*

Reading   *Matthew 2:13–15*

When the magi had departed, behold, the angel of the Lord appeared to Joseph in a dream and said, "Rise, take the child and his mother, flee to Egypt, and stay there until I tell you. Herod is going to search for the child to destroy him." Joseph rose and took the child and his mother by night and departed for Egypt. He stayed there until the death of Herod, that what the Lord had said through the prophet might be fulfilled, / *Out of Egypt I called my son.*

Reflection

This Gospel details the horrendous killing of innocent children. Herod, the tyrant king, feared this "newborn king of the Jews" (Matthew 2). Would this king overthrow his power? Would he disrupt the power hierarchy? We celebrate these innocent martyrs who gave their lives so that Jesus would be spared and, when called out of Egypt, yes, he did disrupt the struggle of power in order to preach the Good News of God's salvation, God's mercy, and God's love. Even today, our world struggles with tyrants seeking power, and many innocent lives are lost in the process.

Prayers   *others may be added*

To God who has visited his people, we pray:

◆ Daybreak from on high, hear our prayer.

May the Church stand in solidarity with the weakest among us, we pray: ◆ May the reign of Christ overthrow the powers of injustice and brutality, we pray: ◆ May leaders of nations work to feed the hungry, protect the innocent, and shelter the homeless, we pray: ◆ May the culture of death be shattered by Christ's unwavering love for all, we pray: ◆

Our Father . . .

God of justice,
you sent your Son to answer the cries
  of the innocent
and to minister to those who call out
  to you for deliverance.
May we never cease to listen to the
  laments of those who suffer
and to trust in your salvation.
We ask this through our Lord Jesus
  Christ, your Son,
who lives and reigns with you
in the unity of the Holy Spirit,
one God, forever and ever.
Amen.

✝ Glory to God in the highest!

✝ Glory to God in the highest!

Canticle of Zechariah   *page 422*

Reading   *1 John 2:3–11*

Beloved: The way we may be sure that we know Jesus is to keep his commandments. Whoever says, "I know him," but does not keep his commandments is a liar, and the truth is not in him. But whoever keeps his word, the love of God is perfected in him. This is the way we are to know we are in union with him: whoever claims to abide in him ought to walk just as he walked.

Beloved, I am writing no new commandment to you but an old commandment that you had from the beginning. The old commandment is the word that you have heard. . . . Whoever says he is in the light, yet hates his brother, is still in the darkness. Whoever loves his brother remains in the light, and there is nothing in him to cause a fall. Whoever hates his brother is in darkness; he walks in darkness and does not know where he is going because the darkness has blinded his eyes.

Reflection

The sign of a healthy Christian community is the love that individual members show one another. Not only do they treat one another with common courtesy, they are also quick to help when someone is in need, no matter what that need is—food, transportation, a friendly visit, anything. To neglect the needs of others is to turn back to the darkness, to turn away from love.

Prayers   *others may be added*

To God who has visited his people, we pray:

◆ **Daybreak from on high, hear our prayer.**

That the Church may be a witness of God's love, we pray: ◆ That political parties work together for the common good of the people, we pray: ◆ That Catholic Charities and other service ministries may be the hands and feet of Christ, we pray: ◆ That converts, whose new Christian faith alienates them from their family and friends, may find love and support in our churches, we pray: ◆

Our Father . . .

Loving Lord,
in baptism we are united to your Body,
    the Church,
which nurtures our life.
Keep us mindful of the ways we can
    nurture others with our loving care.
We ask this through our Lord Jesus
    Christ, your Son,
who lives and reigns with you
in the unity of the Holy Spirit,
one God, forever and ever.
Amen.

✝ Glory to God in the highest!

✝ Glory to God in the highest!

Canticle of Zechariah   *page 422*

Reading   *1 John 2:15–17*

Do not love the world or the things of the world. If anyone loves the world, the love of the Father is not in him. For all that is in the world, sensual lust, enticement for the eyes, and a pretentious life, is not from the Father but is from the world. Yet the world and its enticement are passing away. But whoever does the will of God remains forever.

Reflection

John uses the expression "the world" to sum up everything that is sinful, and contrasts that with everything that comes from God. The world in itself is not bad, but when we become engrossed in material pleasures and selfish ambitions, our love for God dwindles away. We become as empty as our worldly desires. By seeking instead to be filled with God's love, we become part of God, who alone is everlasting.

Prayers   *others may be added*

To God who has visited his people, we pray:

♦ Daybreak from on high, hear our prayer.

That the Church be healed from any earthly ambition, we pray: ♦ That world leaders work to promote the common good and welfare of all people, we pray: ♦ That those who have vowed a life of poverty, share in the richness of God's mercy, we pray: ♦ That those who struggle with addiction and consumerism be set free by God's grace, we pray: ♦

Our Father . . .

Eternal God,
when the things of the world
      feel more real than you,
stir your Spirit within us.
Remind us of what is true
      and lasting.
Fill us with your love.
Help us resist what cannot satisfy
      us in the end.
Through Christ our Lord.
Amen.

✝ Glory to God in the highest!

✝ Glory to God in the highest!

Canticle of Zechariah   *page 422*

Reading   *1 John 2:18–21*

Children, it is the last hour; and just as you heard that the antichrist was coming, so now many antichrists have appeared. Thus we know this is the last hour. They went out from us, but they were not really of our number; if they had been, they would have remained with us. Their desertion shows that none of them was of our number. But you have the anointing that comes from the Holy One, and you all have knowledge. I write to you not because you do not know the truth but because you do, and because every lie is alien to the truth.

Reflection

The antichrists in this passage are not vicious evildoers, but members of the community who have turned away from fundamental Christian teaching. It is always painful and confusing when someone who was part of our community turns away from us. Perhaps they never fully understood or experienced God's love. We are left to reflect on how we can better share God's love and how we too might be drawn away from God's presence.

Prayers   *others may be added*

To God who has visited his people, we pray:

♦ Daybreak from on high, hear our prayer.

May the Church share God's love with wisdom and authenticity, we pray: ♦
May those in public office foster respect and freedom for all believers, we pray: ♦
May God's peace and love come upon all those who have left the Church, we pray: ♦
May each of us be blessed with goodness and health in the coming year, we pray: ♦

Our Father . . .

Holy Lord,
your Spirit makes us one.
When we strain the bonds of fellowship,
strengthen your love within us.
Keep us together as one people
so that others may be drawn to the truth
    of your saving love.
We ask this through our Lord Jesus
    Christ, your Son,
who lives and reigns with you
in the unity of the Holy Spirit,
one God, forever and ever.
Amen.

✝ Glory to God in the highest!

✝ Glory to God in the highest!

Canticle of Zechariah   *page 422*

Reading   *Luke 2:16–20*

The shepherds went in haste to Bethlehem and found Mary and Joseph, and the infant lying in the manger. When they saw this, they made known the message that had been told them about this child. All who heard it were amazed by what had been told them by the shepherds. And Mary kept all these things, reflecting on them in her heart. Then the shepherds returned, glorifying and praising God for all they had heard and seen, just as it had been told to them.

Reflection

Angelic pronouncements about her son clashed with the experience of animals in a stable, the shepherds who came, and the exhaustion Mary experienced. It's no wonder that she pondered what it all meant. God's wondrous promises were unfolding in a way that was utterly insignificant, even burdensome. We should ponder such things in our own hearts. God calls us to be part of his glorious plan, but we can only answer that call by continuing to move forward, no matter how insignificant or burdensome the path before us may be.

Prayers   *others may be added*

To God who has visited his people, we pray:

◆ **Daybreak from on high, hear our prayer.**

May the Church bear Christ to the world with courage and humility, we pray: ◆ May leaders strive in this new year to listen faithfully to the stories of their people, we pray: ◆ May shepherds, veterinarians, and all who work with animals, find joy in their work, we pray: ◆ May those who are faced with challenges find solace in the newborn Christ, we pray: ◆

Our Father . . .

God on high,
Mary bore and raised your Son
    despite the cost.
Give us the courage to do what you
    ask of us.
Fill us with joy
so that nothing may keep us
    from doing your will.
Through Christ our Lord.
Amen.

✝ Glory to God in the highest!

✝ Let the heavens be glad and the earth rejoice!

Psalm 96 *page 413*

Reading *1 John 2:22–28*

Beloved: Who is the liar? Whoever denies that Jesus is the Christ. Whoever denies the Father and the Son, this is the antichrist. Anyone who denies the Son does not have the Father, but whoever confesses the Son has the Father as well.

Let what you heard from the beginning remain in you. If what you heard from the beginning remains in you, then you will remain in the Son and in the Father. And this is the promise that he made us: eternal life. I write you these things about those who would deceive you. As for you, the anointing that you received from him remains in you, so that you do not need anyone to teach you. But his anointing teaches you about everything and is true and not false; just as it taught you, remain in him.

And now, children, remain in him, so that when he appears we may have confidence and not be put to shame by him at his coming.

Reflection

When some people began insisting that Jesus did not perfectly embody God's love, St. John urged his fellow Christians to hold fast to what they had been taught: the Father fully revealed his love in Jesus and brings people into union with him through his Son. If our own faith in God's love seems shaky, then this season of the incarnation is a good time to be still and allow God's love to surround us, fill us, and remain within us.

Prayers *others may be added*

Joyfully, we pray:

◆ Hear us, Savior of the world.

For pastors, teachers, and theologians, we pray: ◆ For local and national leaders, we pray: ◆ For those who do not know God's love, we pray: ◆ For those who wrestle with difficult questions about their faith, we pray: ◆ For those who have died, we pray: ◆

Our Father . . .

O Lord of life,
those who remain in your Son
remain in you and have life itself.
When we waver in faith,
renew us in your love.
Teach us how to encounter your love
   in each moment of our lives.
We ask this through our
   Lord Jesus Christ, your Son,
who lives and reigns with you
in the unity of the Holy Spirit,
one God, forever and ever.
Amen.

✝ Let the heavens be glad and the earth rejoice!

✝ Let the heavens be glad and the earth rejoice!

Psalm 96   *page 413*

Reading   *Matthew 2:1–2, 9–12*

When Jesus was born in Bethlehem of Judea, in the days of King Herod, behold, magi from the east arrived in Jerusalem, saying, "Where is the newborn king of the Jews? We saw his star at its rising and have come to do him homage." . . . After their audience with the king they set out. And behold, the star that they had seen at its rising preceded them, until it came and stopped over the place where the child was. They were over-joyed at seeing the star, and on entering the house they saw the child with Mary his mother. They prostrated themselves and did him homage. Then they opened their treasures and offered him gifts of gold, frankincense, and myrrh. And hav-ing been warned in a dream not to return to Herod, they departed for their country by another way.

Reflection

King Herod and others in Jerusalem were so comfortable with the status quo that they were alarmed rather than excited when the Magi showed up. They forgot their own prophesies, ignored the star, and neglected to bring gifts to the newborn king. As the Christmas season nears its end, we must not forget all we have celebrated. We slowly return to our daily routines, but we bear within us the wonder and joy of the incarnation.

Prayers   *others may be added*

Joyfully, we pray:

◆ Hear us, Savior of the world.

For the Church as she bears the light of the newborn king, we pray: ◆ For those in public office as they work to promote peace and justice, we pray: ◆ For physicists, astronomers, and explorers as they call us to deeper contemplate of God's mystery, we pray: ◆ For those who have lost a sense of wonder, we pray: ◆

Our Father . . .

Lord of glory,
the magi were the first Gentiles
    to witness your salvation.
Christ's saving presence has since spread
    throughout the world.
May we, like the magi,
never cease to celebrate
    the gift of salvation
we have received in your Son,
    our Lord Jesus Christ,
who lives and reigns with you
in the unity of the Holy Spirit,
one God, forever and ever.
Amen.

✝ Let the heavens be glad and the earth rejoice!

☩ Let the heavens be glad and the earth rejoice!

Psalm 96 *page 413*

Reading *Matthew 4:12–17*

When Jesus heard that John had been arrested, he withdrew to Galilee. He left Nazareth and went to live in Capernaum by the sea, in the region of Zebulun and Naphtali, that what had been said through Isaiah the prophet might be fulfilled:

Land of Zebulun and land of Naphtali, / the way to the sea, beyond the Jordan, / Galilee of the Gentiles, / the people who sit in darkness / have seen a great light, / on those dwelling in a land overshadowed by death light has arisen. From that time on, Jesus began to preach and say, "Repent, for the kingdom of heaven is at hand."

Reflection

Most Galilean Jews were poor and uneducated. Still, evidence indicates that they were devoted to their faith despite their lax observance of the Jewish law. The religious leaders in Jerusalem questioned Jesus' authority because he came from this region. Matthew incorporates the quotation from Isaiah to help skeptical hearers see in Jesus the true fulfillment of God's promises. In Jesus, God's "light has arisen."

Prayers *others may be added*

Joyfully, we pray:

◆ Hear us, Savior of the world.

For the Church who proclaims the Gospel in dangerous times and places, we pray: ◆ For people arrested without just cause, we pray: ◆ For Catholic schools, we pray: ◆ For Christians in the Middle East, we pray: ◆ For those who have died, we pray: ◆

Our Father . . .

Faithful God,
the light of your Son is unfading.
Turn our faces toward him
    when we feel surrounded
    by gloom.
Raise us up when we begin falling
    into darkness.
Through Christ our Lord. Amen.

☩ Let the heavens be glad and the earth rejoice!

✝ Let the heavens be glad and the earth rejoice!

Psalm 96 *page 413*

Reading *1 John 4:7–10*

Beloved, let us love one another, because love is of God; everyone who loves is begotten by God and knows God. Whoever is without love does not know God, for God is love. In this way the love of God was revealed to us: God sent his only Son into the world so that we might have life through him. In this is love: not that we have loved God, but that he loved us and sent his Son as expiation for our sins.

Reflection

We apply many adjectives to God—almighty, creator, eternal, all-knowing—but St. John reminds us that God is in essence love. Whatever else is true of God is true only because it follows from God's perfect love. As we cultivate certain virtues or abilities in ourselves, we should likewise ask if these good qualities ultimately flow from our desire to love as freely and as readily as God does.

Prayers *others may be added*

Joyfully, we pray:

◆ Hear us, Savior of the world.

God, grant the Church your perfect love, we pray: ◆ God, grant those who are lost your presence, we pray: ◆ God, grant the unloved and unknown a full heart, we pray: ◆ God, grant those who struggle to be loved peace and comfort, we pray: ◆ God, grant those who have died mercy in your kingdom, we pray: ◆

Our Father . . .

God of love,
you remain steadfast
    in your devotion to us
despite our failure to love you
    whole-heartedly.
Inspire us to persevere
    in our small efforts to grow in love
so as to remain with you in love.
Through Christ our Lord.
Amen.

✝ Let the heavens be glad and the earth rejoice!

✝ Let the heavens be glad and the earth rejoice!

Psalm 96 *page 413*

Reading *1 John 4:11–13, 16–18*

Beloved, if God so loved us, we also must love one another. No one has ever seen God. Yet, if we love one another, God remains in us, and his love is brought to perfection in us.

This is how we know that we remain in him and he in us, that he has given us of his Spirit. . . . We have come to know and to believe in the love God has for us.

God is love, and whoever remains in love remains in God and God in him.

Reflection

God loves perfectly because God loves without the constraint of sin. God is not motivated by self-interest, arrogance, fear or anything else that distorts and inhibits love. There are moments when we could mirror such divine love, but we don't because we fear the cost of loving so freely. Such moments remind us that we must daily call upon God to perfect us in love.

Prayers *others may be added*

Joyfully, we pray:

◆ Hear us, Savior of the world.

May God perfect the Church, we pray: ◆ May God counsel leaders, we pray: ◆ May God protect those who live or work in jails, prisons, and other institutions, we pray: ◆ May God console the anxious, we pray: ◆

Our Father . . .

Loving Father,
you free us from sin and death;
there is nothing left for us to fear.
Forgive our failures to love
    as you love us,
and empower us little by little
to love you and others more fully,
We ask this through our Lord Jesus
    Christ, your Son,
who lives and reigns with you
in the unity of the Holy Spirit,
one God, forever and ever.
Amen.

✝ Let the heavens be glad and the earth rejoice!

✝ Let the heavens be glad and the earth rejoice!

Psalm 96 *page 413*

Reading *1 John 4:19–21*

Beloved, we love God because he first loved us. If anyone says, "I love God," but hates his brother, he is a liar; for whoever does not love a brother whom he has seen cannot love God whom he has not seen. This is the commandment we have from him: Whoever loves God must also love his brother.

Reflection

We are still celebrating the incarnation, when out of perfect love for us, God became human. The Son of God revealed God's love to everyone without exception, and he did so in visible, concrete ways. It is now our turn to do the same, to incarnate God's love to others as perfectly, completely, visibly, and concretely as we can. In this way, we share in God's triumph over evil.

Prayers *others may be added*

Joyfully, we pray:

♦ Hear us, Savior of the world.

For the Church, the sacrament of Christ's presence in the world, we pray: ♦ For local and national leaders called to care for those entrusted to their leadership, we pray: ♦ For those struggling to love after experiencing abuse, violence, or neglect, we pray: ♦ For those seeking healthy physical intimacy, we pray: ♦

Our Father . . .

Son of God,
guide us when we don't know how
to follow you in our love and service
    to others.
Then, when you show us the way,
give us the courage to follow you,
who live and reign with God, the Father,
in the unity of the Holy Spirit,
one God, forever and ever.
Amen.

✝ Let the heavens be glad and the earth rejoice!

✟ Let the heavens be glad and the earth rejoice!

Psalm 96   *page 413*

Reading   *1 John 5:5–9, 13*

Beloved: Who indeed is the victor over the world but the one who believes that Jesus is the Son of God?

This is the one who came through water and Blood, Jesus Christ, not by water alone, but by water and Blood. The Spirit is the one who testifies, and the Spirit is truth. So there are three that testify, the Spirit, the water, and the Blood, and the three are of one accord. If we accept human testimony, the testimony of God is surely greater. Now the testimony of God is this, that he has testified on behalf of his Son.

I write these things to you so that you may know that you have eternal life, you who believe in the name of the Son of God.

Reflection

At Jesus' baptism, God testified that Jesus was his Son. Jesus' crucifixion and death reveal the fullness of Jesus' humanity. God's Spirit confirms that Jesus is both fully human and fully divine, and therefore the only one through whom people are saved. We are so used to this testimony that we forget the enormity of what God has done. God became human and fills us with his own Spirit.

Prayers   *others may be added*

Joyfully, we pray:

◆ Hear us, Savior of the world.

May God's Spirit continue to guide the Church as we testify to the life we have in Christ, we pray: ◆ May those who have rejected Christ listen anew to testimony about him, we pray: ◆ May lawyers, judges, and others who work within judicial systems act with integrity, we pray: ◆ May those seeking God's voice hear the Spirit of truth, we pray: ◆

Our Father . . .

God of salvation,
you have given us your Spirit
so that we might know
    and testify to eternal life.
May we never shy away
    from sharing with others
all that you have done for us.
Through Christ our Lord.
Amen.

✟ Let the heavens be glad and the earth rejoice!

✝ Let the heavens be glad and the earth rejoice!

Psalm 96
page 413

Reading
John 3:23–30

John was also baptizing in Aenon near Salim, because there was an abundance of water there, and people came to be baptized, for John had not yet been imprisoned. Now a dispute arose between the disciples of John and a Jew about ceremonial washings. So they came to John and said to him, "Rabbi, the one who was with you across the Jordan, to whom you testified, here he is baptizing and everyone is coming to him." John answered and said, "No one can receive anything except what has been given him from heaven. You yourselves can testify that I said that I am not the Christ, but that I was sent before him. The one who has the bride is the bridegroom; the best man, who stands and listens for him, rejoices greatly at the bridegroom's voice. So this joy of mine has been made complete. He must increase; I must decrease."

Reflection

When Jesus began his public ministry, it resembled what John the Baptist had been saying. This similarity provoked conflict between the followers of Jesus and the followers of John. Here John keeps the focus entirely on Jesus, insisting that his role has always been a supportive one. The passage invites us to reflect on the role to which God calls us as well as on the limits of that role.

Prayers
others may be added

Joyfully, we pray:

◆ Hear us, Savior of the world.

May the Church keep Christ at the heart of its teaching and ministry, we pray: ◆ May those in public office be steadfast in their commitment to those they serve, we pray: ◆ May the courage of Christ be with those who labor to reconstruct places devastated by war, we pray: ◆ May those preparing for marriage open their hearts to the joy and love of Christ, we pray: ◆

Our Father . . .

Heavenly Father,
all we have is from you.
As we celebrate what you accomplish
    through us,
keep us mindful
    that it is only by your power
that we are able to act at all.
Through Christ our Lord.
Amen.

✝ Let the heavens be glad and the earth rejoice!

✝ Let the heavens be glad and the earth rejoice!

Psalm 96 *page 413*

Reading *Mark 1:7–11*

This is what John the Baptist proclaimed: "One mightier than I is coming after me. I am not worthy to stoop and loosen the thongs of his sandals. I have baptized you with water; he will baptize you with the Holy Spirit."

It happened in those days that Jesus came from Nazareth of Galilee and was baptized in the Jordan by John. On coming up out of the water he saw the heavens being torn open and the Spirit, like a dove, descending upon him. And a voice came from the heavens, "You are my beloved Son; with you I am well pleased."

Reflection

John the Baptist called people to prepare themselves for God's coming. By choosing to be baptized, Jesus expressed his agreement with John, stood in solidarity with his people, and modeled openness to God's plan. In doing so, Jesus hears words of affirmation and empowerment. When we renew our baptismal promises, we proclaim and celebrate how God has affirmed and empowered us in Christ.

Prayers *others may be added*

Joyfully, we pray:

◆ Hear us, Savior of the world.

For the baptized, we pray: ◆ For leaders of nations, we pray: ◆ For godparents, sponsors, and catechists, we pray: ◆ For catechumens and those preparing to be received into full communion, we pray: ◆ For the baptized who remain on the margins of the community, we pray: ◆

Our Father . . .

All-powerful Father,
we have been reborn
    by water and the Holy Spirit.
Forgive our sins.
Keep us steadfast in our commitment
    to grow in holiness.
Through Christ our Lord.
Amen.

✝ Let the heavens be glad and the earth rejoice!

✝ O Lord, our God, how awesome is your name!

Psalm 8 *page 400*

Reading *Hebrews 1:1–6*

Brothers and sisters: In times past, God spoke in partial and various ways to our ancestors through the prophets; in these last days, he spoke to us through the Son, whom he made heir of all things and through whom he created the universe, / *who is the refulgence of his glory, the very imprint of his being, / and who sustains all things by his mighty word. / When he had accomplished purification from sins, / he took his seat at the right hand of the Majesty on high, / as far superior to the angels / as the name he has inherited is more excellent than theirs. /* For to which of the angels did God ever say: / *You are my Son; this day I have begotten you? /* Or again: / *I will be a father to him, and he shall be a Son to me? /* And again, when he leads the first born into the world, he says: / *Let all the angels of God worship him.*

Reflection

The sermon to the Hebrews begins with language that exalts Jesus. There is no one greater than God's Son. No one else fulfills our deepest needs. We might nod our heads in agreement, but sometimes we turn to other things or people for fulfillment. This passage, and the whole work that follows, urges us to commit ourselves daily to God's Son, our only savior. In him God offers us his very self. We should accept nothing less.

Prayers *others may be added*

To Jesus, God's Son in the flesh, we pray:

♦ Hear the prayers of your people, Lord.

For the Church who gives praise to God, we pray: ♦ For those who yearn for truth and meaning, we pray: ♦ For biologists, ecologists, and conservationists, we pray: ♦ For those who have abandoned their faith in Christ, we pray: ♦

Our Father . . .

Lord God,
in the life, death, and glorification
   of your Son
we see your love for us.
May his name be always on our lips.
May we turn to him alone for salvation.
Through Christ our Lord.
Amen.

✝ O Lord, our God, how awesome is your name!

✝ O Lord, our God, how awesome is your name!

Psalm 8   page 400

Reading   *Hebrews 2:5–9*

It was not to the angels that God subjected the world to come, of which we are speaking.

Instead, someone has testified somewhere: / *What is man that you are mindful of him, / or the son of man that you care for him? / You made him for a little while lower than the angels; / you crowned him with glory and honor, / subjecting all things under his feet. /* In "subjecting" all things [to him], he left nothing not "subject to him." Yet at present we do not see "all things subject to him," but we do see Jesus "crowned with glory and honor" because he suffered death, he who "for a little while" was made "lower than the angels," that by the grace of God he might taste death for everyone.

Reflection

Although Jesus, having completed God's will for him, is now crowned with honor and glory, we do not yet see all things subject to him. Some days the world seems untouched by God's grace. In those moments, we may feel tired, sorrowful, and skeptical; we may wonder if we will ever see all things subject to our Lord. We draw strength from Christ, our leader in suffering. To follow him in faith is to walk, one day, into the glory of salvation.

Prayers   *others may be added*

To Jesus, God's Son in the flesh, we pray:

◆ Hear the prayers of your people, Lord.

For all the baptized who face difficult times, we pray: ◆ For leaders of every kind who endure hardships, we pray: ◆ For those with serious illnesses and their caregivers, we pray: ◆ For the patience and perseverance to overcome adversity, we pray: ◆

Our Father . . .

God our Creator,
we long for the completion of
    your kingdom.
When we feel burdened
    or weighed down,
    invigorate us.
Reveal your presence to us
so that we may persevere in faith
and devotion to our Lord Jesus Christ,
    your Son,
who lives and reigns with you
in the unity of the Holy Spirit,
one God, forever and ever.
Amen.

✝ O Lord, our God, how awesome is your name!

✝ O Lord, our God, how awesome is your name!

Psalm 8   *page 400*

Reading   *Hebrews 2:14–18*

Since the children share in blood and Flesh, Jesus likewise shared in them, that through death he might destroy the one who has the power of death, that is, the Devil, and free those who through fear of death had been subject to slavery all their life. Surely he did not help angels but rather the descendants of Abraham; therefore, he had to become like his brothers and sisters in every way, that he might be a merciful and faithful high priest before God to expiate the sins of the people. Because he himself was tested through what he suffered, he is able to help those who are being tested.

Reflection

As we continue to hear from the Letter to the Hebrews, we move from Jesus' divinity to his total humanity, from a presentation of greatness that is beyond our understanding, to utter closeness with us. Jesus even submitted to death itself. In Jesus, God stoops to embrace us at every level of our being. There is no part of us, no aspect of our human nature that God leaves untouched by his grace.

Prayers   *others may be added*

To Jesus, God's Son in the flesh, we pray:

◆ Hear the prayers of your people, Lord.

That the Holy Spirit grants courage to Church leaders, we pray: ◆ That world leaders work to end human trafficking, we pray: ◆ That medical professionals become Christ's healing in the world, we pray: ◆ That those who fear death be comforted by the Spirit, we pray: ◆

Our Father . . .

Gracious Father,
your Son descended to our depths
   out of love for us.
Open our hearts to you.
Fill every part of us with your grace.
Whatever challenges we face,
may we never fail to entrust ourselves
   to you.
Through Christ our Lord.
Amen.

✝ O Lord, our God, how awesome is your name!

✝ O Lord, our God, how awesome is your name!

Psalm 8 *page 400*

Reading *Hebrews 3:7–14*

The Holy Spirit says: / *Oh, that today you would hear his voice, / "Harden not your hearts as at the rebellion / in the day of testing in the desert, / where your ancestors tested and tried me / and saw my works for forty years. / Because of this I was provoked with generations / and I said, 'They have always been of erring heart, / and they do not know my ways.' / As I swore in my wrath, / 'They shall not enter into my rest.'" /* Take care, brothers and sisters, that none of you may have an evil and unfaithful heart, so as to forsake the living God. Encourage yourselves daily while it is still "today," so that none of you may grow hardened by the deceit of sin. We have become partners of Christ if only we hold the beginning of the reality firm until the end.

Reflection

None of the Israelites God freed from slavery in Egypt entered the Promised Land. They kept failing to entrust themselves entirely to him. Their loss is a warning. God also wishes to lead us to a new homeland, but ours is an eternal one. Each day brings us either closer to it or farther away. Each day is thus a choice to try to draw closer to God or to put that task off until it is too late.

Prayers *others may be added*

To Jesus, God's Son in the flesh, we pray:

◆ Hear the prayers of your people, Lord.

For the People of God, we pray: ◆
For local, national, and world leaders, we pray: ◆ For immigrants and refugees, we pray: ◆ For all religious brothers and sisters, we pray: ◆

Our Father . . .

Living God,
you want us to grow closer to you
    each day
and to be with you forever.
Help us to listen to your voice.
Help us to follow our Lord Jesus Christ,
    your Son,
    in faith and obedience,
for he lives and reigns with you
in the unity of the Holy Spirit,
one God, forever and ever.
Amen.

✝ O Lord, our God, how awesome is your name!

✝ O Lord, our God, how awesome is your name!

Psalm 8
page 400

Reading
Hebrews 4:1–5, 11

Let us be on our guard while the promise of entering into his rest remains, that none of you seem to have failed. For in fact we have received the Good News just as our ancestors did. But the word that they heard did not profit them, for they were not united in faith with those who listened. For we who believed enter into that rest, just as he has said: / *As I swore in my wrath,* / *"They shall not enter into my rest,"* / and yet his works were accomplished at the foundation of the world. For he has spoken somewhere about the seventh day in this manner, / *And God rested on the seventh day from all his works;* / and again, in the previously mentioned place, / *They shall not enter into my rest.* /

Therefore, let us strive to enter into that rest, so that no one may fall after the same example of disobedience.

Reflection

We take naps and we sleep. We go on vacations, and eventually we retire. Yet these times of rest are nothing like resting with God. Those who persevere in faith and works will enter an altogether different kind of rest. We cannot fully imagine what such rest is like, but by spending time in quiet prayer we begin not only to imagine it better, we also begin to enter it.

Prayers
others may be added

To Jesus, God's Son in the flesh, we pray:

◆ Hear the prayers of your people, Lord.

For the Church who proclaims the Good News, we pray: ◆ For those hearing the Gospel for the first time, we pray: ◆ For those who have lost hope in the future, we pray: ◆ For those who live or work in retirement homes and nursing facilities, we pray: ◆

Our Father . . .

O Lord of life,
having called us into your rest,
do not let us fall away.
Let no one ever fall away.
Give us all the rest, the perfect peace,
for which we long.
Through Christ our Lord.
Amen.

✝ O Lord, our God, how awesome is your name!

☦ O Lord, our God, how awesome is your name!

Psalm 8 *page 400*

Reading *Hebrews 4:12–13*

The word of God is living and effective, sharper than any two-edged sword, penetrating even between soul and spirit, joints and marrow, and able to discern reflections and thoughts of the heart. No creature is concealed from him, but everything is naked and exposed to the eyes of him, to whom we must render an account.

Reflection

The best scientists in the world do not understand the human brain. We are mysteries to ourselves. Even when we try to act with clear, pure motives, other reasons for our behavior lurk within us. Sometimes we simply lie to ourselves or rationalize poor choices. God alone sees what is really happening. If we wish to act with justice and holiness, then we must allow God to guide us through our conflicting thoughts and feelings.

Prayers *others may be added*

To Jesus, God's Son in the flesh, we pray:

◆ Hear the prayers of your people, Lord.

That the Church may grow in compassion, we pray: ◆ That leaders may grow in sincerity, we pray: ◆ That those with mental illness may grow in peace, we pray: ◆ That each of us may grow in honesty, we pray: ◆

Our Father . . .

Merciful God,
you know how mixed and conflicted
    our minds can be.
Guide us as we seek to
    understand ourselves
and to discern how best to speak
and act each moment of our lives.
We ask this through our Lord Jesus
    Christ, your Son,
who lives and reigns with you
in the unity of the Holy Spirit,
 one God, forever and ever.
Amen.

☦ O Lord, our God, how awesome is your name!

✝ Lord, you will show us the path of life.

Psalm 16   *page 400*

Reading   *John 1:35–42*

John was standing with two of his disciples, and as he watched Jesus walk by, he said, "Behold, the Lamb of God." The two disciples heard what he said and followed Jesus. Jesus turned and saw them following him and said to them, "What are you looking for?" They said to him, "Rabbi"—which translated means Teacher—, "where are you staying?" He said to them, "Come, and you will see." So they went and saw where he was staying, and they stayed with him that day. It was about four in the afternoon. Andrew, the brother of Simon Peter, was one of the two who heard John and followed Jesus. He first found his own brother Simon and told him, "We have found the Messiah"— which is translated Christ. Then he brought him to Jesus. Jesus looked at him and said, "You are Simon the son of John; you will be called Cephas"— which is translated Peter.

Reflection

How would you respond if Jesus asked you, "What are you looking for?" The two disciples ask to spend time with Jesus, who welcomes them into his company. Jesus assures them that as they get to know him, they will want to stay with him forever. We might not be so sure. We may struggle to believe that Jesus will meet our deepest needs. The only way to find out is to spend time with him.

Prayers   *others may be added*

To our high priest, Jesus Christ, we pray:

◆ Lord, have compassion on us.

That the Church may be a place of welcome and comfort, we pray: ◆ That those in public office may have open ears and hearts, we pray: ◆ That those in the hospitality industry may serve with kindness, we pray: ◆ That parishes may be an authentic witness to the Gospel, we pray: ◆

Our Father . . .

Giver of all good gifts,
you fulfill the longing in our hearts.
Help us to spend time
    with your Son.
Help us to listen to him bravely
    and honestly.
Through him,
reveal all that you offer us
and make us eager to accept
    your many gifts.
Through Christ our Lord.
Amen.

✝ Lord, you will show us the path of life.

✝ Lord, you will show us the path of life.

Psalm 16   *page 400*

Reading   *Hebrews 5:1–6*

Brothers and sisters: Every high priest is taken from among men and made their representative before God, to offer gifts and sacrifices for sins. He is able to deal patiently with the ignorant and the erring, for he himself is beset by weakness and so, for this reason, must make sin offerings for himself as well as for the people. No one takes this honor upon himself but only when called by God, just as Aaron was. In the same way, it was not Christ who glorified himself in becoming high priest, but rather the one who said to him: / *You are my Son: / this day I have begotten you; /* just as he says in another place, / *You are a priest forever according to the order of Melchizedek. /*

Reflection

The author of Hebrews begins his presentation of Jesus as our high priest by referring to the Jewish priesthood, an office established by God. Good priests must have been deeply saddened by the sin offerings they had to bring before God, but their awareness of both their own sins and the sins of others would have made them humble and compassionate. We are called to bear that same measure of humility and compassion.

Prayers   *others may be added*

To our high priest, Jesus Christ, we pray:

◆ Lord, have compassion on us.

For bishops, priests, and deacons, we pray: ◆ For leaders everywhere, we pray: ◆ For those discerning their vocation, we pray: ◆ For those with hardened hearts, we pray:

Our Father . . .

Christ the intercessor,
you have never wavered in bearing your
    Father's mercy toward us.
May we, in turn,
    be constant in treating others
with patience and compassion.
We bring this prayer
and all our needs before you,
who live and reign
    with God the Father
in the unity of the Holy Spirit,
one God, forever and ever.
Amen.

✝ Lord, you will show us the path of life.

✝ Lord, you will show us the path of life.

Psalm 16   *page 400*

Reading   *Hebrews 6:10–12*

Brothers and sisters: God is not unjust so as to overlook your work and the love you have demonstrated for his name by having served and continuing to serve the holy ones. We earnestly desire each of you to demonstrate the same eagerness for the fulfillment of hope until the end, so that you may not become sluggish, but imitators of those who, through faith and patience, are inheriting the promises.

Reflection

Earlier in Hebrews, the author warns us not to abandon our Christian faith. God will save those who persevere, no matter how insignificant our gestures of faith seem. God notices even the smallest and simplest acts of love. Not everyone can do big, noticeable works of love and justice, but we can all do things that reveal we are loving and just people. God will not overlook the people we are striving to be.

Prayers   *others may be added*

To our high priest, Jesus Christ, we pray:

♦ Lord, have compassion on us.

That the Holy Spirit sustain the Church in its work for justice and charity, we pray: ♦ That business leaders balance their concern for profit with the needs of people, we pray: ♦ That those who do service be filled with compassion, we pray: ♦ That our families be filled with joy and love, we pray: ♦

Our Father . . .

Just and loving God,
we offer to you our gestures of love
and ask that you accept them
    as signs of our desire
    to be united with you,
    the source of love itself.
May our small efforts in the world
further your reign
    of justice and peace.
We ask this through our Lord Jesus
    Christ, your Son,
who lives and reigns with you
in the unity of the Holy Spirit,
 one God, forever and ever.
Amen.

✝ Lord, you will show us the path of life.

✝ Lord, you will show us the path of life.

Psalm 8   *page 400*

Reading   *Hebrews 7:1–3*

Melchizedek, king of Salem and priest of God Most High, met Abraham as he returned from his defeat of the kings and blessed him. And Abraham apportioned to him *a tenth of everything.* His name first means "righteous king," and he was also "king of Salem," that is, king of peace. Without father, mother, or ancestry, without beginning of days or end of life, thus made to resemble the Son of God, he remains a priest forever.

Reflection

Melchizedek is a mysterious Old Testament figure. Because we know nothing about his life, he remains fixed in our imagination as a permanent priest-king. Melchizedek thus points ahead to the eternal priesthood of Christ. We participate in the priesthood of Christ when we celebrate the sacraments and strive to turn our own lives into an offering to God. This is one of the ways we live out our baptismal anointing as priest, prophet, and king.

Prayers   *others may be added*

To our high priest, Jesus Christ, we pray:

◆ Lord, have compassion on us.

For those who are preparing for ordination, we pray: ◆ For those who promote peace and justice, we pray: ◆ For those who work to resolve conflicts, we pray: ◆ For those who bless and support us, we pray: ◆

Our Father . . .

God Most High,
we encounter your Son in an unparalleled
    way in our celebration of the
    sacraments.
Increase our understanding of these
    ritual actions.
May our love for you grow
    and overflow
into ever greater love for others.
Through Christ our Lord.
Amen.

✝ Lord, you will show us the path of life.

✝ Lord, you will show us the path of life.

Psalm 16 page 400

Reading Hebrews 7:25–28

Jesus is always able to save those who approach God through him, since he lives forever to make intercession for them.

It was fitting that we should have such a high priest: holy, innocent, undefiled, separated from sinners, higher than the heavens. He has no need, as did the high priests, to offer sacrifice day after day, first for his own sins and then for those of the people; he did that once for all when he offered himself. For the law appoints men subject to weakness to be high priests, but the word of the oath, which was taken after the law, appoints a son, who has been made perfect forever.

Reflection

St. Agnes, born in the late third century, wanted to emulate Christ by keeping herself set apart for God. When she refused to marry, she was denounced for being a Christian and was killed. She is a compelling Christian witness for everyone who struggles against overwhelming social pressure to remain faithful to Christ.

Prayers others may be added

To our high priest, Jesus Christ, we pray:

◆ Lord, have compassion on us.

For the Church as she proclaims the Good News, we pray: ◆ For those who suffer from addiction as they seek healing, we pray: ◆ For victims of abuse and sexual violence as they seek strength and courage, we pray: ◆ For engaged and married couples as they learn to love as Christ loves, we pray: ◆

Our Father . . .

Loving God,
though separate from us in his divinity,
your Son entered fully into our humanity.
May we, like St. Agnes,
    follow Christ in holiness.
Protect us from everything
that leads us deeper into sin.
We ask this through our Lord Jesus
    Christ, your Son,
who lives and reigns with you
in the unity of the Holy Spirit,
one God, forever and ever.
Amen.

✝ Lord, you will show us the path of life.

✟ Lord, you will show us the path of life.

Psalm 16 *page 400*

Reading *Mark 3:13–19*

Jesus went up the mountain and summoned those whom he wanted and they came to him. He appointed Twelve whom he also named Apostles that they might be with him and he might send them forth to preach and to have authority to drive out demons: He appointed the Twelve: Simon, whom he named Peter; James, son of Zebedee, and John the brother of James, whom he named Boanerges, that is, sons of thunder; Andrew, Philip, Bartholomew, Matthew, Thomas, James the son of Alphaeus; Thaddeus, Simon the Cananean, and Judas Iscariot who betrayed him.

Reflection

We are so used to hearing about Jesus' call of the Twelve that we forget the significance of that number. Israel emerged from the twelve tribes, or family groups, that had all descended from Abraham. By choosing twelve followers of his own, Jesus symbolically declares that he is forming a new Israel. This new family of God is no longer based on lineage but on faith in Jesus. In Christ, God invites us all to be his chosen people.

Prayers *others may be added*

To our high priest, Jesus Christ, we pray:

◆ Lord, have compassion on us.

For the pope and those who work in the Holy See, we pray: ◆ For bishops and those who assist in the care and administration of dioceses, we pray: ◆ For public officials and those who aid them, we pray: ◆ For ordained ministers and lay staff who collaborate with them, we pray: ◆

Our Father . . .

Lord Jesus,
you summon us to participate
    in the coming of your kingdom.
Lead us to people and places
    most in need of salvation.
Empower us to act in your name,
for you live and reign with God
    the Father
in the unity of the Holy Spirit,
one God, forever and ever.
Amen.

✟ Lord, you will show us the path of life.

✝ Lord, you will show us the path
  of life.

Psalm 16

page 400

Reading

Mark 3:20–21

Jesus came with his disciples into the house. Again the crowd gathered, making it impossible for them even to eat. When his relatives heard of this they set out to seize him, for they said, "He is out of his mind."

Reflection

Jesus' ministry so startles his relatives that they cannot accept it and even interpret it as something unhealthy. When we have carefully discerned God's will for us, our own actions might also surprise friends and family. They may worry and become unsupportive. Often in such moments, our actions must speak for themselves. If we are truly following Christ, others will see him in us.

Prayers

others may be added

To our high priest, Jesus Christ, we pray:

◆ Lord, have compassion on us.

For movements of apostolic life, we pray: ◆ For community activists, we pray: ◆ For those who follow God's call and feel abandoned by others, we pray: ◆ For those discerning God's will, we pray: ◆

Our Father . . .

Holy God,
when we are truly acting
  in accordance with your will,
our actions may upset the status quo
and anger or offend other people.
Keep us faithful to your Spirit
and courageous in our obedience.
Through Christ our Lord.
Amen.

✝ Lord, you will show us the path
  of life.

✝ Lord, may your kindness be
upon us.

Psalm 33 *page 406*

Reading *Mark 1:14–20*

After John had been arrested, Jesus came to Galilee proclaiming the gospel of God: "This is the time of fulfillment. The Kingdom of God is at hand. Repent, and believe in the gospel."

As he passed by the Sea of Galilee, he saw Simon and his brother Andrew casting their nets into the sea; they were fishermen. Jesus said to them, "Come after me, and I will make you fishers of men." Then they left their nets and followed him. He walked along a little farther and saw James, the son of Zebedee, and his brother John. They too were in a boat mending their nets. Then he called them. So they left their father Zebedee in the boat along with the hired men and followed him.

Reflection

Although the sea was a source of livelihood for fishermen, it was also a grave threat. The sea reminded people of the wild and deadly waters of the void, the nothingness, out of which God brought forth creation. Jesus takes the initiative to call and form disciples who will help him rescue people from the abyss of death and give them life forever.

Prayers *others may be added*

With hearts full of hope, we pray:

◆ Lord Jesus, hear our prayer.

That the Church be filled with the gift of courage, we pray: ◆ That world leaders be filled with the gift of stewardship, we pray: ◆ That oceanographers, marine biologists, and those who study freshwater systems be filled with the gift of knowledge, we pray: ◆ That fishermen and others in the fishing industry be filled with the gift of perseverance, we pray: ◆

Our Father . . .

Almighty and ever-living God,
some days our world seems to slip back
    into the abyss.
Empower us to be your disciples today.
By offering your love to others,
help us to draw people out of darkness.
Lead us all into the light and peace of
    your kingdom.
Through Christ our Lord.
Amen.

✝ Lord, may your kindness be
upon us.

✝ Lord, may your kindness be upon us.

Psalm 33 page 406

Reading Mark 16:15–18

Jesus appeared to the Eleven and said to them: "Go into the whole world and proclaim the Gospel to every creature. Whoever believes and is baptized will be saved; whoever does not believe will be condemned. These signs will accompany those who believe: in my name they will drive out demons, they will speak new languages. They will pick up serpents with their hands, and if they drink any deadly thing, it will not harm them. They will lay hands on the sick, and they will recover."

Reflection

In hearing this story, you may recall the passage in which St. Paul is bitten by a venomous snake and remains unharmed (Acts 28:3–4). That story, like today's Gospel, illustrates that God's power works mightily through those who put themselves at God's service. We might not have had the experiences St. Paul did, but God's power is still at work within us. What works will we do in God's name?

Prayers others may be added

With hearts full of hope, we pray:

◆ Lord Jesus, hear our prayer.

For seekers who hear God's word proclaimed, we pray: ◆ For those who are persecuted because of faith, we pray: ◆ For those who are suffering severe illnesses, we pray: ◆ For those who seek God's guidance and love, we pray: ◆

Our Father . . .

Almighty God,
you invite us to share in your
    wondrous power
to bring healing and consolation
    to others.
Open our hearts to your presence.
Fill us with hope and peace
so that we may readily share your saving
    love with others.
Through Christ our Lord.
Amen.

✝ Lord, may your kindness be upon us.

Tuesday, January 26, 2021
Memorial of Sts. Timothy and Titus, Bishops

✝ Lord, may your kindness be upon us.

Psalm 33 page 406

Reading 2 Timothy 1:1–8

Paul, an Apostle of Christ Jesus by the will of God for the promise of life in Christ Jesus, to Timothy, my dear child: grace, mercy, and peace from God the Father and Christ Jesus our Lord.

I am grateful to God, whom I worship with a clear conscience as my ancestors did, as I remember you constantly in my prayers, night and day. I yearn to see you again, recalling your tears, so that I may be filled with joy, as I recall your sincere faith that first lived in your grandmother Lois and in your mother Eunice and that I am confident lives also in you.

For this reason, I remind you to stir into flame the gift of God that you have through the imposition of my hands. For God did not give us a spirit of cowardice but rather of power and love and self-control. So do not be ashamed of your testimony to our Lord, nor of me, a prisoner for his sake; but bear your share of hardship for the Gospel with the strength that comes from God.

Reflection

St. Paul encouraged and guided Timothy and Titus as they learned to share the Gospel and strengthen the faith of their communities. In this passage to Timothy, we are reminded that parents are vital for a child's faith formation. Just as Paul urged Timothy and Titus to persevere in their leadership, so must parents persevere in learning how best to share the Gospel with their children.

Prayers others may be added

With hearts full of hope, we pray:

♦ Lord Jesus, hear our prayer.

For catechists and all involved with formation, we pray: ♦ For pastors and parish staffs, we pray: ♦ For parents, grandparents, and godparents, we pray: ♦ For faith communities under the patronage of St. Timothy and St. Titus, we pray: ♦

Our Father . . .

God our Father,
we thank you for those
    who first taught us about you.
May we be mindful
    of how to inspire faith in others,
especially children.
At each stage of life,
may your Holy Spirit
    rouse our hearts
and strengthen our minds.
Through Christ our Lord.
Amen.

✝ Lord, may your kindness be upon us.

✝ Lord, may your kindness be upon us.

Psalm 33 *page 406*

Reading *Mark 4:3–9*

On another occasion Jesus began to teach by the sea. "Hear this! A sower went out to sow. And as he sowed, some seed fell on the path, and the birds came and ate it up. Other seed fell on rocky ground where it had little soil. It sprang up at once because the soil was not deep. And when the sun rose, it was scorched and it withered for lack of roots. Some seed fell among thorns, and the thorns grew up and choked it and it produced no grain. And some seed fell on rich soil and produced fruit. It came up and grew and yielded thirty, sixty, and a hundredfold." He added, "Whoever has ears to hear ought to hear."

Reflection

Although we are given an interpretation of this parable, we can continue reflecting on its meaning. We could ask ourselves how readily we share our faith. We could ask how securely we are planted and how well we are growing. We could ask if we are ever like the birds, the sun, or the thorns—keeping others or ourselves from growing in faith. A good parable invites us into continual reflection. This is how God's word takes root within us.

Prayers *others may be added*

With hearts full of hope, we pray:

◆ Lord Jesus, hear our prayer.

That the Church may be filled with the Holy Spirit, we pray: ◆ That areas affected by drought may be nourished with rain, we pray: ◆ That farmers may be protected from any harm, we pray: ◆ That the dead may be welcomed into God's Kingdom, we pray: ◆

Our Father . . .

Loving God,
you do all you can
    to instill your word within us.
Keep your word firmly planted within us
so that we may remain firmly planted
    within your divine life.
We ask this through our Lord Jesus
    Christ, your Son,
who lives and reigns with you
in the unity of the Holy Spirit,
one God, forever and ever.
Amen.

✝ Lord, may your kindness be upon us.

✝ Lord, may your kindness be
upon us.

Psalm 33 *page 406*

Reading *Hebrews 10:19–25*

Brothers and sisters: Since through the Blood of Jesus we have confidence of entrance into the sanctuary by the new and living way he opened for us through the veil, that is, his flesh, and since we have "a great priest over the house of God," let us approach with a sincere heart and in absolute trust, with our hearts sprinkled clean from an evil conscience and our bodies washed in pure water. Let us hold unwaveringly to our confession that gives us hope, for he who made the promise is trustworthy. We must consider how to rouse one another to love and good works. We should not stay away from our assembly, as is the custom of some, but encourage one another, and this all the more as you see the day drawing near.

Reflection

St. Thomas Aquinas drove himself to the brink of exhaustion to teach others about God and the Christian faith. Through his teaching and extensive writing, which flow from a deep love for God, the saint inspired people to approach God "with a sincere heart and in absolute trust." Just as St. Thomas inspired whole generations to strive for a greater love for God, so must we "rouse one another to love and good works."

Prayers *others may be added*

With hearts full of hope, we pray:

◆ Lord Jesus, hear our prayer.

That God's love anchor all leaders of the Church, we pray: ◆ That God's life guide all leaders of nations, we pray: ◆ That God's wisdom permeate the minds and hearts of students, faculty, and staff of Catholic universities, we pray: ◆ That God's grace surround all those seeking to know more about Jesus, we pray: ◆

Our Father . . .

Loving Father,
you have brought us close to you
    in Christ.
May we embrace the witness
    of Thomas Aquinas,
who tirelessly committed himself to you.
Deepen our own love for you
so that we, in turn,
may inspire others to follow your Son,
    our Lord Jesus Christ,
who lives and reigns with you
in the unity of the Holy Spirit,
one God, forever and ever.
Amen.

✝ Lord, may your kindness be
upon us.

✝ Lord, may your kindness be upon us.

Psalm 33
page 406

Reading
Hebrews 10:32–36

Remember the days past when, after you had been enlightened, you endured a great contest of suffering. At times you were publicly exposed to abuse and affliction; at other times you associated yourselves with those so treated. You even joined in the sufferings of those in prison and joyfully accepted the confiscation of your property, knowing that you had a better and lasting possession. Therefore, do not throw away your confidence; it will have great recompense. You need endurance to do the will of God and receive what he has promised.

Reflection

From the Letter to the Hebrews it is clear that Christians in the local community were publicly ridiculed, perhaps violently. Others were unjustly imprisoned, and their property and goods were taken from them. The aggressors wanted to discourage others from becoming Christian and provoking those already baptized to renounce their faith. The injustice made some believers even more determined to persevere in following Christ.

Prayers
others may be added

With hearts full of hope, we pray:

◆ Lord Jesus, hear our prayer.

God, protect those who encounter any harm, we pray: ◆ God, stir the hearts of all leaders to serve justly, we pray: ◆ God, comfort those who are imprisoned and falsely accused, we pray: ◆ God, encourage those who are persecuted because of faith, we pray: ◆ God, give rest to all who have died, we pray: ◆

Our Father . . .

Saving God,
we lift up to you
    our brothers and sisters
whose lives are endangered because
    of their faith.
They are signs of endurance for us.
May we be a source of consolation
    for them.
We ask this through Christ
our liberator and friend.
Amen.

✝ Lord, may your kindness be upon us.

✝ Lord, may your kindness be upon us.

Psalm 33 *page 406*

Reading *Hebrews 11:1–2, 8–12*

Brothers and sisters: Faith is the realization of what is hoped for and evidence of things not seen. Because of it the ancients were well attested.

By faith Abraham obeyed when he was called out to a place that he was to receive as an inheritance; he went out, not knowing where he was to go. By faith he sojourned in the promised land as in a foreign country, dwelling in tents with Isaac and Jacob, heirs of the same promise; for he was looking forward to the city with foundations, whose architect and maker is God. By faith he received power to generate, even though he was past the normal age—Sarah herself was sterile—for he thought that the one who had made the promise was trustworthy. So it was that there came forth from one man, himself as good as dead, descendants as numerous as the stars in the sky and as countless as the sands on the seashore.

Reflection

Because faith changes how we act, our faith makes God's promises part of our present, visible reality. By leaving his homeland, Abraham began drawing closer to the homeland God would give to his descendants. By embracing Christ and his way, we draw closer to our heavenly home. By seeking justice and promoting peace, we offer signs of God's Kingdom here on earth. Thus, by acting on our faith, we reveal the presence of God.

Prayers *others may be added*

With hearts full of hope, we pray:

◆ Lord Jesus, hear our prayer.

Holy Spirit, make your Church a sign of God's mercy, we pray: ◆ Holy Spirit, enlighten the hearts and minds of local and national leaders, we pray: ◆ Holy Spirit, protect immigrants and refugees, we pray: ◆ Holy Spirit, open our eyes to see the glory of God, we pray: ◆ Holy Spirit, strengthen the faith of your people, we pray: ◆

Our Father . . .

God of all good gifts,
our ancestors in the faith
reveal your guidance
    and your goodness.
May our own obedience to you
reveal the fulfillment
    of your promises
to those who will come after us.
Through Christ our Lord.
Amen.

✝ Lord, may your kindness be upon us.

✝ Teach me your paths, Lord.

Psalm 25   *page 403*

Reading   *Mark 1:21–28*

[Jesus came to Capernaum with his followers,] and on the sabbath entered the synagogue and taught. The people were astonished at his teaching, for he taught them as one having authority and not as the scribes. In their synagogue was a man with an unclean spirit; he cried out, "What have you to do with us, Jesus of Nazareth? Have you come to destroy us? I know who you are—the Holy One of God!" Jesus rebuked him and said, "Quiet! Come out of him!" The unclean spirit convulsed him and with a loud cry came out of him. All were amazed and asked one another, "What is this? A new teaching with authority. He commands even the unclean spirits and they obey him." His fame spread everywhere throughout the whole region of Galilee.

Reflection

Demon-possession is rare, but confrontations with evil happen every day, sometimes so suddenly we step back, frightened and uncertain how to respond. The moment passes, and we failed to cast the evil out. But new moments will come. We must prepare ourselves. Jesus entrusted his Spirit to us so that we would advance God's reign by opposing evil as boldly as he did.

Prayers   *others may be added*

Trusting in our savior, we pray:

◆ Hear us, Lord Jesus.

Loving God, protect us from evil, we pray: ◆ Holy Wisdom, guide leaders of nations, we pray: ◆ Lord of mercy, lead us away from all that harms us, we pray: ◆ God of healing, show compassion to all those who suffer, we pray: ◆

Our Father . . .

Holy One of God,
in casting evil out of our world
you inaugurated the kingdom of
    your Father.
Teach us how to speak boldly
    in the face of whatever evil
    confronts us.
We draw our strength from you,
    our Lord Jesus Christ,
who live and reign with God
    the Father
in the unity of the Holy Spirit,
one God, forever and ever.
Amen.

✝ Teach me your paths, Lord.

✝ Teach me your paths, Lord.

Psalm 25
page 403

Reading
Hebrews 11:32–38

Brothers and sisters: What more shall I say? I have not time to tell of Gideon, Barak, Samson, of David, Samuel, and the prophets, who by faith conquered kingdoms, did what was righteous, obtained the promises; they closed the mouths of lions, put out raging fires, escaped the devouring sword; out of weakness, they were made powerful, became strong in battle, and turned back foreign invaders. Women received back their dead through resurrection. Some were tortured and would not accept deliverance, in order to obtain a better resurrection. Others endured mockery, scourging, even chains and imprisonment. They were stoned, sawed in two, put to death at sword's point; they went about in skins of sheep or goats, needy, afflicted, tormented. The world was not worthy of them. They wandered about in deserts and on mountains, in caves and in crevices in the earth.

Reflection

Our spiritual ancestors proved their worthiness to become part of a better world by persevering in faith even though they never saw the perfection of God's promises. Although Christ revealed God's Kingdom to us, we also await its completion. The witness of our forebears inspires us to persevere in faith so that our own lives might inspire the next generation.

Prayers
others may be added

Trusting in our Savior, we pray:

◆ Hear us, Lord Jesus.

For the Church and its leaders, we pray: ◆ For all those who are persecuted and oppressed, we pray: ◆ For victims of torture, we pray: ◆ For an end to racism and prejudice, we pray: ◆ For those who have died, we pray: ◆

Our Father . . .

O God of hope,
we are inspired by the courageous
    witness of others,
        both those who have died
        and those who are active in our midst.
May we all find our ultimate rest in you.
We ask this through our Lord Jesus
    Christ, your Son,
who lives and reigns with you
in the unity of the Holy Spirit,
one God, forever and ever.
Amen.

✝ Teach me your paths, Lord.

✝ Teach me your paths, Lord.

Psalm 25 *page 403*

Reading *Luke 2:27–32*

Now there was a man in Jerusalem whose name was Simeon. This man was righteous and devout, awaiting the consolation of Israel, and the Holy Spirit was upon him. It had been revealed to him by the Holy Spirit that he should not see death before he had seen the Christ of the Lord. He came in the Spirit into the temple; and when the parents brought in the child Jesus to perform the custom of the law in regard to him, he took him into his arms and blessed God, saying: / "Now, Master, you may let your servant go / in peace, according to your word, / for my eyes have seen your salvation, / which you prepared in sight of all the peoples, / a light for revelation to the Gentiles, / and glory for your people Israel."

Reflection

Forty days after Christmas, we celebrate a second epiphany, another revelation of Jesus' identity. Our encounter with Jesus ultimately reveals what is in our own hearts because we decide whether to accept or reject his way of life and love. Jesus is thus "a sign that will be contradicted." Some embrace him. Others turn away.

Prayers *others may be added*

Trusting in our Savior, we pray:

◆ Hear us, Lord Jesus.

For the Church, we pray: ◆ For all leaders, we pray: ◆ For the oppressed and marginalized, we pray: ◆ For the poor, we pray: ◆ For refugees and immigrants, we pray: ◆ For newborns, we pray: ◆ For the despondent, we pray: ◆ For the dead, we pray: ◆

Our Father . . .

Lord of light,
illuminate our minds
so that we may know
    and bring to you
those parts of our lives
that are most in need of transformation.
Through Christ our Lord.
Amen.

✝ Teach me your paths, Lord.

✝ Teach me your paths, Lord.

Psalm 25
page 403

Reading
Hebrews 12:7, 11–14

[Brothers and sisters:] Endure your trials as "discipline"; God treats you as his sons. For what "son" is there whom his father does not discipline? At the time, all discipline seems a cause not for joy but for pain, yet later it brings the peaceful fruit of righteousness to those who are trained by it. So strengthen your drooping hands and your weak knees. Make straight paths for your feet, that what is lame may not be dislocated but healed.

Reflection

Persevering in faith requires training that is both mental and physical, just as in preparing to run a race. The race we are running is long. It lasts a lifetime. By praying and reflecting, rooting out sin, engaging in ongoing study and formation, and undertaking works of charity and justice, we train ourselves to stay in this holy race until the end.

Prayers
others may be added

Trusting in our Savior, we pray:

◆ Hear us, Lord Jesus.

Encourage pastors in their ministry of preaching and presiding, we pray: ◆ Strengthen those who advocate for justice and peace, we pray: ◆ Protect athletes, coaches, and trainers, we pray: ◆ Heal conflicts within parishes, families, and neighborhoods, we pray: ◆

Our Father . . .

God our strength,
despite the challenges they faced,
countless men and women
persisted in faith
until they found their rest in you.
When we tire of doing what is right,
enliven us with your Spirit
so that we may also continue forward
    in faith.
We ask this through our Lord Jesus
    Christ, your Son,
who lives and reigns with you
in the unity of the Holy Spirit,
one God, forever and ever.
Amen.

✝ Teach me your paths, Lord.

✝ Teach me your paths, Lord.

Psalm 25 *page 403*

Reading *Hebrews 12:18–19, 21–24*

Brothers and sisters: You have not approached that which could be touched and a blazing fire and gloomy darkness and storm and a trumpet blast and a voice speaking words such that those who heard begged that no message be further addressed to them. Indeed, so fearful was the spectacle that Moses said, "I am terrified and trembling." No, you have approached Mount Zion and the city of the living God, the heavenly Jerusalem, and countless angels in festal gathering, and the assembly of the first-born enrolled in heaven, and God the judge of all, and the spirits of the just made perfect, and Jesus, the mediator of a new covenant, and the sprinkled Blood that speaks more eloquently than that of Abel.

Reflection

Christians live within two worlds. There is the ever-changing world we see around us, and then there's the reign of God that we see with the eyes of faith. As the author of Hebrews describes God's reign with beautiful and uplifting language, he insists that we are already living within it. In God's Kingdom, we are forgiven and perfected, and God draws us so close that we will never again be separated.

Prayers *others may be added*

Trusting in our Savior, we pray:

◆ Hear us, Lord Jesus.

May the Church eloquently profess the salvation we have in Christ, we pray: ◆ May leaders offer amnesty when it will ensure peace within their countries, we pray: ◆ May the peace of God reign in war-torn nations, we pray: ◆ May the Holy Spirit help us live close to God, we pray: ◆

Our Father . . .

Living God,
you alone can transform our world.
Forgive us when we lose sight of you.
Perfect our efforts
    to live with mercy and justice
so that one day
we may join the angels and saints
    in the heavenly Jerusalem.
We ask this through our Lord Jesus
    Christ, your Son,
who lives and reigns with you
in the unity of the Holy Spirit,
one God, forever and ever.
Amen.

✝ Teach me your paths, Lord.

✝ Teach me your paths, Lord.

Psalm 25 *page 403*

Reading *Hebrews 13:1–8*

Let brotherly love continue. Do not neglect hospitality, for through it some have unknowingly entertained angels. Be mindful of prisoners as if sharing their imprisonment, and of the ill-treated as of yourselves, for you also are in the body. Let marriage be honored among all and the marriage bed be kept undefiled, for God will judge the immoral and adulterers. Let your life be free from love of money but be content with what you have, for he has said, / *I will never forsake you or abandon you.* / Thus we may say with confidence: / *The Lord is my helper,* / *and I will not be afraid.* / *What can anyone do to me?* / Remember your leaders who spoke the word of God to you. Consider the outcome of their way of life and imitate their faith. Jesus Christ is the same yesterday, today, and forever.

Reflection

The love of Christ is constant. Our challenge as people baptized in his name is to be constant ourselves in love, faith, and morality. St. Agatha demonstrated such constancy when she endured painful and degrading treatment rather than renounce her love for Christ. She knew Christ's love for her never wavered, and so she never wavered in her love for him. Neither must we.

Prayers *others may be added*

Trusting in our Savior, we pray:

◆ **Hear us, Lord Jesus.**

For those who first revealed God's love to us, we pray: ◆ For those who seek political office, we pray: ◆ For victims of sexual assault and their abusers, we pray: ◆ For married couples and those who counsel them, we pray: ◆ For the sick and suffering and those who care for them, we pray: ◆

Our Father . . .

Eternal God,
you never tire
 of answering our cries for help.
May we always turn to you
 in our need.
Strengthened by your unfailing love,
we will prevail over whatever
 confronts us.
Through Christ our Lord.
Amen.

✝ Teach me your paths, Lord.

✝ Teach me your paths, Lord.

Psalm 25   *page 403*

Reading   *Hebrews 13:15–17, 20–21*

Brothers and sisters: Through Jesus, let us continually offer God a sacrifice of praise, that is, the fruit of lips that confess his name. Do not neglect to do good and to share what you have; God is pleased by sacrifices of that kind.

Obey your leaders and defer to them, for they keep watch over you and will have to give an account, that they may fulfill their task with joy and not with sorrow, for that would be of no advantage to you.

May the God of peace, who brought up from the dead, the great shepherd of the sheep by the Blood of the eternal covenant, furnish you with all that is good, that you may do his will. May he carry out in you what is pleasing to him through Jesus Christ, to whom be glory forever and ever. Amen.

Reflection

St. Paul Miki and his fellow Christians were crucified because they shared the Gospel with the people of sixteenth-century Japan. These martyrs knew the dangers of embracing Christ. God equipped them with all that they needed to confess that Jesus is Lord for the praise and glory of God. What good gifts has God given us? Will we dare to ask for still more so that we, too, may do what pleases him?

Prayers   *others may be added*

Trusting in our Savior, we pray:

◆ Hear us, Lord Jesus.

May God strengthen and protect the Jesuits and Franciscans, and all those in religious life, we pray: ◆ May the Holy Spirit enlighten the hearts of leaders to do what is right for their people, we pray: ◆ May fervor for the Gospel permeate the Christians in Japan, we pray: ◆ May we be graced with courage to come into God's presence, we pray: ◆

Our Father . . .

God of peace,
despite the terrible suffering they endured,
St. Paul Miki and his friends
held fast to faith in your Son.
Reveal to us
    the good that we can do,
the praise and sacrifice
    we can render for your glory.
We ask this through our Lord Jesus
    Christ, your Son,
who lives and reigns with you
in the unity of the Holy Spirit,
one God, forever and ever.
Amen.

✝ Teach me your paths, Lord.

✝ Bless the Lord, my soul.

Psalm 104 *page 415*

Reading *Mark 1:29–39*

On leaving the synagogue Jesus entered the house of Simon and Andrew with James and John. Simon's mother-in-law lay sick with a fever. They immediately told him about her. He approached, grasped her hand, and helped her up. Then the fever left her and she waited on them.

When it was evening, after sunset, they brought to him all who were ill or possessed by demons. The whole town was gathered at the door. He cured many who were sick with various diseases, and he drove out many demons, not permitting them to speak because they knew him.

Rising very early before dawn, he left and went off to a deserted place, where he prayed. Simon and those who were with him pursued him and on finding him said, "Everyone is looking for you." He told them, "Let us go on to the nearby villages that I may preach there also. For this purpose have I come." So he went into their synagogues, preaching and driving out demons throughout the whole of Galilee.

Reflection

Without the benefit of modern medicine, fevers could be life-threatening. Simon's mother-in-law might have thought she was going to die. She must have been astonished when she not only became well, but also was healed instantly. Whatever she felt, she reciprocated as best she could; she offered food and drink to Jesus and his friends. All true disciples do likewise. We express our gratitude for what God has done for us by serving and worshipping him.

Prayers *others may be added*

To the God of heaven and earth,
we pray:

◆ Renew us, O Lord.

Grant us grateful hearts, we pray: ◆ Heal all those who suffer throughout the world, we pray: ◆ Sustain the unemployed and those struggling from addiction, we pray: ◆ Comfort those who experience chronic pain and all illness, we pray: ◆

Our Father . . .

Jesus our healer,
when we are laid low by
    pain, suffering, or doubt,
grasp us by the hand
and raise us up.
Strengthen us
    to serve and follow you,
who live and reign
with God the Father
in the unity of the Holy Spirit,
one God, forever and ever.
Amen.

✝ Bless the Lord, my soul.

✝ Bless the Lord, my soul.

Psalm 104 *page 415*

Reading *Genesis 1:1–8*

In the beginning, when God created the heavens and the earth, the earth was a formless wasteland, and darkness covered the abyss, while a mighty wind swept over the waters.

Then God said, "Let there be light," and there was light. God saw how good the light was. God then separated the light from the darkness. God called the light "day," and the darkness he called "night." Thus evening came, and morning followed—the first day.

Then God said, "Let there be a dome in the middle of the waters, to separate one body of water from the other." And so it happened: God made the dome, and it separated the water above the dome from the water below it. God called the dome "the sky." Evening came, and morning followed—the second day.

Reflection

Today, research has shown how vital the oceans are to the life and health of the planet. In the Old Testament, the vast, unexplored waters symbolized destruction and death. In bringing forth light from darkness and exercising mastery over the water, God creates the space for life to flourish. By sending his Son, who shares in God's creative work, God reveals that he will never let creation fall back into the abyss.

Prayers *others may be added*

To the God of heaven and earth,
we pray:

♦ Renew us, O Lord.

Instill in our hearts a love for creation, we pray: ♦ Guide leaders to promote good stewarding of earth's resources, we pray: ♦ Inspire and renew scientists, researchers, and teachers, we pray: ♦ Shed light and healing upon the darkness that pervades the world, we pray: ♦

Our Father . . .

Loving and creating God,
your son walked across the water
as a sign of his power over evil.
Embolden us to do what is right
so that we might participate
   in your recreation of the world.
We ask this through our Lord Jesus
   Christ, your Son,
who lives and reigns with you
in the unity of the Holy Spirit,
one God, forever and ever.
Amen.

✝ Bless the Lord, my soul.

✝ Bless the Lord, my soul.

Psalm 104   *page 415*

Reading   *Genesis 1:24–28*

Then God said, "Let the earth bring forth all kinds of living creatures: cattle, creeping things, and wild animals of all kinds." And so it happened: God made all kinds of wild animals, all kinds of cattle, and all kinds of creeping things of the earth. God saw how good it was. Then God said: "Let us make man in our image, after our likeness. Let them have dominion over the fish of the sea, the birds of the air, and the cattle, and over all the wild animals and all the creatures that crawl on the ground."

Reflection

In stories of creation from the ancient near east, human beings are presented as savages and slaves of the gods. In this biblical account, however, humans are presented in remarkably different terms. Humanity represents and shares God's creative power. We sometimes struggle to be life giving rather than death dealing, to image goodness instead of evil. Nevertheless, God guides us unfailingly in the work he entrusts to us.

Prayers   *others may be added*

To the God of heaven and earth, we pray:

♦ Renew us, O Lord.

Give us hearts of justice, we pray: ♦ Grant us wisdom, we pray: ♦ Guide us in the way of peace, we pray: ♦ Lead us to your kingdom we pray: ♦ Provide us with a bountiful harvest, we pray: ♦

Our Father . . .

Loving and creating God,
you not only gave us life,
you invite us to participate in your work
     of creation and redemption.
Help us to care for our world,
     other species, and each other
so as to mirror your love.
Through Christ our Lord.
Amen.

✝ Bless the Lord, my soul.

✝ Bless the Lord, my soul.

Psalm 104 *page 415*

Reading *Genesis 2:4b–9*

At the time when the LORD God made the earth and the heavens—while as yet there was no field shrub on earth and no grass of the field had sprouted, for the LORD God had sent no rain upon the earth and there was no man to till the soil, but a stream was welling up out of the earth and was watering all the surface of the ground—the LORD God formed man out of the clay of the ground and blew into his nostrils the breath of life, and so man became a living being.

Then the LORD God planted a garden in Eden, in the east, and he placed there the man whom he had formed. Out of the ground the LORD God made various trees grow that were delightful to look at and good for food, with the tree of life in the middle of the garden and the tree of the knowledge of good and evil.

Reflection

In this second creation story, God shapes and breathes life into a man and places him in the garden. The garden with its fresh, flowing water is a symbol of life. The man—and soon, the woman—have every need provided for. Their life is one of ease, joy, and abundance. Although we read this passage as a story of creation, it is simultaneously a story of the life God wants for us in the end.

Prayers *others may be added*

To the God of heaven and earth,
we pray:

◆ Renew us, O Lord.

Open our eyes to the beauty of creation, we pray: ◆ Encourage community organizers serving the poor and marginalized, we pray: ◆ Nurture gardeners and botanists, we pray: ◆ Raise up new vocations to the Benedictines and all contemplatives, we pray: ◆

Our Father . . .

Loving and creating God,
you provide for our every need.
As we accept one good gift after another,
may we realize that there is no end
    to all that you offer.
Through Christ our Lord.
Amen.

✝ Bless the Lord, my soul.

✝ Bless the Lord, my soul.

Psalm 104   *page 415*

Reading   *Genesis 2:18–23*

The LORD God said: "It is not good for the man to be alone. I will make a suitable partner for him." So the LORD God formed out of the ground various wild animals and various birds of the air, and he brought them to the man to see what he would call them; whatever the man called each of them would be its name. The man gave names to all the cattle, all the birds of the air, and all the wild animals; but none proved to be the suitable partner for the man.

So the LORD God cast a deep sleep on the man, and while he was asleep, he took out one of his ribs and closed up its place with flesh. The LORD God then built up into a woman the rib that he had taken from the man. When he brought her to the man, the man said: "This one, at last is bone of my bones / and flesh of my flesh; / this one shall be called 'woman,' / for out of 'her man' this one has been taken."

Reflection

Out of abundant care for his human creation, God tries fashioning an intimate partner for the man, but the other animals are too different to be a suitable companion. By using part of the man's own body to form the woman, God ensures that the man will have an equal, someone just like him. The woman is someone with whom the man can form a mutually loving and supportive relationship.

Prayers   *others may be added*

To the God of heaven and earth, we pray:

◆ Renew us, O Lord.

For the Church: may she nurture the gifts of the baptized, we pray: ◆ For civil authorities: may they work to eliminate systemic gender inequality, we pray: ◆ For those in unhealthy relationships: grant them courage and healing, we pray: ◆ For zoologists and veterinarians: guide them in their care of the animals of the earth, we pray: ◆

Our Father . . .

Loving and creating God,
we are made for fellowship with you
and with each other.
Keep our hearts open
    to the needs of others,
and help us to acknowledge
    the ways in which our own lives
are enriched by those we get to know.
We ask this through our Lord Jesus
    Christ, your Son,
who lives and reigns with you
in the unity of the Holy Spirit,
one God, forever and ever.
Amen.

✝ Bless the Lord, my soul.

✝ Bless the Lord, my soul.

Psalm 104 *page 415*

Reading *Genesis 3:1–7*

The serpent asked the woman, "Did God really tell you not to eat from any of the trees in the garden?" The woman answered the serpent: "We may eat of the fruit of the trees in the garden; it is only about the fruit of the tree in the middle of the garden that God said, 'You shall not eat it or even touch it, lest you die.'" But the serpent said to the woman: "You certainly will not die! No, God knows well that the moment you eat of it your eyes will be opened and you will be like gods who know what is good and what is evil." The woman saw that the tree was good for food, pleasing to the eyes, and desirable for gaining wisdom. So she took some of its fruit and ate it; and she also gave some to her husband, who was with her, and he ate it. Then the eyes of both of them were opened, and they realized that they were naked; so they sewed fig leaves together and made loincloths for themselves.

Reflection

It is sometimes very hard to figure out what the right course of action is in a given moment. At other times, we know perfectly well what we should do, but we talk ourselves into a poor choice. Those moments reveal our limitations. Only by spending time with God and listening to the wise counsel of others will we make choices we will not regret.

Prayers *others may be added*

To the God of heaven and earth, we pray:

◆ Renew us, O Lord.

Help us confess our limitations and our need for you, O God, we pray: ◆ Guide local and national leaders when shaping new laws and policies, we pray: ◆ Enlighten those who seek wise and holy counsel, we pray: ◆ Safeguard those who are struggling to resist sin, we pray: ◆

Our Father . . .

Merciful Lord,
you offer us intimate friendship with you,
    yet we turn away.
Open our eyes to what is truly pleasing
    and desirable
so that we might make choices that
    ultimately lead to you.
We ask this through our Lord Jesus
    Christ, your Son,
who lives and reigns with you
in the unity of the Holy Spirit,
one God, forever and ever.
Amen.

✝ Bless the Lord, my soul.

✝ Bless the Lord, my soul.

Psalm 104
page 415

Reading
Genesis 3:9–13

The LORD God called to Adam and asked him, "Where are you?" He answered, "I heard you in the garden; but I was afraid, because I was naked, so I hid myself." Then he asked, "Who told you that you were naked? You have eaten, then, from the tree of which I had forbidden you to eat!" The man replied, "The woman whom you put here with me—she gave me fruit from the tree, and so I ate it." The LORD God then asked the woman, "Why did you do such a thing?" The woman answered, "The serpent tricked me into it, so I ate it."

Reflection

Having chosen not to entrust themselves to God's care, the man and woman now hear the terrible question, "Where are you?" This question may be extremely difficult for us to face, but we should ask it of ourselves at the end every day. Where are we in our relationships? Where are we in our personal development? Where are we in our spiritual journey? Above all, where are we heading?

Prayers
others may be added

To the God of heaven and earth, we pray:

◆ Renew us, O Lord.

Holy Spirit, direct ecclesial and political leaders in their pursuit of honest self-appraisal, we pray: ◆ Holy Spirit, comfort those who have never known closeness with God, we pray: ◆ Holy Spirit, help us accept responsibility for our actions, we pray: ◆ Holy Spirit, renew the lives of those suffering from unresolved traumas, we pray: ◆

Our Father . . .

Merciful Lord,
console us with the assurance of your
    unwavering love.
Draw us out of hiding
and into your eternal embrace.
We ask this through our Lord Jesus
    Christ, your Son,
who lives and reigns with you
in the unity of the Holy Spirit,
one God, forever and ever.
Amen.

✝ Bless the Lord, my soul.

✝ Have mercy on me, God,
in your goodness.

Psalm 51 *page 409*

Reading *Mark 1:40–45*

A leper came to Jesus and kneeling down begged him and said, "If you wish, you can make me clean." Moved with pity, he stretched out his hand, touched him, and said to him, "I do will it. Be made clean." The leprosy left him immediately, and he was made clean. Then, warning him sternly, he dismissed him at once.

He said to him, "See that you tell no one anything, but go, show yourself to the priest and offer for your cleansing what Moses prescribed; that will be proof for them."

The man went away and began to publicize the whole matter.

Reflection

According to Jewish law, the leper should not have approached Jesus. Jesus, for his part, should not have touched the leper because by doing so Jesus also became unclean. Yet both men ignore law and custom, and the result is a transformation that transcends physical healing. Too often people feel unworthy to approach God, but the only way to become worthy is to allow God to cleanse us and make us whole.

Prayers *others may be added*

From hearts cleansed by God,
we pray:

◆ God of salvation, hear our prayer.

For those who seek mercy and healing, we pray: ◆ For those who are marginalized and oppressed, we pray: ◆ For all those who care for the sick and suffering, we pray: ◆ For those too ashamed to call upon God in prayer, we pray: ◆

Our Father . . .

Jesus our healer,
give us the courage to approach you when
we feel we have nothing to offer you.
Lift us up
so that we may again rejoice
and praise your goodness,
for you live and reign with God the Father
in the unity of the Holy Spirit,
one God, forever and ever.
Amen.

✝ Have mercy on me, God,
in your goodness.

✝ Have mercy on me, God,
in your goodness.

Psalm 51 *page 409*

Reading *Genesis 4:3–9*

In the course of time Cain brought an offering to the LORD from the fruit of the soil, while Abel, for his part, brought one of the best firstlings of his flock. The LORD looked with favor on Abel and his offering, but on Cain and his offering he did not. Cain greatly resented this and was crestfallen. So the LORD said to Cain: "Why are you so resentful and crestfallen. If you do well, you can hold up your head; but if not, sin is a demon lurking at the door: his urge is toward you, yet you can be his master."

Cain said to his brother Abel, "Let us go out in the field." When they were in the field, Cain attacked his brother Abel and killed him. Then the LORD asked Cain, "Where is your brother Abel?" He answered, "I do not know. Am I my brother's keeper?"

Reflection

In this story of Adam and Eve's offspring, we hear how sin begins spreading from one generation to the next. Where there was perfect communion, now men and women are set against each other and against their environment. As Cain, the farmer, attacks his brother, the shepherd, we are reminded of how various groups oppose each other, sometimes violently. As we prepare for Lent, we confess how much we need God's help to ignore the boundaries we set and to seek common ground.

Prayers *others may be added*

From hearts cleansed by God,
we pray:

◆ **God of salvation, hear our prayer.**

That parish leaders and volunteers may find healthy ways of resolving conflicts, we pray: ◆ That leaders of nations may seek to implement just policies, we pray: ◆ That refugees of war, drought, or oppression, may find security and comfort, we pray: ◆ That those who feel rejected or neglected may know the love of Christ, we pray: ◆

Our Father . . .

O God,
you have blessed us
with friends and family.
May we be quick to help not only those
closest to us,
but also those we barely know.
Through Christ our Lord.
Amen.

✝ Have mercy on me, God,
in your goodness.

✝ Have mercy on me, God,
in your goodness.

Psalm 51 *page 409*

Reading *Genesis 6:5–8*

When the LORD saw how great was man's wickedness on earth, and how no desire that his heart conceived was ever anything but evil, he regretted that he had made man on the earth, and his heart was grieved.

So the LORD said: "I will wipe out from the earth the men whom I have created, and not only the men, but also the beasts and the creeping things and the birds of the air, for I am sorry that I made them." But Noah found favor with the LORD.

Reflection

The sin we commit can be so great that it wrecks everything around us. In this brief, poignant passage, God, who entrusted enormous freedom to human beings, is so heart-broken over the evil perpetuated by the people. The only solution seems to be to allow creation to fall back into nothingness. This passage is a painful reminder of how harmful and far-reaching sin is.

Prayers *others may be added*

From hearts cleansed by God,
we pray:

◆ God of salvation, hear our prayer.

God, grant your people mercy, we pray: ◆
God, grant wisdom to leaders, we pray: ◆
God, open our hearts to your grace,
we pray: ◆ God, grant wisdom to
confessors and spiritual directors,
we pray: ◆

Our Father . . .

Holy God,
you are the source of all goodness.
In the Lenten days ahead,
make us mindful
    of the effect of sin in our lives.
Keep us calling out
    for your saving grace.
We ask this through our Lord Jesus
    Christ, your Son,
who lives and reigns with you
in the unity of the Holy Spirit,
one God, forever and ever.
Amen.

✝ Have mercy on me, God,
in your goodness.

✝ Have mercy on me, God,
in your goodness.

Psalm 51   *page 409*

Reading   *2 Corinthians 5:20—6:2*

Brothers and sisters: We are ambassadors for Christ, as if God were appealing through us. We implore you on behalf of Christ, be reconciled to God. For our sake he made him to be sin who did not know sin, so that we might become the righteousness of God in him.

Working together, then, we appeal to you not to receive the grace of God in vain. For he says: / *In an acceptable time I heard you, / and on the day of salvation I helped you.* / Behold, now is a very acceptable time; behold, now is the day of salvation.

Reflection

St. Paul became a missionary because he had experienced God's mercy so deeply that it changed his life. An ambassador for Christ, he shared the joyous news that God reconciled us to himself, saving us from sin and death. If we have truly accepted God's great mercy, then we must be like Paul: we must be forgiving, patient, and peaceful people, and we must be such people today.

Prayers   *others may be added*

From hearts cleansed by God,
we pray:

◆ God of salvation, hear our prayer.

Show us your gracious mercy, God, we pray: ◆ Strengthen leaders to work for peace, we pray: ◆ Enlighten the elect and their godparents, we pray: ◆ Give your people a spirit of repentance, we pray: ◆

Our Father . . .

Loving Father,
keep us faithful in our Lenten practices
   of prayer, fasting,
   and almsgiving.
Through these and other acts of love,
cleanse our hearts
and fill us with joy in your salvation.
We ask this through our Lord Jesus
   Christ, your Son,
who lives and reigns with you
in the unity of the Holy Spirit,
one God, forever and ever.
Amen.

✝ Have mercy on me, God,
in your goodness.

✝ Have mercy on me, God,
in your goodness.

Psalm 51   *page 409*

Reading   *Deuteronomy 30:15–20a*

Moses said to the people: "Today I have set before you life and prosperity, death and doom. If you obey the command-ments of the LORD, your God, which I enjoin on you today, loving him, and walking in his ways, and keeping his commandments, statutes and decrees, you will live and grow numerous, and the LORD, your God, will bless you in the land you are entering to occupy. If, however, you turn away your hearts and will not listen, but are led astray and adore and serve other gods, I tell you now that you will certainly perish; you will not have a long life on the land that you are crossing the Jordan to enter and occupy. I call heaven and earth today to witness against you: I have set before you life and death, the blessing and the curse. Choose life, then, that you and your descendants may live, by loving the LORD, your God, heeding his voice, and holding fast to him."

Reflection

Before entering the Promised Land, God's people pause to remember all that God has done for them and to recommit themselves to their covenant with God. Although the people solemnly entered this covenant only once, they must choose to stay faithful to it every day. In the same way, each day of our lives is a recommitment, a day in which we choose to remain faithful to God and to enter into the new life God gives us.

Prayers   *others may be added*

From hearts cleansed by God,
we pray:

◆ God of salvation, hear our prayer.

Strengthen pastors and preachers on the journey of faith, we pray: ◆ Protect those who are oppressed and marginalized, we pray: ◆ Grant us the Spirit's grace of counsel as we make decisions, we pray: ◆ Shepherd those who are experiencing difficult transitions, we pray: ◆

Our Father . . .

O God of life,
we don't always see how we turn away
from you.
Reveal where our choices are leading us,
and keep us on the path
that leads to you.
Through Christ our Lord.
Amen.

✝ Have mercy on me, God,
in your goodness.

✝ Have mercy on me, God,
in your goodness.

Psalm 51   *page 409*

Reading   *Isaiah 58:5–7*

[Thus says the Lord GOD]: / Lo, on your fast day you carry out your own pursuits, / and drive all your laborers. / Yes, your fast ends in quarreling and fighting, / striking with wicked claw. / Would that today you might fast / so as to make your voice heard on high! / Is this the manner of fasting I wish, / of keeping a day of penance: / That a man bows / his head like a reed / and lie in sackcloth and ashes? / Do you call this a fast, / a day acceptable to the LORD? / This, rather, is the fasting that I wish: / releasing those bound unjustly, / untying the thongs of the yoke; / Setting free the oppressed, breaking every yoke; / Sharing your bread with the hungry, / sheltering the oppressed and the homeless; / Clothing the naked when you see them, / and not turning your back on your own.

Reflection

Fasting is an ancient practice often used as an expression of repentance. Here, God's people are fasting, but not repenting; grave injustices remain in their society. At the beginning of our Lenten season, we are invited to reflect on the Lenten disciplines of prayer, fasting, and almsgiving. We are also reminded that these practices are only some of the ways in which we participate in the reign of God.

Prayers   *others may be added*

From hearts cleansed by God,
we pray:

◆ **God of salvation, hear our prayer.**

Grant the Church the gift of fortitude to advocate for justice, we pray: ◆ Awaken within us the desire to serve the poor and marginalized, we pray: ◆ Help us persevere on this Lenten journey, we pray: ◆ Sustain and protect those who go without food and shelter, we pray: ◆

Our Father . . .

God of compassion,
you hear those who cry out to you.
Keep our ears attuned to others,
and teach us how best to respond for the
    sake of your kingdom.
Through Christ our Lord.
Amen.

✝ Have mercy on me, God,
in your goodness.

✝ Have mercy on me, God, in your goodness.

Psalm 51
page 409

Reading
Isaiah 58:13–14

[Thus says the LORD:] If you hold back your foot on the sabbath / from following your own pursuits on my holy day; / If you call the sabbath a delight, / and the LORD's holy day honorable; / If you honor it by not following your ways, / seeking your own interests, or speaking with malice— / Then you shall delight in the LORD, / and I will make you ride on the heights of the earth; / I will nourish you with the heritage of Jacob, your father, / for the mouth of the LORD has spoken.

Reflection

How well do we honor the Sabbath? The Sabbath is not merely a day of rest; it is the Lord's day, a day in which we show our dedication to God. Going to Mass is one way we express our commitment, but there may be other ways for us to honor God on the Sabbath, like spending an extra hour reading Scripture or doing an examination of conscience.

Prayers
others may be added

From hearts cleansed by God,
we pray:

◆ God of salvation, hear our prayer.

For overworked pastors and lay ministers, we pray: ◆ For civil authorities striving to protect the rights of workers, we pray: ◆ For those unable to get the rest they need, we pray: ◆ For a spirit of stillness and contemplation, we pray: ◆

Our Father . . .

Holy Lord,
everything we have
    comes from you,
and so it is fitting that we take the time to
    thank and praise you.
May our Sabbath practices
strengthen our devotion to you.
Through Christ our Lord.
Amen.

✝ Have mercy on me, God, in your goodness.

✝ My soul thirsts for you, my God.

Psalm 63 *page 411*

Reading *Mark 1:12–15*

The Spirit drove Jesus out into the desert, and he remained in the desert for forty days, tempted by Satan. He was among wild beasts, and the angels ministered to him.

After John had been arrested, Jesus came to Galilee proclaiming the gospel of God: "This is the time of fulfillment. The kingdom of God is at hand. Repent, and believe in the gospel."

Reflection

Because deserts are physically challenging, they came to represent places of spiritual challenge. Jesus went into the desert to listen, to discern, and to test his spiritual strength. Lent is our time to do the same. No matter the life terrain we are in, if we push ourselves, even just a little, we will discover that with God's help we are far stronger than we think.

Prayers *others may be added*

Calling upon God's name, we pray:

◆ Help us, O Lord.

May the Church grow in wisdom and insight this Lenten season, we pray: ◆ May leaders facing difficult choices entrust themselves to God's guidance, we pray: ◆ May the elect open their hearts to God's love and mercy, we pray: ◆ May we grow in perseverance in the face of temptation, we pray: ◆

Our Father . . .

God our Father,
your Son began his ministry
despite the arrest of
   John the Baptist.
Quiet our own minds and hearts
so that we, too, might hear your call
and bravely go forth to do your will.
Through Christ our Lord.
Amen.

✝ My soul thirsts for you, my God.

✝ My soul thirsts for you, my God.

Psalm 63
page 411

Reading
Matthew 16:13–19

When Jesus went into the region of Caesarea Philippi he asked his disciples, "Who do people say that the Son of Man is?" They replied, "Some say John the Baptist, others Elijah, still others Jeremiah or one of the prophets." He said to them, "But who do you say that I am?" Simon Peter said in reply, "You are the Christ, the Son of the living God." Jesus said to him in reply, "Blessed are you, Simon son of Jonah. For flesh and blood has not revealed this to you, but my heavenly Father. And so I say to you, you are Peter, and upon this rock I will build my Church, and the gates of the netherworld shall not prevail against it. I will give you the keys to the Kingdom of heaven. Whatever you bind on earth shall be bound in heaven; and whatever you loose on earth shall be loosed in heaven."

Reflection

Jesus founded a community to act in his name and established offices or positions of leadership within this community. These offices ensure that his community meet new challenges in ways that reveal his continuing presence in the world. Jesus used the metaphor of keys as well as language about binding and loosing to assure his followers that as long as they are faithful to his Spirit, he upholds their decisions.

Prayers
others may be added

Calling upon God's name, we pray:

◆ Help us, O Lord.

May our pope, bishops, priests, and deacons be ever faithful to the Spirit of Christ, we pray: ◆ May those in public office respect the positions they hold, we pray: ◆ May God's mercy be with those in need of reconciliation, we pray: ◆ May our eyes be opened to see Christ, we pray: ◆

Our Father . . .

Son of the living God,
stand with us,
the community you have gathered
and formed in your name.
Bring all that we do into conformity with
    your will,
for you live and reign
    with God the Father
in the unity of the Holy Spirit,
one God, forever and ever.
Amen.

✝ My soul thirsts for you, my God.

✝ My soul thirsts for you, my God.

Psalm 63 *page 411*

Reading *Isaiah 55:10–11*

Thus says the LORD: / Just as from the heavens / the rain and snow come down / And do not return there / till they have watered the earth, / making it fertile and fruitful, / Giving seed to the one who sows / and bread to the one who eats, / So shall my word be / that goes forth from my mouth; / It shall not return to me void, / but shall do my will, / achieving the end for which I sent it.

Reflection

There are days when it seems like we have only failed God. We have failed to listen, failed to understand, failed to do what is right. At such times, we take heart that God's word is tenacious. God's word takes hold of us and will not let go. God will never stop speaking to us. God will never stop drawing us toward what is good. God will never stop nurturing us and giving us life.

Prayers *others may be added*

Calling upon God's name, we pray:

♦ Help us, O Lord.

For lectors, homilists, and other ministers of the Word, we pray: ♦ For relief agencies and other organizations at work in conflict zones, we pray: ♦ For those who struggle to hear God's voice, we pray: ♦ For the assembly to have hearts to listen attentively to God's life-giving word, we pray: ♦

Our Father . . .

Life-giving Lord,
there are times
    we don't listen to you.
There are even times
    we interrupt you.
Be patient with us.
Gently silence us
until we accept words from you
that sustain and save us.
Through Christ our Lord.
Amen.

✝ My soul thirsts for you, my God.

✝ My soul thirsts for you, my God.

Psalm 63 *page 411*

Reading *Jonah 3:4–10*

Jonah began his journey through the city, and had gone but a single day's walk announcing, "Forty days more and Nineveh shall be destroyed," when the people of Nineveh believed God; they proclaimed a fast and all of them, great and small, put on sackcloth. When the news reached the king of Nineveh, he rose from his throne, laid aside his robe, covered himself with sackcloth, and sat in the ashes. Then he had this proclaimed throughout Nineveh, by decree of the king and his nobles: "Neither man nor beast, neither cattle nor sheep, shall taste anything; they shall not eat, nor shall they drink water. Man and beast shall be covered with sackcloth and call loudly to God; every man shall turn from his evil way and from the violence he has in hand. Who knows, God may relent and forgive, and withhold his blazing wrath, so that we shall not perish." When God saw by their actions how they turned from their evil way, he repented of the evil that he had threatened to do to them; he did not carry it out.

Reflection

Independently each person of Nineveh might have hesitated to heed the warning of a foreign prophet. As they eyed each other and exchanged hushed, anxious words, however, they compelled one another to change until the entire nation bowed its head in repentance. The witness of others strengthens our own resolve, which in turn further strengthens others until the whole community changes for the better.

Prayers *· others may be added*

Calling upon God's name, we pray:

◆ Help us, O Lord.

Give us courage to turn back to you, O God, we pray: ◆ Give wisdom to leaders who work in conflict zones, we pray: ◆ Give comfort to those in isolation, we pray: ◆ Give courage to those in need of healing and reconciliation, we pray: ◆

Our Father . . .

Gracious God,
when we fall into sin,
you reach down to pull us out of it.
May we reach out to others
who have turned away from you
until everyone has turned back
and is calling loudly for your mercy.
Through Christ our Lord.
Amen.

✝ My soul thirsts for you, my God.

✝ My soul thirsts for you, my God.

Psalm 63 *page 411*

Reading *Matthew 7:7–12*

Jesus said to his disciples: "Ask and it will be given to you; seek and you will find; knock and the door will be opened to you. For everyone who asks, receives; and the one who seeks, finds; and to the one who knocks, the door will be opened. Which one of you would hand his son a stone when he asked for a loaf of bread, or a snake when he asks for a fish? If you, who are wicked, know how to give good things to your children, how much more will your heavenly Father give good things to those who ask him.

"Do to others whatever you would have them do to you. This is the law and the prophets."

Reflection

God wants us to ask for good gifts. God wants to welcome us into divine life, to be sought, found, and known. Because God is infinite in goodness, there is no end to the good gifts we will receive. God calls us to be equally generous. Lent is an opportunity to be more intentional about offering what God asks of us, about being found by God, and about welcoming God who is knocking at our door.

Prayers *others may be added*

Calling upon God's name, we pray:

◆ Help us, O Lord.

For ministers of the Church as they share God's goodness with others, we pray: ◆
For those who persevere against systemic corruption and injustice, we pray: ◆
For parents who are unable to care for their children, we pray: ◆ For the wisdom to know what to ask of God, we pray: ◆

Our Father . . .

Heavenly Father,
all that you have, you offer us,
but often we refuse your gifts.
Help us to see how much our lives
are enriched when we accept
  what you offer.
Through Christ our Lord.
Amen.

✝ My soul thirsts for you, my God.

✝ Have mercy on me, God,
  in your goodness.

Psalm 51
page 409

Reading
Ezekiel 18:25–28

You say, "The LORD's way is not fair!"
Hear now, house of Israel: Is it my way
that is unfair, or rather, are not your
ways unfair? When someone virtuous
turns away from virtue to commit iniquity, and dies, it is because of the iniquity he committed that he must die. But
if the wicked, turning from the wickedness he has committed, does what is
right and just, he shall preserve his life;
since he has turned away from all the
sins that he committed, he shall surely
live, he shall not die.

Reflection

God is responding to his people's com-
plaint that they are being punished for
the sins of their ancestors. This belief
in corporate guilt and intergenerational
punishment was strong in Israel. God
responds that he will deal fairly with
each new generation; individuals will
not be punished for the sins of their
ancestors. The people's relief would
have been short-lived, for God declares
that by pointing to the sins of their
ancestors, the people are failing to
admit their own.

Prayers
others may be added

From hearts cleansed by God,
we pray:

◆ God of salvation, hear our prayer.

For pastors, confessors, and spiritual
directors, we pray: ◆ For those who
work in judicial systems, we pray: ◆
For those in prison and for those on
parole, we pray: ◆ For our ancestors,
we pray: ◆ For the Church, we pray: ◆

Our Father . . .

Lord God,
help us recognize
and admit our wrongdoing.
Give us the strength of will
to change our behavior
    no matter how set in our ways
we might seem.
Through Christ our Lord.
Amen.

✝ Have mercy on me, God,
  in your goodness.

✝ My soul thirsts for you, my God.

Psalm 63   *page 411*

Reading   *Deuteronomy 26:16–19*

Moses spoke to the people, saying: "This day the LORD, your God, commands you to observe these statutes and decrees. Be careful, then, to observe them with all your heart and with all your soul. Today you are making this agreement with the LORD: he is to be your God and you are to walk in his ways and observe his statutes, commandments and decrees, and to hearken to his voice. And today the LORD is making this agreement with you: you are to be a people peculiarly his own, as he promised you; and provided you keep all his commandments, he will then raise you high in praise and renown and glory above all other nations he has made, and you will be a people sacred to the LORD, your God, as he promised."

Reflection

As God's people prepare to commit themselves to the covenant, Moses reminds them not only of their obligations, but also of what God will do for them. The people will be bound to God and set apart among all the nations on earth. God will reveal himself to the world through them. By the sacraments of Initiation we have become part of the New Covenant, Christ's Body, through whom God continues revealing himself today.

Prayers   *others may be added*

Calling upon God's name, we pray:

◆ Help us, O Lord.

That the Church hearken to God's voice, we pray: ◆ That civil authorities justly interpret and implement the laws of their nations, we pray: ◆ That sponsors, godparents, and catechists model holiness for those preparing for the Easter sacraments, we pray: ◆ That each of us grow in faith, we pray: ◆

Our Father . . .

Holy Lord,
you entrust to us the work
    of revealing your divine love
so that everyone may become part of your
    holy people.
May we strive each day
    to more faithfully obey your will.
Through Christ our Lord.
Amen.

✝ My soul thirsts for you, my God.

✝ How precious is your love, O God!

Psalm 36 *page 408*

Reading *Mark 9:2–9*

Jesus took Peter, James, and John and led them up a high mountain apart by themselves. And he was transfigured before them, and his clothes became dazzling white, such as no fuller on earth could bleach them. Then Elijah appeared to them along with Moses, and they were conversing with Jesus. Then Peter said to Jesus in reply, "Rabbi, it is good that we are here! Let us make three tents: one for you, one for Moses, and one for Elijah." . . . Then a cloud came, casting a shadow over them; from the cloud came a voice, "This is my beloved Son. Listen to him." Suddenly, looking around, they no longer saw anyone but Jesus alone with them.

As they were coming down from the mountain, he charged them not to relate what they had seen to anyone, except when the Son of Man had risen from the dead.

Reflection

Peter, James, and John do not understand the terrifying moment when Jesus is transfigured on the mountain. They still were unaware that the cross awaited Jesus. Jesus has already spoken of the costs of discipleship, but his followers misunderstand and resist his words. God insists that they listen. It is not easy to follow Jesus. Our hope in the glory to come helps us persevere.

Prayers *others may be added*

We entrust ourselves to God's mercy as we pray:

◆ Gracious God, hear our prayer.

May our Church faithfully follow Christ, we pray: ◆ May those in public office accept the costs of leadership, we pray: ◆ May those facing difficult choices find the strength to do what is right, we pray: ◆ May we allow God's voice to silence our fears, we pray: ◆

Our Father . . .

Lord of heaven and earth,
we do not readily accept
or even understand the challenges
    of following your Son.
As we struggle to be his disciples,
help us persevere in joy and hope.
Through Christ our Lord.
Amen.

✝ How precious is your love, O God!

✝ How precious is your love, O God!

Psalm 36 *page 408*

Reading *Daniel 9:4b–10*

"Lord, great and awesome God, you who keep your merciful covenant toward those who love you and observe your commandments! We have sinned, been wicked and done evil; we have rebelled and departed from your commandments and your laws. We have not obeyed your servants the prophets, who spoke in your name to our kings, our princes, our fathers, and all the people of the land. Justice, O Lord, is on your side; we are shamefaced even to this day: we, the men of Judah, the residents of Jerusalem, and all Israel, near and far, in all the countries to which you have scattered them because of their treachery toward you. O LORD, we are shamefaced, like our kings, our princes, and our fathers, for having sinned against you. But yours, O Lord, our God, are compassion and forgiveness! Yet we rebelled against you and paid no heed to your command, O LORD, our God, to live by the law you gave us through your servants the prophets."

Reflection

If we think that in the Old Testament God is angry and punishing, whereas in the New Testament God is loving and forgiving, we risk taking God's love for granted and treating our sins lightly. As Daniel prays, he speaks earnestly of God's love while starkly confessing his sins and the sins of his people. His prayer is a model for us to follow.

Prayers *others may be added*

We entrust ourselves to God's mercy as we pray:

◆ Gracious God, hear our prayer.

Bestow upon us the grace of repentance, we pray: ◆ Grant wisdom to leaders of nations, we pray: ◆ Give us the gift of prudence and self-awareness, we pray: ◆ Protect confessors and spiritual directors, we pray: ◆

Our Father . . .

Almighty God,
you love us
    despite the sins we commit,
but you also command us to admit
    our failures and to repent.
May we take our sins seriously
so that we may not take your mercy
    for granted.
Through Christ our Lord.
Amen.

✝ How precious is your love, O God!

✝ How precious is your love, O God!

Psalm 36 — page 408

Reading — *Isaiah 1:10, 16–20*

Hear the word of the LORD, / princes of Sodom! / Listen to the instruction of our God / people of Gomorrah!

Wash yourselves clean! / Put away your misdeeds from before my eyes; / cease doing evil; learn to do good. / Make justice your aim: redress the wronged, / hear the orphan's plea, defend the widow.

Come now, let us set things right, says the LORD: / Though your sins be like scarlet / they may become white as snow; / Though they be crimson red, / they may become white as wool. / If you are willing, and obey, / you shall eat the good things of the land; / But if you refuse and resist, / the sword shall consume you: / for the mouth of the LORD has spoken!

Reflection

God's warning is stark and frightening. If his people keep failing to help those in need, then God will allow foreign powers to attack them. There is a link between injustice and destruction. A society that does not care for its weakest members eventually crumbles as the more well-to-do members increasingly look after themselves. Only by living as God intends will we flourish and dwell in comfort and peace.

Prayers — *others may be added*

We entrust ourselves to God's mercy as we pray:

◆ Gracious God, hear our prayer.

Guide the Church to be a prophetic voice for justice in the world, we pray: ◆ Help those in government open their hearts to the poor and marginalized, we pray: ◆ Lead us to share our resources fairly, we pray: ◆ Move us to repent our failings, we pray: ◆

Our Father . . .

O God,
source of all compassion,
you teach us anew how to do what is right.
Grant us clean hearts
and lead us always
to follow your will.
Through Christ our Lord.
Amen.

✝ How precious is your love, O God!

✟ How precious is your love, O God!

Psalm 36 *page 408*

Reading *Matthew 20:25–28*

But Jesus summoned them and said, "You know that the rulers of the Gentiles lord it over them, and the great ones make their authority over them felt. But it shall not be so among you. Rather, whoever wishes to be great among you shall be your servant; whoever wishes to be first among you shall be your slave. Just so, the Son of Man did not come to be served but to serve and to give his life as a ransom for many."

Reflection

Instead of following the example of some people in our culture who seek status, money, or power, Jesus tells us to serve one another. St. Katharine Drexel exemplifies countercultural living: she inherited great wealth and a privileged place in society, but she entered religious life and devoted herself to the needs of minorities. By using Christ as her model of behavior, she became a model for others.

Prayers *others may be added*

We entrust ourselves to God's mercy as we pray:

♦ Gracious God, hear our prayer.

That the Church model humility and service, we pray: ♦ That leaders of nations serve with justice and integrity, we pray: ♦ That minorities and their advocates be strengthened in Christ, we pray: ♦ That low-income families and neighborhoods remain in good health and protected from violence, we pray: ♦

Our Father . . .

Lord of all,
you invite us to live in a world
  in which we all take care
  of each other.
May the example
  of St. Katharine Drexel
keep us steadfast in loving service
as we try to follow the example
  of your Son,
who lives and reigns with you
in the unity of the Holy Spirit,
one God, forever and ever.
Amen.

✟ How precious is your love, O God!

Thursday, March 4, 2021
Lenten Weekday

✝ How precious is your love, O God!

Psalm 36   *page 408*

Reading   *Luke 16:19–25*

Jesus said to the Pharisees: "There was a rich man who dressed in purple garments and fine linen and dined sumptuously each day. And lying at his door was a poor man named Lazarus, covered with sores, who would gladly have eaten his fill of the scraps that fell from the rich man's table. Dogs even used to come and lick his sores. When the poor man died, he was carried away by angels to the bosom of Abraham. The rich man also died and was buried, and from the netherworld, where he was in torment, he raised his eyes and saw Abraham far off and Lazarus at his side. And he cried out, 'Father Abraham, have pity on me. Send Lazarus to dip the tip of his finger in water and cool my tongue, for I am suffering torment in these flames.' Abraham replied, 'My child, remember that you received what was good during your lifetime while Lazarus likewise received what was bad; but now he is comforted here, whereas you are tormented.'"

Reflection

We live in one of the wealthiest nations on earth. If everyone lived as we do, human beings would quickly deplete earth's resources. Our country is like the rich man. We are so accustomed to our level of consumption that we no longer realize how excessive it is and how it blinds us to the needs of others. The parable warns that such self-absorbed consumption is disastrous and irreversible.

Prayers   *others may be added*

We entrust ourselves to God's mercy as we pray:

◆ Gracious God, hear our prayer.

Open our eyes to see the needs of the poor, we pray: ◆ Grant us wisdom to steward earth's resources, we pray: ◆ Change our hearts to serve others with compassion, we pray: ◆ Renew the face of the earth, we pray:

Our Father . . .

Father of the poor,
in the fullness of your reign
     everyone has enough
and no one suffers.
Show us what we must do
to live within your kingdom
so that we might ultimately live with
     you forever.
Through Christ our Lord.
Amen.

✝ How precious is your love, O God!

✝ Have mercy on me, God,
in your goodness.

Psalm 51 *page 409*

Reading *Genesis 37:3–4, 12–13,*
17–19, 26–28

Israel loved Joseph best of all his sons, for he was the child of his old age; and he had made him a long tunic. When his brothers saw that their father loved him best of all his sons, they hated him so much that they would not even greet him.

One day, when his brothers had gone to pasture their father's flocks at Shechem, Israel said to Joseph, "Your brothers, you know, are tending our flocks at Shechem. Get ready; I will send you to them."

So Joseph went after his brothers and caught up with them in Dothan. They noticed him from a distance, and before he came up to them, they plotted to kill him. They said to one another: "Here comes that master dreamer!" . . .

Judah said to his brothers: "What is to be gained by killing our brother and concealing his blood? Rather, let us sell him to these Ishmaelites, instead of doing away with him ourselves. After all, he is our brother, our own flesh." His brothers agreed. They sold Joseph to the Ishmaelites for twenty pieces of silver.

Reflection

When young Joseph, whom Israel loved "best of all his sons," reveals his dreams to his brothers, they are understandably resentful. They let their envy and anger get the better of them, and Joseph nearly dies. This passage invites us to reflect on our own relationships. How have our feelings and behavior provoked tension and caused harm?

Prayers *others may be added*

From hearts cleansed by God,
we pray:

◆ **God of salvation, hear our prayer.**

Strengthen our families in your love, we pray: ◆ Enlighten parents with your wisdom, we pray: ◆ Heal divisions within families by your mercy, we pray: ◆ Rescue those who are filled with envy and hatred, we pray: ◆

Our Father . . .

Heavenly Father,
reveal to us the ways we hurt
those closest to us.
Help us to forgive those we love.
Lead us into mutual understanding,
and strengthen the bonds of familial and
spiritual love.
Through Christ our Lord.
Amen.

✝ Have mercy on me, God,
in your goodness.

✝ How precious is your love, O God!

Psalm 36 *page 408*

Reading *Micah 7:14–15, 18–20*

Shepherd your people with your staff, /
the flock of your inheritance, / That
dwells apart in a woodland, / in the midst
of Carmel. / Let them feed in Bashan
and Gilead; / as in the days of old; / As in
the days when you came from the land
of Egypt, / show us wonderful signs.

Who is there like you, the God who
removes guilt / and pardons sin for the
remnant of his inheritance; / Who does
not persist in anger forever, but delights
rather in clemency, / And will again
have compassion on us, treading underfoot our guilt? / You will cast into the
depths of the sea all our sins; / You will
show faithfulness to Jacob, / and grace
to Abraham, / As you have sworn to our
fathers / from the days of old.

Reflection

No one has God's extraordinary power
to forgive. God, in an outpouring of
love, shares this great gift of forgiveness
with us. Forgiveness frees us from the
burden of anger and hurt; it empowers
us to heal and move forward. Although
forgiveness brings healing and consolation, it is still a gift we often have to ask
for every day.

Prayers *others may be added*

We entrust ourselves to God's mercy
as we pray:

◆ Gracious God, hear our prayer.

For pastors and parish administrators,
we pray: ◆ For those suffering from
debts or any financial crisis, we pray: ◆
For those who have suffered civil
wars, we pray: ◆ For those who seek
reconciliation and forgiveness, we pray: ◆

Our Father . . .

Loving and forgiving God,
your gift of forgiveness helps us
   overcome division
and restore the bonds of fellowship.
May we never cease to ask you
   for this gift.
We ask this through our Lord Jesus
   Christ, your Son,
who lives and reigns with you
in the unity of the Holy Spirit,
one God, forever and ever.
Amen.

✝ How precious is your love, O God!

✝ Merciful and gracious is the Lord.

Psalm 103 *page 414*

Reading *John 2:13–17*

Since the Passover of the Jews was near, Jesus went up to Jerusalem. He found in the temple area those who sold oxen, sheep, and doves, as well as the money changers seated there. He made a whip out of cords and drove them all out of the temple area, with the sheep and oxen, and spilled the coins of the money changers and overturned their tables, and to those who sold doves he said, "Take these out of here, and stop making my Father's house a marketplace." His disciples recalled the words of Scripture, *Zeal for your house will consume me.*

Reflection

Jesus' action and dialogue in the temple point to the temple's eventual destruction and even foreshadow his passion and resurrection. Ultimately, he is teaching the people about God's might. We might think we already have a strong relationship to Christ, but are we really letting him disrupt and overturn our lives?

Prayers *others may be added*

To our Father, whose kindness is forever, we pray:

◆ God of compassion, hear our prayer.

Help the baptized be faithful disciples, we pray: ◆ Guide efforts for ecumenical and interreligious dialogue, we pray: ◆ Guide those who oversee the financial resources of parishes and other ministries, we pray: ◆ Strengthen faith in those preparing for baptism, we pray: ◆

Our Father . . .

Son of God,
you reveal yourself to us in ways that
    we don't always recognize.
Help us to discover your presence
    in our lives
and to entrust more of ourselves to you,
who live and reign with God
    the Father
in the unity of the Holy Spirit,
one God, forever and ever.
Amen.

✝ Merciful and gracious is the Lord.

✝ Merciful and gracious is the Lord.

Psalm 103   *page 414*

Reading   *2 Kings 5:9–11, 12c, 13–14*

Naaman came with his horses and chariots and stopped at the door of Elisha's house. The prophet sent him the message: "Go and wash seven times in the Jordan, and your flesh will heal, and you will be clean." But Naaman went away angry, saying, "I thought that he would surely come out and stand there to invoke the LORD his God, and would move his hand over the spot, and thus cure the leprosy. . . ." [H]e turned about in anger and left.

But his servants came up and reasoned with him. "My father," they said, "if the prophet had told you to do something extraordinary, would you not have done it? All the more now, since he said to you, 'Wash and be clean,' should you do as he said." So Naaman went down and plunged into the Jordan seven times at the word of the man of God. His flesh became again like the flesh of a little child, and he was clean.

Reflection

Naaman is a highly respected and privileged member of a foreign nation who learns that the God of Israel could heal him of his skin ailment. When he makes a visit to God's prophet Elisha, Naaman expects to be received like royalty. He so resents Elisha's response to his arrival that he nearly misses the chance to be healed. We, too, sometimes let our ego and our pride prevent us from experiencing God's life-changing grace.

Prayers   *others may be added*

To our Father, whose kindness is forever, we pray:

◆ **God of compassion, hear our prayer.**

For those who seek God, we pray: ◆
For leaders in the midst of war or conflict, we pray: ◆ For those with incurable illnesses, we pray: ◆ For those filled with resentment or lack hope, we pray: ◆

Our Father . . .

O God,
you alone have given us life.
We can only find strength
and healing in you.
In your mercy, comfort us,
    make us whole, and grant us peace.
We ask this through our Lord Jesus
    Christ your Son, who lives and reigns
    with you in the unity of the Holy
    Spirit, one God, forever and ever.
    Amen.

✝ Merciful and gracious is the Lord.

✝ Merciful and gracious is the Lord.

Psalm 103   *page 414*

Reading   *Matthew 18:23–33*

"[T]he Kingdom of heaven may be likened to a king who decided to settle accounts with his servants. When he began the accounting, a debtor was brought before him who owed him a huge amount. Since he had no way of paying it back, his master ordered him to be sold, along with his wife, his children, and all his property, in payment of the debt. At that, the servant fell down, did him homage, and said, 'Be patient with me, and I will pay you back in full.' Moved with compassion the master of that servant let him go and forgave him the loan. When that servant had left, he found one of his fellow servants who owed him a much smaller amount. He seized him and started to choke him, demanding, 'Pay back what you owe.' Falling to his knees, his fellow servant begged him, 'Be patient with me, and I will pay you back.' But he refused. Instead, he had him put in prison until he paid back the debt. . . . [H]is fellow servants . . . went to their master and reported the whole affair. His master summoned him and said to him . . . 'I forgave you your entire debt . . . Should you not have had pity on your fellow servant, as I had pity on you?'"

Reflection

How do you wish to settle your accounts? Do you want to be paid back in full, or are you willing to cancel all or part of what you're owed? What seems fair? Be careful how you answer: one day you might discover that your own debt—or your own sin—is much greater than you knew.

Prayers   *others may be added*

To our Father, whose kindness is forever, we pray:

◆ God of compassion, hear our prayer.

May our Church leaders model mercy in their pastoral care, we pray: ◆ May world leaders pursue economic policies that benefit everyone, we pray: ◆ May business owners act with integrity and transparency, we pray: ◆ May we make investments that are socially just, we pray:

Our Father . . .

Merciful Lord,
may we never fail to take seriously
the prayer your Son taught us.
Keep us mindful of our own sins,
and make us quick to forgive the sins
   of others.
Through Christ our Lord.
Amen.

✝ Merciful and gracious is the Lord.

✝ Merciful and gracious is the Lord.

Psalm 103   *page 414*

Reading   *Deuteronomy 4:1, 5–9*

Moses spoke to the people and said: "Now, Israel, hear the statutes and decrees which I am teaching you to observe, that you may live, and may enter in and take possession of the land which the LORD, the God of your fathers, is giving you. Therefore, I teach you the statutes and decrees as the LORD, my God, has commanded me, that you may observe them in the land you are entering to occupy. Observe them carefully, for thus will you give evidence of your wisdom and intelligence to the nations, who will hear of all these statutes and say, 'This great nation is truly a wise and intelligent people.' For what great nation is there that has gods so close to it as the LORD, our God, is to us whenever we call upon him?"

Reflection

The laws God gave his chosen people set them apart from other nations. Now it is our turn to distinguish ourselves by how we live. Going to Mass, sustaining our Lenten practices, treating others with kindness and dignity, raising our children to be faithful disciples—these are all ways we set ourselves apart so that others might see in us the holiness of God.

Prayers   *others may be added*

To our Father, whose kindness is forever, we pray:

◆ God of compassion, hear our prayer.

May the Church skillfully articulate the goodness of our faith tradition, we pray: ◆ May lawmakers and judges act wisely and justly, we pray: ◆ May parents and grandparents help their children embrace the Gospel, we pray: ◆ May we be strengthened in difficult times, we pray: ◆

Our Father . . .

Holy Lord,
may our Lenten practices
strengthen us to follow you
    more faithfully.
Show us how best
    to uphold your will
so that others may be drawn to you
and find refuge in the Church,
    the body of Christ, your Son,
who lives and reigns with you
in the unity of the Holy Spirit,
one God, forever and ever.
Amen.

✝ Merciful and gracious is the Lord.

✝ Merciful and gracious is the Lord.

Psalm 103 *page 414*

Reading *Jeremiah 7:23–24*

Thus says the LORD: This is what I commanded my people: Listen to my voice; then I will be your God and you shall be my people. Walk in all the ways that I command you, so that you may prosper.

But they obeyed not, nor did they pay heed. They walked in the hardness of their evil hearts and turned their backs, not their faces, to me. From the day that your fathers left the land of Egypt even to this day, I have sent you untiringly all my servants the prophets. Yet they have not obeyed me nor paid heed; they have stiffened their necks and done worse than their fathers. When you speak all these words to them, they will not listen to you either; when you call to them, they will not answer you. Say to them: This is the nation that does not listen to the voice of the LORD, its God, or take correction. Faithfulness has disappeared; the word itself is banished from their speech.

Reflection

God laments his people's unwillingness to remain faithful to him, but his anger is a sign of his enduring love. God would not bother to send prophets or to punish his people if he did not want them to realize how far they had strayed and how badly they had failed him. When we acknowledge our sins and turn back to God, we will be welcomed back. God will meet us not with rage but with merciful love.

Prayers *others may be added*

To our Father, whose kindness is forever, we pray:

◆ God of compassion, hear our prayer.

For those lost in their sins, we pray: ◆ For those in political office, we pray: ◆ For preachers and prophets among us, we pray: ◆ For those who struggle to hear the Good News, we pray: ◆

Our Father . . .

Faithful Lord,
your Son calls us to be disciples,
but we often turn away
    and choose our own paths.
Help us to listen when you call out.
Show us your countenance
so that we might return to you
and faithfully serve you.
Through Christ our Lord.
Amen.

✝ Merciful and gracious is the Lord.

✝ Have mercy on me, God,
in your goodness.

Psalm 51   *page 409*

Reading   *Hosea 14:2–10*

Thus says the LORD: / Return, O Israel, to the LORD, your God; / you have collapsed through your guilt. / Take with you words, / and return to the LORD; / Say to him, "Forgive all iniquity, / and receive what is good, that we may render / as offerings the bullocks from our stalls. / Assyria will not save us, / nor shall we have horses to mount; / We shall say no more, 'Our god,' / to the work of our hands; / for in you the orphan finds compassion." /

I will heal their defection, says the LORD, / I will love them freely; / for my wrath is turned away from them.

Reflection

As God's people flourished in the Promised Land, they began to worship the gods of the surrounding nations. They forgot it was God who gave them everything. When things are going well for us, we might also neglect to thank God. When things are going badly, we might turn elsewhere for help. Like the Israelites, we must learn to thank and turn to God for everything.

Prayers   *others may be added*

From hearts cleansed by God,
we pray:

◆ God of salvation, hear our prayer.

May the Church model gratitude and trust in God alone, we pray: ◆ May leaders confronted by violence and corruption help justice take root in their land, we pray: ◆ May artists, poets, and musicians helps reveal the beauty of our natural world, we pray: ◆ May we grow in awareness of God's presence, we pray: ◆

Our Father . . .

Almighty God,
all that we have comes from you.
Keep us mindful of all you have done
    for us
and of all that you continue to do in our
    lives and in our world.
Through Christ our Lord.
Amen.

✝ Have mercy on me, God,
in your goodness.

✝ Merciful and gracious is the Lord.

Psalm 103   *page 414*

Reading   *Luke 18:9–14*

Jesus addressed this parable to those who were convinced of their own righteousness and despised everyone else. "Two people went up to the temple area to pray; one was a Pharisee and the other was a tax collector. The Pharisee took up his position and spoke this prayer to himself, 'O God, I thank you that I am not like the rest of humanity—greedy, dishonest, adulterous—or even like this tax collector. I fast twice a week, and I pay tithes on my whole income.' But the tax collector stood off at a distance and would not even raise his eyes to heaven but beat his breast and prayed, 'O God, be merciful to me a sinner.' I tell you, the latter went home justified, not the former; for everyone who exalts himself will be humbled, and the one who humbles himself will be exalted."

Reflection

The parable is bracketed with statements that make us think poorly of the Pharisee, but when we do so, we become equally judgmental. It might be wiser for us to consider the merits of both men. The Pharisee is a model of obedience to God's law: he resists the lure of wealth, he tithes, and he fasts twice a week. The tax collector, meanwhile, confesses his sin without making any excuses for himself. In what ways are we obedient to God?

Prayers   *others may be added*

To our Father, whose kindness is forever, we pray:

♦ God of compassion, hear our prayer.

May the Church speak truly of its sins and failures, we pray: ♦ May governments find ways of correcting social and economic imbalances, we pray: ♦ May sponsors, godparents, and catechists model righteousness and humility, we pray: ♦ May we seek the good in others, we pray: ♦

Our Father . . .

Holy Lord,
you grant us the strength
to persevere in faith.
When others struggle in faith,
grant them peace and comfort.
When we struggle,
lead us back to your embrace.
Through Christ our Lord.
Amen.

✝ Merciful and gracious is the Lord.

✝ The Lord is my light and
my salvation.

Psalm 27 *page 405*

Reading *John 3:14–21*

Jesus said to Nicodemus: "Just as Moses lifted up the serpent in the desert, so must the Son of Man be lifted up, so that everyone who believes in him may have eternal life."

For God so loved the world that he gave his only Son, so that everyone who believes in him might not perish but might have eternal life. For God did not send his Son into the world to condemn the world, but that the world might be saved through him. Whoever believes in him will not be condemned, but whoever does not believe has already been condemned, because he has not believed in the name of the only Son of God. And this is the verdict, that the light came into the world, but people preferred darkness to light, because their works were evil. For everyone who does wicked things hates the light and does not come toward the light, so that his works might not be exposed. But whoever lives the truth comes to the light, so that his works may be clearly seen as done in God.

Reflection

This passage makes it seem as though there are only two types of people in the world: those who live in the light, and those who prefer the darkness. We have only to look at our own lives to know that most people stand somewhere in between. Sometimes our deeds are good, but sometimes we sin. Jesus assures us that despite our failures, if we try to open our eyes and turn to the light, we will find ourselves forever in it.

Prayers *others may be added*

Calling out in faith, we pray:

◆ Lord, show us your face.

That we come to know God's love for the world, we pray: ◆ That local and national leaders act with integrity and transparency, we pray: ◆ That those trapped in darkness be healed and rescued, we pray: ◆ That families grow in God's love, we pray: ◆

Our Father . . .

Son of God,
though we sometimes close our eyes
    to your light,
we long to see your glory.
Strengthen us
so that we may turn toward your light
and keep our eyes fixed on your path,
    for you live and reign
    with God, the Father,
in the unity of the Holy Spirit,
one God, forever and ever.
Amen.

✝ The Lord is my light and
my salvation.

✝ The Lord is my light and
my salvation.

Psalm 27 *page 405*

Reading *Isaiah 65:17–21*

Thus says the LORD: / Lo, I am about to
create new heavens / and a new earth; /
The things of the past shall not be
remembered / or come to mind. /
Instead, there shall always be rejoicing
and happiness / in what I create; For I
create Jerusalem to be a joy / and its
people to be a delight; / I will rejoice in
Jerusalem / and exult in my people. / No
longer shall the sound of weeping be
heard there, / or the sound of crying; /
no longer shall there be in it / an infant
who lives but a few days, / or an old man
who does not round out his full lifetime; /
He dies a mere youth who reaches but
a hundred years, / and he who fails of a
hundred shall be thought accursed. /
They shall live in the houses they
build, / and eat the fruit of the vineyards
they plant.

Reflection

Although this passage was written for
the Jews after their homeland had been
devastated by war and invasion, it holds
forth a promise for every generation.
God will heal our brokenness, rebuild
our lives, and ensure peace and security
so that all people, everywhere, will at
last flourish in health and holiness.

Prayers *others may be added*

Calling out in faith, we pray:

◆ Lord, show us your face.

Purify and renew the Church,
we pray: ◆ Look upon leaders with mercy,
we pray: ◆ Heal those who bear the pain
of miscarriage, we pray: ◆ Strengthen our
hope in your compassion, we pray: ◆

Our Father . . .

Loving Lord,
help us to participate
in your kingdom now
so that we may dwell with you
in its fullness forever.
We ask this through our Lord Jesus
Christ, your Son,
who lives and reigns with you
in the unity of the Holy Spirit,
one God, forever and ever.
Amen.

✝ The Lord is my light and
my salvation.

Tuesday, March 16, 2021
Lenten Weekday

✝ The Lord is my light and
my salvation.

Psalm 27 *page 405*

Reading *John 5:2–9*

Now there is in Jerusalem at the Sheep Gate a pool called in Hebrew Bethesda, with five porticoes. In these lay a large number of ill, blind, lame, and crippled. One man was there who had been ill for thirty-eight years. When Jesus saw him lying there and knew that he had been ill for a long time, he said to him, "Do you want to be well?" The sick man answered him, "Sir, I have no one to put me into the pool when the water is stirred up; while I am on my way, someone else gets down there before me." Jesus said to him, "Rise, take up your mat, and walk." Immediately the man became well, took up his mat, and walked.

Reflection

Rather than tell Jesus, "Yes, I want to be well," the sick man talks about the pool. It does not occur to him that there are other ways he can be healed. When we are facing a difficult time, we might think there is only one way to get through it. Jesus invites us to consider other paths that will lead to healing and wholeness.

Prayers *others may be added*

Calling out in faith, we pray:

◆ Lord, show us your face.

May the members of Christ's body accompany the sick and disabled, we pray: ◆ May national leaders ensure access to medical care for all their people, we pray: ◆ May those with chronic illnesses draw strength and comfort from Christ, we pray: ◆ May we act in ways that foster healing, reconciliation, and peace, we pray: ◆

Our Father . . .

God of our salvation,
we depend on you for guidance
as we strive to follow your Son
    in holiness.
Help us to see our lives as you do.
Show us the paths that lead
    into your kingdom.
We ask this through our Lord Jesus
    Christ, your Son,
who lives and reigns with you
in the unity of the Holy Spirit,
one God, forever and ever.
Amen.

✝ The Lord is my light and
my salvation.

✝ The Lord is my light and
my salvation.

Psalm 27 *page 405*

Reading *Isaiah 49:8–11*

Thus says the LORD: / In a time of favor I answer you, / on the day of salvation I help you; / and I have kept you and given you as a covenant to the people. / To restore the land / and allot the desolate heritages, / Saying to prisoners: Come out! / To those in darkness: Show yourselves! / Along the ways they shall find pasture, / on every bare height shall their pastures be. / They shall not hunger or thirst, / nor shall the scorching wind or the sun strike them; / For he who pities them leads them / and guides them beside springs of water. / I will cut a road through all my mountains, / and make my highways level.

Reflection

In the story of creation, God brought forth light where there was only darkness. Now God gathers and restores his people, bringing them back into the light. Despite terrible things that happen, people are not lost to darkness. We are not lost to emptiness and death. God continually calls people into his light. He provides all we need and ensures that we will find our way forward.

Prayers *others may be added*

Calling out in faith, we pray:

◆ Lord, show us your face.

May we find ways of participating in the Church's care of immigrants and refugees, we pray: ◆ May strong and stable governments help nations devastated by wars and natural disasters, we pray: ◆ May people and places under the patronage of St. Patrick be abundantly blessed, we pray: ◆ May Christians everywhere reach out to those who lack basic needs, we pray: ◆

Our Father . . .

Lord of light,
show us how we can help those who are
falling into darkness.
May we share what we have,
both spiritually and materially,
so that all your people might step forth
into your eternal light.
Through Christ our Lord.
Amen.

✝ The Lord is my light and
my salvation.

✝ The Lord is my light and my salvation.

Psalm 27

page 405

Reading

Exodus 32:7–9

The LORD said to Moses, "Go down at once to your people, whom you brought out of the land of Egypt, for they have become depraved. They have soon turned aside from the way I pointed out to them, making for themselves a molten calf and worshiping it, sacrificing to it and crying out, 'This is your God, O Israel, who brought you out of the land of Egypt!' The LORD said to Moses, "I see how stiff-necked this people is."

Reflection

Since God had led the Israelites out of Egypt, it seemed right to make an image of God that represented his strength. But this image fit the people's hopes and expectations. Like the Israelites, we struggle to accept how much more there is to God than what we understand. God is the ultimate mystery. Although God reveals himself to us in many ways, most especially in Jesus, God remains beyond our understanding and beyond our control.

Prayers

others may be added

Calling out in faith, we pray:

◆ Lord, show us your face.

For the Church to grow in wisdom and compassion, we pray: ◆ For leaders in the world of business and finance, we pray: ◆ For those who cling to idols like wealth and prestige, we pray: ◆ For all those in need of healing, we pray: ◆

Our Father . . .

Lord, mighty God,
you are far beyond
what we could ever comprehend.
As we seek to know and love you,
may we never fail
   to reverence your transcendence.
We ask this through our Lord Jesus
   Christ, your Son,
who lives and reigns with you
in the unity of the Holy Spirit,
one God, forever and ever.
Amen.

✝ The Lord is my light and my salvation.

Friday, March 19, 2021
Solemnity of St. Joseph, Spouse of the Blessed Virgin Mary

✝ Have mercy on me, God,
in your goodness.

Psalm 51 *page 409*

Reading *Matthew 1:18–21*

This is how the birth of Jesus Christ came about. When his mother Mary was betrothed to Joseph, but before they lived together, she was found with child through the Holy Spirit. Joseph her husband, since he was a righteous man, yet unwilling to expose her to shame, decided to divorce her quietly. Such was his intention when, behold, the angel of the Lord appeared to him in a dream and said, "Joseph, son of David, do not be afraid to take Mary your wife into your home. For it is through the Holy Spirit that this child has been conceived in her. She will bear a son and you are to name him Jesus, because he will save his people from their sins."

Reflection

Today's solemnity honors St. Joseph as Mary's spouse. Jesus was not born into isolation but into a network of relationships. After reassuring Joseph, the angel proclaims that Jesus is Emmanuel, "God with us." The God who is with us also wants us to be with each other. Jesus draws people into a new family, a family in which there are no strangers, for all are treated as brothers and sisters, mothers and fathers.

Prayers *others may be added*

From hearts cleansed by God,
we pray:

◆ God of salvation, hear our prayer.

Give us strength, O God, on this Lenten journey, we pray: ◆ Help all leaders, O God, to care for those entrusted to them, we pray: ◆ Show your compassion, O God, to all caregivers, we pray: ◆ Be attentive, O God, to the needs of broken and hurting families, we pray: ◆

Our Father . . .

O God,
you called St. Joseph
to be husband and father.
Help us to trust your call as he did.
May we trust in your Son's vision
of a new family.
Guide us as we bring people into
this family,
and help us to care for those members
who especially need our support.
Through Christ our Lord.
Amen.

✝ Have mercy on me, God,
in your goodness.

✝ The Lord is my light and
my salvation.

Psalm 27 *page 405*

Reading *Jeremiah 11:18–20*

I knew their plot because the LORD
informed me; at that time you, O LORD,
showed me their doings.

Yet I, like a trusting lamb led to
slaughter, had not realized that they
were hatching plots against me: "Let us
destroy the tree in its vigor; / let us cut
him off from the land of the living, / so
that his name will be spoken no more."

But, you, O LORD of hosts, O just
Judge, / searcher of mind and heart, /
Let me witness the vengeance you take
on them, / for to you I have entrusted
my cause!

Reflection

Jeremiah is dismayed that his own people have turned against him. When he
uses the word *vengeance*, he is using
the language of the courtroom. He
wants God to uphold his case, to show
everyone that his words are true. When
we want God to uphold our cause, then
we must be like Jeremiah: as innocent
as lambs and as truthful in our words.

Prayers *others may be added*

Calling out in faith, we pray:

◆ Lord, show us your face.

For the Church as she strives to speak
God's word, we pray: ◆ For communities
suffering internal conflicts and divisions,
we pray: ◆ For those who are bullied
and for those who bully them, we pray: ◆
For the courage to support those who
speak out against wrongdoing, we pray: ◆

Our Father . . .

O just Judge,
make us mindful of the ways we stray
    from the truth.
Summon us back to a righteous path.
When we speak in your name,
help us to speak with passion,
    but also with dignity, gentleness,
    and reverence.
Through Christ our Lord.
Amen.

✝ The Lord is my light and
my salvation.

✝ How precious is your love, O God!

Psalm 36 *page 408*

Reading *John 12:20–24, 31–32*

Some Greeks who had come to worship at the Passover Feast came to Philip, who was from Bethsaida in Galilee, and asked him, "Sir, we would like to see Jesus." Philip went and told Andrew; then Andrew and Philip went and told Jesus. Jesus answered them, "The hour has come for the Son of Man to be glorified. Amen, amen, I say to you, unless a grain of wheat falls to the ground and dies, it remains just a grain of wheat; but if it dies, it produces much fruit." . . .

"Now is the time of judgment on this world; now the ruler of this world will be driven out. And when I am lifted up from the earth, I will draw everyone to myself."

Reflection

Jesus' hour is his crucifixion and resurrection. In the Gospel of John, this hour is one inseparable moment of glorification as God's love is revealed and evil's hold over the world is broken. The universal nature of Jesus' mission is evident in the arrival of the Greeks, the non-Jews who want to see Jesus. They are part of the "everyone" whom Jesus draws to himself. Following Christ means not only accepting God's generous gift of love, but also sharing it, in turn, with everyone.

Prayers *others may be added*

We entrust ourselves to God's mercy as we pray:

◆ Gracious God, hear our prayer.

Transform the Church's suffering into new life, we pray: ◆ Transform the unjust systems that perpetuate oppression, we pray: ◆ Transform those who persecute others, we pray: ◆ Transform hatred into love, we pray: ◆

Our Father . . .

O saving Christ,
you obeyed your Father in everything
and were raised up for the salvation
    of the world.
May we follow you in everything,
rejecting what is evil
and holding fast to all that leads
    to life with you,
who live and reign with God, the Father,
in the unity of the Holy Spirit,
one God, forever and ever.
Amen.

✝ How precious is your love, O God!

✝ How precious is your love, O God!

Psalm 36   *page 408*

Reading   *John 8:3–11*

The scribes and the Pharisees brought [to Jesus] a woman who had been caught in adultery and made her stand in the middle. They said to him, "Teacher, this woman was caught in the very act of committing adultery. Now in the law, Moses commanded us to stone such women. So what do you say?" They said this to test him, so that they could have some charge to bring against him. Jesus bent down and began to write on the ground with his finger. But when they continued asking him, he straightened up and said to them, "Let the one among you who is without sin be the first to throw a stone at her." Again he bent down and wrote on the ground. And in response, they went away one by one, beginning with the elders. So he was left alone with the woman before him. Then Jesus straightened up and said to her, "Woman, where are they? Has no one condemned you?" She replied, "No one, sir." Jesus said, "Neither do I condemn you. Go, and from now on do not sin any more."

Reflection

Where is the man who was with the woman? How did the authorities know when and where to find her? Why must the woman, like a prop, be placed "in the middle" of everyone? Then there is the Gospel writer's own statement that the whole event is a test; it has nothing to do with the woman or her sin. With a single, piercing statement, Jesus stops the whole charade. There may be moments that we, too, must respond to a daunting situation with clearheaded compassion.

Prayers   *others may be added*

We entrust ourselves to God's mercy as we pray:

◆ Gracious God, hear our prayer.

May the Church continue to examine closely its words and actions, we pray: ◆ May lawmakers ensure that both their goals and plans are just, we pray: ◆ May we confess our sins and strive to sin no more, we pray: ◆ May married couples be strengthened in love and mercy, we pray: ◆

Our Father . . .

Divine Judge,
sometimes we are quick
   to find fault in others
and slow to admit our own sins.
Turn our gaze inward
so that we may acknowledge
   our sins, grow in holiness,
   and treat others
with greater compassion.
Through Christ our Lord.
Amen.

✝ How precious is your love, O God!

✝ How precious is your love, O God!

Psalm 36 *page 408*

Reading *Numbers 21:4–9*

From Mount Hor the children of Israel set out on the Red Sea road, to bypass the land of Edom. But with their patience worn out by the journey, the people complained against God and Moses, "Why have you brought us up from Egypt to die in this desert, where there is no food or water? We are disgusted with this wretched food!"

In punishment the LORD sent among the people saraph serpents, which bit the people so that many of them died. Then the people came to Moses and said, "We have sinned in complaining against the LORD and you. Pray the LORD to take the serpents away from us." So Moses prayed for the people, and the LORD said to Moses, "Make a saraph and mount it on a pole, and whoever looks at it after being bitten will live." Moses accordingly made a bronze serpent and mounted it on a pole, and whenever anyone who had been bitten by a serpent looked at the bronze serpent, he lived.

Reflection

How did the Israelites feel when they had to look at the object of their punishment in order to be healed? They probably would have preferred to look at just about anything else in order to be made well, but God does not allow them to find healing any other way. Sometimes the only way to find healing is to face bravely that which makes us suffer.

Prayers *others may be added*

We entrust ourselves to God's mercy as we pray:

◆ Gracious God, hear our prayer.

For ecclesial and civil leaders, we pray: ◆ For hospital chaplains and all who minister to the sick, we pray: ◆ For those who bear hardship, we pray: ◆ For those who struggle to follow Christ, we pray: ◆

Our Father . . .

Lord God,
your Son was lifted upon the cross
    for the salvation of the world.
May we raise our eyes
    to find healing and consolation
    in him, who lives and reigns with you
in the unity of the Holy Spirit,
one God, forever and ever.
Amen.

✝ How precious is your love, O God!

✝ How precious is your love, O God!

Psalm 36   *page 408*

Reading   *Daniel 3:14, 16–17, 19–20, 91–92*

King Nebuchadnezzar said: "Is it true, Shadrach, Meshach, and Abednego, that you will not serve my god, or worship the golden statue that I set up?" . . . Shadrach, Meshach, and Abednego answered King Nebuchadnezzar, "There is no need for us to defend ourselves before you in this matter. If our God, whom we serve, can save us from the white-hot furnace and from your hands, O king, may he save us!" . . .

King Nebuchadnezzar's face became livid with utter rage against Shadrach, Meshach, and Abednego. He ordered the furnace to be heated seven times more than usual and had some of the strongest men in his army bind Shadrach, Meshach, and Abednego and cast them into the white-hot furnace. . . .

Nebuchadnezzar rose in haste and asked his nobles, "Did we not cast three men bound into the fire?" "Assuredly, O king," they answered. "But," he replied, "I see four men unfettered and unhurt, walking in the fire, and the fourth looks like a son of God."

Reflection

Shadrach, Meshach, and Abednego declare that they will remain faithful to God even if the pagan king puts them to death. Would we be as faithful, as courageous as them? Sometimes it seems safer or easier to bow down to something other than God, but it was not an idol that saved the three men. When the king threw them into the fire, the Lord stood by them. God will also accompany us through every challenge and trial we face.

Prayers   *others may be added*

We entrust ourselves to God's mercy as we pray:

◆ Gracious God, hear our prayer.

For all who have given their lives in faithfulness to the Gospel, we pray: ◆ For those who advocate for the freedom of religion, we pray: ◆ For those who are enduring an especially difficult time, we pray: ◆ For our friends and family members who support us in our faith, we pray: ◆

Our Father . . .

God our Savior,
give us the courage of your Son
so that we may entrust our lives to you.
When we feel frightened or alone,
may we always find you walking
    beside us.
Through Christ our Lord.
Amen.

✝ How precious is your love, O God!

✝ May it be done to me according to your word.

Canticle of Mary   *page 421*

Reading   *Luke 1:26–29, 38*

The angel Gabriel was sent from God to a town of Galilee called Nazareth, to a virgin betrothed to a man named Joseph, of the house of David, and the virgin's name was Mary. And coming to her, he said, "Hail, full of grace! The Lord is with you." But she was greatly troubled at what was said and pondered what sort of greeting this might be. . . . Mary said, "Behold, I am the handmaid of the Lord. May it be done to me according to your word."

Reflection

We celebrate Gabriel's visit to Mary nine months before Christmas, which means this solemnity usually falls during Lent. We hear Gabriel announce the incarnation, but in a few days, we will remember Jesus' passion and death. Just as Mary entrusted herself to God's will, so will Jesus when he prays alone in Gethsemane: "Father, not what I will, but what you will." Mary taught her son well. May her words, and now Jesus' words, become our words, every day.

Prayers   *others may be added*

We entrust ourselves to God's mercy as we pray:

◆ Gracious God, hear our prayer.

May the Church humbly and reverently announce the good news, we pray: ◆ May the leaders of divided governments persist in doing what is best for their people, we pray: ◆ May those facing an unplanned pregnancy find support in their family and in the Church, we pray: ◆ May those fearful of carrying out God's will find courage in the Spirit, we pray: ◆

Our Father . . .

Son of the Most High,
may we welcome what angels announce
    to us.
May we walk wherever you lead us.
May we climb upon the crosses
    that confront us,
joining you, who live and reign
    with God the Father
in the unity of the Holy Spirit,
one God, forever and ever.
Amen.

✝ May it be done to me according to your word.

✝ Have mercy on me, God,
  in your goodness.

Psalm 51 *page 409*

Reading *John 10:31–39*

The Jews picked up rocks to stone Jesus. Jesus answered them, "I have shown you many good works from the Father. For which of these are you trying to stone me?" The Jews answered him, "We are not stoning you for a good work but for blasphemy. You, a man, are making yourself God." Jesus answered them, "Is it not written in your law, 'I said, "You are gods"'? If it calls them gods to whom the word of God came, and Scripture cannot be set aside, can you say that the one whom the Father has consecrated and sent into the world blasphemes because I said, 'I am the Son of God'? If I do not perform my Father's works, do not believe me; but if I perform them, even if you do not believe me, believe the works, so that you may realize and understand that the Father is in me and I am in the Father." Then they tried again to arrest him; but he escaped their power.

Reflection

The people who attacked Jesus were understandably offended by his claims to be God's Son. Worshiping a man as God betrayed their monotheistic faith. Although we now understand that Jesus is God's Son, there are other ways in which we fail to recognize him. We sometimes deny that his Spirit is working in and through someone. Jesus invites us to celebrate the good that people do and to honor his Spirit in them.

Prayers *others may be added*

From hearts cleansed by God,
we pray:

◆ **God of salvation, hear our prayer.**

May the Church embrace the movement of the Holy Spirit, we pray: ◆ May local and national leaders strive to do good works, we pray: ◆ May those in conflict with one another find a way to reconcile, we pray: ◆ May our own actions reflect the goodness of God, we pray: ◆

Our Father . . .

God our Father,
help us to discern the presence of your
   Holy Spirit.
Make us quick to commend people
for the good that they do,
and keep us eager to participate
in the movement of your Spirit.
Through Christ sour Lord.
Amen.

✝ Have mercy on me, God,
  in your goodness.

✝ How precious is your love, O God!

Psalm 36   *page 408*

Reading   *Ezekiel 37:21–22, 25–28*

Thus says the Lord GOD: I will take the children of Israel from among the nations to which they have come, and gather them from all sides to bring them back to their land. I will make them one nation upon the land, in the mountains of Israel, and there shall be one prince for them all. Never again shall they be two nations, and never again shall they be divided into two kingdoms.

They shall live on the land that I gave to my servant Jacob, the land where their fathers lived; they shall live on it forever, they, and their children, and their children's children, with my servant David their prince forever. I will make with them a covenant of peace; it shall be an everlasting covenant with them, and I will multiply them, and put my sanctuary among them forever. My dwelling shall be with them; I will be their God, and they shall be my people. Thus the nations shall know that it is I, the LORD, who make Israel holy, when my sanctuary shall be set up among them forever.

Reflection

Ezekiel prophesies unity and peace for God's people under the leadership of a just descendant of David. We will never know perfect unity and peace, however, unless God first cleanses our hearts. Without the gift of God's Spirit, we will continue to act divisively. As we prepare to enter Holy Week and to celebrate the gift of unity and peace that Jesus gives us, we offer our hearts to God, and we pray for the fullness of God's Kingdom.

Prayers   *others may be added*

We entrust ourselves to God's mercy as we pray:

◆ Gracious God, hear our prayer.

For the Church, we pray: ◆ For our pastors, liturgy coordinators, and liturgical ministers, we pray: ◆ For world leaders, we pray: ◆ For the poor and marginalized, we pray: ◆

Our Father . . .

Almighty God,
cleanse our hearts
so that we may accept the unity, justice,
    and peace
that you bring through your Son,
who lives and reigns with you
in the unity of the Holy Spirit,
one God, forever and ever.
Amen.

✝ How precious is your love, O God!

Sunday, March 28, 2021
Palm Sunday of the Passion of the Lord

✝ I trust in you, O Lord.

Psalm 31   *page 405*

Reading   *Mark 11:2, 7–10*

When Jesus and his disciples drew near to Jerusalem, to Bethpage and Bethany at the Mount of Olives, he sent two of his disciples and said to them, "Go into the village opposite you, and immediately on entering it, you will find a colt tethered on which no one has ever sat. Untie it and bring it here." . . . So they brought the colt to Jesus and put their cloaks over it. And he sat on it. Many of the people spread their cloaks on the road, and others spread leafy branches that they had cut from the fields. Those preceding him as well as those following kept crying out: / "Hosanna! / Blessed is he who comes in the name of the Lord! / Blessed is the kingdom of our father David that is to come! / Hosanna in the highest!"

Reflection

After proving himself an adept military leader, David became king of Israel and established Jerusalem as its capital. By entering the city in the dramatic way that he did, Jesus presents himself as David's descendant, who has come to retake the throne. However, Jesus is accompanied by no warriors, and he doesn't even keep the colt. The salvation he brings will disappoint some people, but others will sing hosanna for centuries to come.

Prayers   *others may be added*

Calling out in faith, we pray:

◆ Save us, O Lord.

For presiders and homilists, we pray: ◆ For local and national leaders, we pray: ◆ For those preparing to become Catholic at the Easter Vigil, we pray: ◆ For grace-filled times of communal and individual prayer this week, we pray: ◆

Our Father . . .

God our Father,
just as your Son claimed his authority
    over Jerusalem,
so he enters our own hearts
in order to guide and govern us.
May our Lord Jesus Christ
    reign triumphant
in all that we do
and in every moment of our lives,
for he lives and reigns with you
in the unity of the Holy Spirit,
one God, forever and ever.
Amen.

✝ I trust in you, O Lord.

Monday, March 29, 2021
Monday of Holy Week

✝ The Lord is my light and
my salvation.

Psalm 27 *page 405*

Reading *Isaiah 42:1–7*

Here is my servant whom I uphold, / my chosen one with whom I am pleased, / Upon whom I have put my Spirit; / he shall bring forth justice to the nations, / Not crying out, not shouting, / not making his voice heard in the street. / A bruised reed he shall not break, / and a smoldering wick he shall not quench, / Until he establishes justice on the earth; / the coastlands will wait for his teaching.

Thus says God, the LORD, who created the heavens and stretched them out, / who spreads out the earth with its crops, / Who gives breath to its people / and spirit to those who walk on it: / I, the LORD, have called you for the victory of justice, / I have grasped you by the hand; / I formed you, and set you / as a covenant of the people, / a light for the nations, / To open the eyes of the blind, / to bring out prisoners from confinement, / and from the dungeon, those who live in darkness.

Reflection

As we hear more about the end of Jesus' earthly ministry, we are reminded of the scale and significance of that ministry. Jesus gathered people; he breathed new life into a world afflicted by injustice and violence; he illuminated the way to God. Our risen Lord continues that work today. We pray that God's spirit make servants of us all and help us to follow him into the light.

Prayers *others may be added*

Calling out in faith, we pray:

◆ Lord, show us your face.

May all the members of Christ's body act with patience and compassion, we pray: ◆ May the leaders of nations turn their eyes and ears to the living God, we pray: ◆ May the victims of wrongdoing seek justice over vengeance, we pray: ◆ May we welcome those who have just begun to seek the Lord, we pray: ◆

Our Father . . .

Eternal Creator,
refashion us into the likeness of your Son,
and grasp us by the hand.
May we proclaim your kingdom,
guide people into it,
and remain faithful
until all creation rejoices
in the salvation you have brought us
through our Lord Jesus Christ,
   your Son,
who lives and reigns with you
in the unity of the Holy Spirit,
one God, forever and ever.
Amen.

✝ The Lord is my light and
my salvation.

✝ The Lord is my light and
my salvation.

Psalm 27   *page 405*

Reading   *John 13:31–33, 36–38*

Jesus said, "Now is the Son of Man glorified, and God is glorified in him. If God is glorified in him, God will also glorify him in himself, and he will glorify him at once. My children, I will be with you only a little while longer. You will look for me, and as I told the Jews, 'Where I go you cannot come,' so now I say it to you."

Simon Peter said to him, "Master, where are you going?" Jesus answered him, "Where I am going, you cannot follow me now, although you will follow later." Peter said to him, "Master, why can I not follow you now? I will lay down my life for you." Jesus answered, "Will you lay down your life for me? Amen, amen, I say to you, the cock will not crow before you deny me three times."

Reflection

Peter wants to be brave and accompany Jesus, but what awaits him will be far more difficult than he realizes. Often we are equally bold and well intentioned, but our courage fails us when the critical moment comes. We need the gift of God's Spirit as well as his abundant mercy and patience to follow the way that Jesus first walked.

Prayers   *others may be added*

Calling out in faith, we pray:

◆ Lord, show us your face.

May the Church bravely follow where the Spirit of Christ leads, we pray: ◆ May world leaders hold fast to the pursuit of justice and peace, we pray: ◆ May we accompany those who face difficult times, we pray: ◆ May we model discipleship for our elect and candidates, we pray: ◆

Our Father . . .

Lord of glory,
guide us forward when we fail to listen
for your Spirit,
when we fail to follow your Son.
In all that we do, may we glorify you
so that others might turn to you
and believe.
Through Christ our Lord.
Amen.

✝ The Lord is my light and
my salvation.

✝ The Lord is my light and
  my salvation.

Psalm 27
page 405

Reading
Matthew 26:14–16

One of the Twelve, who was called Judas Iscariot, went to the chief priests and said, "What are you willing to give me if I hand him over to you?" They paid him thirty pieces of silver, and from that time on he looked for an opportunity to hand him over.

Reflection

We will never know for certain why Judas betrayed Jesus. Greed may have been only one of several motives. How well do we understand our own motives? Do we cling to beliefs that are ultimately a betrayal of Jesus and his kingdom? As we enter the holiest time of our liturgical year, we open ourselves to God's scrutiny. We ask God to reveal the ways we conform to his will and the ways we do not.

Prayers
others may be added

Calling out in faith, we pray:

◆ Lord, show us your face.

For the Church's renewal at Easter, we pray: ◆ For leaders of nations to seek common ground among people of different faiths, we pray: ◆ For the sponsors, friends, and families of our elect and candidates, we pray: ◆ For those who have left our community out of anger or misunderstanding, we pray: ◆

Our Father . . .

Holy Lord,
we do not always know what you ask
  of us.
Even when we do,
we struggle to accept your vision
  for our lives and for our world.
As we remember your Son's passion
  and death,
conform our thoughts to his
 so that our lives may more closely
  resemble his own.
Through Christ our Lord.
Amen.

✝ The Lord is my light and
  my salvation.

✝ I will call upon the name of the Lord.

Psalm 116   *page 416*

Reading   *John 13:1–5, 12–15*

Before the feast of Passover, Jesus knew that his hour had come to pass from this world to the Father. He loved his own in the world and he loved them to the end. The devil had already induced Judas, son of Simon the Iscariot, to hand him over. So, during supper, fully aware that the Father had put everything into his power and that he had come from God and was returning to God, he rose from supper and took off his outer garments. He took a towel and tied it around his waist. Then he poured water into a basin and began to wash the disciples' feet and dry them with the towel around his waist. . . .

So when he had washed their feet and put his garments back on and reclined at table again, he said to them, "Do you realize what I have done for you? You call me 'teacher' and 'master,' and rightly so, for indeed I am. If I, therefore, the master and teacher, have washed your feet, you ought to wash one another's feet. I have given you a model to follow, so that as I have done for you, you should also do."

Reflection

As Jesus has his last formal meal with his disciples, he tries to prepare them for what will happen to him by assuming the role of a servant. His crucifixion is not meaningless; it is an act of courageous and selfless love. Whenever we gather to break bread in his name, we do so in gratitude for what Jesus did, but we must also be willing to act with that same brave, sacrificial love.

Prayers   *others may be added*

With longing hearts, we pray:

◆ **Make us holy, O Lord.**

For the elect, godparents, and their families, we pray: ◆ For those whose work is to provide food for the hungry, we pray: ◆ For those who have no one with whom to share a meal, we pray: ◆ For a deeper understanding of and reverence for the Eucharist, we pray: ◆

Our Father . . .

God of holiness,
when we gather at table to break bread
in memory of your Son,
we participate in his passion and death
and pledge to imitate his love.
Keep us mindful of the gift
   he offers us in the Eucharist,
and help us to offer ourselves in return.
Through Christ our Lord.
Amen.

✝ I will call upon the name of the Lord.

✝ Into your hands I commend
my spirit.

Psalm 31 *page 405*

Reading *John 19:31–35*

Since it was preparation day, in order that the bodies might not remain on the cross on the sabbath, for the sabbath day of that week was a solemn one, the Jews asked Pilate that their legs be broken and they be taken down. So the soldiers came and broke the legs of the first and then of the other one who was crucified with Jesus. But when they came to Jesus and saw that he was already dead, they did not break his legs, but one soldier thrust his lance into his side, and immediately blood and water flowed out. An eyewitness has testified, and his testimony is true; he knows that he is speaking the truth, so that you also may come to believe.

Reflection

Although this passage contains allusions to baptism and the Eucharist, the Gospel writer emphasizes the death of Jesus. God's Son submitted fully to the human condition, even to the point of dying and being entombed. God breaks into our lives in the incarnation and shares in our humanity. Even at our lowest point, God is with us.

Prayers *others may be added*

Turning to the Lord, our refuge,
we pray:

◆ Lord, save us in your kindness.

For those who have been harmed by ministers of the Church, we pray: ◆ For those who are attacked and vilified by their own governments, we pray: ◆ For those grieving the death of a loved one, we pray: ◆ For those struggling to make meaning out of suffering, we pray: ◆

Our Father . . .

God, you are love itself.
You incarnated your love
in your Son,
who endured the cross for our sake.
Assure us
of your continuing love for us,
and make us eager to share
your love with others.
Through Christ our Lord.
Amen.

✝ Into your hands I commend
my spirit.

✞ God's mercy endures forever.

Psalm 118   *page 417*

Reading   *Mark 16:1, 5–7*

When the sabbath was over, Mary Magdalene, Mary, the mother of James, and Salome bought spices so that they might go and anoint [Jesus]. . . . On entering the tomb they saw a young man sitting on the right side, clothed in a white robe, and they were utterly amazed. He said to them, "Do not be amazed! You seek Jesus of Nazareth, the crucified. He has been raised; he is not here. Behold the place where they laid him. But go and tell his disciples and Peter, 'He is going before you to Galilee; there you will see him, as he told you.'"

Reflection

The empty tomb is not proof of Jesus' resurrection, but an invitation to faith. The tomb invites us to believe that goodness will ultimately triumph over evil, that Christlike behavior such as patience, nonviolence, compassion, and so on does ultimately defeat evil no matter the form evil takes. The empty tomb, therefore, invites us to step into it, to surrender parts of ourselves to death so that goodness and holiness will rise up within us.

Prayers   *others may be added*

Trusting in God's power, we pray:

◆ Merciful Savior, raise us up.

May we enter into the silence of Christ's death and resurrection, we pray: ◆
May nations in conflict seek creative and peaceful solutions, we pray: ◆
May those who fear death find strength and consolation in the resurrection, we pray: ◆ May the newly baptized remain firm in faith, hope, and love, we pray: ◆

Our Father . . .

Loving and creating God,
as we celebrate this holy day,
help us enter into silent and
    reflective prayer.
Quiet our hearts
so that we can hear you calling us
    to a deeper and bolder faith.
Through Christ our Lord.
Amen.

✞ God's mercy endures forever.

✝ God's mercy endures forever! Alleluia!

Psalm 118   *page 417*

Reading   *John 20:1–9*

On the first day of the week, Mary of Magdala came to the tomb early in the morning, while it was still dark, and saw the stone removed from the tomb. So she ran and went to Simon Peter and to the other disciple whom Jesus loved, and told them, "They have taken the Lord from the tomb, and we don't know where they put him." So Peter and the other disciple went out and came to the tomb. They both ran, but the other disciple ran faster than Peter and arrived at the tomb first; he bent down and saw the burial cloths there, and the cloth that had covered his head, not with the burial cloths but rolled up in a separate place. Then the other disciple also went in, the one who had arrived at the tomb first, and he saw and believed. For they did not yet understand the Scripture that he had to rise from the dead.

Reflection

When Jesus raised Lazarus from the dead, Lazarus emerged bound in burial cloths and had to be untied. By contrast, Jesus needs no help freeing himself from death and the symbols of death. Jesus is life itself. Today we celebrate the root of our hope that life triumphs over death, that goodness triumphs over evil. Our God who empties our tombs will never let us return to them, but will bring us into life with his Son forever.

Prayers   *others may be added*

With joyful hearts, we pray:

♦ Merciful Savior, raise us up.

For the Church who rejoiced in Christ's resurrection, we pray: ♦ For those who strive for justice and peace, we pray: ♦ For the newly baptized, we pray: ♦ For those who are approaching the end of their earthly life, we pray:

Our Father . . .

Loving and creating God,
you have shown us the path to life,
and we celebrate it with joy
   and hope.
Free us from all that leads to death.
Keep us growing in goodness
   and holiness.
We ask this through our Lord Jesus
   Christ, your Son,
who lives and reigns with you
in the unity of the Holy Spirit,
one God, forever and ever.
Amen.

✝ God's mercy endures forever! Alleluia!

✝ God's mercy endures forever!
Alleluia!

Psalm 118
page 417

Reading
Matthew 28:8–14

Mary Magdalene and the other Mary went away quickly from the tomb, fearful yet overjoyed, and ran to announce the news to his disciples. And behold, Jesus met them on their way and greeted them. They approached, embraced his feet, and did him homage. Then Jesus said to them, "Do not be afraid. Go tell my brothers to go to Galilee, and there they will see me."

While they were going, some of the guard went into the city and told the chief priests all that had happened. The chief priests assembled with the elders and took counsel; then they gave a large sum of money to the soldiers, telling them, "You are to say to him, 'His disciples came by night and stole him while we were asleep. And if this gets to the ears of the governor, we will satisfy him and keep you out of trouble.'"

Reflection

Earlier in this Gospel, the authorities place guards at Jesus' tomb to prevent his disciples from stealing his body and claiming that he had been raised. When Jesus—body and all—leaves the tomb anyway, the authorities hastily revise their attempts to undermine the ongoing work of salvation. Their efforts are futile, even comical, when compared to the extraordinary courage that Jesus' followers are to show next in declaring all that has happened.

Prayers
others may be added

With joyful hearts, we pray:

◆ Merciful Savior, raise us up.

May the Church speak with wisdom and patience to those who deny the resurrection, we pray: ◆ May leaders at every level of society speak and act with integrity, we pray: ◆ May those who work in cemeteries and funeral homes know the risen Christ, we pray: ◆ May the newly baptized be filled with joy, we pray: ◆

Our Father . . .

Lord of Life,
just as the women at the tomb greeted our
    risen Lord with joy,
so may we embrace and honor him
each moment of our lives.
Through Christ our Lord.
Amen.

✝ God's mercy endures forever!
Alleluia!

✝ God's mercy endures forever!
Alleluia!

Psalm 118   *page 417*

Reading   *John 20:11–16*

Mary Magdalene stayed outside the tomb weeping. And as she wept, she bent over into the tomb and saw two angels in white sitting there, one at the head and one at the feet where the Body of Jesus had been. And they said to her, "Woman, why are you weeping?" She said to them, "They have taken my Lord, and I don't know where they laid him." When she had said this, she turned around and saw Jesus there, but did not know it was Jesus. Jesus said to her, "Woman, why are you weeping? Whom are you looking for?" She thought it was the gardener and said to him, "Sir, if you carried him away, tell me where you laid him, and I will take him." Jesus said to her, "Mary!" She turned and said to him in Hebrew, "Rabbouni," which means Teacher.

Reflection

In John 10 Jesus says that he calls his sheep by name, and they recognize his voice. When Mary of Magdala meets Jesus near his tomb, he is so transformed by his resurrection that she does not recognize him—until he calls her by name. Sometimes we do not recognize Jesus, either. Only when we stop and listen will we discover that he is with us, though probably in a way we did not expect.

Prayers   *others may be added*

With joyful hearts, we pray:

◆ Merciful Savior, raise us up.

Open our ears to hear your call, O Lord, we pray: ◆ Instill a spirit of compassion into world leaders, O Lord, we pray: ◆ Protect those who work to serve the public, O Lord, we pray: ◆ Rouse the hearts of the baptized, O Lord, we pray: ◆

Our Father . . .

God,
help us to listen
    as your Son calls us by name.
May we rejoice
    when we hear him calling us.
Help us to support one another
as we do your will.
Through Christ our Lord.
Amen.

✝ God's mercy endures forever!
Alleluia!

✝ God's mercy endures forever! Alleluia!

Psalm 118   *page 417*

Reading   *Luke 24:28–32*

As [the disciples] approached the village to which they were going, [Jesus] gave the impression that he was going on farther. But they urged him, "Stay with us, for it is nearly evening and the day is almost over." So he went in to stay with them. And it happened that, while he was with them at table, he took bread, said the blessing, broke it, and gave it to them. With that their eyes were opened and they recognized him, but he vanished from their sight. Then they said to each other, "Were not our hearts burning within us while he spoke to us on the way and opened the Scriptures to us?"

Reflection

These two disciples are leaving Jerusalem with hearts broken by the death of Jesus, in whom they had placed all their hope. The risen Christ appears and helps them understand what has happened. When he breaks bread with them, they realize that Jesus is and always will be with them. Jesus likewise remains with us in word, at table, and in all the ways we are in fellowship with one another.

Prayers   *others may be added*

With joyful hearts, we pray:

◆ Merciful Savior, raise us up.

Lift up and console those who have lost hope, we pray: ◆ Guide local and national leaders who are rebuilding their people's trust, we pray: ◆ Give wisdom to liturgy coordinators, liturgical ministers, and presiders, we pray: ◆ Encourage the newly baptized, we pray: ◆ Grant your Church faith, hope, and love, we pray: ◆

Our Father . . .

Eternal Father,
the risen Jesus accompanies us every
   day of our lives.
Reveal him to us.
Fill us with your Holy Spirit
so that our hearts, too,
may burn in love and fellowship.
Through Christ our Lord.
Amen.

✝ God's mercy endures forever! Alleluia!

✝ God's mercy endures forever!
Alleluia!

Psalm 118   *page 417*

Reading   *Luke 24:35–42*

The disciples of Jesus recounted what had taken place along the way, and how they had come to recognize him in the breaking of bread.

While they were still speaking about this, he stood in their midst and said to them, "Peace be with you." But they were startled and terrified and thought that they were seeing a ghost. Then he said to them, "Why are you troubled? And why do questions arise in your hearts? Look at my hands and my feet, that it is I myself. Touch me and see, because a ghost does not have flesh and bones as you can see I have." And as he said this, he showed them his hands and his feet. While they were still incredulous for joy and were amazed, he asked them, "Have you anything here to eat?" They gave him a piece of baked fish; he took it and ate it in front of them.

Reflection

The disciples had not truly imagined that Jesus would rise from the dead and return to them in a radically transformed way. As they try to make sense out of Jesus' appearance, they assume they are seeing a ghost. By inviting them to touch his wounds and by eating some food, Jesus shows them that he is fully alive. His resurrection is God's promise that he will transform and enliven us in ways we cannot imagine.

Prayers   *others may be added*

With joyful hearts, we pray:

♦ Merciful Savior, raise us up.

For our bishops, priests, and deacons, we pray: ♦ For the leaders of nations that have been devastated by war or a natural disaster, we pray: ♦ For those who research new ways of treating diseases and other chronic illnesses, we pray: ♦ For an increase in faith, we pray: ♦

Our Father . . .

God of power and might,
we do not realize how much you can
    renew our lives.
Help us to offer ourselves to you
so that we can become
    more fully alive.
Through Christ our Lord.
Amen.

✝ God's mercy endures forever!
Alleluia!

✝ God's mercy endures forever!
Alleluia!

Psalm 118   *page 417*

Reading   *John 21:1, 4–7a*

Jesus revealed himself again to his disciples at the Sea of Tiberias. He revealed himself in this way. . . . When it was already dawn, Jesus was standing on the shore; but the disciples did not realize that it was Jesus. Jesus said to them, "Children, have you caught anything to eat?" They answered him, "No." So he said to them, "Cast the net over the right side of the boat and you will find something." So they cast it, and were not able to pull it in because of the number of fish. So the disciple whom Jesus loved said to Peter, "It is the Lord."

Reflection

This passage echoes a story in the Gospel of Luke that comes early in Jesus' ministry. In both stories, Peter and others have been fishing all night, but caught nothing. At the command of Jesus, they cast their nets again, and instantly fill their boats with fish. The fish symbolize life, and Jesus offers it in abundance. Death has not stopped the life that flows from him to all who obey his command.

Prayers   *others may be added*

With joyful hearts, we pray:

◆ Merciful Savior, raise us up.

For the Church, the newly baptized, and all who see the living God, we pray: ◆ For the staff of aid agencies and charitable organizations, we pray: ◆ For children preparing to celebrate their First Holy Communion, we pray: ◆ For those who are struggling with friends and family, we pray: ◆

Our Father . . .

Giver of all good gifts,
in Christ we see your overflowing love.
Fill us with this love so that we,
    in turn,
may overflow with love for others.
In reaching out to help other people,
may we all find life in abundance.
Through Christ our Lord.
Amen.

✝ God's mercy endures forever!
Alleluia!

✝ God's mercy endures forever!
   Alleluia!

Psalm 118 *page 417*

Reading *Acts 4:13–20*

Observing the boldness of Peter and John and perceiving them to be uneducated, ordinary men, the leaders, elders, and scribes were amazed, and they recognized them as the companions of Jesus. Then when they saw the man who had been cured standing there with them, they could say nothing in reply. So they ordered them to leave the Sanhedrin, and conferred with one another, saying, "What are we to do with these men? Everyone living in Jerusalem knows that a remarkable sign was done through them, and we cannot deny it. But so that it may not be spread any further among the people, let us give them a stern warning never again to speak to anyone in this name."

So they called them back and ordered them not to speak or teach at all in the name of Jesus. Peter and John, however, said to them in reply, "Whether it is right in the sight of God for us to obey you rather than God, you be the judges. It is impossible for us not to speak about what we have seen and heard."

Reflection

Even though the religious authorities admit that God is acting through Peter and John, they try to prevent these two apostles from continuing to minister in Jesus' name. They refuse to yield any authority to people they think are unsuitable and to a movement they think is wrong. We, too, sometimes struggle to reevaluate a situation and admit that we are wrong. At such times, we depend upon God's grace to change our hearts.

Prayers *others may be added*

With joyful hearts, we pray:

◆ Merciful Savior, raise us up.

Send your Holy Spirt upon the Church, we pray: ◆ Grant wisdom and patience to leaders, we pray: ◆ Encourage those searching for work, we pray: ◆ Open us to the power of your transformational grace, we pray: ◆

Our Father . . .

Almighty God,
we need your guidance and strength.
Be patient with us
as we try to make changes in our lives
that are in accordance with your will.
Through Christ our Lord.
Amen.

✝ God's mercy endures forever!
   Alleluia!

✝ God's mercy endures forever!
Alleluia!

Psalm 118   *page 417*

Reading   *John 20:19–23*

On the evening of that first day of the week, when the doors were locked, where the disciples were, for fear of the Jews, Jesus came and stood in their midst and said to them, "Peace be with you." When he had said this, he showed them his hands and his side. The disciples rejoiced when they saw the Lord. Jesus said to them again, "Peace be with you. As the Father has sent me, so I send you." And when he had said this, he breathed on them and said to them, "Receive the Holy Spirit. Whose sins you forgive are forgiven them, and whose sins you retain are retained."

Reflection

Jesus did not leave a rulebook for us to follow. Instead, he formed a community and filled it with his Spirit. By dwelling within us, God not only further reveals his great love for us, he also entrusts us with the ongoing work of salvation. God, who has made us worthy of eternal life, empowers us to help other people see and believe that God offers them his life-giving Spirit, too.

Prayers   *others may be added*

With joyful hearts, we pray:

◆ Merciful Savior, raise us up.

Help the Church remain attentive to the Spirit, we pray: ◆ Strengthen leaders working for peace and justice, we pray: ◆ Give wisdom to counselors, therapists, and spiritual directors, we pray: ◆ Open our hearts and minds to the power of the Holy Spirit, we pray: ◆

Our Father . . .

Risen Lord,
you remake what is broken,
enliven what is dying,
and release all that is held captive.
We depend upon your Spirit
    to refashion us and guide us
so that we may at last
    enter your kingdom,
where you live and reign with God,
    the Father,
in the unity of the Holy Spirit,
one God, forever and ever.
Amen.

✝ God's mercy endures forever!
Alleluia!

Monday, April 12, 2021
Easter Weekday

✝ With you is the fountain of life,
   O Lord. Alleluia!

Psalm 36 *page 408*

Reading *John 3:1–8*

There was a Pharisee named Nicodemus, a ruler of the Jews. He came to Jesus at night and said to him, "Rabbi, we know that you are a teacher who has come from God, for no one can do these things that you are doing unless God is with him." Jesus answered and said to him, "Amen, amen, I say to you, unless one is born from above, he cannot see the Kingdom of God." Nicodemus said to him, "How can a man once grown old be born again? Surely he cannot reenter his mother's womb and be born again, can he?" Jesus answered, "Amen, amen, I say to you, unless one is born of water and Spirit he cannot enter the Kingdom of God. What is born of flesh is flesh and what is born of spirit is spirit. Do not be amazed that I told you, 'You must be born from above.' The wind blows where it wills, and you can hear the sound it makes, but you do not know where it comes from or where it goes; so it is with everyone who is born of the Spirit."

Reflection

Nicodemus talks with Jesus at night. The world is so darkened by sin that people struggle to see God's presence. Jesus explains to Nicodemus that people need God's Spirit in order to realize how dark their world is and to move toward the light of God's Kingdom.

God's Spirit helps us discover the darkness that lurks within us so that we can bring our darkness into God's light and be free of it forever.

Prayers *others may be added*

To Christ, our light, we pray:

◆ Lord, hear us in your kindness.

Open our eyes and hearts to see God's kingdom, too, we pray: ◆ Comfort nations and cities affected by war, violence, and catastrophe, we pray: ◆ Enlighten those who feel lost in the darkness, we pray: ◆ Strengthen the newly baptized, we pray: ◆

Our Father . . .

Heavenly Father,
as your Son illuminates our hearts,
he reveals the darkness
   that remains within us.
Cast that darkness out of us.
Deepen our understanding
   of your kingdom
so that we may move toward it
and remain within it forever.
Through Christ our Lord.
Amen.

✝ With you is the fountain of life,
   O Lord. Alleluia!

✝ With you is the fountain of life,
O Lord. Alleluia!

Psalm 36 — page 408

Reading — Acts 4:32–35

The community of believers was of one heart and mind, and no one claimed that any of his possessions was his own, but they had everything in common. With great power the Apostles bore witness to the resurrection of the Lord Jesus, and great favor was accorded them all. There was no needy person among them, for those who owned property or houses would sell them, bring the proceeds of the sale, and put them at the feet of the Apostles, and they were distributed to each according to need.

Reflection

We know that life in the early Church was not always as perfect as this passage makes it seem. The same is true of our parishes and other faith communities. There are aspects of our faith community that conform to God's will, but there are also things that should change. Our role is to make our communities as healthy and as life-giving as they can be, so that others may be drawn to us and may find God in our midst.

Prayers — *others may be added*

To Christ, our light, we pray:

♦ Lord, hear us in your kindness.

O God, heal the divisions within our communities, we pray: ♦ O God, watch over leaders working for justice, we pray: ♦ O God, grant wisdom to development directors, business managers, and accountants, we pray: ♦ O God, enliven all those who volunteer, we pray: ♦

Our Father . . .

God of love,
your Spirit draws us together
and helps us overcome
    our differences.
Guide us as we renew and build up our
    faith communities.
Give us your grace
so that we may always treat
    one another with patience, respect,
    and compassion.
Through Christ our Lord.
Amen.

✝ With you is the fountain of life,
O Lord. Alleluia!

Wednesday, April 14, 2021
Easter Weekday

✝ With you is the fountain of life,
   O Lord. Alleluia!

Psalm 36   *page 408*

Reading   *John 3:16–21*

God so loved the world that he gave his only-begotten Son, so that everyone who believes in him might not perish but might have eternal life. For God did not send his Son into the world to condemn the world, but that the world might be saved through him. Whoever believes in him will not be condemned, but whoever does not believe has already been condemned, because he has not believed in the name of the only-begotten Son of God. And this is the verdict, that the light came into the world, but people preferred darkness to light, because their works were evil. For everyone who does wicked things hates the light and does not come toward the light, so that his works might not be exposed. But whoever lives the truth comes to the light, so that his works may be clearly seen as done in God.

Reflection

In this Gospel, John presents Jesus as being on trial. We hear testimony from Jesus and others about who Jesus is. We are left to render a verdict: Is Jesus God's Son or not? Ultimately our decision about Jesus is really a decision about ourselves, about whether we want to be in the light, whether we want to be saved. We might have decided that Jesus is God's Son, but have we truly turned toward his light?

Prayers   *others may be added*

To Christ, our light, we pray:

◆ Lord, hear us in your kindness.

May all of God's people entrust themselves to the revealing light of Christ, we pray: ◆ May governments seek a balance between justice and mercy in their judicial systems, we pray: ◆ May those who work in the legal profession work for justice, we pray: ◆ May those who struggle with faith find courage in Christ, we pray: ◆

Our Father . . .

Father of light,
we confess faith in your Son
and believe in his saving power.
Support us as we strive to live
    more fully in your light,
and forgive us for those times
    we turn back to the darkness.
Through Christ our Lord.
Amen.

✝ With you is the fountain of life,
   O Lord. Alleluia!

✝ With you is the fountain of life,
O Lord. Alleluia!

Psalm 36 page 408

Reading Acts 5:27–33

When the court officers had brought the Apostles in and made them stand before the Sanhedrin, the high priest questioned them, "We gave you strict orders did we not, to stop teaching in that name. Yet you have filled Jerusalem with your teaching and want to bring this man's blood upon us." But Peter and the Apostles said in reply, "We must obey God rather than men. The God of our ancestors raised Jesus, though you had him killed by hanging him on a tree. God exalted him at his right hand as leader and savior to grant Israel repentance and forgiveness of sins. We are witnesses of these things, as is the Holy Spirit whom God has given to those who obey him."

When they heard this, they became infuriated and wanted to put them to death.

Reflection

After an angel frees the Apostles from jail, they are immediately hauled back before the authorities, who again forbid them from preaching in Jesus' name. The Apostles refuse. There are times that we must speak up and tell the truth, too. Sometimes our words will cost us: we might infuriate people by telling the truth. We might lose friends. In such moments, we should also remember all that we will gain by bearing witness to the truth.

Prayers others may be added

To Christ, our light, we pray:

◆ Lord, hear us in your kindness.

For those who are persecuted or attacked because of their faith, we pray: ◆ For leaders striving to overcome religious divisions in their countries, we pray: ◆ For those who are unjustly imprisoned, we pray: ◆ For those who give their testimony against people who have attacked or assaulted them, we pray: ◆

Our Father . . .

God of truth,
keep us attentive to your word.
Come to our aid
    when our courage fails us
and we hesitate to speak truthfully.
Lead us to others
    who will support us
and who also act with integrity
    and bravery.
Through Christ our Lord.
Amen.

✝ With you is the fountain of life,
O Lord. Alleluia!

Friday, April 16, 2021
Easter Weekday

Psalm 36   page 408

Reading   John 6:5–13

When Jesus raised his eyes and saw that a large crowd was coming to him, he said to Philip, "Where can we buy enough food for them to eat?" He said this to test him, because he himself knew what he was going to do. Philip answered him, "Two hundred days' wages worth of food would not be enough for each of them to have a little." One of his disciples, Andrew, the brother of Simon Peter, said to him, "There is a boy here who has five barley loaves and two fish; but what good are these for so many?" Jesus said, "Have the people recline." Now there was a great deal of grass in that place. So the men reclined, about five thousand in number. Then Jesus took the loaves, gave thanks, and distributed them to those who were reclining, and also as much of the fish as they wanted. When they had had their fill, he said to his disciples, "Gather the fragments left over, so that nothing will be wasted." So they collected them, and filled twelve wicker baskets with fragments from the five barley loaves that had been more than they could eat.

Reflection

Upon seeing the crowd, Jesus does not think, "I need a break from the crowd." Instead, he thinks about their needs, about how they are all probably hungry and cannot easily buy food. Jesus invites them to sit. Then he feeds them. Jesus beckons us to attend to the needs of others, too. We might have to rest first, but then we must raise our eyes and do all we can for those who approach us.

Prayers   *others may be added*

To Christ, our light, we pray:

◆ Lord, hear us in your kindness.

For the Church, we pray: ◆ For world leaders, we pray: ◆ For social workers and counselors, we pray: ◆ For the vulnerable, we pray: ◆

Our Father . . .

Gracious Lord,
your loving kindness is unfailing.
Help us to balance our own needs
with the needs of those around us.
Give us strength to help others
when they are struggling,
and accept their support
when we ourselves need care.
Through Christ our Lord.
Amen.

✝ With you is the fountain of life,
O Lord. Alleluia!

✝ With you is the fountain of life,
O Lord. Alleluia!

Psalm 36 $\qquad$ *page 408*

Reading $\qquad$ *John 6:16–20*

When it was evening, the disciples of Jesus went down to the sea, embarked in a boat, and went across the sea to Capernaum. It had already grown dark, and Jesus had not yet come to them. The sea was stirred up because a strong wind was blowing. When they had rowed about three or four miles, they saw Jesus walking on the sea and coming near the boat, and they began to be afraid. But he said to them, "It is I. Do not be afraid."

Reflection

We pray for God to draw near to us, but it would be quite frightening to watch his Son stride toward us, displaying divine power over stormy waters. When God draws closer to us, we often draw back because we see how small and vulnerable we are. We worry that we will lose ourselves in God, but we ought to worry instead about losing ourselves in the deadly waters that roil around us. God comes to draw us out of this abyss so that we may find ourselves in him.

Prayers $\qquad$ *others may be added*

To Christ, our light, we pray:

◆ Lord, hear us in your kindness.

May we entrust our lives to you, we pray: ◆ May world leaders collaborate to protect oceans, lakes, and coastal areas, we pray: ◆ May those who work on the water be protected, we pray: ◆ May courage fill the hearts of your people, we pray: ◆

Our Father . . .

Lord of all,
we find ourselves in you.
Draw close to us.
Draw us out of whatever
threatens to overwhelm us.
Draw us into you,
for only then will we dwell in safety
and be fully and forever alive.
Through Christ our Lord.
Amen.

✝ With you is the fountain of life,
O Lord. Alleluia!

✝ Blessed are you, O Lord. Alleluia!

Psalm 119   *page 418*

Reading   *Luke 24:44–48*

[Jesus] said to them, "These are my words that I spoke to you while I was still with you, that everything written about me in the law of Moses and in the prophets and psalms must be fulfilled." Then he opened their minds to understand the Scriptures. And he said to them, "Thus it is written that the Christ would suffer and rise from the dead on the third day and that repentance, for the forgiveness of sins, would be preached in his name to all the nations, beginning from Jerusalem. You are witnesses of these things."

Reflection

There is not a passage in the Old Testament that clearly states that the Messiah would die and then rise three days later. If there were, Jesus' followers would not have been so shocked by what happened. Instead, Jesus must help his disciples understand that the Scriptures, taken as a whole, point to him. God, who freed his people from bondage and faithfully cares for the least and the lost, has fully revealed himself in Christ, in whom God draws all people into freedom and life eternal.

Prayers   *others may be added*

With sincere hearts, we pray:

◆ Divine Teacher, hear our prayer.

Deepen our understanding of Scripture, we pray: ◆ Enlighten leaders of nations, we pray: ◆ Grant wisdom to the newly baptized, we pray: ◆ Inspire biblical scholars and theologians, we pray: ◆

Our Father . . .

Faithful Lord,
your risen Son fulfills our deepest
    longings and greatest hopes.
As we come to know you better
    through him,
show us all the ways
    in which you save us,
all the ways in which you fulfill
your promises to your people.
Through Christ our Lord.
Amen.

✝ Blessed are you, O Lord. Alleluia!

✝ Blessed are you, O Lord. Alleluia!

Psalm 119 *page 418*

Reading *Acts 6:8–10, 13–15*

Stephen, filled with grace and power, was working great wonders and signs among the people. Certain members of the so-called Synagogue of Freedmen, Cyreneans, and Alexandrians, and people from Cilicia and Asia, came forward and debated with Stephen, but they could not withstand the wisdom and the Spirit with which he spoke. . . . They presented false witnesses who testified, "This man never stops saying things against this holy place and the law. For we have heard him claim that this Jesus the Nazorean will destroy this place and change the customs that Moses handed down to us." All those who sat in the Sanhedrin looked intently at him and saw that his face was like the face of an angel.

Reflection

In their attempt to get rid of Stephen, people distorted the truth about what he had been saying and others told outright lies. If anyone wondered whether such statements were true, they chose instead to believe the false testimony. The lies became deadly, for Stephen was soon killed. We are left to ponder the lies we tell and to consider how these lies become deadly both to others and to ourselves.

Prayers *others may be added*

With sincere hearts, we pray:

◆ Divine Teacher, hear our prayer.

Strengthen the baptized against the lure of the Father of Lies and Prince of Darkness, we pray: ◆ Help civil and ecclesial leaders govern with integrity, we pray: ◆ Protect all those who encounter violence and bullying, we pray: ◆ Comfort those affected by gossip and false witness, we pray: ◆

Our Father . . .

God of truth,
we often lie out of fear or self-interest.
Correct us when we misrepresent
    ourselves
or speak falsely about others.
Grant us the humility
    to acknowledge the ways
we deceive ourselves,
and lead us onto an upright
    and life-giving path.
Through Christ our Lord.
Amen.

✝ Blessed are you, O Lord. Alleluia!

✝ Blessed are you, O Lord. Alleluia!

Psalm 119
page 418

Reading
Acts 7:55–60

Stephen, filled with the Holy Spirit, looked up intently to heaven and saw the glory of God and Jesus standing at the right hand of God, and Stephen said, "Behold, I see the heavens opened and the Son of Man standing at the right hand of God." But they cried out in a loud voice, covered their ears, and rushed upon him together. They threw him out of the city, and began to stone him. The witnesses laid down their cloaks at the feet of a young man named Saul. As they were stoning Stephen, he called out, "Lord Jesus, receive my spirit." Then he fell to his knees and cried out in a loud voice, "Lord, do not hold this sin against them"; and when he said this, he fell asleep.

Reflection

The ministry of the Apostles resembles the ministry of Jesus in many ways: they preach, heal, and cast out demons. Here, the death of an apostle closely resembles the death of Jesus. Stephen remains faithful to his mission despite the danger looming up against him, and he repeats some of the last words of Jesus as he himself is killed. God also sends each of us, in our different ways, to follow the example of his Son.

Prayers
others may be added

With sincere hearts, we pray:

◆ Divine Teacher, hear our prayer.

Move your Church to serve on the margins, we pray: ◆ Open the hearts and minds of world leaders, we pray: ◆ Console and protect those on death row, we pray: ◆ Inspire young people to healthy vocations, we pray: ◆

Our Father . . .

Merciful Lord,
like the Apostles,
help us be the sacrament of Christ
    in the world.
Guide us when we are not sure where
    to walk.
Give us courage to move forward
when we feel frightened or alone.
May others see in us
    the face of our Lord Jesus Christ,
    your Son,
who lives and reigns with you
in the unity of the Holy Spirit,
one God, forever and ever.
Amen.

✝ Blessed are you, O Lord. Alleluia!

✝ Blessed are you, O Lord. Alleluia!

Psalm 119   *page 418*

Reading   *Acts 8:1b–8*

There broke out a severe persecution of the church in Jerusalem, and all were scattered throughout the countryside of Judea and Samaria, except the Apostles. Devout men buried Stephen and made a loud lament over him. Saul, meanwhile, was trying to destroy the Church; entering house after house and dragging out men and women, he handed them over for imprisonment.

Now those who had been scattered went about preaching the word. Thus Philip went down to the city of Samaria and proclaimed the Christ to them. With one accord, the crowds paid attention to what was said by Philip when they heard it and saw the signs he was doing. For unclean spirits, crying out in a loud voice, came out of many possessed people, and many paralyzed and crippled people were cured. There was great joy in that city.

Reflection

Despite Saul's attack, Philip continues spreading the Gospel. He even goes to the Samaritans, who were longtime enemies of the Jews. The Samaritans might have persecuted him, too, but they do not: the city rejoices at what they see and hear. We will also encounter difficult setbacks. With the aid of the Holy Spirit, we will overcome them and rejoice.

Prayers   *others may be added*

With sincere hearts, we pray:

◆ Divine Teacher, hear our prayer.

May the Church seek common ground with people of other faiths, we pray: ◆ May public officials persist in implementing changes that help people, we pray: ◆ May those who face setbacks remain hopeful, we pray: ◆ May we be filled with the wisdom of the Holy Spirit, we pray: ◆

Our Father . . .

Almighty God,
death had no hold over your Son.
Fill us with patience and fortitude
when it becomes difficult for us
    to complete the good work
    you would have us do.
Keep us steadfast until the end.
Through Christ our Lord.
Amen.

✝ Blessed are you, O Lord. Alleluia!

✝ Blessed are you, O Lord. Alleluia!

Psalm 119   *page 418*

Reading   *Acts 8:27b, 29–31, 36, 38*

Now there was an Ethiopian eunuch . . . who had come to Jerusalem to worship. . . . The Spirit said to Philip, "Go and join up with that chariot." Philip ran up and heard him reading Isaiah the prophet and said, "Do you understand what you are reading?" He replied, "How can I, unless someone instructs me?" So he invited Philip to get in and sit with him. . . . As they traveled along the road they came to some water, and the eunuch said, "Look, there is water. What is to prevent my being baptized?" Then he ordered the chariot to stop, and Philip and the eunuch both went down into the water, and he baptized him.

Reflection

The man Philip talks with is extremely open to hearing the Gospel. He is already studying God's Word, and he welcomes Philip's instruction. Once he understands the meaning of the text, the man himself takes the initiative in seeking baptism. Sometimes as we accompany people in their walk with the Lord, we must take slow, patient steps. At other times, we happily run to keep up.

Prayers   *others may be added*

With sincere hearts, we pray:

◆ Divine Teacher, hear our prayer.

May teachers in the Church instruct us with wisdom and versatility, we pray: ◆
May local and national leaders manage their economies prudently, we pray: ◆
May inquirers and catechumens remain steadfast on their journey, we pray: ◆
May all preachers of the Word share the Good News with joy, we pray: ◆

Our Father . . .

Lord,
help us to support one another
and to keep each other moving along
    the path of holiness.
Quicken our pace when
    we drag our feet.
Join our spirits to your Spirit
so that we may be happily carried along
    by your grace.
Through Christ our Lord.
Amen.

✝ Blessed are you, O Lord. Alleluia!

✝ Blessed are you, O Lord. Alleluia!

Psalm 119   *page 418*

Reading   *Acts 9:1–8*

Saul, still breathing murderous threats against the disciples of the Lord, went to the high priest and asked him for letters to the synagogues in Damascus, that, if he should find any men or women who belonged to the Way, he might bring them back to Jerusalem in chains. On his journey, as he was nearing Damascus, a light from the sky suddenly flashed around him. He fell to the ground and heard a voice saying to him, "Saul, Saul, why are you persecuting me?" He said, "Who are you, sir?" The reply came, "I am Jesus, whom you are persecuting. Now get up and go into the city and you will be told what you must do." The men who were traveling with him stood speechless, for they heard the voice but could see no one. Saul got up from the ground, but when he opened his eyes he could see nothing; so they led him by the hand and brought him to Damascus.

Reflection

Saul was violently persecuting members of the early Church when he encountered the risen Christ. That encounter set Saul, or Paul, on a radically different course. Paul's story reminds us that people can change. Even the bitterest foes can become friends. Such moments are a beautiful testimony to God's grace. Such moments also remind us to keep our hearts open to the possibility of change in others as well as in ourselves.

Prayers   *others may be added*

With sincere hearts, we pray:

◆ Divine Teacher, hear our prayer.

For those who oppose the Gospel, we pray: ◆ For the United Nations in their work of promoting peace, we pray: ◆ For the persecuted and marginalized, we pray: ◆ For peacekeepers and those who specialize in conflict resolution, we pray: ◆

Our Father . . .

God of revelation,
sometimes we oppose your will without
    even knowing it.
When we stand against you,
send your Son to stand beside us.
May he take our hand
    and lead us down the right path.
Through Christ our Lord.
Amen.

✝ Blessed are you, O Lord. Alleluia!

✝ Blessed are you, O Lord. Alleluia!

Psalm 119 *page 418*

Reading *Acts 9:32–33, 36–40*

As Peter was passing through every region, he went down to the holy ones living in Lydda. There he found a man named Aeneas, who had been confined to bed for eight years, for he was paralyzed. Peter said to him, "Aeneas, Jesus Christ heals you. Get up and make your bed." He got up at once. . . .

Now in Joppa there was a disciple named Tabitha. . . . Now during those days she fell sick and died. . . . Since Lydda was near Joppa, the disciples, hearing that Peter was there, sent two men to him with the request, "Please come to us without delay." So Peter got up and went with them. When he arrived, they took him to the room upstairs where all the widows came to him weeping. . . . Peter sent them all out and knelt down and prayed. Then he turned to her body and said, "Tabitha, rise up."

Reflection

Jesus once raised Peter's mother-in-law from her sickbed. Jesus also raised up a girl who had died. People now call upon Peter to do the same thing. Peter acts without hesitation, knowing the Spirit of his master is with him. There are times that we, too, might be called upon to go to someone, pray with him or her, console him or her, and lift him or her up.

Prayers *others may be added*

With sincere hearts, we pray:

◆ Divine Teacher, hear our prayer.

For the Church as she bears the compassion of Christ to the sick and the dying, we pray: ◆ For government officials who strive to provide affordable health care for everyone, we pray: ◆ For those who work in health care and medical research, we pray: ◆ For the sick and the dying and those who care for them, we pray: ◆

Our Father . . .

God our healer,
lift us up when we are laid low.
Renew our strength
so that we can support
    and console others.
We ask this through our Lord Jesus
    Christ, your Son,
who lives and reigns with you
in the unity of the Holy Spirit,
one God, forever and ever.
Amen.

✝ Blessed are you, O Lord. Alleluia!

✝ Sing joyfully to the Lord, all you lands! Alleluia!

Psalm 100
page 414

Reading
John 10:11–16

Jesus said: "I am the good shepherd. A good shepherd lays down his life for the sheep. A hired man, who is not a shepherd and whose sheep are not his own, sees a wolf coming and leaves the sheep and runs away, and the wolf catches and scatters them. This is because he works for pay and has no concern for the sheep. I am the good shepherd, and I know mine and mine know me, just as the Father knows me and I know the Father; and I will lay down my life for the sheep. I have other sheep that do not belong to this fold. These also I must lead, and they will hear my voice, and there will be one flock, one shepherd."

Reflection

Jesus contrasts his care for the sheep with the indifference of those who are merely paid to look after the flock. Unlike hired hands, the shepherd is completely invested in his sheep. The sheep are his livelihood. We think of ourselves as striving to be devoted to our good shepherd, and so we should, but this passage reminds us how devoted the shepherd is to us. Our good shepherd lives for us.

Prayers
others may be added

To our faithful Shepherd, we pray:

♦ Hear the prayers of your flock, O Lord.

May both the laity and ordained strive to bring others into Christ's flock, we pray: ♦ May local and national leaders be sincerely devoted to those they serve, we pray: ♦ May those searching for work find stable and meaningful employment, we pray: ♦ May we entrust our lives to Christ in times of danger, we pray: ♦

Our Father . . .

Good Shepherd,
help us to be as devoted to you
    as you are to us.
Help us also to keep each other within
    the flock.
Gather those who have gone astray.
Lead us all into the fullness of
    your kingdom
where you live and reign with God,
    the Father,
in the unity of the Holy Spirit,
one God, forever and ever.
Amen.

✝ Sing joyfully to the Lord, all you lands! Alleluia!

✝ Sing joyfully to the Lord, all you lands! Alleluia!

Psalm 100   *page 414*

Reading   *Acts 11:1–3*

The Apostles and the brothers who were in Judea heard that the Gentiles too had accepted the word of God. So when Peter went up to Jerusalem the circumcised believers confronted him, saying, "You entered the house of uncircumcised people and ate with them."

Reflection

Centuries ago, God forbid his chosen people from eating certain foods in order to remind them that they were set apart. By keeping his people separate from other nations, God revealed his holiness through them. Now, however, people are made holy by their acceptance of the Gospel and the reception of God's Spirit. This Spirit has dissolved the boundaries between Jew and Gentile. United by God's Spirit, all people shall feast together in friendship and holiness.

Prayers   *others may be added*

To our faithful Shepherd, we pray:

◆ Hear the prayers of your flock, O Lord.

May the Church continually attune itself to the voice of the Spirit, we pray: ◆ May leaders in the Middle East promote peace and justice, we pray: ◆ May nutritionists, dietitians, and those who work in the food industry promote healthy living, we pray: ◆ May our hearts be opened to see new perspectives, we pray: ◆

Our Father . . .

Holy Lord,
you have created all things.
By the transforming power
    of your Spirit,
you make us holy.
Dissolve the boundaries
that we draw between ourselves
and other people.
Draw us instead into peaceful fellowship
    with each other.
Through Christ our Lord.
Amen.

✝ Sing joyfully to the Lord, all you lands! Alleluia!

✝ Sing joyfully to the Lord, all you lands! Alleluia!

Psalm 100 *page 414*

Reading *Acts 11:19–23*

Those who had been scattered by the persecution that arose because of Stephen went as far as Phoenicia, Cyprus, and Antioch, preaching the word to no one but Jews. There were some Cypriots and Cyrenians among them, however, who came to Antioch and began to speak to the Greeks as well, proclaiming the Lord Jesus. The hand of the Lord was with them and a great number who believed turned to the Lord. The news about them reached the ears of the Church in Jerusalem, and they sent Barnabas to go to Antioch. When he arrived and saw the grace of God, he rejoiced and encouraged them all to remain faithful to the Lord in firmness of heart.

Reflection

At first, the Apostles preach to the Jews. The Jews, after all, had the framework for understanding Jesus as the Messiah. A few Apostles, however, decide to step outside their religious circle and share the Gospel with non-Jews. The Gentiles happily accept the witness of the Apostles. We all have our social circles. When we step outside of them, or invite someone to step into them, the result is often wonderfully life-giving.

Prayers *others may be added*

To our faithful Shepherd, we pray:

♦ Hear the prayers of your flock, O Lord.

Encourage and strengthen dialogue with communities of diverse backgrounds, we pray: ♦ Protect and comfort those experiencing religious persecution, we pray: ♦ Guide those who work in the field of communications, we pray: ♦ Sustain healthy relationships, we pray: ♦

Our Father . . .

God of love,
you establish bonds of friendship
that your Spirit makes unbreakable.
Help us to receive
    the friendship of others.
Send us to invite people
    into your Church
so that the Body of Christ
may be continually enriched.
Through Christ our Lord.
Amen.

✝ Sing joyfully to the Lord, all you lands! Alleluia!

✝ Sing joyfully to the Lord, all you lands! Alleluia!

Psalm 100 *page 414*

Reading *Acts 12:24—13:5a*

The word of God continued to spread and grow.

After Barnabas and Saul completed their relief mission, they returned to Jerusalem, taking with them John, who is called Mark.

Now there were in the Church at Antioch prophets and teachers: Barnabas, Symeon who was called Niger, Lucius of Cyrene, Manaen who was a close friend of Herod the tetrarch, and Saul. While they were worshiping the Lord and fasting, the holy Spirit said, "Set apart for me Barnabas and Saul for the work to which I have called them." Then, completing their fasting and prayer, they laid hands on them and sent them off.

So they, sent forth by the Holy Spirit, went down to Seleucia and from there sailed to Cyprus. When they arrived in Salamis, they proclaimed the word of God in the Jewish synagogues.

Reflection

In this passage, the Holy Spirit speaks with remarkable directness, and Christ's followers are listening. They have gathered together and are praying and fasting. They have made themselves ready to listen for God's guidance. During those moments in our lives when we ourselves want God's guidance, we must also prepare ourselves to receive it. Being active members of a faith community as well as spending time in prayer and reflection help us to hear the Spirit.

Prayers *others may be added*

To our faithful Shepherd, we pray:

◆ **Hear the prayers of your flock, O Lord.**

For those preparing for ordination or religious profession, we pray: ◆ For all leaders, we pray: ◆ For parents, catechists, and formators, we pray: ◆ For those discerning their vocation and career, we pray: ◆

Our Father . . .

Heavenly Father,
sometimes we struggle to hear your Spirit
　　speaking within us.
Help us to discipline our bodies
　　and our minds
so that in the stillness of our hearts
we may discern your voice
　　and know your will.
Through Christ our Lord.
Amen.

✝ Sing joyfully to the Lord, all you lands! Alleluia!

Thursday, April 29, 2021
Memorial of St. Catherine of Siena,
Virgin and Doctor of the Church

✝ Sing joyfully to the Lord, all you lands! Alleluia!

Psalm 100 *page 414*

Reading *Acts 13:13–15*

From Paphos, Paul and his companions set sail and arrived at Perga in Pamphylia. But John left them and returned to Jerusalem. They continued on from Perga and reached Antioch in Pisidia. On the sabbath they entered into the synagogue and took their seats. After the reading of the law and the prophets, the synagogue officials sent word to them, "My brothers, if one of you has a word of exhortation for the people, please speak."

Reflection

Paul and the others go to the synagogue out of respect and reverence for their religious heritage. The synagogue officials invite the Apostles to speak, perhaps recognizing their devotion to God. St. Catherine of Siena, who died in 1380, was also devoted to God. She offered her own words of exhortation, especially to those in authority. St. Catherine even wrote letters to the pope, urging certain courses of action. People listened to this holy woman because she addressed them with genuine respect and reverence. If we want people to listen to us, we must address them with love.

Prayers *others may be added*

To our faithful Shepherd, we pray:

♦ Hear the prayers of your flock, O Lord.

May the pope and those who serve in the Holy See govern the Church with humility and wisdom, we pray: ♦ May local and national leaders heed the learning and experience of those they serve, we pray: ♦ May spiritual writers and theologians know the wisdom of God, we pray: ♦ May our community be a fervent witness of the risen Lord, we pray: ♦

Our Father . . .

Loving Lord,
increase our devotion to you.
Fill us with your love
so that we can speak to others
    with genuine reverence
    and respect.
We ask this through our Lord Jesus
    Christ, your Son,
who lives and reigns with you
in the unity of the Holy Spirit,
one God, forever and ever.
Amen.

✝ Sing joyfully to the Lord, all you lands! Alleluia!

✝ Sing joyfully to the Lord, all you lands! Alleluia!

Psalm 100   *page 414*

Reading   *John 14:1–6*

Jesus said to his disciples, "Do not let your hearts be troubled. You have faith in God; have faith also in me. In my Father's house there are many dwelling places. If there were not, would I have told you that I am going to prepare a place for you? And if I go and prepare a place for you, I will come back again and take you to myself, so that where I am you also may be. Where I am going you know the way." Thomas said to him, "Master, we do not know where you are going; how can we know the way?" Jesus said to him, "I am the way and the truth and the life. No one comes to the Father except through me."

Reflection

Jesus came to reveal his Father's perfect love and to bring people into the divine life. Some people do not believe in Jesus while others do not know anything about him. Will God deny these people salvation? Jesus tells us that in his Father's house there are many dwelling places. There is ample room for those who seek the way of love, who confess their need for salvation, and who act in ways that are life-giving rather than harmful.

Prayers   *others may be added*

To our faithful Shepherd, we pray:

♦ Hear the prayers of your flock, O Lord.

For the baptized, we pray: ♦ For leaders of nations, we pray: ♦ For missionaries, retreat directors, and catechists, we pray: ♦ For those who are struggling in their faith, we pray: ♦ For those who have died, we pray: ♦

Our Father . . .

Almighty Father,
you sent your Son
so that all might find the way to you.
Guide the lost and the wayward
    by the light of his love.
Help us all to stay true to the path
that leads to eternal life.
Through Christ our Lord.
Amen.

✝ Sing joyfully to the Lord, all you lands! Alleluia!

✝ Sing joyfully to the Lord, all you lands! Alleluia!

Psalm 100   *page 414*

Reading   *Acts 13:44–48*

On the following sabbath almost the whole city gathered to hear the word of the Lord. When the Jews saw the crowds, they were filled with jealousy and with violent abuse contradicted what Paul said. Both Paul and Barnabas spoke out boldly and said, "It was necessary that the word of God be spoken to you first, but since you reject it and condemn yourselves as unworthy of eternal life, we now turn to the Gentiles. For so the Lord has commanded us, *I have made you a light to the Gentiles, that you may be an instrument of salvation to the ends of the earth.*"

The Gentiles were delighted when they heard this and glorified the word of the Lord.

Reflection

St. Luke wrote his Gospel and the Book of Acts partly to assure the Gentiles that God has included them in salvation. Luke never intended passages like this one to be used to demonize the Jewish people. After all, Jesus and his first followers were Jewish. We who are Christians praise God for offering us salvation, and we honor the Jewish faith tradition from which that salvation has come forth.

Prayers   *others may be added*

To our faithful Shepherd, we pray:

◆ Hear the prayers of your flock, O Lord.

For an end to anti-Semitism and all forms of religious persecution, we pray: ◆ For continued and respectful dialogue between faith leaders, we pray: ◆ For those who have abandoned their search for God, we pray: ◆ For those in our midst who renew the joy of our faith, we pray:

Our Father . . .

God of salvation,
when we take our faith for granted,
renew in us the wonder of your love.
Keep our hearts overflowing with joy
at the salvation we have received
through our Lord Jesus Christ
    your Son,
who lives and reigns with you
in the unity of the Holy Spirit,
one God, forever and ever.
Amen.

◆ Sing joyfully to the Lord, all you lands! Alleluia!

Sunday, May 2, 2021
Fifth Sunday of Easter

✝ May my mouth speak the praise of the Lord. Alleluia!

Psalm 145 *page 420*

Reading *John 15:1–8*

Jesus said to his disciples: "I am the true vine, and my Father is the vine grower. He takes away every branch in me that does not bear fruit, and everyone that does he prunes so that it bears more fruit. You are already pruned because of the word that I spoke to you. Remain in me, as I remain in you. Just as a branch cannot bear fruit on its own unless it remains on the vine, so neither can you unless you remain in me. I am the vine, you are the branches. Whoever remains in me and I in him will bear much fruit, because without me you can do nothing. Anyone who does not remain in me will be thrown out like a branch and wither; people will gather them and throw them into a fire and they will be burned. If you remain in me and my words remain in you, ask for whatever you want and it will be done for you. By this is my Father glorified, that you bear much fruit and become my disciples."

Reflection

By referring to himself as the vine and to us as the branches, Jesus assures us that we have communion with him and draw our life from him. However, we the branches must also be pruned. Even branches that appear healthy need to be trimmed so that new and healthier growth can occur. It is hard to let our Lord cut parts of us away, but when we do, we become fruit-laden branches that help the vine to grow and spread.

Prayers *others may be added*

To our God who draws near, we pray:

◆ Hear us, O Lord.

May the branches of the Church be so fruitful that others are drawn to the vine, we pray: ◆ May governments cut away old practices in order to implement more fruitful policies, we pray: ◆ May farmers reap the benefit of their labor, we pray: ◆ May the newly baptized grow in faith, hope, and love, we pray: ◆

Our Father . . .

Jesus, our True Vine,
without you, we wither and fall.
Nourish us with your Body and Blood.
Trim away the parts of us
that are rotting or unproductive.
Cultivate your life within us
so that we may be joyful,
    fruitful people,
who are united forever with you
who live and reign
    with God, the Father,
in the unity of the Holy Spirit,
one God, forever and ever.
Amen.

✝ May my mouth speak the praise of the Lord. Alleluia!

✟ May my mouth speak the praise
of the Lord. Alleluia!

Psalm 145   *page 420*

Reading   *1 Corinthians 15:1–8*

I am reminding you, brothers and sisters, of the Gospel I preached to you,
which you indeed received and in which
you also stand. Through it you are also
being saved, if you hold fast to the word
I preached to you, unless you believed
in vain. For I handed on to you as of
first importance what I also received:
that Christ died for our sins in accordance with the Scriptures; that he was
buried; that he was raised on the third
day in accordance with the Scriptures;
that he appeared to Cephas, then to the
Twelve. After that, he appeared to more
than five hundred brothers and sisters
at once, most of whom are still living,
though some have fallen asleep. After
that he appeared to James, then to all
the Apostles. Last of all, as to one born
abnormally, he appeared to me.

Reflection

We know little about Philip and James.
As these two men grew in their discipleship, however, it no longer mattered to
them that they themselves be remembered. What mattered was the Gospel.
In ways that have been forgotten over
time, these two Apostles handed on the
faith. The details of our own lives
matter far less than our efforts to grow
as disciples so as to share the Gospel
with others.

Prayers   *others may be added*

To our God who draws near, we pray:

◆ Hear us, O Lord.

Free the Church from selfish desires,
we pray: ◆ Help supervisors and
managers attend to the needs of their
employees, we pray: ◆ Strengthen the
people and communities under the
patronage of Sts. Philip and James,
we pray: ◆ Grant fortitude and wisdom
to your disciples, we pray: ◆

Our Father . . .

Gracious Lord,
through the centuries
    countless men and women
    have handed on
the story of salvation.
May we take our place among them
as we, too, live and share the Gospel.
Through Christ our Lord.
Amen.

✟ May my mouth speak the praise
of the Lord. Alleluia!

✝ May my mouth speak the praise of the Lord. Alleluia!

Psalm 145 *page 420*

Reading *Acts 14:19–22*

In those days, some Jews from Antioch and Iconium arrived and won over the crowds. They stoned Paul and dragged him out of the city, supposing that he was dead. But when the disciples gathered around him, he got up and entered the city. On the following day he left with Barnabas for Derbe.

After they had proclaimed the good news to that city and made a considerable number of disciples, they returned to Lystra and to Iconium and to Antioch. They strengthened the spirits of the disciples and exhorted them to persevere in the faith, saying, "It is necessary for us to undergo many hardships to enter the Kingdom of God."

Reflection

St. Paul's companions must have been horrified to see him being dragged from the city. As they bent over his bruised and bloodied body, they thought he would never arise. To their astonishment —and ours—Paul gets up and continues preaching the Gospel. The story dramatically illustrates how God's plan of salvation will not be thwarted. The story also encourages us to get up and move forward despite the challenges we face.

Prayers *others may be added*

To our God who draws near, we pray:

◆ Hear us, O Lord.

Give courage to the Church to address injustice, we pray: ◆ Open the hearts of government leaders to the needs of the poor and marginalized, we pray: ◆ Comfort and heal those affected by trauma, we pray: ◆ Aid us in our journey of discipleship, we pray: ◆

Our Father . . .

Almighty God,
you lift up those
    who strive to do your will.
You have given us your Holy Spirit
so that we may prevail over
    whatever evil confronts us.
May we cling to your Spirit
so that we might always rise up
and continue following the way of your
    Son, our Lord Jesus Christ,
who lives and reigns with you
in the unity of the Holy Spirit,
one God, forever and ever.
Amen.

✝ May my mouth speak the praise of the Lord. Alleluia!

† May my mouth speak the praise of the Lord. Alleluia!

Psalm 145   page 420

Reading   Acts 15:1–6

Some who had come down from Judea were instructing the brothers, "Unless you are circumcised according to the Mosaic practice, you cannot be saved." Because there arose no little dissension and debate by Paul and Barnabas with them, it was decided that Paul, Barnabas, and some of the others should go up to Jerusalem to the Apostles and presbyters about this question. They were sent on their journey by the Church. . . . When they arrived in Jerusalem, they were welcomed by the Church, as well as by the Apostles and the presbyters, and they reported what God had done with them. But some from the party of the Pharisees who had become believers stood up and said, "It is necessary to circumcise them and direct them to observe the Mosaic law."

The Apostles and the presbyters met together to see about this matter.

Reflection

Christianity began as a Jewish movement. As the Church grew, its leaders were faced with the question of whether the Gentiles had to obey Jewish law. The leaders had to discern how to live the Gospel faithfully under quickly changing circumstances. Their decision was difficult for some to accept, but it safeguarded the unity of the Church and the integrity of the Gospel.

Prayers   others may be added

To our God who draws near, we pray:

◆ Hear us, O Lord.

That the Church may be a place of welcome to the stranger, we pray: ◆ That world leaders may work together to resolve conflicts, we pray: ◆ That hurting families may work toward healing and reconciliation, we pray: ◆ That those struggling with faith may find solace in God's care, we pray: ◆

Our Father . . .

Lord,
we are often slow to discern your will,
and sometimes we disagree
     with each other
about how best to serve you.
Guide us through our disagreements.
As we listen to your Spirit,
lead us toward mutual understanding
     and peaceful resolution.
Through Christ our Lord.
Amen.

† May my mouth speak the praise of the Lord. Alleluia!

✝ May my mouth speak the praise of the Lord. Alleluia!

Psalm 145   *page 420*

Reading   *John 15:9–11*

Jesus said to his disciples: "As the Father loves me, so I also love you. Remain in my love. If you keep my commandments, you will remain in my love, just as I have kept my Father's commandments and remain in his love.

"I have told you this so that my joy might be in you and your joy might be complete."

Reflection

Jesus insists that we remain in his love by obeying his commandments, but in the Gospel of John, Jesus only gives one commandment: love one another. By loving each other as Jesus has loved us, we become part of the love of God. Such love is not easy. We will not like or agree with everyone. As we try to obey Christ's commandment, however, we will see the dignity of every human being and will love him or her as Christ has loved us.

Prayers   *others may be added*

To our God who draws near, we pray:

◆ Hear us, O Lord.

Holy Spirit, lead the Church to the path of healing, reconciliation, and peace, we pray: ◆ Hoy Spirit, guide those in positions of power to seek justice and peace, we pray: ◆ Holy Spirit, break open hardened hearts and teach them how to love, we pray: ◆ Holy Spirit, pour forth your love upon all creation and renew it for the glory of God, we pray: ◆

Our Father . . .

Loving Father,
you want us to draw closer to you.
Reveal the depth of your love;
liberate us from
    fear and selfishness,
and lead us into
    the everlasting joy of life with you.
Through Christ our Lord.
Amen.

✝ May my mouth speak the praise of the Lord. Alleluia!

✝ May my mouth speak the praise of the Lord. Alleluia!

Psalm 145   *page 420*

Reading   *Acts 15:22, 23ac, 25, 27–29, 31*

The Apostles and presbyters, in agreement with the whole Church, decided to choose representatives and to send them to Antioch with Paul and Barnabas. The ones chosen were Judas, who was called Barsabbas, and Silas, leaders among the brothers. This is the letter delivered by them: "[G]reetings. . . . [W]e have with one accord decided to choose representatives and to send them to you along with our beloved Barnabas and Paul. . . . So we are sending Judas and Silas who will also convey this same message by word of mouth: 'It is the decision of the Holy Spirit and of us not to place on you any burden beyond these necessities, namely, to abstain from meat sacrificed to idols, from blood, from meats of strangled animals, and from unlawful marriage. If you keep free of these, you will be doing what is right. Farewell.'" . . .

When the people read it, they were delighted with the exhortation.

Reflection

Having settled the question of whether Gentile converts have to obey Jewish law, the leaders of the early Church notify the Gentiles of their decision in a letter. The letter acknowledges the Gentiles' concerns and sets forth clear guidelines. The letter is also pastorally sensitive as it reflects thoughtful and prayerful deliberation. The Gentiles receive the letter with gratitude and joy. People are much more likely to accept a decision when they know their concerns have been heard and considered.

Prayers   *others may be added*

To our God who draws near, we pray:

◆ Hear us, O Lord.

For the Church, we pray: ◆ For world leaders, we pray: ◆ For the forgotten, we pray: ◆ For catechumens and the newly baptized, we pray: ◆

Our Father . . .

Lord God,
your Spirit guided the early Church
to accommodate the Gentiles.
Your Church will always face new
    questions and challenges.
Send your Spirit to guide our steps.
Through Christ our Lord.
Amen.

✝ May my mouth speak the praise of the Lord. Alleluia!

✝ May my mouth speak the praise of the Lord. Alleluia!

Psalm 145 *page 420*

Reading *Acts 16:4–8*

As [Paul and Timothy] traveled from city to city, they handed on to the people for observance the decisions reached by the Apostles and presbyters in Jerusalem. Day after day the churches grew stronger in faith and increased in number. They traveled through the Phrygian and Galatian territory because they had been prevented by the Holy Spirit from preaching the message in the province of Asia. When they came to Mysia, they tried to go on into Bithynia, but the Spirit of Jesus did not allow them, so they crossed through Mysia and came down to Troas.

Reflection

For most of the Book of Acts, the Apostles rush to keep up with the Spirit. In this passage, the Holy Spirit is a virtual wall, forcing Paul and Timothy to change their plans not once but twice. Sometimes we think we are following the Spirit when we are headed in the wrong direction. We must evaluate our actions humbly and honestly. We might feel a bit embarrassed about our missteps, but the Spirit always stands ready to lead us.

Prayers *others may be added*

To our God who draws near, we pray:

◆ Hear us, O Lord.

Grant your people humble and true hearts, we pray: ◆ Protect travelers and missionaries proclaiming your Word, we pray: ◆ Show your people the path of life, we pray: ◆ Guide those who seek clarity in life, we pray: ◆

Our Father . . .

Almighty God,
you send your Spirit upon creation.
Help us to accept the Spirit's will.
Prevent us from forging our own path;
reveal the path
    you have opened for us.
Grant us courage
    to remain steadfast
on our journey of discipleship.
Through Christ our Lord.
Amen.

✝ May my mouth speak the praise of the Lord. Alleluia!

✝ Blessed are you, O Lord. Alleluia!

Psalm 119 *page 418*

Reading *John 15:12–16*

[Jesus said to his disciples:] "This is my commandment: love one another as I love you. No one has greater love than this, to lay down one's life for one's friends. You are my friends if you do what I command you. I no longer call you slaves, because a slave does not know what his master is doing. I have called you friends, because I have told you everything I have heard from my Father. It was not you who chose me, but I who chose you and appointed you to go and bear fruit that will remain, so that whatever you ask the Father in my name he may give you."

Reflection

If our friends started giving us commandments, they probably would not stay our friends for very long. By giving commandments to his disciples, Jesus defines his friendship with them. Their friendship is not based on mutual interests or life circumstances, but on a love that desires what is best for the other. Friends who love us like this and who desire such love from us in return are friends we would want to keep forever.

Prayers *others may be added*

With sincere hearts, we pray:

◆ Divine Teacher, hear our prayer.

That the Church may be rooted in divine love, we pray: ◆ That entrepreneurs may be rooted in the spirit of generosity, we pray: ◆ That those preparing to celebrate first Communion and confirmation may open their hearts to your grace, we pray: ◆ That friends and family may be roused to proclaim the Gospel of love, we pray: ◆

Our Father . . .

God, you are love itself.
Overturn sin and death
   by the power of your love.
Transform the whole of creation
so that all people may welcome your
   friendship forever.
Through Christ our Lord.
Amen.

✝ Blessed are you, O Lord. Alleluia!

Monday, May 10, 2021
Easter Weekday

✝ Blessed are you, O Lord. Alleluia!

Psalm 119 — page 418

Reading — Acts 16:11–15

We set sail from Troas, making a straight run for Samothrace, and on the next day to Neapolis, and from there to Philippi, a leading city in that district of Macedonia and a Roman colony. We spent some time in that city. On the sabbath we went outside the city gate along the river where we thought there would be a place of prayer. We sat and spoke with the women who had gathered there. One of them, a woman named Lydia, a dealer in purple cloth, from the city of Thyatira, a worshiper of God, listened, and the Lord opened her heart to pay attention to what Paul was saying. After she and her household had been baptized, she offered us an invitation, "If you consider me a believer in the Lord, come and stay at my home," and she prevailed on us.

Reflection

After accepting the Gospel, Lydia immediately extends hospitality to the Apostles. Lydia, a dealer in expensive cloth, puts her great wealth at the service of the Church. Having accepted the Gospel ourselves, we must examine how we spend our time and money. The use of our material resources reveals the disposition of our hearts. We want our hearts to reveal the overflowing love of God.

Prayers — *others may be added*

With sincere hearts, we pray:

◆ Divine Teacher, hear our prayer.

For the many charitable organizations administered by the Church, we pray: ◆ For those who oversee programs that revitalize communities, we pray: ◆ For those who work in the textile industry, we pray: ◆ For those discerning how best to serve the needs of their local community, we pray: ◆

Our Father . . .

Heavenly Father,
you gave your very self to us
	in the person of your Son, Jesus.
Help us to give ourselves back to you.
Open our hands to share
	what we have with others
just as you have shared
	all you have with us.
Through Christ our Lord.
Amen.

✝ Blessed are you, O Lord. Alleluia!

✝ Blessed are you, O Lord. Alleluia!

Psalm 119   *page 418*

Reading   *Acts 16:25–30*

About midnight, while Paul and Silas were praying and singing hymns to God as the prisoners listened, there was suddenly such a severe earthquake that the foundations of the jail shook; all the doors flew open, and the chains of all were pulled loose. When the jailer woke up and saw the prison doors wide open, he drew his sword and was about to kill himself, thinking that the prisoners had escaped. But Paul shouted out in a loud voice, "Do no harm to yourself; we are all here." He asked for a light and rushed in and, trembling with fear, he fell down before Paul and Silas. Then he brought them out and said, "Sirs, what must I do to be saved?" And they said, "Believe in the Lord Jesus and you and your household will be saved."

Reflection

The jailor, thinking he had failed at his duty, was about to kill himself when Paul intervened. The jailor was so impressed by the courage and integrity of the Christians that he immediately asked how to become one. Paul thus saved the jailor's physical life and his eternal life. Our own acts of courage and integrity both draw others to the Gospel and help them to stand fast in the faith.

Prayers   *others may be added*

With sincere hearts, we pray:

◆ Divine Teacher, hear our prayer.

That the baptized may find strength in the Gospel, we pray: ◆ That leaders may persevere in defending human rights, we pray: ◆ That those feeling a loss or depressed may find comfort in Christ, we pray: ◆ That the persecuted and ridiculed may know God's love and mercy, we pray: ◆

Our Father . . .

God our liberator,
there is no place
    your saving hand cannot reach.
Stretch forth your mighty arm
and deliver us
    when we succumb to sin.
Lift us up
so that we may embrace
    the Gospel once again
and inspire others to do the same.
Through Christ our Lord.
Amen.

✝ Blessed are you, O Lord. Alleluia!

✝ Blessed are you, O Lord. Alleluia!

Psalm 119 *page 418*

Reading *Acts 17:22–28*

Then Paul stood up at the Areopagus and said: "You Athenians, I see that in every respect you are very religious. For as I walked around looking carefully at your shrines, I even discovered an altar inscribed, 'To an Unknown God.' What therefore you unknowingly worship, I proclaim to you. The God who made the world and all that is in it, the Lord of heaven and earth, does not dwell in sanctuaries made by human hands, nor is he served by human hands because he needs anything. Rather it is he who gives to everyone life and breath and everything. He made from one the whole human race to dwell on the entire surface of the earth, and he fixed the ordered seasons and the boundaries of their regions, so that people might seek God, even perhaps grope for him and find him, though indeed he is not far from any one of us."

Reflection

As Paul speaks to the Athenians, he mentions the temples and statues dedicated to gods and goddesses that are all over their city. The Athenians are clearly people of faith, but that faith has not found its true source. Paul must guide them. We may find ourselves guiding others who are searching for God's love and truth. Our guidance, like Paul's, must begin not with what we want to tell them, but with what they themselves have already experienced and understand.

Prayers *others may be added*

With sincere hearts, we pray:

◆ Divine Teacher, hear our prayer.

For missionaries and preachers who share the Gospel in different cultural settings, we pray: ◆ For civil servants who maintain communication between nations that are in conflict with each other, we pray: ◆ For those engaged in ecumenism and interreligious dialogue, we pray: ◆ For those who are returning to their Catholic faith and for those who guide them, we pray: ◆

Our Father . . .

Lord of heaven and earth,
people throughout time
   and across the world
have sought the truth
   of who you are.
Inspire those,
   who have stopped seeking you,
to renew their quest.
May we take their hands
   and they ours
as we continue the journey
   into your kingdom.
Through Christ our Lord
Amen.

✝ Blessed are you, O Lord. Alleluia!

✝ God mounts his throne to shouts of joy. Alleluia!

Psalm 47 — page 409

Reading — John 16:16–20

Jesus said to his disciples: "A little while and you will no longer see me, and again a little while later and you will see me." So some of his disciples said to one another, "What does this mean that he is saying to us, 'A little while and you will not see me, and again a little while and you will see me,' and 'Because I am going to the Father'?" So they said, "What is this 'little while' of which he speaks? We do not know what he means." Jesus knew that they wanted to ask him, so he said to them, "Are you discussing with one another what I said, 'A little while and you will not see me, and again a little while and you will see me'? Amen, amen, I say to you, you will weep and mourn, while the world rejoices; you will grieve, but your grief will become joy."

Reflection

Even if Jesus had stated plainly that he was going to be crucified and then raised from the dead, his disciples would not have understood him. It is difficult to accept that someone who was raised up on a cross is also raised up in glory in heaven. In the Gospel of John, however, Jesus' crucifixion is inseparable from his resurrection and ascension. What appears to be a horrible, shameful death reveals itself to be gloriously life-giving.

Prayers — *others may be added*

To Christ who reigns, we pray:

◆ Hear us, king of all the earth.

May the leaders of our Church model Christ's selfless love, we pray: ◆ May global business leaders act in ways that protect both people and the environment, we pray: ◆ May those filled with grief or sadness find comfort in God's presence, we pray: ◆ May the sick and all who suffer be healed by Christ, we pray: ◆

Our Father . . .

O God,
you entrusted the work of salvation to
    your Son, Jesus,
who now reigns at your right hand.
Teach us how to be better disciples
so that we may follow
    in his footsteps.
When we suffer in this life,
assure us of the joy and glory to come.
Through Christ our Lord.
Amen.

✝ God mounts his throne to shouts of joy. Alleluia!

Friday, May 14, 2021
Feast of St. Matthias, Apostle

✝ Blessed are you, O Lord. Alleluia!

Psalm 119 *page 418*

Reading *Acts 1:15–17, 21, 23–26*

[Peter] said, "My brothers and sisters . . . Judas was numbered among us and was allotted a share in this ministry. . . . Therefore, it is necessary that one of the men who accompanied us the whole time the Lord Jesus came and went among us . . . become with us a witness to his resurrection." So they proposed two, Joseph called Barsabbas, who was also known as Justus, and Matthias. Then they prayed, "You, Lord, who know the hearts of all, show which one of these two you have chosen to take the place in this apostolic ministry from which Judas turned away to go to his own place." Then they gave lots to them, and the lot fell upon Matthias, and he was counted with the Eleven Apostles.

Reflection

Jesus had more than twelve followers, but he chose twelve to form his inner circle. These twelve disciples, who represented the twelve tribes of Israel, symbolized the new Israel Jesus was forming. When the early Church was still small and closely connected to Judaism, preserving the symbolism of the Twelve was important. It was thus necessary to replace Judas. The spirit-filled selection of Matthias reminds us that we, too, might be called upon to serve in ways we do not expect.

Prayers *others may be added*

With sincere hearts, we pray:

◆ Divine Teacher, hear our prayer.

May bishops and formation directors listen closely to the Spirit when choosing men for the priesthood, we pray: ◆
May local and national leaders uphold the dignity of their offices, we pray: ◆
For those communities under the patronage of St. Matthias, we pray: ◆
For those who exercise leadership in our faith communities, we pray: ◆

Our Father . . .

Lord God,
you chose St. Matthias to exercise
	leadership within your Church.
Continue to call competent men
	of good character
to be ordained ministers.
May all the baptized find ways
to serve and strengthen the Church.
We ask this through our Lord Jesus
	Christ, your Son,
who lives and reigns with you
in the unity of the Holy Spirit,
one God, forever and ever.
Amen.

✝ Blessed are you, O Lord. Alleluia!

☩ Blessed are you, O Lord. Alleluia!

Psalm 119   *page 418*

Reading   *Acts 18:24–28*

A Jew named Apollos, a native of Alexandria, an eloquent speaker, arrived in Ephesus. He was an authority on the Scriptures. He had been instructed in the Way of the Lord and, with ardent spirit, spoke and taught accurately about Jesus, although he knew only the baptism of John. He began to speak boldly in the synagogue, but when Priscilla and Aquila heard him, they took him aside and explained to him the Way of God more accurately. And when he wanted to cross to Achaia, the brothers encouraged him and wrote to the disciples there to welcome him. After his arrival he gave great assistance to those who had come to believe through grace. He vigorously refuted the Jews in public, establishing from the Scriptures that the Christ is Jesus.

Reflection

Apollos is an inspiring speaker, but his knowledge of the Gospel is incomplete. Priscilla and Aquila discretely take him aside and amend his understanding. Even people who are highly skilled at something still benefit from the wisdom and guidance of others. We might be in need of such guidance or correction. Like Apollos, our work will be strengthened if we accept the wise counsel of other people.

Prayers   *others may be added*

With sincere hearts, we pray:

◆ Divine Teacher, hear our prayer.

For lectors and preachers, we pray: ◆
For world leaders, we pray: ◆ For teachers, catechists, and spiritual directors,
we pray: ◆ For parish leaders, we pray: ◆

Our Father . . .

God of truth,
we all have much to learn.
As we grow in knowledge and wisdom,
may we also grow in humility
    in the understanding
that there is always more to learn.
Through Christ our Lord.
Amen.

☩ Blessed are you, O Lord. Alleluia!

Sunday, May 16, 2021
Solemnity of the Ascension of the Lord
Turn to page 170 if the Seventh Sunday of Easter is celebrated in your (arch)diocese today.

✝ God mounts his throne to shouts of joy. Alleluia!

Psalm 47   *page 409*

Reading   Mark 16:15–20

Jesus appeared to the Eleven and said to them: "Go into the whole world and proclaim the Gospel to every creature. Whoever believes and is baptized will be saved; whoever does not believe will be condemned. These signs will accompany those who believe: in my name they will drive out demons, they will speak new languages. They will pick up serpents with their hands, and if they drink any deadly thing, it will not harm them. They will lay hands on the sick, and they will recover."

Then the Lord Jesus, after he spoke to them, was taken up into heaven and took his seat at the right hand of God. But they went forth and preached everywhere, while the Lord worked with them and confirmed the word through accompanying signs.

Reflection

Having ascended into heaven, Jesus is no longer confined to time and space. The risen Christ now accompanies his followers through the generations and across the earth. As the risen Christ empowers us today, we are probably not going to pick up poisonous animals or quaff toxic drinks, but we can console those who suffer and oppose evil. By letting the power of our risen Lord flow through us, we reveal that Jesus truly is Lord of heaven and earth.

Prayers   *others may be added*

To Christ who reigns, we pray:

◆ Hear us, king of all the earth.

That the Church be a source of compassion and hope, we pray: ◆ That world leaders govern with love and peace, we pray: ◆ That the downtrodden grow in hope, we pray: ◆ That the sick might be strengthened, we pray: ◆

Our Father . . .

Lord of heaven and earth,
you exercise your saving power
through those who have been
    baptized in your name.
Make us holy.
Send us to those people and places
in need of healing, reconciliation,
    and liberation.
Make us living witnesses
    of your eternal glory,
for you live and reign with God,
the Father, in the unity of the Holy Spirit,
one God, forever and ever.
Amen.

✝ God mounts his throne to shouts of joy. Alleluia!

✝ Love one another, alleluia!

Psalm 145   page 420

Reading   *1 John 4:11–16*

Beloved, if God so loved us, we also must love one another. No one has ever seen God. Yet, if we love one another, God remains in us, and his love is brought to perfection in us.

This is how we know that we remain in him and he in us, that he has given us his Spirit. Moreover, we have seen and testify that the Father sent his Son as savior of the world. Whoever acknowledges that Jesus is the Son of God, God remains in him and he in God. We have come to know and to believe in the love God has for us.

God is love, and whoever remains in love remains in God and God in him.

Reflection

When contemplating this passage, you might recall Jesus' commandment to "Love one another. As I have loved you, so you also should love one another" (John 13:34). The author of this Epistle is reminding the Johannine community that love distinguishes those who profess faith in Jesus. Because of his passion, death, and resurrection, which we have been baptized into, we have been forever changed and God's love is what must direct our hearts and minds. By loving our neighbors, we unite our hearts to the heart of Christ. Go forth and love!

Timothy A. Johnston

Prayers   *others may be added*

To Christ who reigns, we pray:

◆ **Loving God, hear us.**

Help the Church to witness the love of Christ, we pray: ◆ Help leaders of nations to love their people, we pray: ◆ Instill within us a deep love for the poor and marginalized, we pray: ◆ Receive into your kingdom those who have died, we pray: ◆

Our Father . . .

O loving God,
you sent your Son, Jesus,
to show us how to live.
Shower us with your Holy Spirit
so that we may forever
be filled with your love and grace.
Through Christ our Lord.
Amen.

✝ Love one another, alleluia!

✝ God's mercy endures forever!
Alleluia!

Psalm 118   *page 417*

Reading   *Acts 19:1b–7*

While Apollos was in Corinth, Paul traveled through the interior of the country and down to Ephesus where he found some disciples. He said to them, "Did you receive the Holy Spirit when you became believers?" They answered him, "We have never even heard that there is a Holy Spirit." He said, "How were you baptized?" They replied, "With the baptism of John." Paul then said, "John baptized with a baptism of repentance, telling the people to believe in the one who was to come after him, that is, in Jesus." When they heard this, they were baptized in the name of the Lord Jesus. And when Paul laid his hands on them, the Holy Spirit came upon them, and they spoke in tongues and prophesied. Altogether there were about twelve men.

Reflection

Jesus brought about a new era of salvation. When the men in this passage are baptized and begin speaking in tongues and prophesying, they reveal that they have become part of this new era. Such dramatic signs probably did not accompany our own baptisms, but the Holy Spirit is no less present within us. We, too, are part of the era of salvation. Our own cooperation with God's Spirit may turn out to be more dramatic than we imagined.

Prayers   *others may be added*

With hearts full of hope, we pray:

◆ Merciful Savior, hear us.

For the pope and bishops as they exercise the teaching office of the Church, we pray: ◆ For young leaders who are discovering their gifts, we pray: ◆ For the newly baptized as they discern the gifts received at baptism, we pray: ◆ For grieving families as they mourn the loss of a loved one, we pray: ◆

Our Father . . .

Almighty Father,
you have brought us into union
    with your Son
and given us a share of your Holy Spirit.
Make us eager to accept
    the Spirit's gifts,
and help us to recognize
    the presence of your Spirit in others.
Through Christ our Lord.
Amen.

✝ God's mercy endures forever!
Alleluia!

✝ God's mercy endures forever!
Alleluia!

Psalm 118   *page 417*

Reading   *John 17:1, 6–10*

[Jesus raised his eyes to heaven and said,] "I revealed your name to those whom you gave me out of the world. They belonged to you, and you gave them to me, and they have kept your word. Now they know that everything you gave me is from you, because the words you gave to me I have given to them, and they accepted them and truly understood that I came from you, and they have believed that you sent me. I pray for them. I do not pray for the world but for the ones you have given me, because they are yours, and everything of mine is yours and everything of yours is mine, and I have been glorified in them."

Reflection

On the eve of Jesus' crucifixion and resurrection, he prayed for his followers. They would face the challenge of living as holy, loving people in a sometimes hostile world. As these first disciples listened to Jesus' prayer, they heard, as we hear, that our Lord remains with us every step of the way. Just as Jesus prayed to his God and glorified God by his life, so do we pray that God be glorified in our lives.

Prayers   *others may be added*

With hearts full of hope, we pray:

♦ Merciful Savior, hear us.

Holy Spirit, renew and heal the Church, we pray: ♦ Holy Spirit, grant wisdom to world leaders, we pray: ♦ Holy Spirit, refresh ministers who are fatigued and disheartened, we pray: ♦ Holy Spirit, enkindle the hearts of the faithful, we pray: ♦

Our Father . . .

O God,
your Son glorified you
through his ministry
    and his Passion and death.
You in turn glorified him
    by restoring him to eternal life.
As we try to imitate our Lord Jesus,
may we reveal his self-giving love
so that people might see Christ in us
and glorify your name.
Through Christ our Lord.
Amen.

✝ God's mercy endures forever!
Alleluia!

✝ God's mercy endures forever!
Alleluia!

Psalm 118 *page 417*

Reading *Acts 20:32–38*

"And now I commend you to God and to that gracious word of his that can build you up and give you the inheritance among all who are consecrated. I have never wanted anyone's silver or gold or clothing. You know well that these very hands have served my needs and my companions. In every way I have shown you that by hard work of that sort we must help the weak, and keep in mind the words of the Lord Jesus who himself said, 'It is more blessed to give than to receive.'"

When he had finished speaking he knelt down and prayed with them all. They were all weeping loudly as they threw their arms around Paul and kissed him, for they were deeply distressed that he had said that they would never see his face again. Then they escorted him to the ship.

Reflection

Preachers of this era expected hospitality and even compensation. Paul reminds his fellow believers that material gain was never what motivated him. Rather, Paul is in love with the Lord, and he wants everyone to experience that same saving love. In his desire to share the good news with as many people as he can, Paul embarks on a new missionary journey. He has done such a good job of sharing God's love in Christ that his friends weep over his departure.

Prayers *others may be added*

With hearts full of hope, we pray:

♦ Merciful Savior, hear us.

May the Church embody our Savior's love, we pray: ♦ May employers provide just wages for their workers, we pray: ♦ May those struggling financially find suitable employment, we pray: ♦ May this community be filled with the zeal of the Holy Spirit, we pray: ♦

Our Father . . .

Loving God,
Paul didn't merely preach
    the Gospel,
he incarnated the love
    that he preached.
Grant us your Son's love
so that people may find joy
    in our presence.
Through Christ our Lord.
Amen.

✝ God's mercy endures forever!
Alleluia!

✞ God's mercy endures forever!
Alleluia!

Psalm 118   *page 417*

Reading   *Acts 23:6–7, 10–11*

[Paul] called out before the Sanhedrin, "My brothers, I am a Pharisee, the son of Pharisees; I am on trial for hope in the resurrection of the dead." When he said this, a dispute broke out between the Pharisees and Sadducees, and the group became divided. . . . The dispute was so serious that the commander . . . ordered his troops to . . . rescue Paul from their midst and take him into the compound. The following night the Lord stood by him and said, "Take courage. For just as you have borne witness to my cause in Jerusalem, so you must also bear witness in Rome."

Reflection

As he stands before the Jewish elders, Paul notes that he is a Pharisee, which gives him credibility. Some accept Paul's words, but others so strongly reject them that Paul is hustled out of the room. Paul then learns that he must go to Rome. Despite his status as a Roman citizen, he will again face dangerous controversy in that city. Paul used his status to continue preaching the Gospel, but in the end, he did not use it to save his life.

Prayers   *others may be added*

With hearts full of hope, we pray:

◆ Merciful Savior, hear us.

For persecuted Christians, we pray: ◆ For those who write policy and enforce the rule of law, we pray: ◆ For those who risk their lives to protect others, we pray: ◆ For spiritual directors, counselors, and confidants, we pray: ◆

Our Father . . .

Lord God,
we do not know where
    or to whom you will next send us.
As we await the guidance of your Spirit,
prepare us to follow where you lead.
Through Christ our Lord.
Amen.

✞ God's mercy endures forever!
Alleluia!

✝ God's mercy endures forever!
Alleluia!

Psalm 118 *page 417*

Reading *John 21:15–17*

[Jesus] said to Simon Peter, "Simon, son of John, do you love me more than these?" He said to him, "Yes, Lord, you know that I love you." He said to him, "Feed my lambs." He then said to him a second time, "Simon, son of John, do you love me?" He said to him, "Yes, Lord, you know that I love you." He said to him, "Tend my sheep." He said to him the third time, "Simon, son of John, do you love me?" Peter was distressed that he had said to him a third time, "Do you love me?" and he said to him, "Lord, you know everything; you know that I love you." Jesus said to him, "Feed my sheep."

Reflection

Simon Peter assures Jesus of his love with a mixture of shame and sorrow. Simon is thinking of the three times he denied knowing his friend and Lord. Jesus not only forgives this remorseful disciple, he gives him a leadership role in the Church. The Good Shepherd entrusts care of the flock to this imperfect follower. In our own love for Jesus, we sometimes fail him, too. Jesus calls us to serve him nonetheless.

Prayers *others may be added*

With hearts full of hope, we pray:

◆ Merciful Savior, hear us.

For our pope, bishops, and priests who shepherd God's people, we pray: ◆ For those who are new to their particular leadership roles, we pray: ◆ For those who feel great shame over their failures, we pray: ◆ For those who struggle to love, we pray: ◆

Our Father . . .

Loving Father,
your Son makes up for
    what is lacking in us.
When we turn away,
    he brings us back.
When we falter, he lifts us up.
Keep us reaching out to him in love
so that he may lead us at last
    into your kingdom
where he lives and reigns with you
in the unity of the Holy Spirit,
one God, forever and ever.
Amen.

✝ God's mercy endures forever!
Alleluia!

✝ God's mercy endures forever!
Alleluia!

Psalm 118   *page 417*

Reading   *Acts 28:16–17, 20, 30–31*

When he entered Rome, Paul was allowed to live by himself, with the soldier who was guarding him.

Three days later he called together the leaders of the Jews. When they had gathered he said to them, "My brothers, although I had done nothing against our people or our ancestral customs, I was handed over to the Romans as a prisoner from Jerusalem. . . . It is on account of the hope of Israel that I wear these chains."

He remained for two full years in his lodgings. He received all who came to him, and with complete assurance and without hindrance he proclaimed the kingdom of God and taught about the Lord Jesus Christ.

Reflection

In the beginning of his Gospel, Luke emphasized that Jesus is the fulfillment of the hope of Israel, indeed, of the whole world. In Luke's second book, Acts of the Apostles, Paul carries this message as far as Rome. Acts concludes with Paul imprisoned, but still preaching the Gospel. The messenger can be chained, but not the message. God has filled the world with his love. Those who believe are forever free.

Prayers   *others may be added*

With hearts full of hope, we pray:

◆ Merciful Savior, hear us.

For those persecuted because of faith, we pray: ◆ For governments to employee just laws, we pray: ◆ For those who are unjustly imprisoned, we pray: ◆ For those within our community burdened by any difficulty, we pray: ◆

Our Father . . .

Almighty and eternal God,
all our hope is in you,
for you fulfill your promises.
We lift our hearts and hands to you.
Break whatever binds us.
Free us to live in unity
    with your Son,
our Lord Jesus Christ,
who lives and reigns with you
in the unity of the Holy Spirit,
one God, forever and ever.
Amen.

✝ God's mercy endures forever!
Alleluia!

✝ Lord, you renew the face of the earth! Alleluia!

Psalm 104   *page 415*

Reading   *John 20:19–23*

On the evening of that first day of the week, when the doors were locked, where the disciples were, for fear of the Jews, Jesus came and stood in their midst and said to them, "Peace be with you." When he had said this, he showed them his hands and his side. The disciples rejoiced when they saw the Lord. Jesus said to them again, "Peace be with you. As the Father has sent me, so I send you." And when he had said this, he breathed on them and said to them, "Receive the Holy Spirit. Whose sins you forgive are forgiven them, and whose sins you retain are retained."

Reflection

After fashioning the first human being, God breathed life into him. After forming his disciples, the risen Christ breathed the Spirit into them and made them his Church. God's Spirit transformed the disciples; they went forth to do wondrous things, which we have been hearing about throughout Easter. Pentecost reminds us that it is now our turn to do amazing things because we, too, have been filled with the Holy Spirit.

Prayers   *others may be added*

Trusting in God's saving power, we pray:

◆ **Come, Holy Spirit.**

Renew the face of the earth, we pray: ◆ Give solace in the midst of woe, we pray: ◆ Bring comfort and healing to the sick and suffering, we pray: ◆ Bend the stubborn heart and lead us to salvation, we pray: ◆

Our Father . . .

O divine Wisdom,
your Son gave us the gift of the Spirit
so that we would have
    your breath of life in us forever.
Teach us how to share your Spirit
    with others.
Enliven and renew all of creation,
and bring us your everlasting peace.
Through Christ our Lord.
Amen.

✝ Lord, you renew the face of the earth! Alleluia!

✝ Lord, you will show us the path to life.

Psalm 16
page 400

Reading
John 19:25–27

Standing by the cross of Jesus were his mother and his mother's sister, Mary the wife of Clopas, and Mary of Magdala. When Jesus saw his mother and the disciple there whom he loved he said to his mother, "Woman, behold, your son." Then he said to the disciple, "Behold, your mother." And from that hour the disciple took her into his home.

Reflection

After the beloved disciple took Mary into his home, the two would have consoled each other upon the death of Jesus. They also would have shared stories about Jesus with each other and the wider community. Today, Mary remains a source of consolation and guidance for God's people. The care that the beloved disciple showed for Mary, and she for him, also reminds us of the care we must show for each other.

Prayers
others may be added

With glad hearts, we pray:

◆ Hear our prayer, O Lord.

May the Church be a place of refuge and hope, we pray: ◆ May women in leadership positions withstand disparagement and harassment, we pray: ◆ May the sick and dying find comfort in God's presence, we pray: ◆ May those who grieve or find themselves alone know the comfort of Christ, we pray: ◆

Our Father . . .

Loving God,
your Spirit brings all the baptized
     into one family.
May we care for each other
     with the same devotion
with which Mary cared for Jesus
and the early disciples.
Through Christ our Lord.
Amen.

✝ Lord, you will show us the path to life.

✝ Lord, you will show us the path to life.

Psalm 16 page 400

Reading *Sirach 35:1–9*

To keep the law is a great oblation, / and he who observes the commandments sacrifices a peace offering. / In works of charity one offers fine flour, / and when he gives alms he presents his sacrifice of praise. / To refrain from evil pleases the LORD, / and to avoid injustice is an atonement. / Appear not before the LORD empty-handed, / for all that you offer is in fulfillment of the precepts. / The just one's offering enriches the altar / and rises as a sweet odor before the Most High. / The just one's sacrifice is most pleasing, / nor will it ever be forgotten. / In a generous spirit pay homage to the LORD, / be not sparing of freewill gifts. / With each contribution show a cheerful countenance, / and pay your tithes in a spirit of joy. / Give to the Most High as he has given to you, / generously, according to your means.

Reflection

Throughout the Old Testament, there is a link between worship and justice. To be in a right relationship with God we do not only go to Mass—for example, we also care for those in need. Because God created and continues to care about all people, so must we. If we do not try to act morally and to care for others, then our worship of God is incomplete and insincere.

Prayers *others may be added*

With glad hearts, we pray:

◆ Hear our prayer, O Lord.

Help the Church witness the compassion of Christ, we pray: ◆ Strengthen the spirit of those who assist the poor and marginalized, we pray: ◆ Grant wisdom to those who work for justice and peace, we pray: ◆ Enlighten the hearts of those who are blind to injustice and racism, we pray: ◆

Our Father . . .

Good and loving God,
no one is beyond
   the reach of your love.
May our love for you flow outward
   into love for others.
May our worship of you
strengthen our communities.
Through Christ our Lord.
Amen.

✝ Lord, you will show us the path to life.

✝ Lord, you will show us the path to life.

Psalm 16 *page 400*

Reading *Sirach 36:1, 4–5a, 14–17*

Come to our aid, O God of the universe, / look upon us, show us the light of your mercies, / and put all the nations in dread of you! / Thus they will know, as we know, / that there is no God but you, O Lord.

Give new signs and work new wonders. . . .

Give evidence of your deeds of old; / fulfill the prophecies spoken in your name, / Reward those who have hoped in you, / and let your prophets be proved true. / Hear the prayer of your servants, / for you are ever gracious to your people; / and lead us in the way of justice. / Thus it will be known to the very ends of the earth / that you are the eternal God.

Reflection

When Philip Neri heard this passage, he might have been thinking less about the other nations than the city of Rome. The people of Rome, especially the clergy, were in a spiritual decline. As Philip encouraged people to recommit themselves to the way of Christ, he spoke with candor and humor. This lighthearted but earnest approach proved effective. People who remain lovingly joyful while helping us admit our sins are great gifts to the Church.

Prayers *others may be added*

With glad hearts, we pray:

◆ Hear our prayer, O Lord.

May the baptized grow in love, we pray: ◆ May world leaders promote justice and peace, we pray: ◆ May the spirit of St. Philip Neri continue to enliven the Oratorians, we pray: ◆ May the joy of the Gospel enlighten our hearts, we pray: ◆

Our Father . . .

God of the universe,
you have revealed
    your saving power
in the resurrection of your Son.
Continue to reveal your gracious
    presence today.
Make us signs of your love
so that others might turn to you in faith.
Through Christ our Lord.
Amen.

✝ Lord, you will show us the path to life.

✝ Lord, you will show us the path to life.

Psalm 16 *page 400*

Reading *Sirach 42:16–17, 23–25*

As the rising sun is clear to all, / so the glory of the LORD fills all his works; / Yet even God's holy ones must fail / in recounting the wonders of the LORD, / Though God has given these, his hosts, the strength / to stand firm before his glory. . . . The universe lives and abides forever; / to meet each need, each creature is preserved. / All of them differ, one from another, / yet none of them has he made in vain; / For each in turn, as it comes, is good; / can one ever see enough of their splendor?

Reflection

It is hard to extol the wisdom of God's creation when we are chasing a spider in our house or recovering from poison ivy. Such moments remind us that we do not control creation; it is a gift. Much of creation remains unexplored. As we strive to learn all we can about our natural world, we also strive to reverence it, for all living things and the earth itself and the whole cosmos are good.

Prayers *others may be added*

With glad hearts, we pray:

◆ Hear our prayer, O Lord.

Open our eyes to the suffering of creation, we pray: ◆ Guide world leaders to work to end climate change, we pray: ◆ Encourage environmental scientists and advocates, we pray: ◆ Help our parish communities become better stewards of creation, we pray: ◆

Our Father . . .

Lord of creation,
we marvel at the work
    of your hands,
from the vastness of the universe
to the tiny animals drifting
    in the ocean.
Each day,
fill us with awe
    at the home you have given us.
May we reverence
    our beautiful world
and do our upmost to protect it.
Through Christ our Lord.
Amen.

✝ Lord, you will show us the path to life.

Friday, May 28, 2021
Weekday

✝ Lord, you will show us the path
to life.

Psalm 16   *page 400*

Reading   *Sirach 44:1, 10–15*

Now will I praise those godly men,
   our ancestors, each in his
      own time: . . .
These also were godly men
   whose virtues have not
      been forgotten;
Their wealth remains in
   their families,
   their heritage with
      their descendants;
Through God's covenant with
      them their family endures,
   their posterity for their sake.

And for all time their progeny
   will endure,
   their glory will never be
      blotted out;
Their bodies are peacefully
   laid away,
   but their name lives on and on.
At gatherings their wisdom is retold,
   and the assembly proclaims
      their praise.

Reflection

In the period of history when the Book of Sirach was composed, God's people did not believe in an afterlife. Instead, they believed that those who upheld God's covenant were rewarded in this life. People who lived justly had a long life, had many descendants, and prospered. After they died, they were remembered and honored. By contrast, those who lived unjustly were entirely forgotten. We who believe in the resurrection must also strive to be remembered as people who lived justly while on earth.

Prayers   *others may be added*

With glad hearts, we pray:

◆ Hear our prayer, O Lord.

May the work of the Church glorify God, we pray: ◆ May the leadership of governments bring forth peace and justice, we pray: ◆ May our good words honor God and all God's people, we pray: ◆ May the dead be raised to new life, we pray: ◆

Our Father . . .

Living God,
in every age men and women have
   modeled holiness and justice.
With these saints as our guides,
help us to live lives worthy
   of remembrance.
Through Christ our Lord.
Amen.

✝ Lord, you will show us the path
to life.

✝ Lord, you will show us the path to life.

Psalm 16 *page XXX*

Reading *Sirach 51:13–18, 20*

When I was young and innocent, / I sought wisdom openly in my prayer / I prayed for her before the temple, / and I will seek her until the end, / and she flourished as a grape soon ripe. / My heart delighted in her, / My feet kept to the level path / because from earliest youth I was familiar with her. / In the short time I paid heed, / I met with great instruction. / Since in this way I have profited, / I will give my teacher grateful praise. / I became resolutely devoted to her— / the good I persistently strove for. . . . My hand opened her gate / and I came to know her secrets. / I directed my soul to her, / and in cleanness I attained her.

Reflection

In the Old Testament, God's wisdom is often personified as Lady Wisdom. Young men were instructed to seek her out and to learn from her. Our lives are a series of choices in which we either seek to live as God intends, or we don't. Even when unexpected and difficult things happen to us, we can still learn from Lady Wisdom. We can still cling to Wisdom as she leads us down the path of life.

Prayers *others may be added*

With glad hearts, we pray:

◆ Hear our prayer, O Lord.

For those discerning a vocation to marriage or religious life, we pray: ◆ For government leaders, we pray: ◆ For those who work with and minister to young people, we pray: ◆ For our parishes, families, and friends, we pray: ◆

Our Father . . .

God of wisdom,
your Son Jesus
   is our teacher and guide.
May we seek him,
learn from him,
and cling to him in all that we do,
for he lives and reigns with you
in the unity of the Holy Spirit,
one God, forever and ever.
Amen.

✝ Lord, you will show us the path to life.

✝ Lord, you renew the face of the earth.

Psalm 104 *page 415*

Reading *Matthew 28:16–20*

The eleven disciples went to Galilee, to the mountain to which Jesus had ordered them. When they saw him, they worshipped, but they doubted. Then Jesus approached and said to them, "All power in heaven and on earth has been given to me. Go, therefore, and make disciples of all nations, baptizing in the name of the Father, and of the Son, and of the Holy Spirit, teaching them to observe all that I have commanded you. And behold, I am with you always, until the end of the age."

Reflection

We acknowledge the Trinity to be holy and perfect, to consist of the Father, the Son, and the Holy Spirit. In this Trinity there is no intrusion of any alien element or of anything from outside, nor is the Trinity a blend of creative and created being. It is a wholly creative and energizing reality, self-consistent and undivided in its active power, for the Father makes all things through the Word and in the Holy Spirit, and in this way the unity of the holy Trinity is preserved. Accordingly, in the Church, one God is preached, one God who is *above all things and through all things and in all things*. God *is above all things* as Father, for he is principle and source; he

is *through all things* through the Word; and he is *in all things* in the Holy Spirit.

*From the first letter to Serapion
by St. Athanasius
(Office of Readings, Trinity Sunday)*

Prayers *others may be added*

United by the Spirit, we pray:

◆ **Triune God, hear our prayer.**

For the ministers of the Church, we pray: ◆ For leaders of the world, we pray: ◆ For married couples, we pray: ◆ For those plagued by doubt and fear, we pray: ◆ For the sick and suffering, we pray: ◆ For the Order of the Most Holy Trinity, we pray: ◆

Our Father . . .

Triune God,
in baptism, we are united to you.
Protect us and bring us deeper
    into the mystery of your divine life
so that we may continue to grow
    in holiness and love.
We ask this through our Lord Jesus
    Christ, your Son,
who lives and reigns with you
in the unity of the Holy Spirit,
one God, forever and ever.
Amen.

✝ Lord, you renew the face of the earth.

Monday, May 31, 2021
Feast of the Visitation of the Blessed Virgin Mary

✝ Let us sing to the Lord as we celebrate the Visitation of the Blessed Virgin Mary.

Psalm 42 *page 408*

Reading *Luke 1:39–47*

Mary set out and traveled to the hill country in haste to a town of Judah, where she entered the house of Zechariah and greeted Elizabeth. When Elizabeth heard Mary's greeting, the infant leaped in her womb, and Elizabeth, filled with the Holy Spirit, cried out in a loud voice and said, "Most blessed are you among women, and blessed is the fruit of your womb. And how does this happen to me, that the mother of my Lord should come to me? For at the moment the sound of your greeting reached my ears, the infant in my womb leaped for joy. Blessed are you who believed that what was spoken to you by the Lord would be fulfilled."

And Mary said: / "My soul proclaims the greatness of the Lord; / my spirit rejoices in God my Savior."

Reflection

Elizabeth recognizes the significance of the child Mary carries in her womb. It would have been customary for Elizabeth to go and honor Mary. Instead, Mary comes to Elizabeth, just as God—in the person of his Son—comes to visit us. St. Bede the Venerable says, "By meditating upon the incarnation, our devotion is kindled, and by remembering the example of God's Mother, we are encouraged to lead a life of virtue" (Office of Readings for the Visitation).

Prayers *others may be added*

With souls thirsting for God, we pray:

◆ God our Savior, hear our prayer.

For priests, religious, and lay missionaries who serve in remote parts of the world, we pray: ◆ For leaders of rural and undeveloped nations, we pray: ◆ For expectant parents and their unborn children, we pray: ◆ For elders and wisdom figures in our communities, we pray: ◆

Our Father . . .

Holy Lord,
we rejoice that you have visited
   your people.
When we lose sight of you,
help us to find you once again.
Hasten us along the path
   that leads to life with you.
Through Christ our Lord.
Amen.

✝ Let us sing to the Lord as we celebrate the Visitation of the Blessed Virgin Mary.

✝ My soul longs for you, O God.

Psalm 42   *page 408*

Reading   *Tobit 2:9–14*

On the night of Pentecost, after I had buried the dead, I, Tobit, went into my courtyard to sleep next to the courtyard wall. My face was uncovered because of the heat. I did not know there were birds perched on the wall above me, till their warm droppings settled in my eyes, causing cataracts. I went to see some doctors for a cure but the more they anointed my eyes with various salves, the worse the cataracts became, until I could see no more. . . .

At that time, my wife Anna worked for hire at weaving cloth, the kind of work women do. When she sent back the goods to their owners, they would pay her. Late in winter on the seventh of Dystrus, she finished the cloth and sent it back to the owners. They paid her the full salary and also gave her a young goat for the table. On entering my house the goat began to bleat.

I called to my wife and said: "Where did this goat come from? Perhaps it was stolen! Give it back to its owners; we have no right to eat stolen food!" She said to me, "It was given to me as a bonus over and above my wages." Yet I would not believe her, and told her to give it back to its owners. I became very angry with her over this. So she retorted: "Where are your charitable deeds now? Where are your virtuous acts? See! Your true character is finally showing itself!"

Reflection

There are many ways to bring people to faith in God. Tobit experienced a number of personal setbacks, yet he tried to maintain his piety. As this passage indicates, he was not always successful. Where the Book of Tobit used dramatic storytelling to inspire faith, St. Justin took a very different approach: philosophy. St. Justin, martyred in 165, drew from different systems of philosophy to demonstrate the truth of the Christian faith. Even in difficult times, we are called to remain steadfast in faith.

Prayers   *others may be added*

With souls thirsting for God, we pray:

♦ God our Savior, hear our prayer.

For those who preach God's word, we pray: ♦ For governments as they work for justice and promote peace, we pray: ♦ For philosophers and theologians, we pray: ♦ For those who seek the living God and yearn to be whole, we pray: ♦

Our Father . . .

Almighty God,
you have revealed yourself
    in creation, in history,
    in your laws, and in stories.
The gift of human reason
    helps us to find you
and to understand you better.
May we who seek you
in our different ways,
grow steadily in knowledge of you,
and in love for you.
Through Christ our Lord.
Amen.

✝ My soul longs for you, O God.

✝ My soul longs for you, O God.

Psalm 42 *page 408*

Reading *Tobit 3:1–3, 6a, 7–8a, 10*

Grief-stricken in spirit, I, Tobit, groaned and wept aloud. Then with sobs I began to pray: / "You are righteous, O Lord, / and all your deeds are just; / All your ways are mercy and truth; / you are the judge of the world. / And now, O Lord, may you be mindful of me, / and look with favor upon me. / Punish me not for my sins, / nor for my inadvertent offenses, / nor for those of my ancestors. . . .

"So now, deal with me as you please, / and command my life breath to be taken from me, / that I may go from the face of the earth into dust. / It is better for me to die than to live, / because I have heard insulting calumnies, / and I am overwhelmed with grief." . . .

On the same day, at Ecbatana in Media, it so happened that Raguel's daughter Sarah also had to listen to abuse, from one of her father's maids. For she had been married to seven husbands, but the wicked demon Asmodeus killed them off before they could have intercourse with her, as it is prescribed for wives. . . .

The girl was deeply saddened that day, and she went into an upper chamber of her house, where she planned to hang herself.

Reflection

Tobit is the descendant of Jews who were forced to leave their homeland during the Babylonian invasion. Tobit and his wife are living in a foreign land where they are mocked because of what happened to their ancestors. Although Tobit remains faithful to God, a series of personal misfortunes compels him to beg God for death. Tobit's prayer is heart-wrenching, yet even in his despair, he still cries aloud to God. In what ways do you call out to God?

Prayers *others may be added*

With souls thirsting for God, we pray:

◆ God our Savior, hear our prayer.

Lead the Church to deeper union with your Son, we pray: ◆ Protect refugees, immigrants, and anyone displaced, we pray: ◆ Console those who mourn and grieve, we pray: ◆ Give hope to those who despair and joy to the downtrodden, we pray: ◆

Our Father . . .

O God,
you are the source
    of all consolation.
Comfort us
    during times of sorrow and doubt.
Lead us through the darkness
    into the joy and comfort
of your light.
Through Christ our Lord.
Amen.

✝ My soul longs for you, O God.

✝ My soul longs for you, O God.

Psalm 42
page 408

Reading
Tobit 8:4–7

When the girl's parents left the bedroom and closed the door behind them, Tobiah arose from bed and said to his wife, "My love, get up. Let us pray and beg our Lord to have mercy on us and to grant us deliverance." She got up, and they started to pray and beg that deliverance might be theirs. . . . "Blessed are you, O God of our fathers, / praised be your name forever and ever. / Let the heavens and all your creation / praise you forever. / You made Adam and you gave him his wife Eve / to be his help and support; / and from these two the human race descended. / You said, 'It is not good for the man to be along; / let us make him a partner like himself.' / Now, Lord, you know that I take this wife of mine / not because of lust, / but for a noble purpose. / Call down your mercy on me and on her, / and allow us to live together to a happy old age."

Reflection

When Charles Lwanga and his companions refused to submit to the abusive practices of their king, the king executed them. These men upheld their integrity at the cost of their lives. Tobiah is also an upright man, and so, on his wedding night, he urges his wife to pray with him. Tobiah prays that his marriage reflect God's covenantal love for his people. He prays that his marriage be fruitful, just, and long-lasting.

Prayers
others may be added

With souls thirsting for God, we pray:

◆ God our Savior, hear our prayer.

For the Church in Africa, we pray: ◆ For civil servants, we pray: ◆ For newly married couples and those preparing for marriage, we pray: ◆ For those who preach the Gospel, we pray: ◆ For missionaries, we pray: ◆

Our Father . . .

Holy Lord,
the martyrdoms of Charles Lwanga
and his fellow Ugandan Christians
inspired others to believe in the Gospel.
Help us to take our own
    courageous stand for truth and justice
so that others may be inspired
    to act with the same faithfulness.
Through Christ our Lord.
Amen.

✝ My soul longs for you, O God.

✝ My soul longs for you, O God.

Psalm 42 *page 408*

Reading *Tobit 11:17*

Tobit proclaimed how God had mercifully restored sight to his eyes. When Tobit reached Sarah, the wife of his son Tobiah, he greeted her: "Welcome, my daughter! Blessed be your God for bringing you to us, daughter! Blessed is your father, and blessed is my son Tobiah, and blessed are you, daughter! Welcome to your home with blessing and joy. Come in, daughter!" That day there was joy for all the Jews who lived in Nineveh.

Reflection

Tobit rejoices in God! At last, his sight is restored and the other miseries he has endured are ending. Tobit's son has returned with his new bride. Despite living miles from his homeland in Israel, Tobit now sees that God is with him. Tobit rejoices in God's faithfulness and goodness. His fellow Jews, who themselves might have felt that God had abandoned them, rejoice at God's enduring presence.

Prayers *others may be added*

With souls thirsting for God, we pray:

◆ God our Savior, hear our prayer.

Help us remain faithful to the Gospel, we pray: ◆ Protect and comfort the poor and marginalized, we pray: ◆ Heal those who are sick and suffering, we pray: ◆ Transform our sorrows into joy and compassion, we pray: ◆

Our Father . . .

God our Father,
just as Tobit came to see his life
　　through new eyes,
so help us to look at our own lives
with ever greater wisdom
and understanding.
Through Christ our Lord.
Amen.

✝ My soul longs for you, O God.

✝ My soul longs for you, O God.

Psalm 42 *page 408*

Reading *Tobit 12:6*

Raphael called . . . [Tobit and Tobiah] aside privately and said to them: "Thank God! Give him the praise and the glory. Before all the living, acknowledge the many good things he has done for you, by blessing and extolling his name in song. Honor and proclaim God's deeds, and do not be slack in praising him.

Reflection

St. Boniface went to what is now Germany because priests and even some bishops had grown slack in their Christian faith. He implemented reforms that renewed the Church throughout the region. His brave efforts brought people back to the Christian faith. St. Boniface, like Raphael in the reading, invites us to consider what changes we should make in our own lives to praise faithfully God in all that we do.

Prayers *others may be added*

With souls thirsting for God, we pray:

◆ God our Savior, hear our prayer.

For formation directors in religious houses and seminaries, we pray: ◆ For nations recovering from war, natural disasters, or poor governance, we pray: ◆ For the people of Germany and others under the patronage of St. Boniface, we pray: ◆ For catechists, teachers, and spiritual directors, we pray: ◆

Our Father . . .

Almighty God,
we praise you for your goodness
and your faithfulness.
We praise you for creation
and for the loving kindness
    you have shown us.
Reveal yourself to us always
so that we may never
    cease to praise your name.
We ask this through our Lord Jesus
    Christ, your Son,
who lives and reigns with you
in the unity of the Holy Spirit,
one God, forever and ever.
Amen.

✝ My soul longs for you, O God.

✝ I will call upon the name of the Lord.

Psalm 116 *page 416*

Reading *Mark 14:22–25*

While they were eating, [Jesus] took bread, said the blessing, broke it, gave it to [the disciples], and said, "Take it; this is my body." Then he took a cup, gave thanks, and gave it to them, and they all drank from it. He said to them, "This is my blood of the covenant, which will be shed for many. Amen, I say to you, I shall not drink again the fruit of the vine until the day when I drink it new in the kingdom of God."

Reflection

As Jesus gathered for his last meal with his disciples, he led them in the traditional Jewish prayers. He thanked God for creation and for leading the Israelites out of Egypt and into a homeland. Then, with a few simple words, Jesus dramatically changed the meaning of the meal. From that moment on, whenever Jesus' followers gathered for a ritual meal; they were to thank God for the life, death, and resurrection of Jesus. Centuries later, we continue to break bread in his name.

Prayers *others may be added*

We raise the cup of salvation as we pray:

◆ Make us holy, O Lord.

In times of need, we pray: ◆ When we encounter the poor and marginalized, we pray: ◆ As we celebrate the Eucharist and serve at the Lord's table, we pray: ◆ When our hears are restless, we pray: ◆

Our Father . . .

Lord Jesus,
when we break bread together
and drink from the cup of salvation,
you are present within
     and among us.
Through the gifts we receive
     from you,
make us holy disciples
who will go forth to be gifts to others.
Nourish us until the day we enter the
     fullness of your kingdom
where you live and reign
     with God, the Father,
in the unity of the Holy Spirit,
one God, forever and ever.
Amen.

✝ I will call upon the name of the Lord.

✝ My heart is steadfast, O God;
my heart is steadfast.

Psalm 108   *page 415*

Reading   *2 Corinthians 1:3–7*

Blessed be the God and Father of our Lord Jesus Christ, the Father of compassion and the God of all encouragement, who encourages us in our every affliction, so that we may be able to encourage those who are in any affliction with the encouragement with which we ourselves are encouraged by God. For as Christ's sufferings overflow to us, so through Christ does our encouragement also overflow. If we are afflicted, it is for your encouragement and salvation; if we are encouraged, it is for your encouragement, which enables you to endure the same sufferings that we suffer. Our hope for you is firm, for we know that as you share in the sufferings, you also share in the encouragement.

Reflection

St. Paul and his companions experience hardships as they share the story of Christ, but they also draw strength from the risen Christ. As they act as Christ would have for those they serve, they share the comfort and consolation that they have received from Christ. In time, the members of the communities that they are forming will learn how to encourage and console each other, just as we try to strengthen and uplift each other today.

Prayers   *others may be added*

With uplifted hearts, we pray:

◆ Help us, O God.

Help the Church imitate Christ, we pray: ◆ Strengthen and encourage community organizers, we pray: ◆ Accompany therapists, hospital chaplains, and hospice workers, we pray: ◆ Enlighten the hearts and minds of your people, we pray: ◆

Our Father . . .

Father of compassion,
as we strive to follow your Son
    in discipleship,
we need encouragement.
We need the support
    of other members of his body.
By guiding and supporting
    each other,
we will overcome
    whatever afflictions we face
until at last we enter the kingdom
of your Son, our Lord Jesus Christ,
who lives and reigns with you
in the unity of the Holy Spirit,
one God, forever and ever.
Amen.

✝ My heart is steadfast, O God;
my heart is steadfast.

✝ My heart is steadfast, O God.

Psalm 108 *page 415*

Reading *Matthew 5:13–16*

Jesus said to his disciples: "You are the salt of the earth. But if salt loses its taste, with what can it be seasoned? It is no longer good for anything but to be thrown out and trampled underfoot. You are the light of the world. A city set on a mountain cannot be hidden. Nor do they light a lamp and then put it under a bushel basket; it is set on a lampstand, where it gives light to all in the house. Just so, your light must shine before others, that they may see your good deeds, and glorify your heavenly Father."

Reflection

Jesus' words invite us to contemplate our lives by using the metaphor of salt and light. Like salt, which enhances the flavor of food and preserves it, our lives must "season" the lives of those we encounter and the work we do to build up the kingdom. We can ask ourselves, Have we lost our zest? Like the light of a lamp, we must radiate with the joy of the Gospel and help illuminate the darkness in our midst; we are not to hide our faith. We must find ways of sharing it so that others may see Christ and be drawn into a deeper and more life-giving relationship with Jesus.

Prayers *others may be added*

With uplifted hearts, we pray:

◆ Help us, O God.

Give zeal to those who share the Gospel, we pray: ◆ Protect those persecuted for their faith, we pray: ◆ Renew those who teach the faith we pray: ◆ Strengthen your people to be salt and light, we pray: ◆

Our Father . . .

Faithful Lord,
people continue to seek you
and to try to know you better.
Teach us how to share our faith
and live proclaiming your goodness.
Through Christ our Lord.
Amen.

✝ My heart is steadfast, O God.

✝ My heart is steadfast, O God;
my heart is steadfast.

Psalm 108   *page 415*

Reading   *2 Corinthians 3:4–11*

Brothers and sisters: Such confidence we have through Christ toward God. Not that of ourselves we are qualified to take credit for anything as coming from us; rather, our qualification comes from God, who has indeed qualified us as ministers of a new covenant, not of letter but of spirit; for the letter brings death, but the Spirit gives life.

Now if the ministry of death, carved in letters on stone, was so glorious that the children of Israel could not look intently at the face of Moses because of its glory that was going to fade, how much more will the ministry of the Spirit be glorious? For if the ministry of condemnation was glorious, the ministry of righteousness will abound much more in glory. Indeed, what was endowed with glory has come to have no glory in this respect because of the glory that surpasses it. For if what was going to fade was glorious, how much more will what endures be glorious.

Reflection

St. Paul began his life as a devout Jew. Once he embraced Christ, however, he spoke of everything as subordinate to the Gospel. He even spoke of the old covenant, the Law given by God to Moses, as obsolete or "dead." Jesus ratified a new covenant and poured out his Spirit so that everyone could become part of it. This Spirit empowers all of us, each in our different ways, to do great things for Christ.

Prayers   *others may be added*

With uplifted hearts, we pray:

◆ Help us, O God.

Renew the zeal of the Church, we pray: ◆
Grant fortitude to ambassadors, diplomats, and other government officials, we pray: ◆
Lift up the poor and lowly, we pray: ◆
Open our hearts to your grace, we pray: ◆

Our Father . . .

Heavenly Father,
through your Son you have made
a new covenant with us.
As we celebrate our life in him,
open our hearts to the Holy Spirit.
Show us how to live more fully
under the Spirit's guidance.
Through Christ our Lord.
Amen.

✝ My heart is steadfast, O God;
my heart is steadfast.

✝ My heart is steadfast, O God;
   my heart is steadfast.

Psalm 108   *page 415*

Reading   *Matthew 5:20–24*

Jesus said to his disciples: "I tell you, unless your righteousness surpasses that of the scribes and Pharisees, you will not enter into the Kingdom of heaven.

"You have heard that it was said to your ancestors, *You shall not kill; and whoever kills will be liable to judgment.* But I say to you, whoever is angry with his brother will be liable to judgment, and whoever says to his brother, *Raqa*, will be answerable to the Sanhedrin, and whoever says, 'You fool,' will be liable to fiery Gehenna. Therefore, if you bring your gift to the altar, and there recall that your brother has anything against you, leave your gift there at the altar, go first and be reconciled with your brother, and then come and offer your gift."

Reflection

Some people accused Jesus of breaking the Jewish law, but in this passage, he deepens it. He insists that it is not only wrong to kill someone, it is also wrong to cling to our rage against another person. We cannot bear hatred against someone and then come before God expecting to receive his merciful love. In order to worship truly the God who is love, we must love and forgive each other.

Prayers   *others may be added*

With uplifted hearts, we pray:

◆ Help us, O God.

Grant us mercy, we pray: ◆ Heal divisions between nations, families, and races, we pray: ◆ Soothe our anger and rage, we pray: ◆ Rouse our hearts to seek forgiveness and reconciliation, we pray: ◆ Awaken the dead to eternal life, we pray: ◆

Our Father . . .

Loving Lord,
we cannot expect mercy from you
without showing mercy to others.
Help us to listen to each other
so that we might grow
   to understand one another.
Teach us how to let go of our anger
and to embrace your lasting peace.
Through Christ our Lord.
Amen.

✝ My heart is steadfast, O God;
   my heart is steadfast.

✝ My heart is steadfast, O God;
my heart is steadfast.

Psalm 108 *page 415*

Reading *John 19:31–35*

Since it was preparation day, in order
that the bodies might not remain on the
cross on the sabbath, for the sabbath day
of that week was a solemn one, the Jews
asked Pilate that their legs be broken
and they be taken down. So the soldiers
came and broke the legs of the first and
then of the other one who was crucified
with Jesus. But when they came to Jesus
and saw that he was already dead, they
did not break his legs, but one soldier
thrust his lance into his side, and immediately blood and water flowed out. An
eyewitness has testified, and his testimony is true; he knows that he is speaking the truth, so that you also may come
to believe.

Reflection

When John wrote that blood flowed
from the side of Jesus, he deliberately
contradicted those who denied that God
became fully human in the person of
his Son. In Jesus, God so fully entered
into our human experience that he
submitted to death itself. The water
symbolized baptism and the gift of the
Holy Spirit. God became one of us so
that we would receive his Spirit and be
enfolded forever into his love.

Prayers *others may be added*

With uplifted hearts, we pray:

♦ Help us, O God.

That the Church deepen its understanding
of sacramentality, we pray: ♦ That world
leaders seek just and nonviolent solutions
to their disagreements, we pray: ♦ That the
sick and suffering rest in God's mercy,
we pray: ♦ That parish communities be
renewed in faith, hope, and love, we pray: ♦

Our Father . . .

God of love,
by becoming human,
Jesus revealed the depths of your heart.
In him,
you gave yourself completely to us.
As we accept the gift of your love,
help us to give our hearts
    completely to you
so that we may abide in your vast
and loving heart forever.
Through Christ our Lord.
Amen.

✝ My heart is steadfast, O God;
my heart is steadfast.

✝ My heart is steadfast, O God;
my heart is steadfast.

Psalm 108 — page 415

Reading — Luke 2:46–51

After three days [Jesus' parents] found him in the temple, sitting in the midst of the teachers, listening to them and asking them questions, and all who heard him were astounded at his understanding and his answers. When his parents saw him, they were astonished, and his mother said to him, "Son, why have you done this to us? Your father and I have been looking for you with great anxiety." And he said to them, "Why were you looking for me? Did you not know that I must be in my Father's house?" But they did not understand what he said to them. He went down with them and came to Nazareth, and was obedient to them; and his mother kept all these things in her heart.

Reflection

It would have been impossible for Mary to understand immediately who her son was. His identity was simply too enormous. Mary did what we must all do: she reflected on the identity of Jesus and on the meaning of his ministry. The more time we spend reading the Gospels, praying, and reflecting on whom Jesus is, the more we will deepen our relationship with him. Day by day, our own hearts will become like his mother's and united to his.

Prayers — *others may be added*

With uplifted hearts, we pray:

♦ Help us, O God.

Grant us gracious hearts, we pray: ♦
Fill leaders with your wisdom and perseverance, we pray: ♦ Strengthen those who are differently abled and those who care for them, we pray: ♦ Protect those affected by violence, we pray: ♦

Our Father . . .

God our Father,
Mary loved your Son deeply,
even when she didn't fully understand
    who he was.
Deepen our own understanding of Jesus,
and strengthen our love for him.
Prepare our minds and hearts
    to know and love him
as he truly is.
Through Christ our Lord.
Amen.

✝ My heart is steadfast, O God;
my heart is steadfast.

☩ The seed is the word of God, Christ is the sower. All who come to him will live forever.

Psalm 16 *page 400*

Reading *Mark 4:26–34*

Jesus said to the crowds: "This is how it is with the kingdom of God; it is as if a man were to scatter seed on the land and would sleep and rise night and day and the seed would sprout and grow, he knows not how. Of its own accord the land yields fruit, first the blade, then the ear, then the full grain in the ear. And when the grain is ripe, he wields the sickle at once, for the harvest has come."

He said, "To what shall we compare the kingdom of God, or what parable can we use for it? It is like a mustard seed that, when it is sown in the ground, is the smallest of all the seeds on the earth. But once it is sown, it springs up and becomes the largest of plants and puts forth large branches, so that the birds of the sky can dwell in its shade." With many such parables he spoke the word to them as they were able to understand it. Without parables he did not speak to them, but to his own disciples he explained everything in private.

Reflection

Mark seems to have written his Gospel for Christians who were persecuted for their faith. These Christians might have felt scared, weary, or doubtful. There may be days when we wonder if upholding our Christian values has any impact on others. This little parable reminds us that more is happening in the hearts of others than we know. Even the simplest thing that we do is likely to have a greater impact than we realize.

Prayers *others may be added*

Trusting in our Lord, we pray:

◆ Faithful God, hear our prayer.

That the Church teaches with wisdom and patience, we pray: ◆ That leaders uphold just policies, we pray: ◆ That farmers bountifully reap what is sown, we pray: ◆ That those who are ridiculed or persecuted gain strength and hope through Christ, we pray: ◆

Our Father . . .

Faithful God,
through your Son's paschal mystery,
your kingdom has taken root.
Keep us patient
    as your kingdom grows
in ways we cannot see.
If we become weary
    of doing what is right,
nourish us with your grace.
Bring us at last
    into the harvest of eternal life.
Through Christ our Lord.
Amen.

☩ The seed is the word of God, Christ is the sower. All who come to him will live forever.

✝ A lamp to my feet is your word,
a light to my path.

Psalm 27 — page 405

Reading — 2 Corinthians 6:1–10

Brothers and sisters: As your fellow workers, we appeal to you not to receive the grace of God in vain. For he says: / *In an acceptable time I heard you, / and on the day of salvation I helped you.* / Behold, now is a very acceptable time; behold, now is the day of salvation. We cause no one to stumble in anything, in order that no fault may be found with our ministry; on the contrary, in everything we commend ourselves as ministers of God, through much endurance, in afflictions, hardships, constraints, beatings, imprisonments, riots, labors, vigils, fasts; by purity, knowledge, patience, kindness, in the Holy Spirit, in unfeigned love, in truthful speech, in the power of God; with weapons of righteousness at the right and at the left; through glory and dishonor, insult and praise. We are treated as deceivers and yet are truthful; as unrecognized and yet acknowledged; as dying and behold we live; as chastised and yet not put to death; as sorrowful yet always rejoicing; as poor yet enriching many; as having nothing and yet possessing all things.

Reflection

St. Paul's words prompt us to ask questions of ourselves. What are we willing to endure for the sake of Christ? In what ways have we welcomed the power of God in us? Do we believe that love and goodness will triumph despite setbacks and apparent failures? By imitating St. Paul's love of Christ, we, too, will gain all things.

Prayers — *others may be added*

Hear us, O Lord, as we pray:

◆ Lord, hear our prayer.

For those in the Church who endure hardships for the sake of the Gospel, we pray: ◆ For government leaders who care for the poorest members of society, we pray: ◆ For those who administer aid to people living in isolated areas, we pray: ◆ For God's grace when we face difficult times, we pray: ◆

Our Father . . .

Lord of all,
throughout the ages,
    Christians have endured
    countless hardships
for the sake of the Gospel.
Impassion us with the same love
    for your Son that they had.
By embracing your Spirit in us,
may we too gain all things
in our Lord Jesus Christ your Son,
who lives and reigns with you
in the unity of the Holy Spirit,
one God, forever and ever.
Amen.

✝ A lamp to my feet is your word,
a light to my path.

✝ I give you a new commandment:
love one another as I have
loved you.

Psalm 36 *page 408*

Reading *2 Corinthians 8:1–4, 7–8*

We want you to know, brothers and sisters, of the grace of God that has been given to the churches of Macedonia, for in a severe test of affliction, the abundance of their joy and their profound poverty overflowed in a wealth of generosity on their part. For according to their means, I can testify, and beyond their means, spontaneously, they begged us insistently for the favor of taking part in the service to the holy ones. . . . Now as you excel in every respect, in faith, discourse, knowledge, all earnestness, and in the love we have for you, may you excel in this gracious act also.

I say this not by way of command, but to test the genuineness of your love by your concern for others.

Reflection

St. Paul wants the Christians in Corinth to contribute generously to his fundraising efforts for the impoverished Jerusalem church. He appeals to their competitive spirit by praising the generosity of the Christians in Macedonia. He then tries to persuade them by making a theological argument. He writes that Christ freely gave himself to enrich people with grace and life. Do such reasons persuade us? More importantly, are we listening?

Prayers *others may be added*

Trusting in God's kindness, we pray:

◆ Graciously hear us, O Lord.

For the poor and oppressed, we pray: ◆ For peoples affected by famine, war, and corruption, we pray: ◆ For the sick of our community, we pray: ◆ For those who are struggling financially, we pray: ◆

Our Father . . .

Giver of all good gifts,
open our hearts and our hands
so that we may be as generous
with others as you are with us.
Turn our attention to those
in our midst who need our help,
and make us quick to respond.
Through Christ our Lord.
Amen.

✝ I give you a new commandment:
love one another as I have
loved you.

✝ Whoever loves me will keep my word, and my Father will love him and we will come to him.

Psalm 31 — page 405

Reading — *Matthew 6:1, 5–6*

Jesus said to his disciples: "Take care not to perform righteous deeds in order that people may see them; otherwise, you will have no recompense from your heavenly Father. . . .

"When you pray, do not be like the hypocrites, who love to stand and pray in the synagogues and on street corners so that others may see them. Amen, I say to you, they have received their reward. But when you pray, go to your inner room, close the door, and pray to your Father in secret. And your Father who sees in secret will repay you."

Reflection

In today's Gospel, Jesus instructs his disciples regarding their behavior before God. He invites us to consider our prayer life, which is a conversation with God. Some in the community, as Jesus notes, transformed this moment of prayer into an opportunity to be noticed by others in the community. The community rewarded them for proclaiming what would otherwise remain concealed. Consider your own practice of prayer, whether it be with the assembly at Mass, in a small community, with your spouse, or alone. When we come before the Lord, may we have the proper attitude of humility and love.

Prayers — *others may be added*

With humble hearts, O Lord, we pray:

◆ Lord, hear our pray.

For our Church, that our daily lives reveal the Mystery to the world, we pray: ◆ For our nation's leaders, that they humbly provide witness in both word and deed, we pray: ◆ For all those who find prayer to be difficult and a great effort, that they come to know God's voice, we pray: ◆ For those who long for authentic relationships, that they find support in a community of faith, we pray: ◆

Our Father . . .

Lord God,
you know what is hidden
    in the depths of our hearts.
Allow us to make known the mystery
    of how you work in our lives,
through the words we speak
and by how we love our neighbor.
May each encounter draw us closer to
    you and your will for our life.
Through Christ our Lord.
Amen.

✝ Whoever loves me will keep my word, and my Father will love him and we will come to him.

✝ You have received a spirit of adoption as sons through which we cry: Abba! Father!

Psalm 96 *page 413*

Reading *Matthew 6:7–15*

Jesus said to his disciples: "In praying, do not babble like the pagans, who think that they will be heard because of their many words. Do not be like them. Your Father knows what you need before you ask him.

"This is how you are to pray: / 'Our Father who art in heaven, / hallowed be thy name, / thy Kingdom come, / thy will be done, / on earth as it is in heaven. / Give us this day our daily bread; / and forgive us our trespasses, / as we forgive those who trespass against us; / and lead us not into temptation, / but deliver us from evil.'

"If you forgive men their transgressions, your heavenly Father will forgive you. But if you do not forgive men, neither will your Father forgive your transgressions."

Reflection

The Lord's Prayer is recited at every Mass. It is prayed often by the faithful, so much so, that it has potential to become a stale habit rather than a living conversation with God. Let us pause to reflect on the words that our Lord gave us as a model for prayer. The first lines of the prayer are concerned about our relationship with God: his name, his kingdom, and his will. Jesus wants to unite his followers to his Father, by how we address God, how we dwell in the kingdom, and how we live out God's plan for our life. The final verses of the prayer focus on our relationship with our brothers and sisters: our bread, our forgiveness, and our delivery from the evil one. This prayer calls us to be active participants in restoring our relationship with God and among God's people.

Prayers *others may be added*

To God who takes care of all our needs, we pray:

◆ Lord, hear our prayer.

For the Church, that we may practice forgiveness and reconciliation among communities and within families, we pray: ◆ For the leaders of our nation, that they continue to work towards harmony and peace for all people, we pray: ◆ For those who are overwhelmed by the temptations of daily life, that they find strength in Christ, we pray: ◆ For those who seek the Lord with a humble heart, we pray:

Our Father . . .

Father of all,
we come to you
    seeking the joy of the Kingdom,
and asking for you to guide us
to know your will for us.
May each encounter
    with our brothers and sisters
draw us closer to you.
Through Christ our Lord.
Amen.

✝ You have received a spirit of adoption as sons through which we cry: Abba! Father!

✝ Blessed are the poor in spirit; for theirs is the Kingdom of heaven.

Psalm 96 *page 413*

Reading *Matthew 6:19–23*

Jesus said to his disciples: "Do not store up for yourselves treasures on earth, where moth and decay destroy, and thieves break in and steal. But store up treasures in heaven, where neither moth nor decay destroys, nor thieves break in and steal. For where your treasure is, there also will your heart be.

"The lamp of the body is the eye. If your eye is sound, your whole body will be filled with light; but if your eye is bad, your whole body will be in darkness. And if the light in you is darkness, how great will the darkness be."

Reflection

Jesus cautions the disciples not to be concerned about earthly treasures that have no lasting value, rather we should value and cherish that which is centered in God. If I am guarding my possessions so that they retain value and are kept safe, am I also able to see the presence of God in my daily existence and trust that God will take care of my needs? Or does the clutter of those assets and the work of gathering, storing, and hoarding them contribute to the buildup of the darkness and the inability to experience the Light?

Prayers *others may be added*

Lord God, you know the desires of hearts, hear us as we pray:

♦ Lord, hear our prayer.

For our Church leaders, that they may guide us to see with the eyes of faith, we pray: ♦ For the leaders of nations, that they may seek to share resources among all peoples, we pray: ♦ For our communities, that we may care for all aspects of creation, we pray: ♦ For those who suffer in decay and darkness, may they experience the light of Christ, we pray: ♦

Our Father . . .

O God, you are the giver of all gifts, remove from my life
all of the unnecessary aspects
    that do not serve you
    or your will for me.
Help me place all my trust in you.
Through Christ our Lord.
Amen.

✝ Blessed are the poor in spirit; for theirs is the Kingdom of heaven.

Saturday, June 19, 2021
Weekday

✝ Jesus Christ became poor although he was rich, so that by his poverty you might become rich.

Psalm 31 *page 405*

Reading *Matthew 6:24–27*

Jesus said to his disciples: "No one can serve two masters. He will either hate one and love the other, or be devoted to one and despise the other. You cannot serve God and mammon.

"Therefore I tell you, do not worry about your life, what you will eat or drink, or about your body, what you will wear. Is not life more than food and the body more than clothing? Look at the birds in the sky; they do not sow or reap, they gather nothing into barns, yet your heavenly Father feeds them. Are not you more important than they? Can any of you by worrying add a single moment to your life-span?"

Reflection

Jesus instructs the disciples to look at the birds of the sky, or the beauty of the wild flowers, to know how much more each of us is valued in God's Kingdom. God knows what we need. If we seek the Kingdom of God, all that we need will be given to us. Worry can consume the mind and have an impact on the body and our well-being. When we allow our energy to be spent on the anxiety of life, we are not able to use that strength, that power, or that time on the work of the Kingdom of God.

Prayers *others may be added*

Lord, we bring our cares and worries to you, as we pray:

♦ Lord, hear our prayer.

For those in the Church who work to build the Kingdom, we pray: ♦ For the leaders in our country who work to care for God's children, we pray: ♦ For those who are crippled by worry and fear, that they find hope in the Lord, we pray: ♦ For those who are weak in body, mind, or spirit, that they find strength in the Lord, we pray: ♦

Our Father . . .

O God,
you transform the doubts
and worries within our hearts.
Guide us away from what troubles us
    when we face uncertainty or fear
and lead us into your peace.
Through Christ our Lord.
Amen.

✝ Jesus Christ became poor although he was rich, so that by his poverty you might become rich.

✝ May the Father of our Lord Jesus Christ enlighten the eyes of our mind, so that we can see what hope his call holds for us.

Psalm 100   *page 414*

Reading   *Mark 4:35–41*

On that day, as evening drew on, Jesus said to them, "Let us cross to the other side." Leaving the crowd, they took him with them in the boat just as he was. And other boats were with him. A violent squall came up and waves were breaking over the boat, so that it was already filling up. Jesus was in the stern, asleep on a cushion. They woke him and said to him, "Teacher, do you not care that we are perishing?" He woke up, rebuked the wind, and said to the sea, "Quiet! Be still!" The wind ceased and there was great calm. Then he asked them, "Why are you terrified? Do you not yet have faith?" They were filled with great awe and said to one another, "Who then is this whom even wind and sea obey?"

Reflection

Jesus was asleep in the midst of a violent squall. The disciples woke him to question whether he cared about what was happening. We too have found ourselves in the midst of powerful and dangerous storms, where we have no control over the strong, driving wind or the waves that are crashing around us. Where is the Lord in the midst of this storm? Does it appear he is sleeping? Do we assume he is absent from the situation if we do not hear him rebuking what terrifies us? Do we have faith to trust that God is the calm that we find when we enter into the quiet and stillness?

Prayers   *others may be added*

Lord, our strength and refuge, we turn to you as we pray:

◆ Lord, hear our prayer.

For the Church to remain a safe harbor for those who seek shelter from the storms of life, we pray: ◆ For our nation's leaders, to welcome those who encounter difficult journeys, we pray: ◆ For those who seek calm, but instead find chaos, may they rest in the presence of God, we pray: ◆ For those who care for the sick, that they bring healing and your peace, we pray: ◆

Our Father . . .

Lord of all creation,
you command all elements of nature
to abide by your holy plan.
Protect your people
   as we seek refuge;
grant us your peace
   in what can be a hectic
   and confusing world.
Through Christ our Lord.
Amen.

✝ May the Father of our Lord Jesus Christ enlighten the eyes of our mind, so that we can see what hope his call holds for us.

✝ The word of God is living and effective; able to discern reflections and thoughts of the heart.

Psalm 108   *page 415*

Reading   *Matthew 7:1–5*

Jesus said to his disciples: "Stop judging, that you may not be judged. For as you judge, so will you be judged, and the measure with which you measure will be measured out to you. Why do you notice the splinter in your brother's eye, but do not perceive the wooden beam in your own eye? How can you say to your brother, 'Let me remove that splinter from your eye,' while the wooden beam is in your eye? You hypocrite, remove the wooden beam from your eye first; then you will see clearly to remove the splinter from your brother's eye."

Reflection

It is not possible to have an actual wooden beam in your eye, but if your eye is injured by the same size splinter found in your brother's eye, your perception may obscure the size and weight of the wood. When we experience a painful wound, even from a tiny fragment, the discomfort may consume us. Yet when our brother has the same grievance, do we allow him the same compassion and empathy that we expected or are we dismissive because it does not directly affect us? Does your pain affect your ability to be in right relationship with others?

Prayers   *others may be added*

Trusting in the power of forgiveness, we pray:

◆ Lord, hear our prayer.

For those who are called to serve in community, that they may see with clear vision, we pray: ◆ For the Church, that we may practice mercy toward our brothers and sisters, we pray: ◆ For those who suffer chronic pain and are unable to find relief, that they may find comfort in the Lord, we pray: ◆ For those who are in need of mercy, may they receive the grace of reconciliation, we pray: ◆

Our Father . . .

Lord God,
who gives sight to the blind,
grant eyes of faith to your people,
so that we may recognize you
    in the face of everyone we meet.
Lead us to be a people of compassion and
    reconciliation.
Through Christ our Lord.
Amen.

✝ The word of God is living and effective; able to discern reflections and thoughts of the heart.

Tuesday, June 22, 2021
Weekday

✝ I am the light of the world, says the Lord; whoever follows me will have the light of life.

Psalm 31 page 405

Reading Matthew 7:6, 12–14

Jesus said to his disciples: "Do not give what is holy to dogs, or throw your pearls before swine, lest they trample them underfoot, and turn and tear you to pieces.

"Do to others whatever you would have them do to you. This is the Law and the Prophets.

"Enter through the narrow gate; for the gate is wide and the road broad that leads to destruction, and those who enter through it are many. How narrow the gate and constricted the road that leads to life. And those who find it are few."

Reflection

We know that God wants to have a loving relationship with his people. He offers us words, through the Law and the prophets on how we are to treat our brothers and sisters. Other faith traditions, beyond Judaism and Christianity, also possess a version of the Golden Rule, "Do to others whatever you would have them do to you." Why is this saying, which seems to be so countercultural, known to other denominations and in other cultures? This Great Law or New Commandment is given to God's people so that we know the loving response God desires from his people.

Prayers *others may be added*

Turning to God who gives us his law of love, we pray:

◆ Lord, hear our prayer.

That the Church may witness the presence of God, we pray: ◆ That those in need may receive what is needed, we pray: ◆ That families may receive the grace to live holy lives, we pray: ◆ That those who struggle to make decisions may receive the gift of wisdom and discernment, we pray: ◆

Our Father . . .

Lord God,
you gave us the Law and the prophets
to prepare us for the gift of your Son.
Help us to know Jesus
    as our model for how to love,
so that our lives may be filled with joy.
Through Christ our Lord.
Amen.

✝ I am the light of the world, says the Lord; whoever follows me will have the light of life.

✝ Remain in me, as I remain in you, says the Lord; whoever remains in me will bear much fruit.

Psalm 26   *page 404*

Reading   *Matthew 7:15–20*

Jesus said to his disciples: "Beware of false prophets, who come to you in sheep's clothing, but underneath are ravenous wolves. By their fruits you will know them. Do people pick grapes from thornbushes, or figs from thistles? Just so, every good tree bears good fruit, and a rotten tree bears bad fruit. A good tree cannot bear bad fruit, nor can a rotten tree bear good fruit. Every tree that does not bear good fruit will be cut down and thrown into the fire. So by their fruits you will know them."

Reflection

During a strong windstorm, a large tree in our yard fell over. We had no idea how decayed the trunk had become. The tree had once been solid and strong, with branches that towered over our house. How do we distinguish a rotten tree from a healthy one? How do we recognize those who are false prophets? Jesus counsels that it is by their fruits that we will know them. How do we train our eyes to examine and observe that which is worthy? Jesus warns us to beware so as not to encounter thorns or thistles, or even to face a wolf under the guise of a sheep.

Prayers   *others may be added*

Lord, seeking wisdom and guidance, we pray:

◆ Lord, hear our prayer.

For those who govern, that they may lead with sincerity and authenticity, we pray: ◆ For those who shepherd our Church, that they may offer comfort and care to God's people, we pray: ◆ For those in our community who are blind to the needs of their brothers and sisters, we pray: ◆ For those who bear false witness, may they come to know the Gospel truth, we pray: ◆

Our Father . . .

Lord of all goodness,
you call us to bear good fruit.
Help us remain in you,
so that we may know
    the goodness of others
and recognize you in our living.
Through Christ our Lord.
Amen.

✝ Remain in me, as I remain in you, says the Lord; whoever remains in me will bear much fruit.

✝ You, child, will be called prophet of the Most High, for you will go before the Lord to prepare his way.

Psalm 118   *page 417*

Reading   *Luke 1:57–66*

When the time arrived for Elizabeth to have her child she gave birth to a son. Her neighbors and relatives heard that the Lord had shown his great mercy toward her, and they rejoiced with her. When they came on the eighth day to circumcise the child, they were going to call him Zechariah after his father, but his mother said in reply, "No. He will be called John." But they answered her, "There is no one among your relatives who has this name." So they made signs, asking his father what he wished him to be called. He asked for a tablet and wrote, "John is his name," and all were amazed.

Reflection

God showed mercy toward Elizabeth, as her neighbors and relatives rejoiced at the birth of her son. The spirit moved this child to leap for joy in his mother's womb because the Lord was near. This story is rich with joy at the birth of this child. Joy is mixed with wonder as the community considers what God's plan would be for this child. It is important for us to discern God's will as it unfolds in our lives. How we minister to one another and how we live will affect the community. How have you experienced God's mercy, joy, or the movement of the Holy Spirit this week?

Prayers   *others may be added*

With hearts full of hope, we turn to you, as we pray:

◆ Lord, hear our prayer.

For catechists, teachers, and spiritual directors, we pray: ◆ For those preparing to receive a sacrament, we pray: ◆ For couples awaiting the birth of a child, we pray: ◆ For those who labor proclaiming the joy of the Gospel, we pray: ◆

Our Father . . .

Lord God,
you called John the Baptist
    from the womb,
to be a herald in the desert
and prepare your people
    for the coming of the Messiah.
May the words of this prophet
allow us to recognize the Lamb of God.
Through Christ our Lord.
Amen.

✝ You, child, will be called prophet of the Most High, for you will go before the Lord to prepare his way.

✝ Christ took away our infirmities and bore our diseases.

Psalm 8 *page 400*

Reading *Matthew 8:1–4*

When Jesus came down from the mountain, great crowds followed him. And then a leper approached, did him homage, and said, "Lord, if you wish, you can make me clean." He stretched out his hand, touched him, and said, "I will do it. Be made clean." His leprosy was cleansed immediately. Then Jesus said to him, "See that you tell no one, but go show yourself to the priest, and offer the gift that Moses prescribed; that will be proof for them."

Reflection

A leper was considered unclean and would be forced to live apart from the public. They would be isolated from the community, their families, and temple worship. Jewish law had specific rules for lepers and for the ritual cleansing of the skin. Jesus moved beyond the law; he allowed the leper to be near him and to speak to him. Then, Jesus stretched out his hand to touch, heal, and restore the leper. This restorative gesture returned the leper to life with the community and with his God. What is the barrier keeping you from coming to Jesus and allowing him to heal you?

Prayers *others may be added*

Lord of all healing, we turn to you as we pray:

◆ Hear us, Lord.

For those who are marginalized and ostracized, we pray: ◆ For those who care for the poor and downtrodden, we pray: ◆ For those who live in fear and loneliness, we pray: ◆ For those who are afflicted with disease and illness, we pray: ◆ For those who have died, we pray: ◆

Our Father . . .

Lord of mercy,
who touches, who heals, who loves,
grant us the grace
   to be among your chosen people.
Heal us of all that is unclean
and unworthy of being
   in your presence.
Keep us forever firmly in your love.
Through Christ our Lord.
Amen.

✝ Christ took away our infirmities and bore our diseases.

✝ Christ took away our infirmities and bore our diseases.

Psalm 60   *page 410*

Reading   *Matthew 8:5–11*

When Jesus entered Capernaum, a centurion approached him and appealed to him, saying, "Lord, my servant is lying at home paralyzed, suffering dreadfully." He said to him, "I will come and cure him." The centurion said in reply, "Lord, I am not worthy to have you enter under my roof; only say the word and my servant will be healed. For I too am a man subject to authority, with soldiers subject to me. And I say to one, 'Go,' and he goes; and to another, 'Come here,' and he comes; and to my slave, 'Do this,' and he does it." When Jesus heard this, he was amazed and said to those following him, "Amen, I say to you, in no one in Israel have I found such faith. I say to you, many will come from the east and the west, and will recline with Abraham, Isaac, and Jacob at the banquet in the Kingdom of heaven."

Reflection

It may be easy to think that God's Word is only proclaimed at the liturgy or we may even forget the power of God's Word. However, in this story, Jesus reminds us that his word saves and heals. Because of his station, the centurion understood the power of a spoken command. He recognized the power of Jesus' words. Do I allow the authority of God's Word to be present to me? Have I allowed God's Word to ease my suffering and heal what is broken in my life?

Prayers   *others may be added*

To our Lord, who heals us with his Word, we pray:

◆ Hear us, Lord.

For those who preach God's Word, we pray: ◆ For those who are paralyzed physically, emotionally, or mentally, we pray: ◆ For those who long for the comfort of human touch, a kind word, or a caring smile, we pray: ◆ For those who work to heal body, mind, and soul, we pray: ◆

Our Father . . .

God of all compassion,
you sent your Son among us
    to heal and to restore.
Allow us to be moved to kindness
and care for those in our own lives
who are in need of your mercy
    and love.
Through Christ our Lord.
Amen.

✝ Christ took away our infirmities and bore our diseases.

✝ God, you lift up the lowly.

Psalm 31   *page 405*

Reading   *Mark 5:22–23, 35–36, 38–42*

One of the synagogue officials, named Jairus, came forward. Seeing [Jesus] he fell at his feet and pleaded earnestly with him, saying, "My daughter is at the point of death. Please, come lay your hands on her that she may get well and live." . . .

While he was still speaking, people from the synagogue official's house arrived and said, "Your daughter has died; why trouble the teacher any longer?" Disregarding the message that was reported, Jesus said to the synagogue official, "Do not be afraid; just have faith." . . . When they arrived at the house of the synagogue official. . . . [Jesus] went in and said to them, "Why this commotion and weeping? The child is not dead but asleep." And they ridiculed him. Then he put them all out. He took along the child's father and mother . . . and entered the room where the child was. He took the child by the hand and said to her, "*Talitha koum*," which means, "Little girl, I say to you, arise!" The girl, a child of twelve, arose immediately and walked around. At that they were utterly astounded.

Reflections

What is amazing in this healing story is that Jesus drops everything to go to Jarius' house. Certainly, Jesus could have healed the girl from afar, but his presence, his gesture of compassion, reveals God's grace of healing. Ask yourself, Am I aware of Christ's healing presence? Then consider ways in which your presence might aid the healing of others.

Prayers   *others may be added*

To the Lord of healing, we pray:

◆ Lord, hear our prayer.

For catechists and youth ministers, we pray: ◆ For hospice volunteers, we pray: ◆ For grieving families, we pray: ◆ For the sick and suffering, we pray: ◆ For those who request our prayers, we pray: ◆

Our Father . . .

O divine Healer,
you bring new life through your Son.
Allow every encounter with him,
to bring restoration
     to all that needs healing
in our own lives.
Through Christ our Lord.
Amen.

✝ God, you lift up the lowly.

✝ If today you hear his voice, harden not your hearts.

Psalm 51 *page 409*

Reading *Matthew 8:18–22*

When Jesus saw a crowd around him, he gave orders to cross to the other shore. A scribe approached and said to him, "Teacher, I will follow you wherever you go." Jesus answered him, "Foxes have dens and birds of the sky have nests, but the Son of Man has nowhere to rest his head." Another of his disciples said to him, "Lord, let me go first and bury my father." But Jesus answered him, "Follow me, and let the dead bury their dead."

Reflection

Jesus is about to cross to the other side of the lake. A disciple makes what seems to be a reasonable request of him, "Lord, let me go first and bury my father." Jesus' response seems harsh and demanding. How often do we ask Jesus to wait because we are not quite ready to proceed? Jesus calls us, and we want to follow him even if life as a disciple is difficult for us. It is easy for us to be concerned with our own plans, our own agenda, so much so that they prevent us from following the Lord.

Prayers *others may be added*

To the Lord who calls us to discipleship, we pray:

◆ Hear us, Lord.

That we may have ears to hear God's call, we pray: ◆ That the Church might graciously share its gifts, we pray: ◆ That our parishes grow in living the corporal and spiritual works of mercy, we pray: ◆ That restless hearts may be calmed by God's presence, we pray: ◆

Our Father . . .

Lord God,
you call us by name to follow you.
May we have the trust and courage
   to go wherever you lead.
Help us not to worry
   about where we live or rest,
so that we may simply dwell
   in your presence.
Through Christ our Lord.
Amen.

✝ If today you hear his voice, harden not your hearts.

✝ You are Peter and upon this rock
I will build my church.

Psalm 145 *page 420*

Reading *Matthew 16:13–19*

When Jesus went into the region of Caesarea Philippi he asked his disciples, "Who do people say that the Son of Man is?" They replied, "Some say John the Baptist, others Elijah, still others Jeremiah or one of the prophets." He said to them, "But who do you say that I am?" Simon Peter said in reply, "You are the Christ, the Son of the living God." Jesus said to him in reply, "Blessed are you, Simon son of Jonah. For flesh and blood has not revealed this to you, but my heavenly Father. And so I say to you, you are Peter, and upon this rock I will build my Church, and the gates of the netherworld shall not prevail against it. I will give you the keys to the Kingdom of heaven. Whatever you bind on earth shall be bound in heaven; and whatever you loose on earth shall be loosed in heaven."

Reflection

Peter is told that he is the rock upon which the Church will be built. A rock is strong and solid, not considered fragile or weak. Yet that is how we often see Peter when he is faced with challenges or in moments of fear. He sinks into the depths of the waters, denies Jesus three times, and reveals his weakness and brokenness. Yet the Lord uses Peter, as he uses each of us despite our shortcomings, to build up the Church. Let us be grateful that God calls us as disciples and embraces us in our limitations.

Prayers *others may be added*

To our God who calls us to follow him to the Kingdom, we pray:

♦ Lord, hear our prayer.

For the pope, we pray: ♦ For missionaries, we pray: ♦ For the imprisoned, we pray: ♦ For the neglected and abandoned, we pray: ♦ For the dead, we pray: ♦

Our Father . . .

Lord God,
you called Peter and Paul
to preach the Good News.
Like the Apostles,
may we faithfully follow you
and share the Gospel.
Through Christ our Lord.
Amen.

✝ You are Peter and upon this rock
I will build my church.

✝ All peoples, clap your hands. Cry to God with shouts of joy!

Psalm 47   *page 409*

Reading   *Matthew 8:28–34*

When Jesus came to the territory of the Gadarenes, two demoniacs who were coming from the tombs met him. They were so savage that no one could travel by that road. They cried out, "What have you to do with us, Son of God? Have you come here to torment us before the appointed time?" Some distance away a herd of many swine was feeding. The demons pleaded with him, "If you drive us out, send us into the herd of swine." And he said to them, "Go then!" They came out and entered the swine, and the whole herd rushed down the steep bank into the sea where they drowned. The swineherds ran away, and when they came to the town they reported everything, including what had happened to the demoniacs. Thereupon the whole town came out to meet Jesus, and when they saw him they begged him to leave their district.

Reflection

Why do you think the townspeople "begged" Jesus to leave their district after he freed the two men from the demons? Is it because they lost their herd of swine that drowned themselves in the sea? Or is it because they are afraid that Jesus might discover something in them that needs to be transformed? While the first proposition makes logical sense, it is probable that the second accounts for more of their fear. When we see other people entering into the process of conversion—a person who stops drinking, someone who loses a substantial amount of weight, a friend who falls in love—it is often the case that we become jealous because we know that we need to change as well but are afraid to do so. May we let go of all jealousy and fear.

Rev. Stephen Wilbricht, CSC (Daily Prayer 2015)

Prayers   *others may be added*

To the Lord who gives us new life, we pray:

◆ Hear us, Lord.

That the Church may be delivered from all evil, we pray: ◆ That the Church may glory in God's mercy, we pray: ◆ That the afflicted may be healed, we pray: ◆ That those imprisoned in any way may be freed, we pray: ◆

Our Father . . .

O God of life,
your Son conquered sin and death.
Guide our steps
so that we may walk as children of the
    light and reject evil.
Help us proclaim your goodness.
Through Christ our Lord.
Amen.

✝ All peoples, clap your hands. Cry to God with shouts of joy!

✝ God was reconciling the world to himself in Christ and entrusting to us the message of reconciliation.

Psalm 108   *page 415*

Reading   *Matthew 9:1–8*

After entering a boat, Jesus made the crossing, and came into his own town. And there people brought to him a paralytic lying on a stretcher. When Jesus saw their faith, he said to the paralytic, "Courage, child, your sins are forgiven." At that, some of the scribes said to themselves, "This man is blaspheming." Jesus knew what they were thinking, and said, "Why do you harbor evil thoughts? Which is easier, to say, 'Your sins are forgiven,' or to say, 'Rise and walk'? But that you may know that the Son of Man has authority on earth to forgive sins"—he then said to the paralytic, "Rise, pick up your stretcher, and go home." He rose and went home. When the crowds saw this they were struck with awe and glorified God who had given such authority to men.

Reflection

A paralytic is brought to Jesus. The Lord sees his faith and forgives his sins. The scribes who witness this event think to themselves that Jesus is a blasphemer. The paralysis seems to be in the hearts and minds of those who are gathered, not just the legs of the man lying on the stretcher. The sin in our life is the greater handicap than any physical disability that we might experience. Jesus comes to restore all aspects of our lives, beginning with what separates us from him. Jesus seeks to heal the most wounded aspects of our nature.

Prayers   *others may be added*

We come to you, Lord, seeking reconciliation, as we pray:

♦ Lord, hear our prayer.

May the Church be a source of mercy and healing, we pray: ♦ May government leaders work to promote peace and justice, we pray: ♦ May estranged family members be welcomed home, we pray: ♦ May anxious people be comforted, we pray: ♦ May the sick and suffering be healed by Christ, we prayer: ♦

Our Father . . .

Gentle and loving God,
you look with kindness on your children,
and in your mercy,
    offer us love and forgiveness.
Help us see one another
    with eyes of love and compassion.
Through Christ our Lord.
Amen.

✝ God was reconciling the world to himself in Christ and entrusting to us the message of reconciliation.

Friday, July 2, 2021
Weekday

✝ Come to me, all you who labor and are burdened, and I will give you rest, says the Lord.

Psalm 35   *page 407*

Reading   *Matthew 9:9–13*

As Jesus passed by, he saw a man named Matthew sitting at the customs post. He said to him, "Follow me." And he got up and followed him. While he was at table in his house, many tax collectors and sinners came and sat with Jesus and his disciples. The Pharisees saw this and said to his disciples, "Why does your teacher eat with tax collectors and sinners?" He heard this and said, "Those who are well do not need a physician, but the sick do. Go and learn the meaning of the words, *I desire mercy, not sacrifice.* I did not come to call the righteous but sinners."

Reflection

Jesus sits and eats with tax collectors and sinners; Jesus' presence among sinners shows that there is a place for everyone at the table, even those who were considered unclean and unacceptable by Jewish law. During the time of Jesus, the people would make a ritual sacrifice at the temple, an offering that expressed their relationship with God. This offering is a gesture to atone for sins, or a sign to give God thanks for a blessing. Jesus is a model of God's desire for relationships that are steeped in mercy. Our relationship with God is also lived in how we love our brothers and sisters.

Prayers   *others may be added*

Lord God, with humble hearts, we pray:

◆ Lord, hear our prayer.

Help us welcome the stranger and treat them as Christ, we pray: ◆ Grant wisdom to those who assist refugees and immigrants, we pray: ◆ Increase vocations to the religious life, priesthood, and diaconate, we pray: ◆ Enlighten those who seek the living God, we pray: ◆

Our Father . . .

O God,
you revealed your compassion
    in the ministry of Jesus,
    your Son.
Send your Holy Spirit upon on us
when we hesitate to sit among
    sinners or outcasts,
so that, strengthened by love,
we may bear witness to your mercy.
Through Christ our Lord.
Amen.

✝ Come to me, all you who labor and are burdened, and I will give you rest, says the Lord.

Saturday, July 3, 2021
Feast of St. Thomas, Apostle

✝ Come, let us worship the Lord,
the King of the apostles.

Psalm 63   *page 411*

Reading   *John 20:24–29*

Thomas, called Didymus, one of the Twelve, was not with them when Jesus came. So the other disciples said to him, "We have seen the Lord." But Thomas said to them, "Unless I see the mark of the nails in his hands and put my finger into the nailmarks and put my hand into his side, I will not believe." Now a week later his disciples were again inside and Thomas was with them. Jesus came, although the doors were locked, and stood in their midst and said, "Peace be with you." Then he said to Thomas, "Put your finger here and see my hands, and bring your hand and put it into my side, and do not be unbelieving, but believe." Thomas answered and said to him, "My Lord and my God!" Jesus said to him, "Have you come to believe because you have seen me? Blessed are those who have not seen and have believed."

Reflection

Thomas is absent when the risen Christ appears to the Apostles. He does not believe their account of seeing the Lord, thus earning the nickname "Doubting Thomas." He further goes on to place stipulations to his believing that the Lord has risen. Thomas wants to place his finger in the nail marks and his hand into Christ's side, or he will not believe. What conditions do we place on our relationship with Jesus? What do we expect from God in order for us to respond? No matter the response, he continues to offer his mercy, his love, and his peace.

Prayers   *others may be added*

With grateful hearts, we pray:

◆ Lord, hear our prayer.

For lay and ordained leaders within the Church, we pray: ◆ For the leaders of nations, we pray: ◆ For the sick, suffering, shut-ins, and all who are alone, we pray: ◆ For those who do not believe in Christ, we pray: ◆

Our Father . . .

Lord God,
you called Thomas to follow you.
Grant us the grace to believe
   in the risen Lord
and to not doubt your presence
   in our neighbors or in our lives.
Through Christ our Lord.
Amen.

✝ Come, let us worship the Lord,
the King of the apostles.

Renew *DAILY PRAYER* *Today!*

Order *Daily Prayer 2022* today and continue to bring ritual, reflection, and prayer into your daily life.

DAILY PRAYER 2022

LTP

Single copy: **$13**

Bulk pricing available on 2 or more copies. For pricing and to place a bulk order, please call 800-933-1800, or order online at www.LTP.org.

☐ Bill my card   ☐ Check enclosed

Make checks payable to Liturgy Training Publications.

Name

Address

City, State   Zip

Phone   E-mail

Card #

Exp. date

Signature

☐ Visa   ☐ MC   ☐ Discover   ☐ American Express

Quantity	Order Code	Item/Description	Cost
1	DP22	**Daily Prayer 2022**	$13
		Illinois residents add 10.25% sales tax.	
		Subtotal	
		Shipping	$5
		Total	

For orders to be shipped outside the U.S., please call customer service at 800-933-1800. Prices are in U.S. dollars and are subject to change without notice.

ORDERING INFORMATION

- **MAIL**   Liturgy Training Publications
  Order Department
  3949 South Racine Avenue, Chicago, IL 60609

- **PHONE**   800-933-1800
  8:30 a.m. to 4:30 p.m. Central Time

- **FAX**   1-800-933-7094 *Any Time Day or Night*

- **EMAIL**   orders@LTP.org   • ONLINE www.LTP.org

Two Ways to Pay:

- **CREDIT CARD** Visa, Mastercard, American Express, and Discover Card
- **CHECK**

I21DR1M

✝ The Spirit of the Lord is upon me for he sent me to bring glad tidings to the poor.

Psalm 63 *page 411*

Reading *Mark 6:1–6*

Jesus departed from there and came to his native place, accompanied by his disciples. When the sabbath came he began to teach in the synagogue, and many who heard him were astonished. They said, "Where did this man get all this? What kind of wisdom has been given him? What mighty deeds are wrought by his hands! Is he not the carpenter, the son of Mary, and the brother of James and Joseph and Judas and Simon? And are not his sisters here with us?" And they took offense at him. Jesus said to them, "A prophet is not without honor except in his native place and among his own kin and in his own house." So he was not able to perform any mighty deed there, apart from curing a few sick people by laying his hands on them. He was amazed at their lack of faith.

Reflection

Jesus returns to his home of Nazareth. The Sabbath finds him in the synagogue where he begins to teach. Those present were astonished at what he was saying. What is the source of his wisdom and mighty deeds? They took offense at him. They were not able to see how God was present in Jesus and how God was working in his life. Because of their lack of faith, Jesus could perform no mighty deeds there. Are there areas of your life where faith is lacking, where God is unable to work?

Prayers *others may be added*

Source of all goodness, we turn to you as we pray:

◆ Lord, hear our prayer.

That members of the Church may know the joy of the Gospel, we pray: ◆ That preachers and missionaries may grow in wisdom, we pray: ◆ That our families and friends may know God's love and mercy, we pray: ◆ That God's peace and justice reign throughout the world, we pray: ◆

Our Father . . .

Lord God,
your Word transforms and sustains us.
Bless us with Holy Wisdom
so that we may recognize
    Christ's presence
    in the Word proclaimed
and in the community in which we live.
Through Christ our Lord.
Amen.

✝ The Spirit of the Lord is upon me for he sent me to bring glad tidings to the poor.

✝ O Lord, open my lips.
And my mouth will proclaim
your praise.

Psalm 8
page 400

Reading
Matthew 9:20–22

A woman suffering hemorrhages for twelve years came up behind him and touched the tassel on his cloak. She said to herself, "If only I can touch his cloak, I shall be cured." Jesus turned around and saw her, and said, "Courage, daughter! Your faith has saved you." And from that hour the woman was cured.

Reflection

A sign of great humility is often seen in the woman who suffered from hemorrhages. She seems to want to blend in, not get noticed. But what if this was not out of humility but fear? Her condition was considered a sign of being "unclean"; therefore, she was an outcast. The Law of Moses would have stated that she was to isolate herself from others. This makes Jesus' response all the more significant: by acknowledging her he states boldly that no one is an outcast. It is also interesting to note that the same law that labeled the woman unclean was also the law that prescribed the wearing of tassels on the corners of one's garment as a reminder to keep the commandments. Here is a subtle hint at how Christ fulfills the law and makes it perfect, for the law of God, as St. Paul observes, was established to teach us God's love. Christ takes notice of even the marginalized because God's love incorporates all.

Rev. Michael J. K. Fuller (Daily Prayer 2008)

Prayers
others may be added

Lord, in confidence we pray:

◆ Hear us, Lord.

For the Church, we pray: ◆ For world leaders, we pray: ◆ For the sick and dying, we pray: ◆ For victims of violence, we pray: ◆

Our Father . . .

God of mercy,
your Son, Jesus,
reveals your transforming love.
Open our heart to your mercy
so that we may praise your name.
Through Christ our Lord.
Amen.

✝ O Lord, open my lips.
And my mouth will proclaim
your praise.

✝ I am the good shepherd, says the Lord; I know my sheep, and mine know me.

Psalm 23   page 402

Reading   *Matthew 9:32–38*

A demoniac who could not speak was brought to Jesus, and when the demon was driven out the mute man spoke. The crowds were amazed and said, "Nothing like this has ever been seen in Israel." But the Pharisees said, "He drives out demons by the prince of demons."

Jesus went around to all the towns and villages, teaching in their synagogues, proclaiming the Gospel of the Kingdom, and curing every disease and illness. At the sight of the crowds, his heart was moved with pity for them because they were troubled and abandoned, like sheep without a shepherd. Then he said to his disciples, "The harvest is abundant but the laborers are few; so ask the master of the harvest to send out laborers for his harvest."

Reflection

A sheep without a shepherd is vulnerable to predators, incapable of finding clean water or a sustaining pasture and susceptible to wounds, briers, and thistles. A shepherd is one who is strong and gentle, capable of defending the flock, of adapting to their needs, of bearing them in his arms. This image of shepherd and sheep captures for us the heart of what it means to be in relationship with Jesus. He is moved to pity for the people as he recognizes that they are troubled and abandoned. Jesus invites us to share in the same care and compassion that he had for others.

Prayers   *others may be added*

Lord God, looking for healing, we turn to you as we pray:

◆ Lord, hear our prayer.

For the Church who, with love and mercy, seeks the lost and forgotten, we pray: ◆ For those who are discerning their spiritual gifts, we pray: ◆ For catechists who share the Gospel, we pray: ◆ For those who are lost, alone, and afraid, we pray: ◆

Our Father . . .

O God,
through your Son, Jesus,
you show us your care for us.
Give us a compassionate heart
so that we may care for others
in our work of building up
     the Kingdom of heaven.
Through Christ our Lord.
Amen.

✝ I am the good shepherd, says the Lord; I know my sheep, and mine know me.

✝ The Kingdom of God is at hand: repent and believe in the Gospel.

Psalm 33 *page 406*

Reading *Matthew 10:1, 5–7*

Jesus summoned his Twelve disciples and gave them authority over unclean spirits to drive them out and to cure every disease and every illness. . . .

Jesus sent out these Twelve after instructing them thus, "Do not go into pagan territory or enter a Samaritan town. Go rather to the lost sheep of the house of Israel. As you go, make this proclamation: 'The Kingdom of heaven is at hand.'"

Reflection

Matthew lists the names of the Twelve Apostles. The number twelve is found repeatedly in the Old and New Testaments. It is the perfect number; it symbolizes God's power, authority and, completeness. Jesus is giving the Twelve authority over unclean spirits, to drive them out and to cure every disease and every illness. He sends them out on a mission: to heal and to announce the Good News. To be delivered from unclean spirits and freed from disease and illness would certainly make one proclaim, "The Kingdom of heaven is at hand." How has God called and sent you to be among those who bring his healing love to a wounded world?

Prayers *others may be added*

To the Lord who preaches the Kingdom, we pray:

◆ Lord, hear our prayer.

For all who share the Gospel, we pray: ◆
For missionaries, teachers, catechists, and spiritual directors, we pray: ◆
For pastoral ministers, we pray: ◆
For those who are sick and in need of healing, we pray: ◆

Our Father . . .

Lord of power and might,
you gave the Apostles
    authority over unclean spirits
and the command to cure
    every disease and every illness.
May we listen as you call our name
and invite us to share
    in your mission
and to proclaim that
'the Kingdom of heaven is at hand.'
Through Christ our Lord.
Amen.

✝ The Kingdom of God is at hand: repent and believe in the Gospel.

✝ The Kingdom of God is at hand:
repent and believe in the Gospel.

Psalm 31   *page 405*

Reading   *Matthew 10:7–13*

Jesus said to his Apostles: "As you go, make this proclamation: 'The Kingdom of heaven is at hand.' Cure the sick, raise the dead, cleanse the lepers, drive out demons. Without cost you have received; without cost you are to give. Do not take gold or silver or copper for your belts; no sack for the journey, or a second tunic, or sandals, or walking stick. The laborer deserves his keep. Whatever town or village you enter, look for a worthy person in it, and stay there until you leave. As you enter a house, wish it peace. If the house is worthy, let your peace come upon it; if not, let your peace return to you."

Reflection

Jesus continues to give instructions to the Twelve about their mission of proclaiming the Kingdom of God. They are to take no gold or silver, no sack, or a second tunic, or sandals or a walking stick. This journey is dependent upon the Apostles' ability to trust God and to trust the people they will encounter as they move from each town or village. The Apostles will be unrestricted by those extra belongings so that they may be free and open, better able to receive God's mercy, love, and peace.

Prayers   *others may be added*

With grateful hearts, we pray:

◆ Lord, hear us.

Transform our hearts, we pray: ◆
Strengthen our gifts, we pray: ◆
Protect us from all harm, we pray: ◆
Help us to trust you, we pray: ◆
Raise up the dead, we pray: ◆

Our Father . . .

Loving God,
your incarnate Word lives within us.
May your Holy Spirit strengthen us
as we go forth sharing the Gospel.
Help us to bear witness
to the joy and freedom
    of the Christian life.
Through Christ our Lord.
Amen.

✝ The Kingdom of God is at hand:
repent and believe in the Gospel.

Friday, July 9, 2021
Weekday

✝ When the Spirit of truth comes, he will guide you to all truth and remind you of all I told you.

Psalm 51   *page 409*

Reading   *Matthew 10:16–23*

Jesus said to his Apostles: "Behold, I am sending you like sheep in the midst of wolves; so be shrewd as serpents and simple as doves. But beware of men, for they will hand you over to courts and scourge you in their synagogues, and you will be led before governors and kings for my sake as a witness before them and the pagans. When they hand you over, do not worry about how you are to speak or what you are to say. You will be given at that moment what you are to say. For it will not be you who speak but the Spirit of your Father speaking through you. Brother will hand over brother to death, and the father his child; children will rise up against parents and have them put to death. You will be hated by all because of my name, but whoever endures to the end will be saved. When they persecute you in one town, flee to another. Amen, I say to you, you will not finish the towns of Israel before the Son of Man comes."

Reflection

Jesus warns the Twelve that he is sending them out like sheep in the midst of wolves. Jesus assures them that there is nothing that they will lack as they are sent forth. They are not to worry about what to say, as the Spirit of God will speak through them. Jesus also warns his Apostles about the hostility and dangers they may encounter on their mission, yet those that endure will be saved. The sheep may walk through a dark valley, but they do not need to fear, they are not alone; the Lord guides them.

Prayers   *others may be added*

Confident in your Holy Spirit, we pray:

◆ Lord, hear our prayer.

Have mercy on those who preach the Gospel, we pray: ◆ Comfort the lost and forsaken, we pray: ◆ Heal the divisions in families and communities, we pray: ◆ Refresh the spirit of those who are sick, we pray: ◆

Our Father . . .

Lord of heaven and earth,
you send us forth to preach your Word
    and speak your holy name.
Guard us and keep us on the right path,
so that we may bear witness
to the power of our God.
Through Christ our Lord.
Amen.

✝ When the Spirit of truth comes, he will guide you to all truth and remind you of all I told you.

Saturday, July 10, 2021
Weekday

✝ If you are insulted for the name of Christ, blessed are you, for the Spirit of God rests upon you.

Psalm 8
page 400

Reading
Matthew 10:24–33

Jesus said to his Apostles: "No disciple is above his teacher, no slave above his master. It is enough for the disciple that he become like his teacher, for the slave that he become like his master. If they have called the master of the house Beelzebul, how much more those of his household!

"Therefore do not be afraid of them. Nothing is concealed that will not be revealed, nor secret that will not be known. What I say to you in the darkness, speak in the light; what you hear whispered, proclaim on the housetops. And do not be afraid of those who kill the body but cannot kill the soul; rather, be afraid of the one who can destroy both soul and body in Gehenna. Are not two sparrows sold for a small coin? Yet not one of them falls to the ground without your Father's knowledge." Even all the hairs of your head are counted. So do not be afraid; you are worth more than many sparrows. Everyone who acknowledges me before others I will acknowledge before my heavenly Father. But whoever denies me before others, I will deny before my heavenly Father.

Reflection

To encourage the disciples, Jesus tells them not to be afraid. He then tells them to fear "the one who can destroy body and soul." It is a brief warning surrounded by the protective love of God. Jesus tells us that "even all the hairs of your head are counted"; what a deep, personal, and complete love God has for us. The disciples are sent out in the protective hands of God to prepare them for what is to come.

Prayers
others may be added

In times of distress, we turn to you, Lord, as we pray:

♦ Lord, hear our prayer.

For the Church that it may be a beacon of hope, we pray: ♦ For world leaders that they work for justice, we pray: ♦ For faith communities that they grow in love and mercy, we pray: ♦ For those who are persecuted that they may find courage in Christ, we pray: ♦

Our Father . . .

Lord of all creation,
we, your children,
    are made in your image.
Grant us rest in your loving care
as we share the saving works
    of your Son, Jesus.
Through Christ our Lord.
Amen.

✝ If you are insulted for the name of Christ, blessed are you, for the Spirit of God rests upon you.

Sunday, July 11, 2021
Fifteenth Sunday in Ordinary Time

✟ May the Father of our Lord Jesus Christ enlighten the eyes of our hearts, that we may know what is the hope that belongs to our call.

Psalm 63   *page 411*

Reading   *Mark 6:7–13*

Jesus summoned the Twelve and began to send them out two by two and gave them authority over unclean spirits. He instructed them to take nothing for the journey but a walking stick—no food, no sack, no money in their belts. They were, however, to wear sandals but not a second tunic. He said to them, "Wherever you enter a house, stay there until you leave. Whatever place does not welcome you or listen to you, leave there and shake the dust off your feet in testimony against them." So they went off and preached repentance. The Twelve drove out many demons, and they anointed with oil many who were sick and cured them.

Reflection

Jesus sends the Twelve out to preach, teach, and heal. Consider what it must have been like for them to have spent all that time hearing the words spoken by Jesus and to have seen him heal people; now they themselves are the ones preaching the Good News, teaching about the Kingdom, and healing others. We too have spent time with the Word of God. We have experienced healing in the sacraments. How is God calling you to preach, teach, and heal in the world today?

Prayers   *others may be added*

Lord, our foundation and source, we turn to you in prayer:

◆ Hear us, O God.

May the Gospel lead us to conversion, we pray: ◆ Open our hearts to hear and receive the Word of God, we pray: ◆ Heal those who suffer from disease, we pray: ◆ Forgive our sins and strengthen us to act justly, we pray: ◆

Our Father . . .

Lord God,
source of all life and goodness,
you call your disciples
    to live in community,
and to assist one another on the journey.
Help us learn how to support each other
    on our mission,
so that all your people may know the joy
    of the Good News.
Through Christ our Lord.
Amen.

✟ May the Father of our Lord Jesus Christ enlighten the eyes of our hearts, that we may know what is the hope that belongs to our call.

Monday, July 12, 2021
Weekday

✝ Blessed are they who are persecuted for the sake of righteousness, for theirs is the Kingdom of heaven.

Psalm 127   *page 418*

Reading   *Matthew 10:34–36*

Jesus said to his Apostles: "Do not think that I have come to bring peace upon the earth. I have come to bring not peace but the sword. For I have come to set a man against his father, / a daughter against her mother, and a daughter-in-law against her mother-in-law; / and one's enemies will be those of his household."

Reflection

Jesus tells his disciples that he has not come to bring peace to the world, but the sword. Shocking words to hear! He speaks about those who prefer a father or mother to the Lord. That individual is not worthy of being a disciple. God calls us to be a part of a family, he also calls us to extend our family to those outside our home. In all relationships, we are called to put God first. Sometimes the Good News will cause division and discord in our community and in our own home with those we love.

Prayers   *others may be added*

Lord of all unity, we pray:

◆ Lord, hear our prayer.

For the Church to be a herald of peace in the world, we pray: ◆ For leaders of nations to work together in building goodwill among all people, we pray: ◆ For the grace to live the demanding challenges of discipleship, we pray: ◆ For healing of division between families, neighbors, and parish communities, we pray: ◆

Our Father . . .

Lord God,
you call us to unity with you
    and one another.
Guide us as disciples
when we are compelled
    to live the Gospel
in a radical way.
Through Christ our Lord.
Amen.

✝ Blessed are they who are persecuted for the sake of righteousness, for theirs is the Kingdom of heaven.

✝ If today you hear his voice, harden not your hearts.

Psalm 35   *page 407*

Reading   *Matthew 11:20–24*

Jesus began to reproach the towns where most of his mighty deeds had been done, since they had not repented. "Woe to you, Chorazin! Woe to you, Bethsaida! For if the mighty deeds done in your midst had been done in Tyre and Sidon, they would long ago have repented in sackcloth and ashes. But I tell you, it will be more tolerable for Tyre and Sidon on the day of judgment than for you. "And as for you, Capernaum:

Will you be exalted to heaven? / You will go down to the netherworld. / For if the mighty deeds done in your midst had been done in Sodom, it would have remained until this day. But I tell you, it will be more tolerable for the land of Sodom on the day of judgment than for you."

Reflection

Jesus speaks to the cities that were not open to hearing and accepting the Word of God. It is uncomfortable to hear these words proclaimed. We are most accustomed to a peaceful and loving Jesus; instead, we encounter our Lord who seems to be more critical and judgmental. The Gospel is supposed to challenge us and make us uncomfortable, especially when we know that we have not heeded the Word and lived up to what God is calling us to for our life. Lord, allow me to be counted among your faithful ones.

Prayers   *others may be added*

Confident that our mighty God walks with us, we pray:

◆ Hear us, O God.

Guide those who work in the ministry of healing, we pray: ◆ Open our hearts to your Word, we pray: ◆ Bring relief to the poor and those affected by violence, we pray: ◆ Raise up all who have died, we pray: ◆

Our Father . . .

God of Abraham,
in every age
your Word transforms the hearts
and lives of your people.
May the proclamation
    of the living Word
draw people from every nation,
    town, and district to you.
Through Christ our Lord.
Amen.

✝ If today you hear his voice, harden not your hearts.

✝ Blessed are the pure of heart,
for they shall see God.

Psalm 33 *page 406*

Reading *Matthew 11:25–27*

At that time Jesus exclaimed: "I give praise to you, Father, Lord of heaven and earth, for although you have hidden these things from the wise and the learned you have revealed them to the childlike. Yes, Father, such has been your gracious will. All things have been handed over to me by my Father. No one knows the Son except the Father, and no one knows the Father except the Son and anyone to whom the Son wishes to reveal him."

Reflection

God has a preferential option for the small. In the Scriptures, we find many examples of the power and might of God found within the small and the hidden. The youngest ones among us recognize the strength and power of God that are found within those humble moments and in people who seem too small. Where have you seen God revealed? When you did not expect it?

Prayers *others may be added*

King of heaven and earth, rejoicing with you, we pray:

♦ Lord, hear us.

That the Church may be transparent and truthful, we pray: ♦ That leaders may honestly serve their people, we pray: ♦ That the smallest and weakest in society may be protected from harm, we pray: ♦ That parishes may be filled with wonder and awe in God's presence, we pray: ♦

Our Father . . .

Divine Creator,
you reveal yourself to us
    through your Son, Jesus Christ.
Guide us to recognize
    all the ways in which
    you are made known to us
so that we may know the beauty
    of your Kingdom.
Through Christ our Lord.
Amen.

✝ Blessed are the pure of heart,
for they shall see God.

✝ Come to me, all you who labor and are burdened, and I will give you rest, says the Lord.

Psalm 26   *page 404*

Reading   *Matthew 11:28–30*

Jesus said to the crowds: "Come to me, all you who labor and are burdened, and I will give you rest. Take my yoke upon you and learn from me, for I am meek and humble of heart; and you will find rest for yourselves. For my yoke is easy, and my burden light."

Reflection

Burdens weigh us down. We often carry the weight of our sins, a millstone causing great weariness. We find ourselves seeking rest through our own means, through other people, or through a broken world. Jesus tells us that his yoke is easy, and his burden is light. He invites us to come to him and experience the relief and the joy that can only be found in him. The rest that Jesus offers is a quiet rest. This rest is an opportunity to refresh, restore, and find a new strength after the fatigue of our labors.

Prayers   *others may be added*

O God, we turn to you in prayer:

◆ **Lord, hear our prayer.**

Help the Church be a place of rest for God's people, we pray: ◆ Transform our aggression and arrogance, we pray: ◆ Refresh those who are burdened in any way, we pray: ◆ Grant rest to all who labor, we pray: ◆

Our Father . . .

O God,
you care for your people
and offer us rest
    when we are weary.
May we know
    that relief and freedom,
which comes from laying down
    our yoke and being joined
    to your Son.
Through Christ our Lord.
Amen.

✝ Come to me, all you who labor and are burdened, and I will give you rest, says the Lord.

✝ My sheep hear my voice, says the Lord; I know them, and they follow me.

Psalm 108   *page 415*

Reading   *Matthew 12:1–8*

Jesus was going through a field of grain on the sabbath. His disciples were hungry and began to pick the heads of grain and eat them. When the Pharisees saw this, they said to him, "See, your disciples are doing what is unlawful to do on the sabbath." He said to them, "Have you not read what David did when he and his companions were hungry, how he went into the house of God and ate the bread of offering, which neither he nor his companions but only the priests could lawfully eat? Or have you not read in the law that on the sabbath the priests serving in the temple violate the sabbath and are innocent? I say to you, something greater than the temple is here. If you knew what this meant, *I desire mercy, not sacrifice*, you would not have condemned these innocent men. For the Son of Man is Lord of the sabbath."

Reflection

The Pharisees were critical of Jesus' disciples who disobeyed Jewish law by violating the Sabbath. One was not allowed to pick grain and eat it on the Sabbath. They were concerned with the details of the law and making sure that others followed the law, so much so that they did not understand the spirit of the law or Jesus' proclamation that the Son of Man is the Lord of the Sabbath. Jesus knows the Law by heart, and his heart was filled with compassion and mercy. Do our responses and reactions perpetuate conflict, or do they offer mercy and love?

Prayers   *others may be added*

Merciful God grant us your kindness, as we pray:

◆ Have mercy, Lord.

When the Church fails to bear witness to love and mercy, we pray: ◆ When elected officials waver in their work for justice, we pray: ◆ When we fail to see Christ in others, we pray: ◆ When we refuse to accompany the poor and marginalized, we pray: ◆ When our scruples blind us to the joy of the Gospel, we pray: ◆

Our Father . . .

God of truth,
you gave your Son
   to help us know your Law.
May your Law of love
   reign in our hearts
and lead us to everlasting life.
Through Christ our Lord.
Amen.

✝ My sheep hear my voice, says the Lord; I know them, and they follow me.

✝ God was reconciling the world to himself in Christ, and entrusting to us the message of reconciliation.

Psalm 127 *page 418*

Reading *Matthew 12:14–21*

The Pharisees went out and took counsel against Jesus to put him to death.

When Jesus realized this, he withdrew from that place. Many people followed him, and he cured them all, but he warned them not to make him known. This was to fulfill what had been spoken through Isaiah the prophet:

Behold, my servant whom I have chosen, / my beloved in whom I delight; / I shall place my Spirit upon him, / and he will proclaim justice to the Gentiles. / He will not contend or cry out, / nor will anyone hear his voice in the streets. / A bruised reed he will not break, / a smoldering wick he will not quench, / until he brings justice to victory. / And in his name the Gentiles will hope.

Reflection

Jesus is the fulfillment of Isaiah's prophecy of the Suffering Servant. God delights in his Servant; the Spirit is upon him. This is reminiscent of the words the Father has for Jesus at his baptism, "You are my Son, the Beloved; with you I am well pleased" (Luke 3:22, NRSVCE). The Suffering Servant is one who comes for all those who live in the margins of society: the weak and the bruised, those who seek liberty and justice, those who long for courage and hope. Jesus witnesses not with a loud cry but with a gentle love.

Prayers *others may be added*

To the Lord, who is our strength, we pray:

◆ Hear us, O Christ.

For the Church to be a source of all that is fair and just in the world, we pray: ◆ For legislators to address human dignity and the common good in society, we pray: ◆ For the vulnerable and weak to know the strength of God, we pray: ◆ For those affected by abuse and violence, we pray: ◆

Our Father . . .

God of power and might, we look to your beloved Son to show us how to live as servants in today's world. May our efforts in his name, bring hope to all people. Through Christ our Lord. Amen.

✝ God was reconciling the world to himself in Christ, and entrusting to us the message of reconciliation.

✟ My sheep hear my voice, says the Lord; I know them, and they follow me.

Psalm 23 *page 402*

Reading *Mark 6:30–34*

The apostles gathered together with Jesus and reported all they had done and taught. He said to them, "Come away by yourselves to a deserted place and rest a while." People were coming and going in great numbers, and they had no opportunity even to eat. So they went off in the boat by themselves to a deserted place. People saw them leaving and many came to know about it. They hastened there on foot from all the towns and arrived at the place before them.

When Jesus disembarked and saw the vast crowd, his heart was moved with pity for them, for they were like sheep without a shepherd; and he began to teach them many things.

Reflection

Much like the shepherd in Psalm 23, who leads his flock to green pastures, Jesus invites the disciples to a deserted place for rest. Unfortunately, before they arrive, the crowds overwhelm them. Moved to pity, Jesus begins to teach them. Jesus is teaching the Apostles that it is important to take time to pause and reflect upon the mission. Too often, that mission to follow Christ involves placing the needs of others before our own. In baptism, we are called to put on Christ. How will you live out this call today?

Prayers *others may be added*

We turn to you, God, as we pray:

◆ Hear us, O Christ.

For bishops and priests who are called to smell like the sheep, we pray: ◆ For those needing sabbatical and rest, we pray: ◆ For children who need the love and protection of the Shepherd, we pray: ◆ For those who need guidance in their discernment, we pray: ◆

Our Father . . .

O God,
you are the Shepherd of our hearts.
Protect us in our work
and guide us to places of rest
    when we become weary.
Help us to share your love
    with those who are feeling
alone and isolated.
Through Christ our Lord.
Amen.

✟ My sheep hear my voice, says the Lord; I know them, and they follow me.

Monday, July 19, 2021
Weekday

☩ If today you hear his voice, harden not your hearts.

Psalm 26   *page 404*

Reading   *Matthew 12:38–42*

Some of the scribes and Pharisees said to Jesus, "Teacher, we wish to see a sign from you." He said to them in reply, "An evil and unfaithful generation seeks a sign, but no sign will be given it except the sign of Jonah the prophet. Just as Jonah was in the belly of the whale three days and three nights, so will the Son of Man be in the heart of the earth three days and three nights. At the judgment, the men of Nineveh will arise with this generation and condemn it, because they repented at the preaching of Jonah; and there is something greater than Jonah here. At the judgment the queen of the south will arise with this generation and condemn it, because she came from the ends of the earth to hear the wisdom of Solomon; and there is something greater than Solomon here."

Reflection

What is the sign of Jonah? The Jewish crowd could answer this question. Jonah's message to the Ninevites was, "Repent!" They listened and were saved. Jesus' message, "Repent, the Kingdom of God is at hand," is the same, but they do not listen. This is the irony, a Jewish prophet's message changes the hearts and minds of the pagans, and they are saved. The Messiah has the same message for his people, but the leaders reject it. We look back at both and consider what our response will be to the invitation to repent?

Prayers   *others may be added*

In mercy, we turn to you and pray:

◆ Hear us, O Christ.

For the Church, we pray: ◆ For leaders, we pray: ◆ For travelers, we pray: ◆ For peacemakers, we pray: ◆ For the poor, we pray: ◆ For confessors, we pray: ◆

Our Father . . .

Lord God,
you call us to repent and be saved.
May the words of the prophet Jonah
remind us of your coming Kingdom.
Through Christ our Lord.
Amen.

☩ If today you hear his voice, harden not your hearts.

✝ Whoever loves me will keep my word, and my Father will love him and we will come to him.

Psalm 33 *page 406*

Reading *Matthew 12:46–50*

While Jesus was speaking to the crowds, his mother and his brothers appeared outside, wishing to speak with him. Someone told him, "Your mother and your brothers are standing outside, asking to speak with you." But he said in reply to the one who told him, "Who is my mother? Who are my brothers?" And stretching out his hand toward his disciples, he said, "Here are my mother and my brothers. For whoever does the will of my heavenly Father is my brother, and sister, and mother."

Reflection

When Jesus is told his mother and brothers were waiting outside to speak with him, the response he gives seems to imply that he disowns his family members. Jesus is actually expanding his family to include those beyond his mother and brothers, to include all those who do the will of his heavenly Father. We surely want to be included in this clan, but membership in this family requires us to do God's will. How do we know God's will for us? Would others recognize us as members of Jesus' company of disciples?

Prayers *others may be added*

In love, we pray:

◆ Lord, hear our prayer.

For the newly baptized, we pray: ◆ For those who are alone and outcasts, we pray: ◆ For friends and family, we pray: ◆ For those who are persecuted, we pray: ◆ For those who seek the living God, we pray: ◆

Our Father . . .

Loving Father,
you called us as members of your family,
to do your will.
Guide us to listen to your Word
and to discern our role
    in the plan of salvation.
Through Christ our Lord.
Amen.

✝ Whoever loves me will keep my word, and my Father will love him and we will come to him.

✝ The seed is the word of God, Christ is the sower; all who come to him will live for ever.

Psalm 85   *page 413*

Reading   *Matthew 13:1–9*

On that day, Jesus went out of the house and sat down by the sea. Such large crowds gathered around him that he got into a boat and sat down, and the whole crowd stood along the shore. And he spoke to them at length in parables, saying: "A sower went out to sow. And as he sowed, some seed fell on the path, and birds came and ate it up. Some fell on rocky ground, where it had little soil. It sprang up at once because the soil was not deep, and when the sun rose it was scorched, and it withered for lack of roots. Some seed fell among thorns, and the thorns grew up and choked it. But some seed fell on rich soil and produced fruit, a hundred or sixty or thirtyfold. Whoever has ears ought to hear."

Reflection

The Word of God does not always bear fruit in my life. Some days my current situation resembles rocky ground; it may allow the heat of a moment to weaken or crush what had potential for growth; or even become entrapped by thorns. Nevertheless, that does not prevent Jesus from speaking his Word to me, even from an unusual place like a boat. Today's parable offers us great hope in knowing that we, too, can be a part of the crowd that stands along the shore, wanting to have the ears to hear and become the rich and fruitful soil. Let us be open to hearing the Word, even if it is proclaimed in an uncommon setting.

Prayers   *others may be added*

Let us call upon the Lord:

◆ Hear us, O Christ.

For all ministers of the Word, we pray: ◆ For those distracted from seeing your goodness, we pray: ◆ For those who strain to hear the Word of God in today's world, we pray: ◆ For farmers and all those who work with the earth, we pray: ◆

Our Father . . .

God of abundance,
you prepare our hearts
    to receive your Word.
Help it take root and grow
so that we may produce
    a hundred or sixty or thirtyfold.
Through Christ our Lord.
Amen.

✝ The seed is the word of God, Christ is the sower; all who come to him will live for ever.

✝ I saw the glory of the risen Christ,
I saw his empty tomb.

Psalm 108 — *page 415*

Reading — *John 20:11–13*

Mary Magdalene stayed outside the tomb weeping. As she wept, she bent over the tomb and saw two angels in white sitting there, one at the head and one at the feet where the Body of Jesus had been. And they said to her, "Woman, why are you weeping?" She said to them, "They have taken my Lord, and I don't know where they laid him." When she had said this, she turned around and saw Jesus there, but did not know it was Jesus.

Reflection

Mary Magdalene is one of the first witnesses to the resurrection. She comes to the tomb in the early morning hours, but does not know it is the Lord; instead, she believes she is speaking to the gardener. In her grief, she asks him to tell her where Jesus' body has been taken. Because of her great sorrow, she is weeping, but she is still seeking the Lord. It is not until he speaks her name that she is able to recognize him. She is given her mission, to go to Peter and the other disciples and to tell them that she has seen the Lord. Are we able to share with others what we have seen and heard after an encounter with the risen Christ?

Prayers — *others may be added*

To God our Father who raised Jesus from the dead, we pray:

◆ Lord, hear our prayer.

That the Church fervently witness to the resurrection, we pray: ◆ That missionaries and preachers joyfully share the Gospel, we pray: ◆ That those filled with sorrow may find joy in the risen Lord, we pray: ◆ That faith communities respond in faith to God's voice, we pray: ◆

Our Father . . .

Saving God,
you freed Mary Magdalene
    to witness the resurrection
and share the Good News
    with the disciples.
Help us proclaim the risen Christ
and tell our brothers and sisters
about the greatness of our God.
Through Christ our Lord.
Amen.

✝ I saw the glory of the risen Christ,
I saw his empty tomb.

Friday, July 23, 2021
Weekday

✝ Blessed are they who have kept the word with a generous heart and yield a harvest through perseverance.

Psalm 23 *page 402*

Reading *Matthew 13:18–23*

Jesus said to his disciples: "Hear the parable of the sower. The seed sown on the path is the one who hears the word of the Kingdom without understanding it, and the Evil One comes and steals away what was sown in his heart. The seed sown on rocky ground is the one who hears the word and receives it at once with joy. But he has no root and lasts only for a time. When some tribulation or persecution comes because of the word, he immediately falls away. The seed sown among thorns is the one who hears the word, but then worldly anxiety and the lure of riches choke the word and it bears no fruit. But the seed sown on rich soil is the one who hears the word and understands it, who indeed bears fruit and yields a hundred or sixty or thirtyfold."

Reflection

The sower is generous with the seed, allowing it to fall everywhere: upon a path, on rocky ground, amid the thorns. There are days that seem to be filled with obstacles for my hearing and understanding the Word of God, and I am weak in removing the threat to the growth of that seed that has been sown in my heart. At some moment in our life, we can identify with each of the types of soil described in today's Gospel. God is generous and allows us to make choices. How am I able to enjoy the abundance of God's love sown in my life today?

Prayers *others may be added*

Turning to the Lord, we pray:

◆ Lord, hear our prayer.

For the Church in her ministry of preaching, we pray: ◆ For world leaders working for peace, we pray: ◆ For catechists and teachers who share the Good News, we pray: ◆ For catechumens as they learn God's Word, we pray: ◆

Our Father . . .

Ever-living God,
your Word resounds in the hearts
    of your faithful ones.
Guard and protect us from evil
so that your Word may always
be a source of joy and consolation.
Through Christ our Lord.
Amen.

✝ Blessed are they who have kept the word with a generous heart and yield a harvest through perseverance.

✝ Humbly welcome the word that has been planted in you and is able to save your souls.

Psalm 70   *page 411*

Reading   *Matthew 13:24–30*

Jesus proposed another parable to the crowds, saying: "The Kingdom of heaven may be likened to a man who sowed good seed in his field. While everyone was asleep his enemy came and sowed weeds all through the wheat, and then went off. When the crop grew and bore fruit, the weeds appeared as well. The slaves of the householder came to him and said, 'Master, did you not sow good seed in your field? Where have the weeds come from?' He answered, 'An enemy has done this.' His slaves said to him, 'Do you want us to go and pull them up?' He replied, 'No, if you pull up the weeds you might uproot the wheat along with them. Let them grow together until harvest.'"

Reflection

There are moments when it is difficult to distinguish the weeds from the wheat. How can we discern the weeds entangled with the wheat of our own lives? In an effort to detach the weeds from the wheat, the wheat can be damaged. The wheat represents the good work God has accomplished in us. God is able to differentiate between good and evil; God will separate the two when it is time.

Prayers   *others may be added*

May we be faithful to your Word,
as we pray:

◆ Lord, hear our prayer.

Help the Church proclaim the Gospel, we pray: ◆ Grant wisdom to world leaders, we pray: ◆ Give courage to your people, we pray: ◆ Heal all who suffer from any affliction, we pray: ◆ Raise up those who have died, we pray: ◆

Our Father . . .

God of all goodness,
may your Word take root
    during this season of growth.
Use our strengths
as well as our weaknesses
    to hasten the Kingdom.
Through Christ our Lord.
Amen.

✝ Humbly welcome the word that has been planted in you and is able to save your souls.

✝ A great prophet has risen in our midst. God has visited his people.

Psalm 118 *page 417*

Reading *John 6:11–15*

Then Jesus took the loaves, gave thanks, and distributed them to those who were reclining, and also as much of the fish as they wanted. When they had had their fill, he said to his disciples, "Gather the fragments left over, so that nothing will be wasted." So they collected them, and filled twelve wicker baskets with fragments from the five barley loaves that had been more than they could eat. When the people saw the sign he had done, they said, "This is truly the Prophet, the one who is to come into the world." Since Jesus knew that they were going to come and carry him off to make him king, he withdrew again to the mountain alone.

Reflection

The boy's five barley loaves and two fish are not enough to feed the gathered crowd. The miracle performed by Jesus is a reminder of his abundant love and mercy for us. With grateful hearts, we thank God that he is able to take the little that we are able to offer him and do so much good with our small efforts. How can our actions help our neighbors?

Prayers *others may be added*

Lord, you satisfy all our hungers, as we pray:

◆ Lord, hear our prayer.

For the Church who nourishes with the Word of God, we pray: ◆ For our elected officials that they may work to end hunger, we pray: ◆ For the sick and suffering that they may be comforted, we pray: ◆ For the hungry, the destitute, and imprisoned, we pray: ◆

Our Father . . .

O God, source of our nourishment, you have blessed us in abundance through the gift of your Son, Jesus. Open our hearts to see those
in most need
so that, filled with your grace, we may accompany them
on this pilgrimage.
Through Christ our Lord.
Amen.

✝ A great prophet has risen in our midst. God has visited his people.

Monday, July 26, 2021
Memorial of Sts. Joachim and Anne, Parents
of the Blessed Virgin Mary

✝ They yearned for the comforting
of Israel, and the Holy Spirit rested
upon them.

Psalm 47 *page 409*

Reading *Matthew 13:31–35*
Jesus proposed a parable to the crowds.
"The Kingdom of heaven is like a mustard seed that a person took and sowed
in a field. It is the smallest of all the
seeds, yet when full-grown it is the largest of plants. It becomes a large bush,
and the 'birds of the sky come and dwell
in its branches.'"

He spoke to them another parable.
"The Kingdom of heaven is like yeast
that a woman took and mixed with three
measures of wheat flour until the whole
batch was leavened."

All these things Jesus spoke to the
crowds in parables. He spoke to them
only in parables, to fulfill what had been
said through the prophet: / *I will open
my mouth in parables, / I will announce
what has lain hidden from the foundation of the world.*

Reflection
Jesus said that when the seed is planted
in the soil, it becomes the largest of
plants. It is so big that the birds come and
make their nests in its branches. Birds
will only make their nests in strong and
sturdy places. Jesus said that the Kingdom of heaven is like this. The birds eat
seeds, yet in this parable, the seed has
grown and transformed into something
that provides shelter and rest for the birds
of the sky. There is great harmony in all
of God's creation. How does this help me
in understanding the Kingdom of God?

Prayers *others may be added*
We turn to God as we pray:

◆ Lord, hear our prayer.

For the Church, we pray: ◆ For parents
and children, we pray: ◆ For catechists
and those who study and proclaim sacred
Scripture, we pray: ◆ For the least among
us, we pray: ◆ For farmers, we pray: ◆

Our Father . . .

O God,
through your Son, Jesus,
you revealed your Kingdom.
Grant each of us,
    especially the least among us,
an awareness to see your presence.
Through Christ our Lord.
Amen.

✝ They yearned for the comforting
of Israel, and the Holy Spirit rested
upon them.

✝ The seed is the word of God, Christ is the sower; all who come to him will live for ever.

Psalm 8   *page 400*

Reading   *Matthew 13:36–41*

Jesus dismissed the crowds and went into the house. His disciples approached him and said, "Explain to us the parable of the weeds in the field." He said in reply, "He who sows good seed is the Son of Man, the field is the world, the good seed the children of the Kingdom. The weeds are the children of the Evil One, and the enemy who sows them is the Devil. The harvest is the end of the age, and the harvesters are angels. Just as weeds are collected and burned up with fire, so will it be at the end of the age. The Son of Man will send his angels, and they will collect out of his Kingdom all who cause others to sin and all evildoers. They will throw them into the fiery furnace, where there will be wailing and grinding of teeth. Then the righteous will shine like the sun in the Kingdom of their Father. Whoever has ears ought to hear."

Reflection

The disciples approach Jesus asking for an explanation about the parable of the weeds in the field. It is difficult to sow good seed in an evil world. Consider the weeds in your life. What needs to be done to clear the weeds? Sometimes we do not know until the time of the harvest if it is a weed or wheat. Is there a way for the field of my life to contain more wheat and less of the evil one?

Prayers   *others may be added*

Merciful Lord, we turn to you and pray:

◆ Lord, hear our prayer.

For the ministers of the Church who plant seeds of love and mercy, we pray: ◆ For world leaders who sow seeds of peace and justice, we pray: ◆ For the sick and suffering who reveal God's compassion, we pray: ◆ For the parish community who sends laborers into the field to sow and reap, we pray: ◆

Our Father . . .

Loving God,
Jesus teaches us
    about the Kingdom
through parables.
Open our hearts and minds
    to your Word,
so we may hear all that you proclaim.
Through Christ our Lord.
Amen.

✝ The seed is the word of God, Christ is the sower; all who come to him will live for ever.

✝ I call you my friends, says the Lord, for I have made known to you all that the Father has told me.

Psalm 60   *page 410*

Reading   *Matthew 13:44–46*

Jesus said to his disciples: "The Kingdom of heaven is like a treasure buried in a field, which a person finds and hides again, and out of joy goes and sells all that he has and buys that field. Again, the Kingdom of heaven is like a merchant searching for fine pearls. When he finds a pearl of great price, he goes and sells all that he has and buys it."

Reflection

Why do you think the merchant sells everything he owns when he finds this special pearl? The author does not tell us if the merchant found other pearls during his quest, but we do know that this one pearl caused him to change. Jesus tells this story to invite us to contemplate the Kingdom of God, our pearl of great price. It is not easy to give up all we own, but the treasure of eternal life is worth more than anything we can imagine.

Prayers   *others may be added*

Longing for the Kingdom, we pray:

◆ Hear us, O Christ.

For all who seek the Kingdom of God, we pray: ◆ For all who live under unjust leadership, we pray: ◆ For all workers who seek just compensation and equal employment, we pray: ◆ For those who lack food, shelter, and clothing, we pray: ◆

Our Father . . .

God of all endeavors,
you offer us the dignity of work
so that all may have basic rights
and that we may give you glory.
May all our efforts
    hasten the work of the Kingdom.
Through Christ our Lord.
Amen.

✝ I call you my friends, says the Lord, for I have made known to you all that the Father has told me.

✝ I am the light of the world, says the Lord; whoever follows me will have the light of life.

Psalm 60 *page 410*

Reading *John 11:19–27*

Many of the Jews had come to Martha and Mary to comfort them about their brother [Lazarus, who had died]. When Martha heard that Jesus was coming, she went to meet him; but Mary sat at home. Martha said to Jesus, "Lord, if you had been here, my brother would not have died. But even now I know that whatever you ask of God, God will give you. Jesus said to her, "Your brother will rise." Martha said to him, "I know he will rise, in the resurrection on the last day." Jesus told her, "I am the resurrection and the life; whoever believes in me, even if he dies, will live, and anyone who lives and believes in me will never die. Do you believe this?" She said to him, "Yes, Lord. I have come to believe that you are the Christ, the Son of God, the one who is coming into the world."

Reflection

Martha tells Jesus that if he had been present, her brother would not have died. She seeks a miracle from Jesus, the one she knows as the source of life. Jesus' assurance that he is the resurrection and life moves Martha to make a profession of faith; she states that he is the Christ. Consider how your life and encounter with Christ moves you to make a profession of faith.

Prayers *others may be added*

In moments of despair, we turn to you, Lord, as we pray:

♦ Hear us, O Christ.

For the Church who proclaims Jesus as the resurrection and the life, we pray: ♦ For those mourning who seek comfort and peace, we pray: ♦ For families who seek reconciliation and renewal, we pray: ♦ For our community of faith who yearns for the Kingdom, we pray: ♦

Our Father . . .

Eternal Father,
we celebrate the resurrection
    of your Son
at every Eucharistic liturgy.
May our lives be a witness
    to the presence of the risen Lord
in our midst.
Through Christ our Lord.
Amen.

✝ I am the light of the world, says the Lord; whoever follows me will have the light of life.

✝ The word of the Lord remains
forever; this is the word that has
been proclaimed to you.

Psalm 8   *page 400*

Reading   *Matthew 13:54–58*

Jesus came to his native place and taught
the people in their synagogue. They
were astonished and said, "Where did
this man get such wisdom and mighty
deeds? Is he not the carpenter's son? Is
not his mother named Mary and his
brothers James, Joseph, Simon, and
Judas? Are not his sisters all with us?
Where did this man get all this?" And
they took offense at him. But Jesus said
to them, "A prophet is not without honor
except in his native place and in his own
house." And he did not work many
mighty deeds there because of their lack
of faith.

Reflection

Jesus' teaching in the synagogue astonished those who knew him from his
youth. They do not recognize him as
anything other than the carpenter's son.
They took offense at him. It must have
been difficult and even painful for Jesus
to visit this sacred space, which had
been a sanctuary for him, only to find
it filled with disapproval, critique, and
judgement. Lord, allow me to be transformed by your presence in my life.

Prayers   *others may be added*

Lord of all comfort, we turn to you as
we pray:

◆ Lord, hear our prayer.

For the Church in her mission of
preaching, we pray: ◆ For those who are
shunned from the community or ignored
within the family, we pray: ◆ For the
ability to recognize God's presence in
unexpected places, we pray: ◆ For those
in our community who feel isolated,
especially the elderly and infirmed,
we pray: ◆

Our Father . . .

God of consolation,
we come to you bearing our hurt
    and loneliness.
Grant us the grace
    of resting in your mercy.
Through Christ our Lord.
Amen.

✝ The word of the Lord remains
forever; this is the word that has
been proclaimed to you.

✝ Blessed are the poor in spirit, for theirs is the Kingdom of heaven.

Psalm 8   page 400

Reading   *Matthew 14:3–10*

Herod had arrested John, bound him, and put him in prison on account of Herodias, the wife of his brother Philip, for John had said to him, "It is not lawful for you to have her." Although he wanted to kill him, he feared the people, for they regarded him as a prophet. But at a birthday celebration for Herod, the daughter of Herodias performed a dance before the guests and delighted Herod so much that he swore to give her whatever she might ask for. Prompted by her mother, she said, "Give me here on a platter the head of John the Baptist." The king was distressed, but because of his oaths and the guests who were present, he ordered that it be given, and he had John beheaded in the prison.

Reflection

Herod's title as tetrarch or governor meant that he had authority and power over the region, over the people living in that province and ultimately in his own palace. Herod's acts of power displayed in today's Gospel seem to be born from a weakness and cowardice. John is arrested for the unlawful relationship between Herod and his brother's wife. John's death is carried out because of Herod's prideful promise to his niece; besides, he did not want to be embarrassed in front of the guests at his banquet. His weakness and sin affect his family, his leadership, and the innocent of the world.

Prayers   *others may be added*

Lord of all power and life, we turn to you as we pray:

◆ Lord, hear our prayer.

For those who hold authority in the Church and in the world, we pray: ◆ For those who find themselves in situations of manipulation and intimidation, we pray: ◆ For families who make efforts to live in holiness and peace, we pray: ◆ For those who work to provide basic necessities for the least among us, we pray: ◆ For Jesuits and their apostolates, we pray ◆

Our Father . . .

God of justice and mercy,
you call us to preach your Word
    and to witness your love
    in the world.
Bring hope to those moments
    filled with despair
so that you may be all in all.
Through Christ our Lord.
Amen.

✝ Blessed are the poor in spirit, for theirs is the Kingdom of heaven.

Sunday, August 1, 2021
Eighteenth Sunday in Ordinary Time

✝ One does not live on bread alone,
but by every word that comes forth
from the mouth of God.

Psalm 8 *page 400*

Reading *Exodus 16:2–4, 12*

The whole Israelite community grumbled against Moses and Aaron. The Israelites said to them, "Would that we had died at the LORD's hand in the land of Egypt, as we sat by our fleshpots and ate our fill of bread! But you had to lead us into this desert to make this whole community die of famine!"

Then the LORD said to Moses, "I will rain down bread from heaven for you. Each day the people are to go out and gather their daily portion; thus will I test them, to see whether they follow my instructions or not.

"I have heard the grumbling of the Israelites. Tell them: In the evening twilight you shall eat flesh, and in the morning you shall have your fill of bread, so that you may know that I, the LORD, am your God."

Reflection

The Israelites discovered that hunger could lead to discomfort and irritability, leaving the body weak and empty. Still, God tells Moses, "I will now rain down bread from heaven for you." The Lord is generous in describing the abundance of food, letting them know that he will give them a deluge of bread, so that they will not know hunger. In our moments of emptiness and weakness, may we turn to the One who fulfills our needs, comforts and strengthens us.

Prayers *others may be added*

Lord who provides for all of our
needs, we come to you in prayer:

◆ Lord, hear our prayer.

For the Church, we pray: ◆ For leaders of nations, we pray: ◆ For families, we pray: ◆ For grumblers, we pray: ◆ For the lost and forsaken, we pray: ◆

Our Father . . .

Bread of life,
who gives us strength
    for the journey,
lead us to your table,
where we may be nourished
    by your banquet of love.
Through our Lord Jesus Christ
    who lives and reigns with you
in unity of the Holy Spirit,
one God for ever and ever.
Amen

✝ One does not live on bread alone,
but by every word that comes forth
from the mouth of God.

Monday, August 2, 2021
Weekday

✠ One does not live on bread alone, but on every word that comes forth from the mouth of God.

Psalm 8   page 400

Reading   Matthew 14:15–20

When it was evening, the disciples approached [Jesus] and said, "This is a deserted place and it is already late; dismiss the crowds so that they can go to the villages and buy food for themselves." Jesus said to them, "There is no need for them to go away; give them some food yourselves." But they said to him, "Five loaves and two fish are all we have here." Then he said, "Bring them here to me," and he ordered the crowds to sit down on the grass. Taking the five loaves and the two fish, and looking up to heaven, he said the blessing, broke the loaves, and gave them to the disciples, who in turn gave them to the crowds. They all ate and were satisfied, and they picked up the fragments left over—twelve wicker baskets full.

Reflection

Jesus takes five loaves and two fish, raises his eyes to heaven and says a blessing, and then breaks the bread. This gesture foreshadows what will happen at the Last Supper, and what we experience today in the Eucharist. The Gospel tells us that after everyone ate as much as they wanted, twelve baskets of scraps are collected. The Lord in his abundant love for us will give us all that we need; he will provide for all our hungers if we only draw near to him. The Eucharist is so rich, that as we reflect upon that encounter with the risen Christ, it continues to feed and transform for us.

Prayers   others may be added

God of all blessings, we turn to you as we pray:

◆ Lord, hear our prayer.

For bishops, priests, deacons, and religious, we pray: ◆ For the hungry in body and soul, we pray: ◆ For the poor and brokenhearted, we pray: ◆ For farmers, fisherman and those whose work is to provide food for communities, we pray: ◆

Our Father . . .

Almighty God,
from such meager gifts you offer an
    abundant feast for your people.
Allow us to gather near to you
so that our hungers may be satisfied
and we may be strengthened
    for the work
of building up the Kingdom.
Through Christ our Lord.
Amen

✠ One does not live on bread alone, but on every word that comes forth from the mouth of God.

✝ Rabbi, you are the Son of God; you
are the King of Israel.

Psalm 8   *page 400*

Reading   *Matthew 14:22–27*

Jesus made the disciples get into a boat
and precede him to the other side of the
sea, while he dismissed the crowds.
After doing so, he went up on the mountain by himself to pray. When it was
evening he was there alone. Meanwhile
the boat, already a few miles offshore,
was being tossed about by the waves,
for the wind was against it. During the
fourth watch of the night, he came
toward them, walking on the sea. When
the disciples saw him walking on the
sea they were terrified. "It is a ghost,"
they said, and they cried out in fear. At
once Jesus spoke to them, "Take courage, it is I; do not be afraid."

Reflection

Fear can overcome us when we are
tossed about by the waves and the wind
blows strong against us. It is in these
difficult situations, sometimes the dark-
est moments of life, when Jesus speaks
to our hearts. How are we able to recognize his voice and his presence amid
the crashing waves and deafening wind?
To recognize his voice, we must listen
carefully as he calls our name. If we
reach for the Word of God, we will find
comfort and assurance as he tells us, "It
is I. Do not be afraid."

Prayers   *others may be added*

Lord of all goodness, we turn to you as
we pray:

◆ Lord, hear our prayer.

For those harmed by the Church,
we pray: ◆ For the hungry and homeless,
we pray: ◆ For those who are dying,
we pray: ◆ For those who live with
anxiety, worry, and fear, we pray: ◆

Our Father . . .

Mighty God,
we come to you
when we are overcome with fear
and seek shelter from the chaos
    of the world.
Reach out to us
    when we are distracted
    by the world and turn away
from your mercy and love.
Through Christ our Lord.
Amen.

✝ Rabbi, you are the Son of God; you
are the King of Israel.

✝ A great prophet has arisen in our midst and God has visited his people.

Psalm 63　　　　　　　page 411

Reading　　　　　Matthew 15:21–28

At that time Jesus withdrew to the region of Tyre and Sidon. And behold, a Canaanite woman of that district came and called out, "Have pity on me, Lord, Son of David! My daughter is tormented by a demon." But he did not say a word in answer to her. His disciples came and asked him, "Send her away, for she keeps calling out after us." He said in reply, "I was sent only to the lost sheep of the house of Israel." But the woman came and did him homage, saying, "Lord, help me." He said in reply, "It is not right to take the food of the children and throw it to the dogs." She said, "Please, Lord, for even the dogs eat the scraps that fall from the table of their masters." Then Jesus said to her in reply, "O woman, great is your faith! Let it be done for you as you wish." And her daughter was healed from that hour.

Reflection

The Canaanite woman is persistent in crying out to Jesus, even when he does not respond to her first request and the disciples dismiss her. She recognizes his power and believes that Jesus would heal her daughter. Even though he is reluctant to respond, this does not diminish the faith that she has in Jesus. Like the disciples, we may find ourselves being dismissive to those whom we judge as unworthy. How do our unkind words block another person's heart in being open to and hearing the Word of God?

Prayers　　　　　others may be added

God of all healing, we turn to you as we pray:

◆ Hear us, O Christ.

Protect those threatened by hatred and injustice, we pray: ◆ Renew the Church in its vocation, we pray: ◆ Shelter the immigrant and refugee, we pray: ◆ Comfort the lost and forsaken, we pray: ◆

Our Father . . .

Lord Jesus,
you answered the Canaanite woman's
　plea for healing.
Help us to be hospitable
　in welcoming the stranger
and those in need of healing.
Pour out your mercy upon us,
for you live and reign with God,
　the Father,
in the unity of the Holy Spirit,
one God, for ever and ever.
Amen.

✝ A great prophet has arisen in our midst and God has visited his people.

✝ You are Peter, and upon this rock I will build my Church, and the gates of the nether world shall not prevail against it.

Psalm 63   *page 411*

Reading   *Matthew 16:13–20*

Jesus went into the region of Caesarea Philippi and he asked his disciples, "Who do people say that the Son of Man is?" They replied, "Some say John the Baptist, others Elijah, still others Jeremiah or one of the prophets." He said to them, "But who do you say that I am?" Simon Peter said in reply, "You are the Christ, the Son of the living God." Jesus said to him in reply, "Blessed are you, Simon son of Jonah. For flesh and blood has not revealed this to you, but my heavenly Father. And so I say to you, you are Peter, and upon this rock I will build my Church, and the gates of the netherworld shall not prevail against it. I will give you the keys to the Kingdom of heaven. Whatever you bind on earth shall be bound in heaven; and whatever you loose on earth shall be loosed in heaven." Then he strictly ordered his disciples to tell no one that he was the Christ.

Reflection

Peter proclaims that Jesus is the Christ, the Son of the living God. Jesus tells him that he will be a rock, a strong foundation for the Church. Only moments later, Peter is concerned for Jesus' humanity and what awaits them in Jerusalem. This rock is now a stumbling stone, an obstacle to the Lord. As disciples, we strive to build up the Kingdom, but are confronted by the limits of our humanity. Even in our weakness may our words and actions profess Jesus as Lord, so that he may transform the brokenness of our life to a life of complete joy.

Prayers   *others may be added*

Lord God, we come to you as we pray:

◆ Hear us, O Christ.

For those preparing to enter the Catholic Church, we pray: ◆ For civic leaders and volunteers, we pray: ◆ For the sick and dying, we pray: ◆ For the hungry, we pray: ◆ For victims of violence and sexual assault, we pray: ◆

Our Father . . .

Lord God,
you call your chosen people
   to a covenant relationship.
May we continue to discover you,
grow in our understanding of you,
and deepen our love for you.
Through Christ our Lord.
Amen

✝ You are Peter, and upon this rock I will build my Church, and the gates of the nether world shall not prevail against it.

✝ This is my beloved Son, with whom I am well pleased; listen to him.

Psalm 80   *page 412*

Reading   *Mark 9:2–7*

Jesus took Peter, James, and his brother John, and led them up a high mountain apart by themselves. And he was transfigured before them, and his clothes became dazzling white, such as no fuller on earth could bleach them. Then Elijah appeared to them along with Moses, and they were conversing with Jesus. Then Peter said to Jesus in reply, "Rabbi, it is good that we are here! Let us make three tents: one for you, one for Moses, and one for Elijah." He hardly knew what to say, they were so terrified. Then a cloud came, casting a shadow over them; from the cloud came a voice, "This is my beloved Son. Listen to him."

Reflection

Near the end of his public ministry, Jesus takes Peter, James, and John to the top of a high mountain, where his clothes become dazzling white, and he converses with Moses and Elijah. The apostles are terrified at this glimpse of the glory of the Lord. The Transfiguration prepares them for another hilltop experience where Jesus is stripped of his clothes, thieves surround him, and darkness consumes the day. How do two very different images shape and transform your relationship with him?

Prayers   *others may be added*

God of glory and might, hear us as we pray:

◆ Lord, hear our prayer.

For those who are discerning their vocation, we pray: ◆ For the dying and those who care for them, we pray: ◆ For those with prophetic voices in our midst, we pray: ◆ For those who find change difficult, we pray: ◆

Our Father . . .

Almighty and ever-living God,
you allowed Peter, James, and John
to see a glimpse of your radiant glory.
Reveal to us
    the presence of your beloved Son
    in both the mountaintop
and valley moments of our life.
Through Christ our Lord.
Amen

✝ This is my beloved Son, with whom I am well pleased; listen to him.

Saturday, August 7, 2021
Weekday

✝ Our Savior Jesus Christ has destroyed death and brought life to light through the Gospel.

Psalm 103   *page 414*

Reading   *Matthew 17:14–20*

A man came up to Jesus, knelt down before him, and said, "Lord, have pity on my son, who is a lunatic and suffers severely; often he falls into fire, and often into water. I brought him to your disciples, but they could not cure him." Jesus said in reply, "O faithless and perverse generation, how long will I be with you? How long will I endure you? Bring the boy here to me." Jesus rebuked him and the demon came out of him, and from that hour the boy was cured. Then the disciples approached Jesus in private and said, "Why could we not drive it out?" He said to them, "Because of your little faith. Amen, I say to you, if you have faith the size of a mustard seed, you will say to this mountain, 'Move from here to there,' and it will move. Nothing will be impossible for you."

Reflection

Jesus tells his disciples that it is their little faith that prohibited them from curing the boy with a demon. If their faith had been the size of a mustard seed, the smallest of all seeds, they could have moved a mountain. There are days when my words and deeds do not demonstrate my faith, and do not express the relationship I have with Jesus. How do you respond to impossible circumstances? Am I able to respond as someone who believes and trusts in God?

Prayers   *others may be added*

Faithful Lord, we bring our needs before you as we pray:

◆ Lord, hear our prayer.

For those who seek healing and mercy, we pray: ◆ For missionaries, we pray: ◆ For doctors, nurses, and all those who care for the sick and dying, we pray: ◆ For those who seek clarity as they struggle with questions of faith, we pray: ◆

Our Father . . .

Mighty Lord,
you call your children
    to life in your Kingdom.
We come to you with our doubts,
    weaknesses, and fears.
Strengthen our faith
and may we bear witness
    to your power and presence
at work in our lives.
Through Christ our Lord.
Amen

✝ Our Savior Jesus Christ has destroyed death and brought life to light through the Gospel.

✝ I am the living bread that came down from heaven, says the Lord; whoever eats this bread will live forever.

Psalm 8   page 400

Reading   *John 6:41–51*

[Jesus said to the crowds:] "No one can come to me unless the Father who sent me draw him, and I will raise him on the last day. It is written in the prophets: / *They shall all be taught by God.* / Everyone who listens to my Father and learns from him comes to me. Not that anyone has seen the Father except the one who is from God; he has seen the Father. Amen, amen, I say to you, whoever believes has eternal life. I am the bread of life. Your ancestors ate the manna in the desert but they died; this is the bread that comes from heaven so that one may eat it and not die. I am the living bread that came down from heaven; whoever eats this bread will live forever; and the bread that I will give is my flesh for the life of the world."

Reflection

The Jews are murmuring about Jesus' claim to be the bread of life. This bread is not like the bread that their ancestors ate in the desert. When the manna fell, the Israelites only gathered enough for one day, it provided nourishment for a short time. Jesus is the living bread and whoever eats this bread with live forever. We are called to the table to partake in and be nourished by this holy meal.

Prayers   *others may be added*

Lord, source of all life, we pray:

◆ Lord, hear our prayer.

For those in the Church who seek formation and opportunities to grow in their faith, we pray: ◆ For leaders of nations who strive to justly provide for their people, we pray: ◆ For those caregivers who offer love and compassion to family members who are ill, we pray: ◆ For those mothers and fathers who are deprived of sleep as they care for their children, we pray: ◆

Our Father . . .

Lord of life,
you nourish us
    with Bread from Heaven
so that we may one day join you
    in the Kingdom
for a feast that will never end.
Through Christ our Lord.
Amen

✝ I am the living bread that came down from heaven, says the Lord; whoever eats this bread will live forever.

✝ God has called you through the Gospel to possess the glory of our Lord Jesus Christ.

Psalm 42   *page 408*

Reading   *Matthew 17:24–27*

When they [Jesus and his disciples] came to Capernaum, the collectors of the temple tax approached Peter and said, "Does not your teacher pay the temple tax?" "Yes," he said. When he came into the house, before he had time to speak, Jesus asked him, "What is your opinion, Simon? From whom do the kings of the earth take tolls or census tax? From their subjects or from foreigners?" When he said, "From foreigners," Jesus said to him, "Then the subjects are exempt. But that we may not offend them, go to the sea, drop in a hook, and take the first fish that comes up. Open its mouth and you will find a coin worth twice the temple tax. Give that to them for me and for you."

Reflection

It was hard for the disciples to hear Jesus speak about the suffering that awaits him in Jerusalem. The conversation that follows between Jesus and Peter is another example of how we are to be dependent on God. God will provide for our spiritual growth and our earthly needs. Jesus uses this question about payment of tolls and taxes to remind Peter that God will provide. Miraculous things, like finding a coin in the mouth of a fish, happen when we have a relationship with Christ.

Prayers   *others may be added*

Savior, we ask you to deliver us, as we pray:

◆ Hear us, O Christ.

For harmony among the Church and civic leaders, we pray: ◆ For justice to reign in all aspects of society, we pray: ◆ For the wisdom to be good stewards of God's gifts, we pray: ◆ For joy and hope to fill those who despair, we pray: ◆

Our Father . . .

Lord God,
you give your children laws
so that we might live in your love.
Gift us with the power of your presence
so that we may always follow
    the spirit of your law of love,
and in doing so, know complete joy.
Through Christ our Lord.
Amen.

✝ God has called you through the Gospel to possess the glory of our Lord Jesus Christ.

✝ Whoever follows me will not walk in darkness but will have the light of life, says the Lord.

Psalm 42 *page 408*

Reading *John 12:24–26*

Jesus said to his disciples: "Amen, amen, I say to you, unless a grain of wheat falls to the ground and dies, it remains just a grain of wheat; but if it dies, it produces much fruit. Whoever loves his life loses it, and whoever hates his life in this world will preserve it for eternal life. Whoever serves me must follow me, and where I am, there also will my servant be. The Father will honor whoever serves me."

Reflection

Jesus loved his friends and family and wanted to prepare them for his death. He knew that his dying would be very hard for them and that they would have a difficult time understanding why it had to happen. In today's Gospel, Jesus told a parable that would help his friends understand: he spoke of a grain of wheat that falls to the ground and dies. Unless this seed dies, it could only remain that one small seed. But if it dies, something amazing happens. As we come to Mass, we experience the life, death, and resurrection of Jesus in celebration, and it makes our lives fuller through our transformation.

Prayers *others may be added*

Lord of all life, we turn to you and pray:

◆ Lord, hear us.

For those who shepherd our families through times of illness and mourning, we pray: ◆ For those who care for the sick and dying, we pray: ◆ For those in hospice care, we pray: ◆ For those who grieve, we pray: ◆

Our Father . . .

Lord of all,
you call us to listen to your Word
and help us to ponder
   the paschal mystery of Jesus.
Keep us mindful that the life, death,
   and resurrection of Jesus
is celebrated daily
   within each of our lives
and transforms our hearts.
Through Christ our Lord.
Amen.

✝ Whoever follows me will not walk in darkness but will have the light of life, says the Lord.

✝ God was reconciling the world
to himself in Christ, and entrusting
to us the message of reconciliation.

Psalm 8   *page 400*

Reading   *Matthew 18:15–18*

Jesus said to his disciples: "If your brother sins against you, go and tell him his fault between you and him alone. If he listens to you, you have won over your brother. If he does not listen, take one or two others along with you, so that every fact may be established on the testimony of two or three witnesses. If he refuses to listen to them, tell the Church. If he refuses to listen even to the Church, then treat him as you would a Gentile or a tax collector. Amen, I say to you, whatever you bind on earth shall be bound in heaven, and whatever you loose on earth shall be loosed in heaven."

Reflection

So much of Jesus' ministry and teaching was dedicated to the exercise of reconciliation between people(s). Many of his parables and his gestures of concern were about the healing of hearts and the forgiveness of sins. This passage seems to outline a particular ritual for the community on how to restore unity when a member sins against another. One thing is clear: Jesus wants the one who has sinned and the one who has been wronged to return to a peaceful relationship once again. This is to be done with honesty and respect for each other, and it is to include the others, who are the Church. It is not easy to ask for forgiveness or to extend forgiveness. But the message of the Gospel is clear—that is precisely what must happen if the community of believers is to live in the love of God.

Phil Horrigan (Daily Prayer 2009)

Prayers   *others may be added*

Turning to God, we pray:

◆ Lord, hear our prayer.

For those whose lives are filled with conflict, we pray: ◆ For those in the most need of God's healing and mercy, we pray: ◆ For those elected to civil service, we pray: ◆ For those who profess a vowed life as a Poor Clare, we pray: ◆

Our Father . . .

Lord of mercy,
we turn to you, the one who brings
    forgiveness and peace.
Keep us mindful
    of the opportunities for us
to serve as ministers of your peace
to a hurting and injured world.
Through Christ our Lord.
Amen.

✝ God was reconciling the world
to himself in Christ, and entrusting
to us the message of reconciliation.

✝ Let your countenance shine upon your servant and teach me your statutes.

Psalm 72   *page 412*

Reading   *Matthew 18:21–22*

Peter approached Jesus and said to him, "Lord, if my brother sins against me, how often must I forgive him? As many as seven times?" Jesus answered, "I say to you, not seven times but seventy-seven times."

Reflection

Whether we are forgiving another person or forgiving ourselves, forgiveness can be difficult. Forgiveness and mercy can bring healing and restoration where there is brokenness and pain. How do I seek forgiveness from my brother or sister while I continue to reflect upon those comments, actions, and decisions that I am not proud of and regret in my own heart? Jesus asks us to forgive from the heart. To begin to forgive our self, to forgive one another, and to seek forgiveness from the Lord, pray the Our Father and think about how you can live the words "Forgive us our trespasses, as we forgive those who trespass against us."

Prayers   *others may be added*

Merciful Lord, we come to you seeking healing, as we pray:

♦ Lord, hear our prayer.

For the Church to be an instrument of healing and peace, we pray: ♦ For those who are wounded by the deeds and words of others, we pray: ♦ For those who carry the burden of debt, we pray: ♦ For those affected by poverty, we pray: ♦

Our Father . . .

Good and gracious God,
when we are weighed down
    by the hardships of life;
may we find comfort and solace
    by resting in your Word.
May your grace and healing
    wash over us and cleanse us
from all that causes us pain.
Through Christ our Lord.
Amen.

✝ Let your countenance shine upon your servant and teach me your statutes.

✝ Receive the word of God, not as the word of men, but as it truly is, the word of God.

Psalm 35   *page 407*

Reading   *Matthew 19:3–6*

Some Pharisees approached Jesus, and tested him, saying, "Is it lawful for a man to divorce his wife for any cause whatever?" He said in reply, "Have you not read that from the beginning the Creator *made them male and female* and said, *For this reason a man shall leave his father and mother and be joined to his wife, and the two shall become one flesh?* So they are no longer two, but one flesh. Therefore, what God has joined together, man must not separate."

Reflection

The Pharisees approach Jesus to test him on the laws regarding marriage and divorce. Jesus' reply indicates that no matter what our state is in life, married or single, we are all called to love. While the plan of God includes marriage, we know the reality is that every family has been touched by the pain of broken relationships. We are called to show care and compassion to one another as we deal with the loss and sorrow of ending a relationship. May we pray today for all those who are struggling in their marriages.

Prayers   *others may be added*

Lord of love, as we work for the Kingdom, we pray:

♦ Lord, hear us.

For the Church to be an instrument of grace for all those seeking a covenant relationship, we pray: ♦ For those couples who are dealing with pain and sorrow in their relationships, we pray: ♦ For those discerning their vocation, may they trust God and his plan for their life, we pray: ♦ For those who are lonely and in need of companionship, may we seek to include them in the life of our community, we pray: ♦

Our Father . . .

Holy God,
in the waters of baptism,
we have been united
     to your Son, Jesus.
Help us to love one another
     as you love us
and may our lives give you glory.
Through Christ our Lord.
Amen.

✝ Receive the word of God, not as the word of men, but, as it truly is, the word of God.

✝ Blessed are you, Father, Lord of heaven and earth; you have revealed to little ones the mysteries of the Kingdom.

Psalm 60 *page 410*

Reading *Matthew 19:13–15*

Children were brought to Jesus that he might lay his hands on them and pray. The disciples rebuked them, but Jesus said, "Let the children come to me, and do not prevent them; for the Kingdom of heaven belongs to such as these." After he placed his hands on them, he went away.

Reflection

The child leads the adult to enter the Kingdom of God. How does that happen? We see wonder alive in the child. The sense of wonder is one of the child's deepest and most serious capacities. Wonder is a deep emotional response of joy, gratitude, and awe. Wonder is what draws us to God, like a starry night draws us out into the mystery of the universe. The child notices the details often overlooked by the busy and over stimulated adult. Only through contemplating and observing our reality, can we become conscious of the mysteries contained within.

Prayers *others may be added*

With awe and wonder, we pray:

◆ Lord, hear our prayer.

For parents and catechists, we pray: ◆ For creative and innovative people, we pray: ◆ For the poor and neglected, we pray: ◆ For children preparing to receive the sacraments, we pray: ◆ For victims of war, violence, and abuse, we pray: ◆

Our Father . . .

O wondrous God,
you reveal the mystery of
    the Kingdom in your Son, Jesus.
Rouse our hearts
    to live with wonder and awe
at your presence
so that forever we may give you glory.
Through Christ our Lord.
Amen.

✝ Blessed are you, Father, Lord of heaven and earth; you have revealed to little ones the mysteries of the Kingdom.

✝ Mary is taken up to heaven;
a chorus of angels exults.

Psalm 8   *page 400*

Reading   *Luke 1:39–45*

Mary set out in those days and traveled to the hill country in haste to a town of Judah, where she entered the house of Zechariah and greeted Elizabeth. When Elizabeth heard Mary's greeting, the infant leaped in her womb, and Elizabeth, filled with the Holy Spirit, cried out in a loud voice and said, "Blessed are you among women, and blessed is the fruit of your womb. And how does this happen to me, that the mother of my Lord should come to me? For at the moment the sound of your greeting reached my ears, the infant in my womb leaped for joy. Blessed are you who believed that what was spoken to you by the Lord would be fulfilled."

Reflection

Mary and Elizabeth lived a good distance from one another and were of different ages, but in the Gospel, they appear to have a very close relationship. The power of the Holy Spirit is a power that brings mysterious knowledge to Elizabeth who knew immediately that Mary was the "mother of her Lord." Baby John knew the Lord was near because he leapt in his mother's womb. The Holy Spirit brings new life, joy, and new knowledge.

Prayers   *others may be added*

Lord of all, we turn to you and pray:

◆ **Lord, hear our prayer.**

May the Church be a model of Mary's joy, we pray: ◆ May world leader provide safety for their people, we pray: ◆ May families witness compassion in the world, we pray: ◆ May those who are pregnant rest in God's protection, we pray: ◆

Our Father . . .

O God,
creator and source of all that is good,
you made us in the divine image.
Grant us the grace
to recognize your Son, Jesus,
in those we meet
and in all our work.
Through Christ our Lord.
Amen.

✝ Mary is taken up to heaven;
a chorus of angels exults.

☦ Blessed are the poor in spirit; for theirs is the Kingdom of heaven.

Psalm 96 *page 413*

Reading *Matthew 19:16–22*

A young man approached Jesus and said, "Teacher, what good must I do to gain eternal life?" . . . Jesus said to him, "If you wish to be perfect, go, sell what you have and give to the poor, and you will have treasure in heaven. Then come, follow me." When the young man heard this statement, he went away sad, for he had many possessions.

Reflection

The young man seeks to be close to God, but he finds great security in his possessions and wealth. As we strive to be close to the Lord, what would it mean for us to sell all we have and give to the poor? Is Jesus actually asking us to let go of all that we own? Or are there other things that would be beneficial for us to let go of (i.e., bad attitudes, unhealthy habits, gripes about my coworker, procrastination or laziness)? It would be much easier to serve the poor and to gain eternal life if we were not burdened with that which may seem comforting, but in actuality does not bring life.

Prayers *others may be added*

Lord of all, we turn to you as we pray:

◆ Lord, hear our prayer.

For all the baptized in the ongoing journey of conversion, we pray: ◆ For the poor and homeless in their pursuit of justice, we pray: ◆ For the sick and dying who share in Christ's passion and resurrection, we pray: ◆ For judges and lawyers who work for the common good, we pray: ◆

Our Father . . .

Eternal God,
you give us the gift of salvation.
Help us to see the path
    that leads us to the Kingdom
and give us wisdom and strength
to follow you.
Through Christ our Lord.
Amen

☦ Blessed are the poor in spirit; for theirs is the Kingdom of heaven.

✝ Jesus Christ became poor although he was rich so that by his poverty you might become rich.

Psalm 33   *page 406*

Reading   *Matthew 19:23–26*

Jesus said to his disciples: "Amen, I say to you, it will be hard for one who is rich to enter the Kingdom of heaven. Again I say to you, it is easier for a camel to pass through the eye of a needle than for one who is rich to enter the Kingdom of God." When the disciples heard this, they were greatly astonished and said, "Who then can be saved?" Jesus looked at them and said, "For men this is impossible, but for God all things are possible."

Reflection

Jesus tells his disciples that there will be great difficulty for the rich to enter the Kingdom of heaven. It will be easier for a camel to pass through the eye of a needle. The eye of the needle is a figure of speech for a very small or narrow passageway. It would seem an impossible task for a camel. Moreover, it would be a radical change for a wealthy person to be separated from his or her riches and possessions. What is Jesus asking of me, does it seem unreasonable or unbearable for my life? What does he want me to know about God's Kingdom?

Prayers   *others may be added*

In confidence, we pray:

♦ **Lord, hear our prayer.**

For the Church who witnesses the providential love of God, we pray: ♦ For world leaders who care for the poor, we pray: ♦ For the sick who reveal the compassion of God, we pray: ♦ For the baptized who seek the living God, we pray: ♦

Our Father . . .

Lord God,
the world attempts
    to pull us away from you.
Give us strength
so that our words and actions
may express our absolute trust in
your Son, our Lord Jesus Christ
who lives and reigns with you
in unity of the Holy Spirit,
one God for ever and ever.
Amen.

✝ Jesus Christ became poor although he was rich so that by his poverty you might become rich.

✝ The word of God is living and effective, able to discern reflections and thoughts of the heart.

Psalm 85　　　　　page 413

Reading　　　　　*Matthew 20:8–15*

[Jesus said:] "When it was evening the owner of the vineyard said to his foreman, 'Summon the laborers and give them their pay, beginning with the last and ending with the first.' When those who had started about five o'clock came, each received the usual daily wage. So when the first came, they thought that they would receive more, but each of them also got the usual wage. And on receiving it they grumbled against the landowner, saying, 'These last ones worked only one hour, and you have made them equal to us, who bore the day's burden and the heat.' He said to one of them in reply, 'My friend, I am not cheating you. Did you not agree with me for the usual daily wage? Take what is yours and go. What if I wish to give this last one the same as you? Or am I not free to do as I wish with my own money? Are you envious because I am generous?'"

Reflection

The landowner asks, "Are you envious because I am generous?" It is easy to identify with the workers who grumble against the landowner and feel cheated by his generosity. Are we able to rejoice in the good fortune of our brothers and sisters? Is it difficult for us to be grateful for God's fairness and generosity?

God calls each person to participate in his Kingdom through the joy and labor of work, no matter if they arrive early in the morning or show up late in the afternoon.

Prayers　　　*others may be added*

Generous Lord, we turn to you as we pray:

◆ Lord, hear our prayer.

That the dignity and rights of workers be upheld, we pray: ◆ That elected officials may lead with kindness rather than criticism, we pray: ◆ That we may be filled with compassion for others, we pray: ◆ That the poor may find hope in the Lord, we pray: ◆

Our Father . . .

O God,
you are kind and merciful
and you invite us to work
　　in the vineyard as colaborers
　　in building the Kingdom.
Help us to respond to you
　　with grateful hearts,
Through Christ our Lord.
Amen.

✝ The word of God is living and effective, able to discern reflections and thoughts of the heart.

✝ If today you hear his voice, harden not your hearts.

Psalm 116   *page 416*

Reading   *Matthew 22:2–3, 8–9, 10ac, 11–14*

[Jesus said:] "The Kingdom of heaven may be likened to a king who gave a wedding feast for his son. He dispatched his servants to summon the invited guests to the feast, but they refused to come. . . . Then the king said to his servants, 'The feast is ready, but those who were invited were not worthy to come. Go out, therefore, into the main roads and invite to the feast whomever you find.' The servants went out into the streets and gathered all they found, . . . and the hall was filled with guests. But when the king came in to meet the guests he saw a man there not dressed in a wedding garment. He said to him, 'My friend, how is it that you came in here without a wedding garment?' But he was reduced to silence. Then the king said to his attendants, 'Bind his hands and feet, and cast him into the darkness outside, where there will be wailing and grinding of teeth.' Many are invited, but few are chosen."

Reflection

The guest is speechless when confronted by the king. The man's lack of response lands him in the darkness, alone. Had he asked for mercy, would the king have welcomed him to remain at the banquet? The Lord continues to call us. We are chosen to come to the feast. He gives us the opening, the grace to make things different, to restore our relationship. We respond as a community, "Lord, I am not worthy that you should enter under my roof, but only say the word and my soul shall be healed." The feast awaits.

Prayers   *others may be added*

Merciful Lord, we turn to you as we pray:

◆ Lord, hear our prayer.

That we may be hospitable, we pray: ◆ That governments lead with justice, we pray: ◆ That the sick might be comforted, we pray: ◆ That we might seek forgiveness, we pray: ◆

Our Father . . .

Loving God,
we come to you seeking shelter,
and long to see your face.
Do not let us be taken
   from your presence.
Through Christ our Lord.
Amen.

✝ If today you hear his voice, harden not your hearts.

✝ Teach me your paths, my God,
guide me in your truth.

Psalm 47   *page 409*

Reading   *Matthew 22: 34–40*

When the Pharisees heard that Jesus had silenced the Sadducees, they gathered together, and one of them a scholar of the law, tested him by asking, "Teacher, which commandment in the law is the greatest?" Jesus said to him, "You shall love the Lord, your God, with all your heart, with all your soul, and with all your mind. This is the greatest and the first commandment. The second is like it: You shall love your neighbor as yourself. The whole law and the prophets depend on these two commandments."

Reflection

God desires that we love him with all of our heart, soul, and mind, echoing the words from the book of Deuteronomy (6:5). Jesus goes further. He gave us a new commandment: "Love one another as I have loved you." Jesus wants to be a model for how we are to love. He invites us to observe how he loves and to love our brothers and sisters in the same way. If we are able to love as Jesus loves, then we will have a life of complete joy. A life filled with his joy.

Prayers   *others may be added*

Lord of love, we come to you,
as we pray:

◆ Hear us, O God.

Help the Church to live out the corporal works of mercy, we pray: ◆ Strengthen civic leaders in their work of caring for those in need, we pray: ◆ Heal and bring comfort to the sick and suffering, we pray: ◆ Enliven our parishes to bring love to the world, we pray: ◆

Our Father . . .

Lord Jesus,
you gave us the great commandment
so that we would know how we are to live
    in response to the Father's love,
and in turn, give him glory.
You live and reign with God the Father,
in unity with the Holy Spirit,
one God for ever and ever.
Amen.

✝ Teach me your paths, my God,
guide me in your truth.

✝ You have but one Father in heaven;
you have but one master, the Christ.

Psalm 100   *page 414*

Reading   *Matthew 23:1–12*

Jesus spoke to the crowds and to his disciples, saying, "The scribes and the Pharisees have taken their seat on the chair of Moses. Therefore, do and observe all things whatsoever they tell you, but do not follow their example. For they preach but they do not practice. They tie up heavy burdens hard to carry and lay them on people's shoulders, but they will not lift a finger to move them. All their works are performed to be seen. They widen their phylacteries and lengthen their tassels. They love places of honor at banquets, seats of honor in synagogues, greetings in marketplaces, and the salutation 'Rabbi.' As for you, do not be called 'Rabbi.' You have but one teacher, and you are all brothers. Call no one on earth your father; you have but one Father in heaven. Do not be called 'Master'; you have but one master, the Christ. The greatest among you must be your servant. Whoever exalts himself will be humbled; but whoever humbles himself will be exalted."

Reflection

Jesus tells the people that titles and the status that accompany them are not important. The last title listed in today's Gospel is that of servant. While the scribe, Pharisee, teacher, and rabbi all have a role within the community, it is the humble servant who lives the law of love. The role of the disciple is to serve his brother and sister, and not to sit back and expect to be waited upon. May we accept the role of the servant, so that we may also serve our Master, Jesus Christ.

Prayers   *others may be added*

Servant of all, we turn to you as we pray:

◆ Lord, hear our prayer.

For bishops and pastors, that they may be humble servants to God's people, we pray: ◆ For world leaders, that they may not abuse the power and status of their position, we pray: ◆ For laborers, that they may receive God's grace, we pray: ◆ For families, that their divisions may be healed, we pray: ◆

Our Father . . .

Lord Jesus,
you call us to be your disciple
   and to live a life of service.
May we be faithful witnesses
   to your power and presence
   in the world,
and in doing so,
give the Father glory.
You live and reign with God
   the Father,
in unity with the Holy Spirit,
one God for ever and ever.
Amen.

✝ You have but one Father in heaven;
you have but one master, the Christ.

✝ Your words, Lord, are Spirit and life; you have the words of everlasting life.

Psalm 8   *page 400*

Reading   *John 6:60–69*

Many of the disciples of Jesus who were listening said, "This saying is hard; who can accept it?" Since Jesus knew that his disciples were murmuring about this, he said to them, "Does this shock you? What if you were to see the Son of Man ascending to where he was before? It is the Spirit that gives life, while the flesh is of no avail. The words I have spoken to you are Spirit and life. But there are some of you who do not believe." Jesus knew from the beginning the ones who would not believe and the one who would betray him. And he said, "For this reason I have told you that no one can come to me unless it is granted him by my Father."

As a result of this, many of his disciples returned to their former way of life and no longer walked with him. Jesus then said to the Twelve, "Do you also want to leave?" Simon Peter answered him, "Master, to whom shall we go? You have the words of eternal life. We have come to believe and are convinced that you are the Holy One of God."

Reflection

Jesus' followers found his teaching on the bread of life difficult to understand. Some chose that moment to walk away from him and return to their former life. Jesus then turns to his disciples and asks them if they too want to leave. Peter responds with the proclamation that Jesus has the words of eternal life. Even though Peter may not have fully comprehended what the Lord was telling him, he realized that Jesus was the Holy One of God. When faced with the difficulties and problems of life, to whom do we go? Do we turn to Scripture as a source for understanding, guidance and life?

Prayers   *others may be added*

Path of life, we come to you,
as we pray:

◆ Lord, hear our prayer.

For the Church, that she may work toward solidarity among all people, we pray: ◆ For elected leaders, that they create communities where unity and love prevail, we pray: ◆ For those who no longer practice the faith, that they may return to the table of the Lord, we pray: ◆ For those who face isolation from their families, that they know the presence of God, we pray: ◆

Our Father . . .

O God,
you call us to follow you as disciples.
Even when we our challenged
   by the task before us,
help us to respond to that call,
   with a joyful heart.
You live and reign with God the Father,
in unity with the Holy Spirit,
one God for ever and ever.
Amen.

✝ Your words, Lord, are Spirit and life; you have the words of everlasting life.

Monday, August 23, 2021
Optional Memorial of St. Rose of Lima, Virgin

✝ My sheep hear my voice, says the Lord; I know them, and they follow me.

Psalm 42
page 408

Reading
Matthew 23:13

Jesus said to the crowds and to his disciples: "Woe to you, scribes and Pharisees, you hypocrites. You lock the Kingdom of heaven before men. You do not enter yourselves, nor do you allow entrance to those trying to enter."

Reflection

Jesus accuses the scribes and Pharisees of actually blocking the entrance to the Kingdom of God. I would like to think that the Lord is using my words, my actions, my gifts to further the work of his Kingdom; but in reality, there may be times when my own thoughts, behavior, and comments have been an obstacle to those who long to draw near to God. Let us ask the Lord for mercy as we work to hasten the coming of the Kingdom.

Prayers
others may be added

Lord of all power and life, we turn to you as we pray:

◆ Lord, hear our prayer.

For those who preach the Gospel in word and deed, we pray: ◆ For world leaders who work for justice, we pray: ◆ For young people who seek wisdom and truth, we pray: ◆ For those who experience chronic pain and discomfort, we pray: ◆

Our Father . . .

Eternal Father,
help us in our disbelief
so that we draw close to your Son
    and follow him,
who is the way, the truth,
and the life.
Through Christ our Lord.
Amen.

✝ My sheep hear my voice, says the Lord; I know them, and they follow me.

☩ Rabbi, you are the Son of God;
you are the King of Israel.

Psalm 116   *page 416*

Reading   *John 1:45–49*

Philip found Nathanael and told him, "We have found the one about whom Moses wrote in the law, and also the prophets, Jesus son of Joseph, from Nazareth." But Nathanael said to him, "Can anything good come from Nazareth?" Philip said to him, "Come and see." Jesus saw Nathanael coming toward him and said of him, "Here is a true child of Israel. There is no duplicity in him." Nathanael said to him, "How do you know me?" Jesus answered and said to him, "Before Philip called you, I saw you under the fig tree." Nathanael answered him, "Rabbi, you are the Son of God; you are the King of Israel."

Reflection

Today the Church celebrates the apostle Bartholomew, who is identified with Nathaniel, mentioned in today's Gospel. Philip brings Nathaniel to Jesus, telling him that this is the promised Messiah. Though Nathaniel is skeptical at first, when he comes face to face with Jesus, he finds that Jesus knows him already: "I saw you under the fig tree." Nathaniel responds at once, with a profession of faith that goes even deeper than Philip's. Philip recognized the one about whom prophets spoke; Nathaniel recognizes "the Son of God," "the King of Israel." And Jesus promises Nathaniel a vision more wonderful even than the ladder Jacob dreamed about—the heavens opened, and he saw the angels "ascending and descending on the Son of Man." On the hill of Calvary, that vision would be fulfilled.

Daily Prayer 2010

Prayers   *others may be added*

Lord of love, we turn to you as we pray:

♦ Lord, hear our prayer.

For those who teach the Word of God, we pray: ♦ For those who advocate for peace and justice, we pray: ♦ For those who are homeless, we pray: ♦ For those who advocate for the dignity of workers, we pray: ♦

Our Father . . .

Lord Jesus,
you called Bartholomew
   to follow you,
and you gave him authority
   to teach and preach
   in your name.
Grant us wisdom and courage
to share the Good News
   of your salvation.
You live and reign with God
   the Father,
in unity with the Holy Spirit,
one God for ever and ever.
Amen.

☩ Rabbi, you are the Son of God;
you are the King of Israel.

✝ Whoever keeps the word of Christ,
the love of God is truly perfected
in him.

Psalm 70   *page 411*

Reading   *I Thessalonians 2:9–13*

You recall, brothers and sisters, our toil
and drudgery. Working night and day
in order not to burden any of you, we
proclaimed to you the Gospel of God.
You are witnesses, and so is God, how
devoutly and justly and blamelessly we
behaved toward you believers. As you
know, we treated each one of you as a
father treats his children, exhorting and
encouraging you and insisting that you
walk in a manner worthy of the God who
calls you into his Kingdom and glory.

   And for this reason we too give thanks
to God unceasingly, that, in receiving
the word of God from hearing us, you
received it not as the word of men, but
as it truly is, the word of God, which is
now at work in you who believe.

Reflection

Paul is not bragging about his work and
his mission; rather, he is offering
encouragement for continuing efforts to
proclaim the Gospel. We can only imagine how difficult it must have been for
the fledgling communities of faith to
keep up their hope and enthusiasm for
this new way of life. Perhaps we take it
for granted that living and proclaiming
the message of the Gospel is easy, since
we are not subject to any great persecution in our part of the world. That is
not the case everywhere. Yet we need
encouragement in our mission; we can
be discouraged when our efforts don't
seem to instill excitement or acceptance
by others. These words of Paul can be a
good affirmation of our task as disciples
and a reminder to pray daily for those
who continue to preach the Gospel, even
when it is difficult and dangerous.

Phil Horrigan (Daily Prayer 2009)

Prayers   *others may be added*

   Lord, we turn to you and pray:

◆ **Hear us, O Christ.**

Grant the Church wisdom and
understanding, we pray: ◆ Grant leaders
knowledge and counsel, we pray: ◆
Grant fortitude to those who are
persecuted, we pray: ◆ Grant piety and
counsel to those making decision,
we pray: ◆

Our Father . . .

Good and gracious God,
in times of trouble,
we place our lives in your hands.
Heal us and give us the grace
   to speak the Good News
in every corner of the world.
Through Christ our Lord.
Amen.

✝ Whoever keeps the word of Christ,
the love of God is truly perfected
in him.

✝ Stay awake! For you do not know when the Son of Man will come.

Psalm 60 *page 410*

Reading *Matthew 24:42–44*

Jesus said to his disciples: "Stay awake! For you do not know on which day your Lord will come. Be sure of this: if the master of the house had known the hour of night when the thief was coming, he would have stayed awake and not let his house be broken into. So too, you also must be prepared, for at an hour you do not expect, the Son of Man will come."

Reflection

It is easy to become caught up in the details and the busyness of our day-to-day living, so much so that we neglect to "stay awake," to pray, to pay attention to our relationship with the Lord. We do not know the hour when the Master will return, but we want to be prepared for his arrival. We need to spend each day nurturing the relationship with the Master, so that when he does come back, we may be ready and he may recognize us as that faithful and prudent servant.

Prayers *others may be added*

Gracious God, we turn to you and pray:

◆ O God, hear us.

That the Church may be a faithful servant, we pray: ◆ That preachers be sustained by God's Word, we pray: ◆ That the baptized cooperate with God's grace to build up the Kingdom, we pray: ◆ That the lonely and afraid may find comfort in our parishes, we pray: ◆

Our Father . . .

Lord and Master of my life,
grant us the wisdom
   to recognize your presence.
In my coming and going,
   in my waking and sleeping,
   in my joy and in my sorrow,
stay with me O Lord,
and hold me close to your heart.
Amen.

✝ Stay awake! For you do not know when the Son of Man will come.

✝ Be vigilant at all times and pray, that you may have the strength to stand before the Son of Man.

Psalm 36 *page 408*

Reading *Matthew 25:1–13*

Jesus told his disciples this parable: "The Kingdom of heaven will be like ten virgins who took their lamps and went out to meet the bridegroom. Five of them were foolish and five were wise. The foolish ones, when taking their lamps, brought no oil with them, but the wise brought flasks of oil with their lamps. Since the bridegroom was long delayed, they all became drowsy and fell asleep. At midnight, there was a cry, 'Behold, the bridegroom! Come out to meet him!' Then all those virgins got up and trimmed their lamps. The foolish ones said to the wise, 'Give us some of your oil, for our lamps are going out.' But the wise ones replied, 'No, for there may not be enough for us and you. Go instead to the merchants and buy some for yourselves.' While they went off to buy it, the bridegroom came and those who were ready went into the wedding feast with him. Then the door was locked. Afterwards the other virgins came and said, 'Lord, Lord, open the door for us!' But he said in reply, 'Amen, I say to you, I do not know you.' Therefore, stay awake, for you know neither the day nor the hour."

Reflection

In the depth of the darkness, we groan, "Lord, Lord, open the door for us!" That was the cry of the five foolish virgins only to hear the response, "Amen, I say to you, I do not know you." How devastating to be standing at the door to the wedding feast and be told by the bridegroom that he does not know you. The bridesmaids in this parable had a particular role to fulfill. They greeted and lit the way for the bridegroom as he came to the feast. We too have a particular role to prepare for the Kingdom of God. How can we hasten the coming of the Kingdom and ensure that we enter the feast?

Prayers *others may be added*

Lord of light, we turn to you and pray:

◆ Hear us, O Christ.

For the Church, that she may be a light for all to see, we pray: ◆ For those preparing for sacramental anointing, that they may encounter the risen Christ, we pray: ◆ For those who live in poverty, that they may receive needed assistance, we pray: ◆ For mothers, that they always care for their children with love, we pray: ◆

Our Father . . .

Merciful Father,
in baptism we received the light of Christ.
Help us prepare and ready our light,
so that it may shine for all to see.
Make us ready
    for the eternal banquet.
Through Christ our Lord.
Amen.

✝ Be vigilant at all times and pray, that you may have the strength to stand before the Son of Man.

Saturday, August 28, 2021
Memorial of St. Augustine, Bishop and Doctor of the Church

✝ I give you a new commandment: love one another as I have loved you.

Psalm 145 *page 420*

Reading *Matthew 25:14–15, 19–21*
Jesus told his disciples this parable: "A man going on a journey called in his servants and entrusted his possessions to them. To one he gave five talents; to another, two; to a third, one—to each according to his ability. Then he went away. . . . After a long time the master of those servants came back and settled accounts with them. The one who had received five talents came forward bringing the additional five. He said, 'Master, you gave me five talents. See, I have made five more.' His master said to him, 'Well done, my good and faithful servant. Since you were faithful in small matters, I will give you great responsibilities. Come, share your master's joy.'"

Reflection
In Biblical times, a talent meant a large sum of money. The talents are entrusted to the servants. The servants are expected to develop the talents on behalf of the Master. God has given each of us gifts and talents. It is our responsibility as baptized Christians to use those gifts of the Spirit, to develop them, to share them, in order to hasten the coming of the Kingdom and enter into the fullness of the Master's joy. What would happen if someone did not use the talent that God has given them?

Prayers *others may be added*
Spirit of life, we turn to you as we pray:

◆ Lord, hear our prayer.

For the Church to care for the vulnerable among us, we pray: ◆ For leaders of nations to be just in the distribution of resources, we pray: ◆ For the elderly to find strength in Christ, we pray: ◆ For those who seek just employment, we pray: ◆

Our Father . . .

Generous Father,
you have entrusted your servants
   with gifts and talents.
Awaken in us a desire
   to use our gifts to build up
   the Kingdom.
Through Christ our Lord.
Amen.

✝ I give you a new commandment: love one another as I have loved you.

Sunday, August 29, 2021
Twenty-Second Sunday in Ordinary Time

† The Father willed to give us birth by the word of truth that we may be a kind of firstfruits of his creatures.

Psalm 8   *page 400*

Reading   *Deuteronomy 4:1–2, 6–8*

Moses said to the people: "Now, Israel, hear the statutes and decrees which I am teaching you to observe, that you may live, and may enter in and take possession of the land which the LORD, the God of your fathers, is giving you. In your observance of the commandments of the LORD, your God, which I enjoin upon you, you shall not add to what I command you nor subtract from it. Observe them carefully, for thus will you give evidence of your wisdom and intelligence to the nations, who will hear of all these statutes and say, 'This great nation is truly a wise and intelligent people.' For what great nation is there that has gods so close to it as the LORD, our God, is to us whenever we call upon him? Or what great nation has statutes and decrees that are as just as this whole law which I am setting before you today?"

Reflection

When we think of laws, we may imagine a list of what is restricted. The purpose of the law found in the Book of Deuteronomy was to draw people closer to God. After captivity in Egypt, the community experiences freedom. They had no idea of how to live and needed the limits found within the law to guide their actions and their hearts. God cares

for his chosen people and wants to be in an intimate relationship with them.

Prayers   *others may be added*

Turning our hearts toward God, we pray:

◆ Lord, hear our prayer.

For leaders in the Church, we pray: ◆
For leaders of nations, we pray: ◆
For those in prison, we pray: ◆ For those with scrupulous hearts, we pray: ◆ For the sick and dying, we pray: ◆

Our Father . . .

Lord,
instill in all of those entrusted
with preaching the Gospel,
your wisdom and justice
so that all generations
may come to know the Living Word,
your Son, our Lord Jesus Christ,
who lives and reigns with you
in unity of the Holy Spirit,
one God for ever and ever.
Amen.

† The Father willed to give us birth by the word of truth that we may be a kind of firstfruits of his creatures.

✝ The Spirit of the Lord is upon me;
he has sent me to bring glad tidings
to the poor.

Psalm 34 — page 406

Reading — Luke 4:16–21

Jesus came to Nazareth, where he had grown up, and went according to his custom into the synagogue on the sabbath day. He stood up to read and was handed a scroll of the prophet Isaiah. He unrolled the scroll and found the passage where it was written:

The Spirit of the Lord is upon me, / because he has anointed me / to bring glad tidings to the poor. / He has sent me to proclaim liberty to captives / and recovery of sight to the blind, / to let the oppressed go free, / and to proclaim a year acceptable to the Lord. / Rolling up the scroll, he handed it back to the attendant and sat down, and the eyes of all in the synagogue looked intently at him. He said to them, "Today this Scripture passage is fulfilled in your hearing."

Reflection

Jesus takes the words of the prophet Isaiah and applies them to himself when he proclaims, "Today this Scripture passage is fulfilled in your hearing." Those who listened in the synagogue that day were filled with fury. There are moments in our own lives when we do not meet the expectations of our family, neighbors, and coworkers. We may have had moments when we hold tightly to our misguided presumptions about another person. When we judge others, do we allow ourselves the ability to recognize the work of the Holy Spirit? Let us carry the words of St. Teresa of Calcutta with us, "If you judge people, you have no time to love them."

Prayers — others may be added

Turning to the Lord, we pray:

◆ Lord, hear our prayer.

For ministers of the Word, we pray: ◆
For judges and lawmakers, we pray: ◆
For the sick and suffering, we pray: ◆
For the parish community, we pray: ◆

Our Father . . .

We turn to your Word, O God,
when we seek comfort, solace,
    and guidance for our daily living.
Make us attentive to Scripture
as we make decisions
    that impact our family,
our world, and our own relationship
    with your Son,
our Lord Jesus Christ,
who lives and reigns with you
in unity of the Holy Spirit,
one God for ever and ever.
Amen.

✝ The Spirit of the Lord is upon me;
he has sent me to bring glad tidings
to the poor.

✝ A great prophet has arisen in our midst and God has visited his people.

Psalm 127   *page 418*

Reading   *Luke 4:31–37*

Jesus went down to Capernaum, a town of Galilee. He taught them on the sabbath, and they were astonished at his teaching because he spoke with authority. In the synagogue there was a man with the spirit of an unclean demon, and he cried out in a loud voice, "What have you to do with us, Jesus of Nazareth? Have you come to destroy us? I know who you are—the Holy One of God!" Jesus rebuked him and said, "Be quiet! Come out of him!" Then the demon threw the man down in front of them and came out of him without doing him any harm. They were all amazed and said to one another, "What is there about his word? For with authority and power he commands the unclean spirits, and they come out." And news of him spread everywhere in the surrounding region.

Reflection

Jesus spoke with such power and authority that the unclean demon was silenced and came out of the man without doing him any harm. In what ways do we allow Jesus to have authority over our lives? When we recognize the presence of evil in the world, do we give in to worry and doubt, or do we trust in the presence and power of the risen Christ to protect and heal? Let us pray for all those who seek to be freed from what traps, binds, and destroys their life with Jesus.

Prayers   *others may be added*

Author of life, we turn to you as we pray:

◆ Hear us, O God.

That peace may overcome those filled with fear and anxiety, we pray: ◆ That healing grace may be given to those who suffer, we pray: ◆ That wisdom and right judgement fill civic leaders, we pray: ◆ That eternal life be granted to all those who have died, we pray: ◆

Our Father . . .

Holy God,
you offer us freedom and life
so that we may live
     as your covenant people.
Help us to enter into
     the wonder and awe
     that comes from following
your Son, our Lord Jesus Christ,
who lives and reigns with you
in unity of the Holy Spirit,
one God for ever and ever.
Amen.

✝ A great prophet has arisen in our midst and God has visited his people.

✝ The Lord sent me to bring glad tidings to the poor and to proclaim liberty to captives.

Psalm 127   *page 418*

Reading   *Luke 4:38–44*

After Jesus left the synagogue, he entered the house of Simon. Simon's mother-in-law was afflicted with a severe fever, and they interceded with him about her. He stood over her, rebuked the fever, and it left her. She got up immediately and waited on them.

At sunset, all who had people sick with various diseases brought them to him. He laid his hands on each of them and cured them. And demons also came out from many, shouting, "You are the Son of God." But he rebuked them and did not allow them to speak because they knew that he was the Christ.

At daybreak, Jesus left and went to a deserted place. The crowds went looking for him, and when they came to him, they tried to prevent him from leaving them. But he said to them, "To the other towns also I must proclaim the good news of the Kingdom of God, because for this purpose I have been sent." And he was preaching in the synagogues of Judea.

Reflection

Healing can occur in the family home, allowing those who dwell there to be restored to wholeness and even serve one another. Healing can occur within a community, allowing those who are weakened by disease to be restored to life. Healing can occur at daybreak, at sunset; it can be realized in cities and towns and deserted places. What aspects of my own life are in need of Jesus' healing touch? Who in my home or community need my loving support and my healing presence today?

Prayers   *others may be added*

God of all mercies, we ask you:

◆ Hear, our prayer, O God.

For those who care for the sick, homebound, and anyone suffering, we pray: ◆ For those who lack food, shelter, and medicine, we pray: ◆ For those who have restless hearts, we pray: ◆ For families who seek healing, we pray: ◆

Our Father . . .

O healing God,
we come to you seeking wholeness
    for the places and moments
where brokenness
    and disorder reside.
Transform and restore us
so that my service may hasten
    the work of the Kingdom.
Through Christ our Lord.
Amen.

✝ The Lord sent me to bring glad tidings to the poor and to proclaim liberty to captives.

✝ Come after me, says the Lord,
and I will make you fishers of men.

Psalm 127   *page 418*

Reading   *Luke 5:4–7,10b*

[Jesus] said to Simon, "Put out into deep water and lower your nets for a catch." Simon said in reply, "Master, we have worked hard all night and have caught nothing, but at your command I will lower the nets." When they had done this, they caught a great number of fish and their nets were tearing. They signaled to their partners in the other boat to come to help them. They came and filled both boats so that the boats were in danger of sinking. . . . Jesus said to Simon, "Do not be afraid; from now on you will be catching men." When they brought their boats to the shore, they left everything and followed him.

Reflection

Jesus invites Simon to lower his net in the deep water. The result is a catch of fish so large that the nets begin to tear, and Simon fears the boat may sink. He calls his friends to come and assist with their boats. Soon the abundance of the catch of fish puts the safety of both boats in peril. Alone, Simon nearly sinks and is unable to complete the task. Like Simon, we need the help of our friends to accomplish the mission before us. The Word of God calls us into relationship with him and with one another. How has the Word and the efforts of your community assisted you in times of risk or danger? When has the Word and your neighbor called you to mission? Do you share the abundance of God's grace and mercy with your friends and neighbors?

Prayers   *others may be added*

Lord God, we call to you as we pray:

◆ Lord, hear our prayer.

For those who preach the Gospel, we pray: ◆ For all leaders, we pray: ◆ For the sick and suffering, we pray: ◆ For those who lack faith, we pray: ◆ For the poor and hungry, we pray: ◆

Our Father . . .

Lord of abundance,
you call us to listen to your Word
and strengthen us for the mission.
Allow me to see your presence
     in the heart of those
     who journey with me
and in the face of those
     who seek you.
Through Christ, our Lord.
Amen.

✝ Come after me, says the Lord,
and I will make you fishers of men.

✝ I am the light of the world, says
the Lord; whoever follows me will
have the light of life.

Psalm 33 *page 406*

Reading *Luke 5:33–39*

The scribes and Pharisees said to Jesus,
"The disciples of John the Baptist fast
often and offer prayers, and the disciples
of the Pharisees do the same; but yours
eat and drink." Jesus answered them,
"Can you make the wedding guests fast
while the bridegroom is with them? But
the days will come, and when the bridegroom is taken away from them, then
they will fast in those days." And he
also told them a parable. "No one tears
a piece from a new cloak to patch an old
one. Otherwise, he will tear the new and
the piece from it will not match the old
cloak. Likewise, no one pours new wine
into old wineskins. Otherwise, the new
wine will burst the skins, and it will be
spilled, and the skins will be ruined.
Rather, new wine must be poured into
fresh wineskins. And no one who has
been drinking old wine desires new, for
he says, 'The old is good.'"

Reflection

Winemaking and the fermentation process pushes and stretches the wineskins.
Anyone who has owned a leather garment knows that, as time goes on, the
leather stiffens and becomes rigid. We
are the wineskins; Christ is the new
wine. He is going to push and stretch us
as we grow in our faith. We may respond
by either stretching and growing or by
being rigid and eventually torn by the
pressure. Christ desires that we be a people that grow with him. How is Christ
challenging us to stretch and grow today?

Prayers *others may be added*

Lord, we seek your grace as we pray:

◆ Lord, hear our prayer.

Make the Church humble in its service,
we pray: ◆ Protect persecuted Christians,
we pray: ◆ Free those who are paralyzed
by fear, we pray: ◆ Raise up those who
have died, we pray: ◆

Our Father . . .

O God,
you call your sons and daughters
to collaborate with you
    in your great plan for salvation.
You invite us to bear your light
    in dark places.
Give us courage to do your will
and to hasten the coming
    of the Kingdom.
Through Christ our Lord.
Amen.

✝ I am the light of the world, says
the Lord; whoever follows me will
have the light of life.

✝ I am the way and the truth and the life, says the Lord; no one comes to the Father except through me.

Psalm 8 *page 400*

Reading *Luke 6:1–5*

While Jesus was going through a field of grain on a sabbath, his disciples were picking the heads of grain, rubbing them in their hands, and eating them. Some Pharisees said, "Why are you doing what is unlawful on the sabbath?" Jesus said to them in reply, "Have you not read what David did when he and those who were with him were hungry? How he went into the house of God, took the bread of offering, which only the priests could lawfully eat, ate of it, and shared it with his companions?" Then he said to them, "The Son of Man is lord of the sabbath."

Reflection

The Sabbath is a day of rest, but the Pharisees work very hard to see whether Jesus and his disciples are obeying the letter of the Law. When the Pharisees question Jesus, he is quick to respond that David himself also did what he is accused of when taking the temple bread to feed his hungry soldiers. Jesus proclaims that the Son of Man is the Master of the Sabbath. How does that influence your view of and practice of the Sabbath?

Prayers *others may be added*

Lord of the Sabbath:

◆ Hear our prayer:

Send your Holy Spirit upon the Church, we pray: ◆ Bring the peace of Christ upon all that is tumultuous, we pray: ◆ Grant your people the sevenfold gifts of the Holy Spirit, we pray: ◆ Heal the sick and raise up the dying, we pray: ◆

Our Father . . .

Master of the Sabbath,
you give your people a day of rest
so that we may honor you
   in all we are and all we do.
May the Sabbath become a time of
recapturing the reverence
   of living in your love.
We ask this
   in your most holy name.
Amen.

✝ I am the way and the truth and the life, says the Lord; no one comes to the Father except through me.

✝ Jesus proclaimed the Gospel of the kingdom and cured every disease among the people.

Psalm 8   *page 400*

Reading   *Mark 7:31–37*

Again Jesus left the district of Tyre and went by way of Sidon to the Sea of Galilee, into the district of the Decapolis. And people brought to him a deaf man who had a speech impediment and begged him to lay his hand on him. He took him off by himself away from the crowd. He put his finger into the man's ears and, spitting, touched his tongue; then he looked up to heaven and groaned, and said to him, "*Ephphatha*!" —that is, "Be opened!"—And immediately the man's ears were opened, his speech impediment was removed, and he spoke plainly. . . . They were exceedingly astonished and they said, "He has done all things well. He makes the deaf hear and the mute speak."

Reflection

Jesus opened the ears of the deaf man and commanded that his tongue be freed from its obstruction. Jesus is not afraid to get his hands dirty; he reaches into the man's ears and touches his tongue. His contact is physical. He wholly gives of himself to transform the woundedness of others. We, in our brokenness, are called to do the same. We must encounter and draw close to those who are weak; in doing so, we hasten the coming of the Kingdom. In baptism, Jesus touches our ears and mouth so that we might be opened to hear and proclaim the Good News.

Prayers   *others may be added*

Lord of all healing, we pray:

◆ Lord, hear our prayer.

For members of the Church who seek mercy, we pray: ◆ For world leaders working for justice, we pray: ◆ For those who are differently-abled in body and mind, we pray: ◆ For the imprisoned who seek pardon, we pray: ◆

Our Father . . .

O God,
you surround us with your love
    and presence.
Help us as we approach the obstacles
    of this day.
Teach us joy and kindness
as we face any difficulties.
Through Christ our Lord.
Amen.

✝ Jesus proclaimed the Gospel of the kingdom and cured every disease among the people.

✝ My sheep hear my voice, says the Lord; I know them, and they follow me.

Psalm 26 *page 404*

Reading *Luke 6:6–11*

On a certain sabbath Jesus went into the synagogue and taught, and there was a man there whose right hand was withered. The scribes and the Pharisees watched him closely to see if he would cure on the sabbath so that they might discover a reason to accuse him. But he realized their intentions and said to the man with the withered hand, "Come up and stand before us." Then Jesus said to them, "I ask you, is it lawful to do good on the sabbath rather than to do evil, to save life rather than to destroy it?" Looking around at them all, he then said to him, "Stretch out your hand." He did so and his hand was restored. But they became enraged and discussed what they might do to Jesus.

Reflection

Care and compassion for our neighbor should be a priority over laws and regulations. One could argue that Jesus did indeed break the Pharisee's understanding of the Law, but he did not break God's understanding of the Law. God is love. Jesus' love outweighs any law, and that is evident in his dealing with the man with the withered hand. The Pharisees, in their passion and enthusiasm for the law, are really bringing about the opposite of what God wanted to establish with the Law. God is love and the great Law he gives his people is to love him and love your neighbor.

Prayers *others may be added*

Loving God, we pray:

♦ Hear us, O God.

For lawyers both civil and ecclesial, we pray: ♦ For leaders, we pray: ♦ For all who hunger and thirst, we pray: ♦ For those who seek God's healing mercy, we pray: ♦

Our Father . . .

Almighty God,
you gave us your great Law of love
so that we would know
   how to live in your Kingdom.
May we seek to love our neighbor
and live in peace and harmony,
as we await the time
   when God will be all in all.
We ask this through Christ our Lord.
Amen.

✝ My sheep hear my voice, says the Lord; I know them, and they follow me.

✝ I chose you from the world, that you may go and bear fruit that will last, says the Lord.

Psalm 26   page 404

Reading   Luke 6:12–19

Jesus departed to the mountain to pray, and he spent the night in prayer to God. When day came, he called his disciples to himself, and from them he chose Twelve, whom he also named Apostles: Simon, whom he named Peter, and his brother Andrew, James, John, Philip, Bartholomew, Matthew, Thomas, James the son of Alphaeus, Simon who was called a Zealot, and Judas the son of James, and Judas Iscariot, who became a traitor.

And he came down with them and stood on a stretch of level ground. A great crowd of his disciples and a large number of the people from all Judea and Jerusalem and the coastal region of Tyre and Sidon came to hear him and to be healed of their diseases; and even those who were tormented by unclean spirits were cured. Everyone in the crowd sought to touch him because power came forth from him and healed them all.

Reflection

Jesus has a big decision to make in who will journey with him and carry on his mission. We have many decisions to make in the course of a day, of a week; in the course of a month, of a year; in the course of our life. As Jesus is about to make a big decision, he spends the night in prayer. He shows us the importance of prayer in our lives; he assists us when we are faced with decisions and offers us counsel and guidance. We do not have to limit it to the big decisions in our lives; God should be a part of every decision of our lives.

Prayers   others may be added

Seeking your counsel, we come to you, Lord:

◆ Lord, hear our prayer.

For those discerning vocations to the priesthood and religious life, we pray: ◆
For managers and leaders, we pray: ◆
For the elderly and alone, we pray: ◆
For spiritual directors and counselors, we pray: ◆

Our Father . . .

Lord Jesus Christ,
you call us to follow you
and to tell others about your love.
May we find great joy in the beauty
and mystery of your Kingdom,
where you live and reign,
for ever and ever.
Amen.

✝ I chose you from the world, that you may go and bear fruit that will last, says the Lord.

✝ Blessed are you, holy Virgin Mary, deserving of all praise; from you rose the sun of Justice, Christ our God.

Psalm 8 *page 400*

Reading *Matthew 1:18–21*

This is how the birth of Jesus Christ came about. When his mother Mary was betrothed to Joseph, but before they lived together, she was found with child through the Holy Spirit. Joseph her husband, since he was a righteous man, yet unwilling to expose her to shame, decided to divorce her quietly. Such was his intention when, behold, the angel of the Lord appeared to him in a dream and said, "Joseph, son of David, do not be afraid to take Mary your wife into your home. For it is through the Holy Spirit that this child has been conceived in her. She will bear a son and you are to name him Jesus, because he will save his people from their sins."

Reflection

There are three moments recorded in Scripture where an angel appears to Joseph. In this dream, Joseph is called to action, and his response to the angel's words is immediate. Joseph himself does not speak any words in Scripture. Even though his words are hidden from us, his actions and attributes are not. We know him as a faithful, just, and righteous protector of the Holy Family. The actions of this humble servant are done to fulfill Isaiah's prophecy, which allows Emmanuel to continue to "be with us"

today in his Word, in the Eucharist, and in our love for one another.

Prayers *others may be added*

With trust, we pray:

◆ Hear us, O Christ.

May members of the Church model Mary's obedience, we pray: ◆ May civic leaders be just in all they do, we pray: ◆ May children be protected from all harm, we pray: ◆ May families be strengthened in your love and mercy, we pray: ◆

Our Father . . .

Loving God,
a plan has always existed to bring
all creation to fullness of life.
May we, your children
collaborate in all efforts toward unity
as we prepare for Jesus' return.
We ask this through your Son,
our Lord, Jesus Christ.
Amen.

✝ Blessed are you, holy Virgin Mary, deserving of all praise; from you rose the sun of Justice, Christ our God.

✝ If you love one another, God remains in us, and his love is brought to perfection in us.

Psalm 26   page 404

Reading   Luke 6:27–31, 35

Jesus said to his disciples: "To you who hear I say, love your enemies, do good to those who hate you, bless those who curse you, pray for those who mistreat you. To the person who strikes you on one cheek, offer the other one as well, and from the person who takes your cloak, do not withhold even your tunic. Give to everyone who asks of you, and from the one who takes what is yours do not demand it back. Do to others as you would have them do to you . . . love your enemies and do good to them, and lend expecting nothing back; then your reward will be great and you will be children of the Most High, for he himself is kind to the ungrateful and the wicked."

Reflection

Jesus says, "Love your enemies." Sometimes we do not even love our brothers and sisters, the people in our own families or our friends who we are expected to hold dear. Does the Lord ask us to do something that is seemingly impossible? He allows us to turn to him in those times, as challenging as they may be, and offers us his own strength. When Jesus invites us to love our enemies, does he mean for us to do this alone? Are there ways Jesus can help us to love our enemies?

Prayers   *others may be added*

Father of all understanding, we come to you in prayer:

◆ Lord, hear our prayer.

For members of the Church to reconcile with one another and with God, we pray: ◆
For leaders to seek peace and harmony among families, peoples, and nations, we pray: ◆ For those who hold anger and bitterness in their hearts, we pray: ◆
For those who have difficulty with communication and social skills, we pray: ◆

Our Father . . .

In your wisdom Lord,
you guide us with words of truth and love
so that we may live a life of peace
among our brothers and sisters.
Give us the grace to walk the path
    of goodness and kindness,
until that day when we walk with you in
    the Kingdom.
We ask in your Most Holy Name.
Amen.

✝ If you love one another, God remains in us, and his love is brought to perfection in us.

✝ Your words, O Lord, are truth;
consecrate us in the truth.

Psalm 25
page 403

Reading
Luke 6:39–42

Jesus told his disciples a parable: "Can a blind person guide a blind person? Will not both fall into a pit? No disciple is superior to the teacher; but when fully trained, every disciple will be like his teacher. Why do you notice the splinter in your brother's eye, but do not perceive the wooden beam in your own? How can you say to your brother, 'Brother, let me remove that splinter in your eye,' when you do not even notice the wooden beam in your own eye? You hypocrite! Remove the wooden beam from your eye first; then you will see clearly to remove the splinter in your brother's eye."

Reflection

Jesus' parable invites us to contemplate what obscures our vision. We have to be able to see our own blindness and areas where we do not have clarity of vision. How do we see? What things blind us from seeing the world the way that God envisions? How does God's grace open our eyes, and ultimately our hearts, to allow us to offer his kindness and charity to our brothers and sisters?

Prayers
others may be added

Grant us eyes of faith as we pray:

◆ Lord, hear our prayer.

For the Church in its ministry to the poor, we pray: ◆ For the most vulnerable in our community, we pray: ◆ For those who have been unfairly judged, condemned, and criticized, we pray: ◆ For those who seek reconciliation and for those in need of forgiveness, we pray: ◆

Our Father . . .

Good and gracious God,
we ask you to have mercy upon us
    in our weakness.
Give us a compassionate heart
    in dealing with our neighbor
so that we may see them
    as you see them.
Through Christ our Lord.
Amen.

✝ Your words, O Lord, are truth;
consecrate us in the truth.

✝ Whoever loves me will keep my word, and my Father will love him, and we will come to him.

Psalm 8   *page 400*

Reading   *Luke 6:43–45*

Jesus said to his disciples: "A good tree does not bear rotten fruit, nor does a rotten tree bear good fruit. For every tree is known by its own fruit. For people do not pick figs from thorn bushes, nor do they gather grapes from brambles. A good person out of the store of goodness in his heart produces good, but an evil person out of a store of evil produces evil; for from the fullness of the heart the mouth speaks."

Reflection

Jesus, the master teacher, skillfully made use of vivid images from daily life to communicate essential truths to his disciples; images that have not lost their power. Today's Gospel offers two rich examples. Just as every tree is known by the fruit it bears, so will each of us be known. Unless we are nourished by the Word of God and prayer, our behavior and actions quickly betray us. Good fruit cannot be faked or forced. The wisdom of building a house on a strong foundation seems fairly obvious, but it takes extra time and effort. What is God helping you to build?

Mary Frances Flesichaker, OP
(Daily Prayer 2016)

Prayers   *others may be added*

Lord, we turn to you and pray:

◆ Lord, hear our prayer.

For those preparing for baptism, we pray: ◆ For those affected by natural disasters, we pray: ◆ For those preparing for the fall harvest, we pray: ◆ For those who are spiritually hungry, we pray: ◆ For immigrants and refugees, we pray: ◆

Our Father . . .

Ever-living God,
you nourish us with all that we need.
May your Word live in our hearts
and be proclaimed to all those
who long to hear the Good News.
Through Christ our Lord.
Amen.

✝ Whoever loves me will keep my word, and my Father will love him, and we will come to him.

✝ May I never boast except in the cross of our Lord through which the world has been crucified to me and I to the world.

Psalm 96 *page 413*

Reading *Mark 8:27–31, 32b–34*

Jesus and his disciples set out for the villages of Caesarea Philippi. Along the way he asked his disciples, "Who do people say that I am?" They said in reply, "John the Baptist, others Elijah, still others one of the prophets." And he asked them, "But who do you say that I am?" Peter said to him in reply, "You are the Christ." Then he warned them not to tell anyone about him. . . .

Then Peter took him aside and began to rebuke him. At this he turned around and, looking at his disciples, rebuked Peter and said, "Get behind me, Satan. You are thinking not as God does, but as human beings do."

He summoned the crowd with his disciples and said to them, "Whoever wishes to come after me must deny himself, take up his cross, and follow me."

Reflection

Just as he asked Peter, Jesus asks us today, "Who do you say that I am?". Peter is a reminder to all of us that even when we stumble in our relationship with Jesus, his love, his light, and his risen life will restore us to him, and define who we are in him.

Prayers *others may be added*

Turning to the risen Lord, we pray:

◆ Lord, hear our prayer.

For the pope and bishops, we pray: ◆ For world leaders, we pray: ◆ For those who struggle to see Christ, we pray: ◆ For those who struggle to carry their cross, we pray: ◆

Our Father . . .

O Christ,
you call your disciples to follow you.
The path is difficult,
and we may falter.
Grant that we come to find
  our strength in you,
the anointed one.
We ask this
  in your most holy name.
Amen.

✝ May I never boast except in the cross of our Lord through which the world has been crucified to me and I to the world.

✝ God so loved the world that he gave his only-begotten Son, so that everyone who believes in him might have eternal life.

Psalm 8   *page 400*

Reading   *Luke 7:1–7*

When Jesus had finished all his words to the people, he entered Capernaum. A centurion there had a slave who was ill and about to die, and he was valuable to him. When he heard about Jesus, he sent elders of the Jews to him, asking him to come and save the life of his slave. They approached Jesus and strongly urged him to come, saying, "He deserves to have you do this for him, for he loves our nation and he built the synagogue for us." And Jesus went with them, but when he was only a short distance from the house, the centurion sent friends to tell him, "Lord, do not trouble yourself, for I am not worthy to have you enter under my roof. Therefore, I did not consider myself worthy to come to you; but say the word and let my servant be healed."

Reflection

In this Gospel, we hear some familiar words we recite at Mass. Before we receive Communion, the assembly recites the centurion's words, "Lord, I am not worthy that you should enter under my roof." It is when we discover our great need for the Lord—acknowledging our poverty and our brokenness—that we come to understand our preciousness in the sight of the Lord. Let us pray the prayer of St. John Chrysostom: "I am not worthy that you should come into my soul, but I am glad that you have come to me because in your loving kindness you desire to dwell in me."

Prayers   *others may be added*

Lord of all goodness:

◆ Hear our prayer.

That the baptized might grow in their love of the Eucharist, we pray: ◆ That the poor and marginalized be comforted in Christ's presence, we pray: ◆ That those burdened by shame may surrender to your love, we pray: ◆ That those affected by violence come to know Christ's peace, we pray: ◆

Our Father . . .

Almighty and powerful God,
you provide for us in many ways.
We come to you with humble hearts,
seeking healing and wholeness
in our homes and in our lives.
Through Christ our Lord.
Amen.

✝ God so loved the world that he gave his only-begotten Son, so that everyone who believes in him might have eternal life.

☦ We adore you, O Christ, and we bless you, because by your Cross you have redeemed the world.

Psalm 8   *page 400*

Reading   *John 3:13–17*

Jesus said to Nicodemus: "No one has gone up to heaven except the one who has come down from heaven, the Son of Man. And just as Moses lifted up the serpent in the desert, so must the Son of Man be lifted up, so that everyone who believes in him may have eternal life.

"For God so loved the world that he gave his only Son, so that everyone who believes in him might not perish but might have eternal life. For God did not send his Son into the world to condemn the world, but that the world might be saved through him."

Reflection

On the Feast of the Exaltation of the Holy Cross we celebrate the death and resurrection of Jesus, which conquers all sin and death. The cross is the symbol of salvation; a holy sign, it invites us to contemplate God's abounding love for us. Cyril of Jerusalem observed how the Sign of the Cross on the forehead signified that the candidate belonged to Christ. He says, "Let us not be ashamed of the Cross of Christ, but even if someone else conceals it, do you carry its mark on your forehead, so that the demons, seeing the royal sign, trembling, may fly far away. Make this sign when you eat and when you drink, when you sit down, when you go to bed, when

you get up, when you speak—in a word, on all occasions."

Prayers   *others may be added*

Saving Lord, we pray:

◆ Hear us, O Christ.

For the Church and her faithful to continue to live their baptismal promises, we pray: ◆ For healing and peace among people whose ethnicity, race, or creed cause division, we pray: ◆ For the sick and suffering, may they find solace in the cross of Christ, we pray: ◆ For those who are persecuted for their beliefs, we pray: ◆

Our Father . . .

Lord Jesus,
you gave your life as a gift,
no one could take it from you.
May your act of great love
    give us strength
when we are weak,
and bring us to new life with you.
Who lives and reigns with God the
    Father, in unity of the Holy Spirit,
one God, for ever and ever.
Amen

☦ We adore you, O Christ, and we bless you, because by your Cross you have redeemed the world.

☩ Your words, Lord, are Spirit and life, you have the words of everlasting life.

Psalm 16
page 400

Reading
John 19:25–27

Standing by the cross of Jesus were his mother and his mother's sister, Mary the wife of Clopas, and Mary of Magdala. When Jesus saw his mother and the disciple there whom he loved he said to his mother, "Woman, behold, your son." Then he said to the disciple, "Behold, your mother." And from that hour the disciple took her into his home.

Reflection

Mary and John stand at the foot of the cross. United in sorrow and grief, they continue to be a model for us as we watch, wait, and pray when a loved one nears death. That Jesus entrusts Mary and John to one another symbolizes the care of the Christian community for one another. Mary and John demonstrate for us how we are to be faithful in our love by trusting in God's care and compassion to the very end.

Prayers
others may be added

Trusting in you, O Lord, we pray:

♦ Hear us, O Christ.

For the Church that seeks to comfort and console those who mourn, we pray: ♦ For mothers who seek to share the Good News, we pray: ♦ For those who work in hospice care who seek to reveal God's mercy, we pray: ♦ For pastoral ministers that work to build up God's Kingdom, we pray: ♦

Our Father . . .

Lord Jesus,
as you hung upon the cross,
you continued to provide for your
    Mother and Beloved Disciple.
We thank you for never leaving us,
never forsaking us,
and always loving us.
May you guide us
    all the days of our lives.
We ask this in your Most Holy Name,
    Amen.

☩ Your words, Lord, are Spirit and life, you have the words of everlasting life.

Thursday, September 16, 2021
Memorial of St. Cornelius, Pope, and Cyprian, Bishop, Martyrs

† Come to me, all you who labor and are burdened and I will give you rest, says the Lord.

Psalm 96 *page 413*

Reading *Luke 7:36–39, 44–47*

A Pharisee invited Jesus to dine with him, and he entered the Pharisee's house and reclined at table. Now there was a sinful woman in the city who learned that he was at table in the house of the Pharisee. Bringing an alabaster flask of ointment, she stood behind him at his feet weeping and began to bathe his feet with her tears. Then she wiped them with her hair, kissed them, and anointed them with the ointment. When the Pharisee who had invited him saw this he said to himself, "If this man were a prophet, he would know who and what sort of woman this is who is touching him, that she is a sinner." . . . Then he [Jesus] turned to the woman and said to Simon, "Do you see this woman? When I entered your house you did not give me water for my feet, but she has bathed them with her tears and wiped them with her hair. You did not give me a kiss, but she has not ceased kissing my feet since the time I entered. You did not anoint my head with oil, but she anointed my feet with ointment. So I tell you, her many sins have been forgiven; hence, she has shown great love. But the one to whom little is forgiven, loves little."

Reflection

The sinful woman, an uninvited and unwelcome guest, seeks Jesus at the house of the Pharisee. The guests all know who she is and what she has done to place herself in this position. She is willing to face their abuse and hostility, so that she can encounter Jesus. She further draws attention to herself with the oil; the aroma of it and the lavish use of it, all speak to the depth of her sinfulness. Humbly, she anoints Jesus' feet as a sign of her contrition. Her tears express her sorrow and humility. Jesus forgives her and sends her away in peace.

Prayers *others may be added*

We come to you, Lord, with contrite hearts, as we pray:

◆ Hear us, O Christ.

For the Church who seeks forgiveness, we pray: ◆ For those in power who seek reconciliation, we pray: ◆ For those who work within the justice system who strive for justice, we pray: ◆ For the destitute and lonely who seek comfort and healing, we pray: ◆

Our Father . . .

Lord Jesus,
you lifted the woman from her sinfulness,
and offered her forgiveness and peace.
Do not let fear and desperation
keep us from your mercy.
Through Christ our Lord.
Amen.

† Come to me, all you who labor and are burdened and I will give you rest, says the Lord.

✝ Blessed are you, Father, Lord
of heaven and earth; you have
revealed to little ones the mysteries
of the Kingdom.

Psalm 108   *page 415*

Reading   *Luke 8:1–3*

Jesus journeyed from one town and village to another, preaching and proclaiming the good news of the Kingdom
of God. Accompanying him were the
Twelve and some women who had been
cured of evil spirits and infirmities.
Mary, called Magdalene, from whom
seven demons had gone out, Joanna, the
wife of Herod's steward Chuza, Suzanna,
and many others who provided for them
out of their resources.

Reflection

Luke's Gospel account stresses the uni-
versality of God's plan of salvation to
include Gentiles as well as Jews, women
as well as men, the poor as well as the
wealthy. This may be one reason why
there is more attention to the role of
women in the life and ministry of Jesus
in Luke than in the other three Gospel
accounts. Today's selection records the
names of three women who traveled
with Jesus and the Apostles, minister-
ing to their needs. Despite the patriar-
chy of the first century, these women,
and others like them, were welcomed
by Jesus to participate in his mission.
That Good News continues to inspire
and encourage many, even today.

Mary Frances Flesichaker, OP
(Daily Prayer 2016)

Prayers   *others may be added*

With loving hearts, we turn to God
and pray:

- ◆ Lord, hear our prayer.

For the women who minister in the
Church, we pray: ◆ For those who offer
support to community leaders, we pray: ◆
For those marginalized because of race,
gender, economic status, and education,
we pray: ◆ For hospital chaplains,
counselors, and medical professionals,
we pray: ◆

Our Father . . .

O Living Word,
you preached the Gospel
to every heart that would listen.
Open our eyes and ears
   to your word,
which you share with us today.
Who lives and reigns with God
   the Father,
in unity of the Holy Spirit,
one God, for ever and ever.
Amen.

✝ Blessed are you, Father, Lord
of heaven and earth; you have
revealed to little ones the mysteries
of the Kingdom.

✝ Blessed are they who have kept the word with a generous heart and yield a harvest through perseverance.

Psalm 103   *page 414*

Reading   *Luke 8:4–8*

When a large crowd gathered, with people from one town after another journeying to Jesus, he spoke in a parable. "A sower went out to sow his seed. And as he sowed, some seed fell on the path and was trampled, and the birds of the sky ate it up. Some seed fell on rocky ground, and when it grew, it withered for lack of moisture. Some seed fell among thorns, and the thorns grew with it and choked it. And some seed fell on good soil, and when it grew, it produced fruit a hundredfold." After saying this, he called out, "Whoever has ears to hear ought to hear."

Reflection

Jesus' parables used familiar images, ideas, and metaphors to communicate his lesson. Here, he uses an agrarian metaphor. The heart and mind is the soil in which the seed, God's Word, is planted and takes root. We need to ask ourselves, Is my heart rocky or is it well prepared and cultivated to receive the seed of God's Word? No matter the ground, whether lush and fertile or scarce and shabby, God continues to give generously to his people.

Prayers   *others may be added*

Turn to Christ, we pray:

◆ Christ, hear us.

For those who preach the Good News, we pray: ◆ For those who suffer famine and drought, we pray: ◆ For those who suffer from food borne allergies and illnesses, we pray: ◆ For those who labor in the field to plant and harvest, we pray: ◆ For those who seek to receive God's word, we pray: ◆

Our Father . . .

O Word of God,
you provide nourishment
    and strength
for the spiritually famished
    and weak.
May all who hear the Gospel
welcome the Good News
into their heart and home.
We ask this in your most holy name.
Amen.

✝ Blessed are they who have kept the word with a generous heart and yield a harvest through perseverance.

☩ God has called us through the Gospel to possess the glory of our Lord Jesus Christ.

Psalm 63 *page 411*

Reading *Mark 9:30–35*

Jesus and his disciples left from there and began a journey through Galilee, but he did not wish anyone to know about it. He was teaching his disciples and telling them, "The Son of Man is to be handed over to men and they will kill him, and three days after his death he will rise." But they did not understand the saying, and they were afraid to question him.

They came to Capernaum and, once inside the house, he began to ask them, "What were you arguing about on the way?" But they remained silent. They had been discussing among themselves on the way who was the greatest. Then he sat down, called the Twelve, and said to them, "If anyone wishes to be first, he shall be the last of all and the servant of all." Taking a child he placed it in their midst, and putting his arms around it he said to them, "Whoever receives one child such as this in my name, receives me; and whoever receives me, receives not me but the One who sent me."

Reflection

When we welcome the child, we welcome Christ. At the time of Jesus, the child was considered a lowly member of society. To serve a child was a great act of humility. Jesus wants the disciples to know that if they are to lead others to the Kingdom, they are called to a life of service. Called to follow Jesus, we too assume the role of a servant. Whom are we called to serve today? The baptized serve those who do not offer us status but honor us with the witness of their vulnerability and weakness. We serve the lonely, the elderly, the ill, and the poor, as well as the child. May the least among us draw us closer to Christ. When we welcome the child, we welcome Christ.

Prayers *others may be added*

To the Lord, who calls us to serve one another, we pray:

◆ Lord, hear our prayer.

For catechists and the children they accompany, we pray: ◆ For the voiceless, abandoned, and neglected weak, we pray: ◆ For the terminally ill and their families, we pray: ◆ For victims of child sex trafficking and abuse, we pray: ◆

Our Father . . .

Lord of all,
your children often disagree or even
squabble with one another.
May your grace help us be courteous
within our home
and workplaces,
in our neighborhoods
and on social media.
We ask this through your Son,
Jesus Christ, our Lord.
Amen.

☩ God has called us through the Gospel to possess the glory of our Lord Jesus Christ.

Monday, September 20, 2021

Memorial of Sts. Andrew Kim Tae-gŏn, Priest, and Paul Chŏng Ha-sang, and Companions, Martyrs

✝ Let your light shine before others, that they may see your good deeds and glorify your heavenly Father.

Psalm 36   *page 408*

Reading   *Luke 8:16–18*

Jesus said to the crowd: "No one who lights a lamp conceals it with a vessel or sets it under a bed; rather, he places it on a lampstand so that those who enter may see the light. For there is nothing hidden that will not become visible, and nothing secret that will not be known and come to light. Take care, then, how you hear. To anyone who has, more will be given, and from the one who has not, even what he seems to have will be taken away."

Reflection

A city built on a hill would offer advantages, including protection during times of war, access to water that could be kept from your enemies; it would also be a beacon for those pilgrims in search of the light. The light of Christ beckons us. We are called to be a child of the light, to walk in that light. God gives us the light, and when it is placed on a lampstand, it benefits all who see it. To hide it is a degradation of the light. How will you share the light of Christ this week?

Prayers   *others may be added*

Lord of light, we come to you and pray:

◆ Lord, hear our prayer.

That the Church may be a beacon of hope for all those who seek the Lord, we pray: ◆ That world leaders may seek you first in their lives when making difficult decisions, we pray: ◆ That the brokenhearted may know the peace of Christ, we pray: ◆ That those who live in fear and darkness may know comfort and live as children of the light, we pray: ◆

Our Father . . .

Christ our light,
shine upon us,
and allow your light to enter
    the dark corners of our lives
so that nothing may be hidden,
and we may be covered in the grace
of your light and your love.
We ask this in your Most Holy Name,
Amen.

✝ Let your light shine before others, that they may see your good deeds and glorify your heavenly Father.

✝ We praise you, O God, we acclaim you as Lord; the glorious company of Apostles praise you.

Psalm 36 *page 408*

Reading *Matthew 9:9–13*

As Jesus passed by, he saw a man named Matthew sitting at the customs post. He said to him, "Follow me." And he got up and followed him. While he was at table in his house, many tax collectors and sinners came and sat with Jesus and his disciples. The Pharisees saw this and said to his disciples, "Why does your teacher eat with tax collectors and sinners?" He heard this and said, "Those who are well do not need a physician, but the sick do. Go and learn the meaning of the words, / *I desire mercy, not sacrifice.* / I did not come to call the righteous but sinners."

Reflection

The Lord calls people in unexpected ways. He calls us where we are, in the midst of the ordinary, and despite the obstacles of the world. Matthew is sitting at the customs post, carrying on his business, when Jesus calls him. We have two choices: to accept the invitation or to remain locked in the roles and expectations that the world places upon us. Are there obstacles or excuses that keep us from answering the Lord's call? When we follow him, we can become something even greater in Christ.

Prayers *others may be added*

To the Lord, who calls us by name to follow him, we pray:

◆ Lord, hear our prayer.

For those who are in need of God's mercy and forgiveness, we pray: ◆ For the poor and lonely, we pray: ◆ For those discerning next steps, we pray: ◆ For those who are searching for the light of faith, we pray: ◆

Our Father . . .

O God,
you reveal your love and mercy
through Jesus Christ, your Son.
Help us to answer your call
and to be ever-faithful
    to your promises.
We ask this through your Son,
Jesus Christ, our Lord.
Amen.

✝ We praise you, O God, we acclaim you as Lord; the glorious company of Apostles praise you.

✝ Blessed are those who hear the word of God and observe it.

Psalm 31   *page 405*

Reading   *Luke 9:1–6*

Jesus summoned the Twelve and gave them power and authority over all demons and to cure diseases, and he sent them to proclaim the Kingdom of God and to heal the sick. He said to them, "Take nothing for the journey, neither walking stick, nor sack, nor food, nor money, and let no one take a second tunic. Whatever house you enter, stay there and leave from there. And as for those who do not welcome you, when you leave town, shake the dust from your feet in testimony against them." Then they set out and went from village to village proclaiming the good news and curing diseases everywhere.

Reflection

Possessions can give us a false sense of security. When we have enough money saved in the bank, plenty of food in the pantry, and new clothes in our closets, it is harder to remember that not all people have what they need. Having too many possessions can also cause us to forget that our dependence should not be on things but on God. While we should be thankful we have the things we need, we must keep this in tension with the fact that these things can be fleeting. Illness, loss of a job, or a bad investment can quickly lead us from a life of luxury to a life of poverty. Yet, even when all things vanish, today's Gospel reminds us that ultimately God is the one who will provide for his people. Only God gives security.

Latisse Heerwig (Daily Prayer 2009)

Prayers   *others may be added*

O God, we come to you with our needs, and pray:

◆ Lord, hear our prayer.

For all the Church's ministers who preach the Gospel, we pray: ◆ For leaders who work to reunite families and bring harmony among peoples, we pray: ◆ For those who suffer alone and are entrapped by sin, we pray: ◆ For those who lack faith and trust in God, we pray: ◆

Our Father . . .

Jesus,
you invite us to listen to your voice
and follow you.
May we seek you in all that we do,
and may your Word resound deep
    within us
so that we might be counted among
    the family of God.
We ask this in your most holy name.
Amen.

✝ Blessed are those who hear the word of God and observe it.

✝ I am the way and the truth and the life, says the Lord; no one comes to the Father except through me.

Psalm 72 *page 412*

Reading *Luke 9:7–9*

Herod the tetrarch heard about all that was happening and he was greatly perplexed because some were saying, "John has been raised from the dead"; others were saying, "Elijah has appeared"; still others, "One of the ancient prophets has arisen." But Herod said, "John I beheaded. Who then is this about whom I hear such things?" And he kept trying to see him.

Reflection

"He kept trying to see him." If the Tetrarch, backed by the Roman Empire, wanted to see someone, he could have made it happen. How many of us desire a deeper, richer relationship with Jesus, but not right now? We may be like Herod, embarrassed by our sins and reluctant to change. However, what Jesus offers is liberation and freedom, freedom from our sin, from our shame, from the weaknesses of our past. Herod does meet Jesus during the Passion, but it is too late and Jesus remains silent. Let us go now to find Jesus and allow his presence to transform our lives.

Prayers *others may be added*

In unity of heart, we turn and pray:

◆ Lord, hear our prayer.

That the Church may be a place of refuge for the faithful, we pray: ◆ That world leaders may have ears to hear God's Word, we pray: ◆ That those in bondage to sin may receive mercy, we pray: ◆ That catechumens may grow in faith, we pray: ◆

Our Father . . .

Lord of lords,
we hear of your great mercy
and long to be restored by your grace.
May we never miss an opportunity
to encounter the living God,
we pray through Christ our Lord.
Amen.

✝ I am the way and the truth and the life, says the Lord; no one comes to the Father except through me.

Friday, September 24, 2021
Weekday

✝ Blessed are those who hear the word of God and observe it.

Psalm 127   *page 418*

Reading   *Luke 9:18–22*

Once when Jesus was praying in solitude, and the disciples were with him, he asked them, "Who do the crowds say that I am?" They said in reply, "John the Baptist; others, Elijah; still others, 'One of the ancient prophets has arisen.'" Then he said to them, "But who do you say that I am?" Peter said in reply, "The Christ of God." He rebuked them and directed them not to tell this to anyone. He said, "The Son of Man must suffer greatly and be rejected by the elders, the chief priests, and the scribes, and be killed and on the third day be raised."

Reflection

We do not always understand the full impact of the words we use. While the disciples correctly name Jesus "the Christ of God," Jesus knows that they do not understand that the Messiah must suffer, die, and rise. This does not mean that the disciples were poor followers of Christ, but rather that they could not fully comprehend the greatness of Christ and held certain preconceived notions of what the Messiah was to be. Like the disciples, we also struggle to understand the message of Christ and the words that he used to explain his kingdom. Scripture often confronts us with the reality that we are sinners and our lives must be changed. While this may be a frightening truth, it is the only way that we can begin to gain a deeper understanding of Christ and who he is calling us to be. Today, let us consider the sins that are holding us back from living the truth and ask that Christ will lead us to embrace the fullness of his Gospel.

Latisse Heerwig (Daily Prayer 2009)

Prayers   *others may be added*

To our Father, who calls us to action we pray:

◆ Lord, hear our prayer.

That the Church may be a witness of a living faith, we pray: ◆ That our world may hear the word of God, and be moved by it, we pray: ◆ That those on the margins might hear the word of God, we pray: ◆ That our children may know and follow Jesus, we pray: ◆

Our Father . . .

Creator of all,
we thank you for inviting us
     into your holy family.
Give us the strength and courage
to be noble sons and daughters
     of such a gracious Father.
Through Christ our Lord.
Amen.

✝ Blessed are those who hear the word of God and observe it.

✝ The Son of Man came to serve and to give his life as a ransom for many.

Psalm 22 *page 401*

Reading *Luke 9:43b–45*

While they were all amazed at his every deed, Jesus said to his disciples, "Pay attention to what I am telling you. The Son of Man is to be handed over to men." But they did not understand this saying; its meaning was hidden from them so that they should not understand it, and they were afraid to ask him about this saying.

Reflection

Often, when we hear of Jesus predicting his future passion and his death, we think of it as a teaching moment. Jesus is trying to prepare his disciples for what is to come. What is ironic, though, is that when it does come, the disciples do not seem to be prepared. They are scared, they have doubts, they run away. But that is really not altogether true, is it? It was natural, after all, for the disciples to be scared and to be confused, because nothing could have prepared them for what actually happened; they had to live through the cross, just like every disciple. But they also did not abandon each other; they gathered together in the upper room, on the way to Emmaus. And so they were prepared, not for the actual events of the cross— as no people can be prepared for them in their lives—but for how to live through the experience of the cross, in community, in prayer, and in trusting what the Lord has said.

Rev. Michael J. K. Fuller (Daily Prayer 2008)

Prayers *others may be added*

In prayer, we turn to God and pray:

◆ Lord, hear our prayer.

That the Church might see with eyes of faith, we pray: ◆ That leaders might see and care for the poor and marginalized, we pray: ◆ That the blind might know the light of Christ, we pray: ◆ That the faithful may always see Christ in their neighbors, we pray: ◆

Our Father . . .

O God,
we thank you
for revealing yourself to us.
In this world of distractions
and false gods,
may we always see you
and love you.
Through Christ our Lord.
Amen.

✝ The Son of Man came to serve and to give his life as a ransom for many.

Sunday, September 26, 2021
Twenty-Sixth Sunday in Ordinary Time

✝ Come quickly to help me, my Lord and my salvation.

Psalm 51
page 409

Reading
Mark 9:47–48

"If your hand causes you to sin, cut it off. It is better for you to enter into life maimed than with two hands to go into Gehenna, into the unquenchable fire. And if your foot causes you to sin, cut it off. It is better for you to enter into life crippled than with two feet to be thrown into Gehenna. And if your eye causes you to sin, pluck it out. Better for you to enter into the kingdom of God with one eye than with two eyes to be thrown into Gehenna, where 'their worm does not die, and the fire is not quenched.'"

Reflection
Jesus offers dramatic solutions to combat sin. The imagery he uses seems contrary to the nature of Jesus, but totally fits the deadly nature of sin. Our opposition to sin has to be radical and dramatic. Victims of vice can easily describe the pain and suffering it causes. We often live with our sin, hoping it will do us no harm. We should passionately surrender our sin to the healing balm of Reconciliation. We must celebrate the sacraments, and lean on our friends and family to help us as we reject our sinfulness. Whom will you turn to today?

Prayers
others may be added

To our healing Redeemer, we lift our hearts in prayer:

◆ Lord, hear our prayer.

For leaders of the Church, we pray: ◆ For world leaders, we pray: ◆ For those trapped by sin, we pray: ◆ For counselors, confessors, and spiritual directors, we pray: ◆

Our Father . . .

Holy God,
we stand before you
    weakened by sin
and we ask for the strength
    and wisdom
to combat sin in our life.
Heal us and wrap us in your love.
Through Christ our Lord.
Amen.

✝ Come quickly to help me, my Lord and my salvation.

✝ The Son of Man came to serve and to give his life as a ransom for many.

Psalm 144 *page 419*

Reading *Luke 9:46–48*

An argument arose among the disciples about which of them was the greatest. Jesus realized the intention of their hearts and took a child and placed it by his side and said to them, "Whoever receives this child in my name receives me, and whoever receives me receives the one who sent me. For the one who is least among all of you is the one who is the greatest."

Reflection

Jesus makes the concept of greatness personal. It is found when we embrace the insignificant and vulnerable; this is where God is found. The disciples want a greatness that will exclude others; it places them in positions of honor. Jesus rejects this vision quickly to welcome all those that use his name for the greater good of all. Have we ever excluded others because they are not a part of our group? Have we surrendered our power so that others may know the greatness of God?

Prayers *others may be added*

To the Lamb of God, who walks with the weak and wounded, we pray:

◆ Lord, hear our prayer.

That the Church become a safe haven for those overlooked by the world, we pray: ◆ That the world care for all like precious beloved children, we pray: ◆ That we work with all who strive to do good, we pray: ◆ That we welcome children and nurture them in the faith, we pray: ◆

Our Father . . .

Good and loving God,
Jesus reveals your love for us.
Help us to be humble of heart
and to put the needs of others
    before our own.
Through Christ our Lord.
Amen.

✝ The Son of Man came to serve and to give his life as a ransom for many.

Tuesday, September 28, 2021

Optional Memorial of St. Wenceslaus, Martyr

✝ The Son of Man came to serve and to give his life as a ransom for many.

Psalm 144   *page 419*

Reading   *Matthew 10:34–36*
This Gospel is taken from the Proper for St. Wenceslaus.

Jesus said to his Apostles: "Do not think that I have come to bring peace upon the earth. I have come to bring not peace but the sword. For I have come to set a man against his father, / a daughter against her mother, / and a daughter-in-law against her mother-in-law; / and one's enemies will be those of his household."

Reflection

This Gospel text never gets any easier to hear. Jesus warns his Apostles that faith in him will sometimes become a cause of division, a "sword" that will divide us, even from those closest to us. Our love for God must come first— before our love for father and mother, son and daughter. This is difficult to imagine, but the lives of the saints are full of such "swords" when they had to endure separation even from their nearest and dearest to follow Christ and conscience. Jesus does not promise an easy path. No matter how we are circumstanced, we will carry the cross.

Ward Johnson and Corinna Laughlin
(Daily Prayer 2010)

Prayers   *others may be added*

God of life, we come to you and pray:

◆ Lord, hear our prayer.

For healing within the Church, we pray: ◆
For healing of a divided world, we pray: ◆
For healing of divisions within families, we pray: ◆ For healing for those estranged from God, we pray: ◆

Our Father . . .

Loving God,
whose truth makes us free,
let us put no other gods before you;
let even the bonds of flesh and blood
fall away if they do not serve you.
Grant us courage to do your will,
to walk in the way of your Son,
and to bear his cross daily
as a witness to our faith.
Through Christ our Lord.
Amen.

✝ The Son of Man came to serve and to give his life as a ransom for many.

✝ Bless the Lord, all you angels,
  you ministers, who do his will.

Psalm 26   *page 404*

Reading   *John 1:47–51*

Jesus saw Nathanael coming toward him and said of him, "Here is a true child of Israel. There is no duplicity in him." Nathanael said to him, "How do you know me?" Jesus answered and said to him, "Before Philip called you, I saw you under the fig tree." "Rabbi, you are the Son of God; you are the King of Israel." Jesus answered and said to him, "Do you believe because I told you that I saw you under the fig tree? You will see greater things than this." And he said to him, "Amen, amen, I say to you, you will see heaven opened and the angels of God ascending and descending on the Son of Man."

Reflection

Nathaniel is straightforward with Jesus, and Jesus celebrates Nathaniel's integrity. We live in a world of masks that protect us and keep others at a comfortable distance. Jesus longs to see us without our masks, so that we might share an honest, holy relationship with him and others. Taking off our masks and revealing our true self might surprise those around us, but, once stripped away, we become free precious children of God. How do people know us when we are honest with God and our neighbor?

Prayers   *others may be added*

To the Savior of the world that sees the very best of us, we pray:

◆ Lord, hear our prayer.

That the Archangels watch over us, we pray: ◆ That the superficial give way to a world of true faith, we pray: ◆ That those who hide behind masks gain the courage to lay them down, we pray: ◆ That the faithful come to know you, we pray: ◆

Our Father . . .

To the God who sees us
    in unexpected ways,
we ask you to give us the courage
    to walk as your holy people,
in Christ's name.
Amen.

✝ Bless the Lord, all you angels,
  you ministers, who do his will.

✝ In you, Lord I have found my peace.

Psalm 60   *page 410*

Reading   *Luke 10:1–12*

Jesus appointed seventy-two other disciples whom he sent ahead of him in pairs to every town and place he intended to visit. He said to them, "The harvest is abundant but the laborers are few; so ask the master of the harvest to send out laborers for his harvest. Go on your way; behold, I am sending you like lambs among wolves. Carry no money bag, no sack, no sandals; and greet no one along the way. Into whatever house you enter, first say, 'Peace to this household.' If a peaceful person lives there, your peace will rest on him; but if not, it will return to you. Stay in the same house and eat and drink what is offered to you, for the laborer deserves payment. Do not move about from one house to another. Whatever town you enter and they welcome you, eat what is set before you, cure the sick in it and say to them, 'The Kingdom of God is at hand for you.' Whatever town you enter and they do not receive you, go out into the streets and say, 'The dust of your town that clings to our feet, even that we shake off against you.' Yet know this: the Kingdom of God is at hand. I tell you, it will be more tolerable for Sodom on that day than for that town."

Reflection

Jesus sends the disciples out to prepare the places he intends to visit. Jesus' command is to offer peace to each household and see if they are welcomed. If they are welcomed, the disciple remains to partake in the offered hospitality. This challenges us to consider whether we are a people of peace. Do I strive to reconcile my differences with those around me? When I have experienced injustice, is my first response one of anger and hostility or meekness? If the gift of peace came to my home, would I welcome it?

Prayers   *others may be added*

With open hearts, we pray:

◆ God of peace, hear us.

That the Church may be a place of peace and reconciliation, we pray: ◆ That world leaders may come together to work for peace, we pray: ◆ That parish communities may be a place of peace and welcome, we pray: ◆ That missionaries may faithfully proclaim God's justice and peace, we pray: ◆

Our Father . . .

O God,
Jesus, your Son,
invites us to reap what has been sown.
May we all work diligently
to bring in your harvest
as we share the Good News.
Through Christ our Lord.
Amen.

✝ In you, Lord I have found my peace.

✝ In the heart of the Church I will be love.

Psalm 60 *page 410*

Reading *Song of Song 8:6–7*

This reading is taken from the Common of Virgins.

Set me as a seal on your heart, / as a seal on your arm; / For stern as death is love, / relentless as the nether world is devotion; / its flames are a blazing fire. / Deep waters cannot quench love, / nor floods sweep it away. / Were one to offer all he owns to purchase love, / he would be roundly mocked.

Reflection

Since my longing for martyrdom was powerful and unsettling, I turned to the epistles of St. Paul in the hope of finally finding my answer. . . . I read that not everyone can be an apostle, prophet, or teacher, that the Church is composed of a variety of members. . . . Even with such an answer revealed before me, I was not satisfied and did not find peace.

I persevered in the reading and did not let my mind wander until I found this encouraging theme: *Set your desires on the greater gifts. And I will now show you the way which surpasses all others.* . . . Love appeared to me to be the hinge for my vocation.

From the autobiography of St. Thérèse of the Child Jesus (Office of Readings)

Prayers *others may be added*

Prince of Peace, may we always know and share your gift of peace, we pray:

◆ Lord, hear our prayer.

Help the Church to love as St. Thérèse loved you, we pray: ◆ Grant compassion to world leaders, we pray: ◆ Shower this community of faith with your grace, we pray: ◆ Open the hearts of the faithful to desire great gifts, we pray: ◆

Our Father . . .

Loving God,
you reveal your care for us
in the paschal mystery of Christ.
Open our hearts to the mystery
    of your love
so that, with joyful hearts,
we may forever give you praise.
Through Christ our Lord.
Amen.

✝ In the heart of the Church I will be love.

☩ Bless the Lord, all you angels,
you ministers, who do his will.

Psalm 24
page 402

Reading
Matthew 18:1–5, 10

The disciples approached Jesus and said, "Who is the greatest in the Kingdom of heaven?" He called a child over, placed it in their midst, and said, "Amen, I say to you, unless you turn and become like children, you will not enter the Kingdom of heaven. Whoever humbles himself like this child is the greatest in the Kingdom of heaven. And whoever receives one child such as this in my name receives me.

"See that you do not despise one of these little ones, for I say to you that their angels in heaven always look upon the face of my heavenly Father."

Reflection

On this Memorial of the Guardian Angels, we should consider the great gift they are to us. God has bestowed a spiritual protector upon us to light our way, to lead us home, to guide us through this life, and to guard us against the evil one and his demons. The prayer to our guardian angel is a great comfort; it reminds us to call upon our angel often. When was the last time you asked your angel for guidance and support?

Prayers
others may be added

God of mercy, we turn to you as we pray:

◆ Lord, hear our prayer.

That the guardian angels watch over the Church, we pray: ◆ That the guardian angels protect the world from all harm, we pray: ◆ That the guardian angels guide children on the path of faith, we pray: ◆ That the guardian angels accompany those who die, we pray: ◆

Our Father . . .

O marvelous Light,
you open the eyes of your people
to see the miracle of life around them.
May we always be students
of what is truly great in God's eyes.
Through Christ our Lord.
Amen.

☩ Bless the Lord, all you angels,
you ministers, who do his will.

✝ May the Lord bless us all the days of our lives.

Psalm 8 *page 400*

Reading *Mark 10:2–8*

The Pharisees approached Jesus and asked, "Is it lawful for a husband to divorce his wife?" They were testing him. He said to them in reply, "What did Moses command you?" They replied, "Moses permitted a husband to write a bill of divorce and dismiss her." But Jesus told them, "Because of the hardness of your hearts he wrote you this commandment. But from the beginning of creation, *God made them male and female. For this reason a man shall leave his father and mother and be joined to his wife, and the two shall become one flesh.* So they are no longer two but one flesh. Therefore what God has joined together, no human being must separate."

Reflection

As Jesus answers the Pharisees' question, he looks to Genesis for the teaching. In the Sacrament of Matrimony, we believe, as Jesus teaches, that two become one, and yes, that can be messy. Nevertheless, this sacramental union becomes an icon of our loving God. The man and woman become a living witness of love in the world; the couple reveals God's love for his people and teaches us the power of love. Love is creative, forgiving, merciful, and sacrificial. Love is never easy, but the reward is profound communion with the divine.

Prayers *others may be added*

God of love, we pray:

◆ Lord, hear our prayer.

That the Church may give witness to God's love, we pray: ◆ That the world may be transformed by God's love, we pray: ◆ That married couples may grow in God's love and grace, we pray: ◆ That those in need of healing may know the love of Christ, we pray: ◆

Our Father . . .

To the loving Father,
who anticipates the union
    of the Bridegroom
    with his holy Bride,
give us strength
    to wait in peace for his coming.
Through Christ our Lord.
Amen.

✝ May the Lord bless us all the days of our lives.

Monday, October 4, 2021
Memorial of St. Francis of Assisi, Religious

✝ Through the cross the world has
been crucified.

Psalm 104 *page 415*

Reading *Galatians 6:14–18*

This reading is taken from the Proper for St. Francis.

Brothers and sisters: May I never boast
except in the cross of our Lord Jesus
Christ, through which the world has
been crucified to me, and I to the world.
For neither does circumcision mean
anything, nor does uncircumcision, but
only a new creation. Peace and mercy
be to all who follow this rule and to the
Israel of God.

From now on, let no one make troubles for me; for I bear the marks of Jesus
on my body.

The grace of our Lord Jesus Christ
be with your spirit, brothers and sisters.
Amen.

Reflection

The idea that our salvation is tied up
with the salvation of the world permeates Catholic theology. We do not
believe in a personal Savior alone. God's
plan of redemption is for all. We are
forever linked to our brothers and sisters
throughout the earth, and our practice
should reflect this belief. St. Francis
devoted himself to all of creation and
all people, especially the sick, the poor,
and the forgotten.

Sara McGinnis Lee (Daily Prayer 2011)

Prayers *others may be added*

In the spirit of humility, we pray:

♦ Lord, hear our prayer.

Transform and renew your Church,
we pray: ♦ Send prophets to speak among
us and call us to new life, we pray: ♦
Open our ears to hear the Gospel,
we pray: ♦ Grant us joyful hearts,
we pray: ♦ Strengthen Franciscans
throughout the world, we pray: ♦ Lift up
the lowly, we pray: ♦

Our Father . . .

O God,
your servant, Francis,
was filled with the joy of the Gospel
and compassion for the poor.
Renew your Spirit within us
so that, like St. Francis,
we may work to build up the Church.
Through Christ our Lord.
Amen.

✝ Through the cross the world has
been crucified.

✝ Guide me, Lord, along the everlasting way.

Psalm 22   *page 401*

Reading   *Luke 10:38–42*

Jesus entered a village where a woman whose name was Martha welcomed him. She had a sister named Mary who sat beside the Lord at his feet listening to him speak. Martha, burdened with much serving, came to him and said, "Lord, do you not care that my sister has left me by myself to do the serving? Tell her to help me." The Lord said to her in reply, "Martha, Martha, you are anxious and worried about many things. There is need of only one thing. Mary has chosen the better part and it will not be taken from her."

Reflection

Martha extends the invitation, but Mary enjoys the company of Jesus. Martha serves, while Mary listens. Martha complains, while Mary sits at Jesus' feet. The powerful contrast between these two women is easy to spot. Martha could have enjoyed the time with Jesus, but the expectation of others gets in her way. When Jesus is present, do we listen or get busy with the demands of the world? The first path leads to relationship and salvation, the second leads us back out into world, filled with distractions and emptiness. Which path is the better one?

Prayers   *others may be added*

O God, we turn to you and pray:

◆ Lord, hear our prayer.

That the Church grow to become a place of hospitality, we pray: ◆ That the anxious world may find peace in Christ, we pray: ◆ That arguments between siblings be resolved in Christ's love, we pray: ◆ That those who labor may offer thanks for times of rest, we pray: ◆

Our Father . . .

God of peace,
you allow us to respond,
    in our own way,
to Jesus' presence,
give us the wisdom and courage
to choose the path that will lead us
to the greatest good in our life.
Through Christ our Lord.
Amen.

✝ Guide me, Lord, along the everlasting way.

✝ Go out to all the world, and tell the Good News.

Psalm 63 *page 411*

Reading *Luke 11:1–4*

Jesus was praying in a certain place, and when he had finished, one of his disciples said to him, "Lord, teach us to pray just as John taught his disciples." He said to them, "When you pray, say:

Father, hallowed be your name, / your Kingdom come. / Give us each day our daily bread / and forgive us our sins / for we ourselves forgive everyone in debt to us, / and do not subject us to the final test."

Reflection

Although the disciples would have prayed at the synagogue and at home, they still ask Jesus to teach them to pray. What is this about? In this important moment, Jesus is revealing an intimate way to address God and a prayer that would sustain the disciples in their ministry. Jesus' truth reveals the essential elements of prayer. It begins with the intimate relations he desires we share with God, Father. It is followed with praise, petition, forgiveness, and hope before the final test. Does this rich formula serve as the foundation of our prayer life as we pray regularly and passionately with our God?

Prayers *others may be added*

Son of the Most High, we turn to you and pray:

◆ Lord, hear our prayer.

For the baptized, we pray: ◆ For world leaders, we pray: ◆ For the hungry, we pray: ◆ For families, we pray: ◆ For the lost and forsaken, we pray: ◆ For the dead, we pray: ◆

Our Father . . .

Good and loving God,
send your Holy Spirit upon us
to enliven and rouse our hearts
to approach you in prayer.
Give us lips to speak your praise
and ears to hear your voice.
Through Christ our Lord.
Amen.

✝ Go out to all the world, and tell the Good News.

Thursday, October 7, 2021
Memorial of Our Lady of the Rosary

✝ Go out to all the world, and tell the Good News.

Psalm 63

page 411

Reading

Luke 1:38

This reading is taken from the Proper for today's Memorial.

[Mary said,] "Behold, I am the handmaid of the Lord. May it be done to me according to your word."

Reflection

Yesterday, we meditated on the prayer Christ gave as a gift to his followers—the Lord's Prayer. Today we meditate on the prayer of his mother Mary: the Rosary. The linked beads of the rosary embody a marvelous sequence of prayers. We touch the cross and we profess our faith. We call on God as our Father. We greet Mary and adore the child in her womb. We lift our hearts to heaven in praise of the Blessed Trinity. Through the Rosary, the mysteries of faith come to life in our hearts, minds, and imaginations as we ponder those moments in the life of Christ and his mother—joyful, luminous, sorrowful, and glorious—where heaven and earth met, where divine and human came together. Our Lady of the Rosary, pray for us.

Ward Johnson and Corinna Laughlin
(Daily Prayer 2010)

Prayers

others may be added

Through the intercession of Our Lady of the Rosary, we pray:

◆ Hear us, O God.

Renew the Church's prayer, we pray: ◆ Shower the world with the gifts of your Holy Spirit, we pray: ◆ Rouse the hearts of your faithful to share the Gospel, we pray: ◆ Teach us how to follow you, we pray: ◆

Our Father . . .

Gracious and loving God,
your Holy Spirit stirs in our hearts
    the desire to pray.
Inspired by the Blessed Virgin,
may we always be obedient
    to your will;
may contemplation
    of the mysteries of our faith
bring unceasing prayers to our lips.
Reveal yourself to us
    through these mysteries;
let us celebrate in prayer
the miraculous story of salvation.
Through Christ our Lord.
Amen.

✝ Go out to all the world, and tell the Good News.

✝ The Lord will remember his
covenant for ever.

Psalm 34   *page 406*

Reading   *Luke 11:23–26*

[Jesus said:] "Whoever is not with me
is against me, and whoever does not
gather with me scatters.

"When an unclean spirit goes out of
someone, it roams through arid regions
searching for rest but, finding none, it
says, 'I shall return to my home from
which I came.' But upon returning, it
finds it swept clean and put in order.
Then it goes and brings back seven other
spirits more wicked than itself who move
in and dwell there, and the last condition
of that man is worse than the first."

Reflection

The image Jesus provides in this passage invites us to consider our heart and
soul. How have they been kept? Are
they a welcome home for Jesus? When
we rid ourselves of sin and death, with
what do we fill our hearts? Surely, God's
Word is the beacon that calls us to be
attentive to the Spirit in our lives and
to guard off evil. It should consume
us as it transforms us. Instead of filling
the "house" with the seven deadly sins,
fill the void with the seven virtues of
our faith.

Prayers   *others may be added*

God of mercy, hear us as we pray:

◆ Lord, hear our prayer.

That the Church be a shelter for all,
we pray: ◆ That divisions in the world
may cease, we pray: ◆ That those held
captive by sin be set free by Jesus Christ,
we pray: ◆ That the imprudent may grow
in wisdom, we pray: ◆

Our Father . . .

To the Lord of lords,
may your scattered children
be brought back into the fold
by your faithful people
and protected by your Holy Spirit.
Through Christ our Lord.
Amen.

✝ The Lord will remember his
covenant for ever.

✝ The Lord will remember his covenant for ever.

Psalm 34 *page 406*

Reading *Luke 11:27–28*

While Jesus was speaking, a woman from the crowd called out and said to him, "Blessed is the womb that carried you and the breasts at which you nursed." He replied, "Rather, blessed are those who hear the word of God and observe it."

Reflection

In saying this, is Jesus saying something negative about his mother? Certainly, this is not the case. Mary, by definition, is blessed, not for conceiving Christ but because she first heard the Word of God and observed it. Recall her words, "May it be done to me according to your word" (Luke 1:38); later, in the manger, Mary reflects on all these things in her heart. In the tradition of the Church, the prayer of *lectio divina* reinforces all of this in four stages. First, we must hear the word, and so we read (*lectio*) the Scriptures. Second, we ponder on these words, meditating on what they mean: What are they calling us to do? To be? Third, we ask for God's help that his will may come to pass. Finally, we contemplate what the Lord is saying by sitting in silence. In this prayer, which is found in the sacred liturgy and in daily prayer, we hear the Word of God and observe it. In this way we, too, like Mary, become blessed by God's grace.

Rev. Michael J.K. Fuller (Daily Prayer 2008)

Prayers *others may be added*

Source of love, we pray:

◆ Hear us, O Christ.

Bless your Church with ears to hear, we pray: ◆ Open the hearts of civic leaders to the needs of the poor, we pray: ◆ Strengthen families as they strive to live the Gospel, we pray: ◆ Heal all who suffer and long to see your face, we pray: ◆

Our Father . . .

O Word of God,
you reveal the love of the Father.
Hear us, we pray,
as we call upon you
to open our hearts to your saving words.
Who live and reign with God
    the Father
in the unity of the Holy Spirit,
one God, for ever and ever.
Amen.

✝ The Lord will remember his covenant for ever.

Sunday, October 10, 2021
Twenty-Eighth Sunday in Ordinary Time

✝ Fill us with your love, O Lord,
and we will sing for joy.

Psalm 25   page 403

Reading   Mark 10:17–22

As Jesus was setting out on a journey, a man ran up, knelt down before him, and asked him, "Good teacher, what must I do to inherit eternal life?" Jesus answered him, "Why do you call me good? No one is good but God alone. You know the commandments: *You shall not kill; you shall not commit adultery; you shall not steal; you shall not bear false witness; you shall not defraud; honor your father and your mother.*" He replied and said to him, "Teacher, all of these I have observed from my youth." Jesus, looking at him, loved him and said to him, "You are lacking in one thing. Go, sell what you have, and give to the poor and you will have treasure in heaven; then come, follow me." At that statement his face fell, and he went away sad, for he had many possessions.

Reflection

With love, Jesus invites each of us to set aside all that hinders our ability to follow him. It seems to be a simple three-step process. First, sell what you have. Second, give to the poor. Third, follow him. St. Francis certainly took these words seriously, but we might ask what Jesus is asking of us today. Surely, he does not ask us to give up everything, does he? What Jesus is asking, it seems, is that we must divest ourselves of all those things, material and nonmaterial, that inhibit our discipleship. The truth of what Jesus shares is that when we follow him with our whole being, we will share in his life, his joy.

Prayers   *others may be added*

Loving God, we pray:

◆ Hear us, O Christ.

Help the Church become poor and humble, we pray: ◆ Free leaders from the snares of greed and power, we pray: ◆ Bless the hungry, the poor, and the marginalized, we pray: ◆ Strengthen our community in discipleship, we pray: ◆

Our Father . . .

Heavenly Father,
we know it is impossible
    to earn your divine blessing.
Instruct and guide us
so that we might be able
    to let go of everything
    that keeps us
from your holy presence.
Through Christ our Lord.
Amen.

✝ Fill us with your love, O Lord,
and we will sing for joy.

✝ If today you hear his voice, harden not your hearts.

Psalm 22   *page 401*

Reading   *Luke 11:29–32*

While still more people gathered in the crowd Jesus said to them, "This generation is an evil generation; it seeks a sign, but no sign will be given it, except the sign of Jonah. Just as Jonah became a sign to the Ninevites, so will the Son of Man be to this generation. At the judgment the queen of the south will rise with the men of this generation and she will condemn them, because she came from the ends of the earth to hear the wisdom of Solomon, and there is something greater than Solomon here. At the judgment the men of Nineveh will arise with this generation and condemn it, because at the preaching of Jonah they repented, and there is something greater than Jonah here."

Reflection

Jonah was successful in his call to the Ninevites to repent. They listened and were saved. Jesus shares the same message of repentance, but God's chosen people choose not to listen. As a result, they miss the Messiah. Jesus' message is one of salvation. He is greater than Jonah. The invitation is to repent and follow Christ to share in eternal life. This will number us among those who repented during the time of Jonah. We must be vulnerable enough to acknowledge our sins to repent and seek forgiveness.

Prayers   *others may be added*

Merciful God, we pray:

◆ Lord, hear our prayer.

That the Church be healed from its sins, we pray: ◆ That world leaders be granted courage to work for peace, we pray: ◆ That suffering hearts be strengthened in God's love, we pray: ◆ That our hearts be transformed to be more loving and forgiving, we pray: ◆

Our Father . . .

Redeemer,
who never gives up on his children,
save us from our foolishness
and give us a longing
to restore our relationship with you.
Through Christ our Lord.
Amen.

✝ If today you hear his voice, harden not your hearts.

Tuesday, October 12, 2021
Weekday

✝ Let your mercy come to me, O Lord.

Psalm 31 *page 405*

Reading *Luke 11:37–41*

After Jesus had spoken, a Pharisee invited him to dine at his home. He entered and reclined at table to eat. The Pharisee was amazed to see that he did not observe the prescribed washing before the meal. The Lord said to him, "Oh you Pharisees! Although you cleanse the outside of the cup and the dish, inside you are filled with plunder and evil. You fools! Did not the maker of the outside also make the inside? But as to what is within, give alms, and behold, everything will be clean for you."

Reflection

Jesus is an invited guest and, by not following the traditional purification ritual before meals, he scandalizes the Pharisee. Jesus' response provokes the Pharisee and should provoke us. Peripheral things cannot consume us; we must be attentive to the whole. Empty rituals lead us nowhere. We can be fussy that all the rules are followed, but is our heart prepared, ready to receive Christ. Have we been fussy or intentional about attending to the purity of heart and mind? Are we focused on Christ, the real substance of our life?

Prayers *others may be added*

With contrite heart, we pray:

◆ Lord, hear our prayer.

That the Church might be cleansed of its sin, we pray: ◆ That world leaders might grow in wisdom, we pray: ◆ That foolish people may desire a better understanding of God's will, we pray: ◆ That the faithful may be changed by Jesus, and share his wisdom, we pray: ◆

Our Father . . .

Loving God,
you search us and you know us.
In your mercy,
cleanse our hearts
and lead us to know you more deeply.
Through Christ our Lord.
Amen.

✝ Let your mercy come to me, O Lord.

✝ Those that follow you, Lord, will have the light of life.

Psalm 27   *page 405*

Reading   *Luke 11:42–46*

The Lord said: "Woe to you Pharisees! You pay tithes of mint and of rue and of every garden herb, but you pay no attention to judgment and to love for God. These you should have done, without overlooking the others. Woe to you Pharisees! You love the seat of honor in synagogues and greetings in marketplaces. Woe to you! You are like unseen graves over which people unknowingly walk."

Then one of the scholars of the law said to him in reply, "Teacher, by saying this you are insulting us too." And he said, "Woe also to you scholars of the law! You impose on people burdens hard to carry, but you yourselves do not lift one finger to touch them."

Reflection

The leaders of the day were caught up in following the human letter of the Law; they had lost sight of its spirit. It is interesting that Jesus mentions judgment right next to love for God. Judgment today is often used in a negative manner, but here Jesus uses it as an expression of love. When a neighbor is engaged in harmful actions that may damage self and others, we have a responsibility to reach out and offer love and support. Let the love of God move us to love of neighbor.

Prayers   *others may be added*

Loving God, we pray:

◆ Lord, hear our prayer.

Grant the Church the spirit of discernment, we pray; ◆ Grant world leaders the spirit of right judgment, we pray: ◆ Grant the poor and lonely the spirit of fortitude, we pray: ◆ Grant the faithful the spirit of wisdom, we pray: ◆

Our Father . . .

Saving God,
you have placed your law
   on the hearts of your people.
Grant us wisdom to know your law
and perseverance to follow it.
Through Christ our Lord.
Amen.

✝ Those that follow you, Lord, will have the light of life.

Thursday, October 14, 2021
Weekday

✝ The Lord has made known his salvation.

Psalm 72 *page 412*

Reading *Luke 11:47–52*

The Lord said: "Woe to you who build the memorials of the prophets whom your fathers killed. Consequently, you bear witness and give consent to the deeds of your ancestors, for they killed them and you do the building. Therefore, the wisdom of God said, 'I will send to them prophets and Apostles; some of them they will kill and persecute' in order that this generation might be charged with the blood of all the prophets shed since the foundation of the world, from the blood of Abel to the blood of Zechariah who died between the altar and the temple building. Yes, I tell you, this generation will be charged with their blood! Woe to you, scholars of the law! You have taken away the key of knowledge. You yourselves did not enter and you stopped those trying to enter."

Reflection

Again, in today's reading, the tensions between Jesus and the Pharisees continue to unfold. Jesus' words confront the Pharisees' understanding of the Law and their belief that they are the arbiters of the Law. However, Jesus strongly challenges this notion when he talks about building memorials. The prophets of old were killed for sharing God's message, and their sons now build monuments over their tombs. These monuments show their approval and that these prophets can no longer disturb the status quo. Jesus has a different understanding. He has come to challenge the misinterpretation of the Law. His very life is a testament that God's will is stronger than being scrupulous and petty. The Kingdom shall be proclaimed and those who hear will be saved.

Prayers *others may be added*

O Source of Wisdom, we pray:

◆ Lord, hear our prayer.

That the Church may speak the truth of the Gospel, we pray: ◆ That courage fill today's prophets, we pray: ◆ That wisdom fill those who seek truth, we pray: ◆ That love and mercy emanate from our parishes, we pray: ◆

Our Father . . .

Prince of Peace,
empower your disciples
    to bravely stand in the world
and witness your love, forgiveness,
and righteousness.
Who live and reign with God
    the Father
in the unity of the Holy Spirit,
one God, for ever and ever.
Amen.

✝ The Lord has made known his salvation.

Friday, October 15, 2021
Memorial of St. Teresa of Jesus, Virgin and Doctor of the Church

✝ May your kindness, Lord, be upon us.

Psalm 31
page 405

Reading
Luke 12:5b–7

Jesus began to speak, first to his disciples, . . . "Be afraid of the one who after killing has the power to cast into Gehenna; yes, I tell you, be afraid of that one. Are not five sparrows sold for two small coins? Yet not one of them has escaped the notice of God. Even the hairs of your head have all been counted. Do not be afraid. You are worth more than many sparrows."

Reflection

We know Jesus tells us, "Be not afraid," but in this passage, he tells us what to fear. We are admonished to fear what is destructive. The relativism of our day tells us there is no truth, so we are free to do as we please. These beliefs separate and drive us from our God. If God chooses to care for the simple sparrow, then imagine how much more he will care for Jesus' disciples. Jesus' message in today's Gospel is reminding us to be faithful to God in everything we do and say, to follow the Lord and not what can lead to destruction.

Prayers
others may be added

God of compassion, we pray:

◆ Lord, hear our prayer.

For the Church, that she remains fervent in proclaiming the Word, we pray: ◆ For the world, that the light of Christ may shine in its dark places, we pray: ◆ For those who fear death, that they be comforted by God's loving presence, we pray: ◆ For the baptized, that we boldly share our peace with the lost and forsaken, we pray: ◆

Our Father . . .

Loving Father,
you know every facet of creation.
Grant us the grace to follow you;
fill us with your wisdom;
show us the way to eternal life.
Through Christ our Lord.
Amen.

✝ May your kindness, Lord, be upon us.

Saturday, October 16, 2021
Weekday

✝ May your kindness, Lord, be upon us.

Psalm 31 *page 405*

Reading *Romans 4:13, 16–18*

Brothers and sisters: It was not through the law that the promise was made to Abraham and his descendants that he would inherit the world, but through the righteousness that comes from faith. For this reason, it depends on faith, so that it may be a gift, and the promise may be guaranteed to all his descendants, not to those who only adhere to the law but to those who follow the faith of Abraham, who is the father of all of us, as it is written, *I have made you father of many nations.* He is our father in the sight of God, in whom he believed, who gives life to the dead and calls into being what does not exist. He believed, hoping against hope, that he would become *the father of many nations,* according to what was said, *Thus shall your descendants be.*

Reflection

Paul returns to his common themes of the law and faith. The law does not provide salvation, righteousness, or justification. All of these come through faith. Law has its place but so does mercy. In The *Joy of the Gospel*, Pope Francis quotes Thomas Aquinas regarding mercy: "The foundation of the New Law is in the grace of the Holy Spirit, who is manifested in the faith which works through love" (37).

Mary C. Dumm and Randall R. Phillips
(Daily Prayer 2017)

Prayers *others may be added*

With trusting hearts, we pray:

◆ **Hear us, O God.**

Renew the Church, we pray: ◆ Lift up the poor and lowly, we pray: ◆ Strengthen leaders, we pray: ◆ Raise up the dead, we pray: ◆ Enlighten your people, we pray: ◆

Our Father . . .

Merciful God,
you show us the path of life
　through Jesus.
Guide us on our journey
and open us to your Holy Spirit
who leads us in faith
and showers us with your grace.
Through Christ our Lord.
Amen.

✝ May your kindness, Lord, be upon us.

Sunday, October 17, 2021
Twenty-Ninth Sunday in Ordinary Time

✝ The Lord hears the cry of the poor.

Psalm 25 *page 403*

Reading *Mark 10:42–45*

Jesus summoned the Twelve and said to them, "You know that those who are recognized as rulers over the Gentiles lord it over them, and their great ones make their authority over them felt. But it shall not be so among you. Rather, whoever wishes to be great among you will be your servant; whoever wishes to be first among you will be the slave of all. For the Son of Man did not come to be served but to serve and to give his life as a ransom for many."

Reflection

"Who is the greatest?" That is a question that pulls at each one of us. It is rooted in pride and is the gateway to all the other vices. But Jesus offers us a solution, it is pure, simple, and effective: be a servant. A servant is humble and seeks to satisfy the needs of those they are called to minister to. Then Jesus gives us a glimpse of God's standards— the greatest is "the slave of all." Humility is the gateway to the other virtues, do it well and we become that which God created us to be.

Prayers *others may be added*

With humble hearts, we pray:

◆ Lord, hear our prayer.

For the Church's leaders, we pray: ◆ For world leaders, we pray: ◆ For the poor and marginalized, we pray: ◆ For refugees and immigrants, we pray: ◆ For the parish family, we pray: ◆

Our Father . . .

O God,
source of all goodness,
you call us to humble ourselves
to be servants as we build up
    the Kingdom.
Send your Holy Spirit
to transform our hearts
and strengthen us in our mission
    of sharing the Good News.
Through Christ our Lord.
Amen.

✝ The Lord hears the cry of the poor.

✝ I choose you from the world,
to go and bear fruit that will last,
says the Lord.

Psalm 60 page 410

Reading Luke 10:1–9

The Lord Jesus appointed seventy-two disciples whom he sent ahead of him in pairs to every town and place he intended to visit. He said to them, "The harvest is abundant but the laborers are few; so ask the master of the harvest to send out laborers for his harvest. Go on your way; behold, I am sending you like lambs among wolves. Carry no money bag, no sack, no sandals; and greet no one along the way. Into whatever house you enter, first say, 'Peace to this household.' If a peaceful person lives there, your peace will rest on him; but if not, it will return to you. Stay in the same house and eat and drink what is offered to you, for the laborer deserves payment. Do not move about from one house to another. Whatever town you enter and they welcome you, eat what is set before you, cure the sick in it and say to them, 'The Kingdom of God is at hand for you.'"

Reflection

Do you know what a wolf does to a lamb? It is not pretty. However, a lamb that is protected by a good shepherd is led to green pastures and safety. Jesus sends forth his disciples, who are completely dependent on and protected by God. They witness to the Kingdom on behalf of Jesus and come back with stories of how God worked through them. Are we willing to be vulnerable in the world and dependent on God? What miraculous encounters could we have if we answered Jesus' call and went out into the world like lambs among wolves?

Prayers others may be added

To the Master of the harvest, we pray:

◆ Lord, hear our prayer.

For missionary disciples, we pray: ◆ For world leaders, we pray: ◆ For an increase in vocations to priesthood, religious life, and lay ecclesial ministry, we pray: ◆ For families that do not know peace, we pray: ◆

Our Father . . .

Master of the harvest,
we come to you with nothing
but our brokenness
and we ask for healing,
through your Son,
Jesus Christ our Lord.
Amen.

✝ I choose you from the world,
to go and bear fruit that will last,
says the Lord.

Tuesday, October 19, 2021

Memorial of Sts. John de Brébeuf and Isaac Jogues, Priests, and Companions, Martyrs

✝ Be vigilant at all times and pray.

Psalm 63   *page 411*

Reading   *Luke 12:35–38*

Jesus said to his disciples: "Gird your loins and light your lamps and be like servants who await their master's return from a wedding, ready to open immediately when he comes and knocks. Blessed are those servants whom the master finds vigilant on his arrival. Amen, I say to you, he will gird himself, have them recline at table, and proceed to wait on them. And should he come in the second or third watch and find them prepared in this way, blessed are those servants."

Reflection

As we near the end of the liturgical year, the readings focus on the Second Coming of Christ. In this story, Jesus again reminds us to ready ourselves for the return of the Master. We are called to be vigilant in our faith in this life so we are ready to encounter God on that final day. But there is more to this story. Jesus' words call community leaders to humble themselves enough to truly serve those in their care. Part of our readiness is serving our neighbor.

Prayers   *others may be added*

With joyful hearts, we pray:

◆ Lord, hear our prayer.

May the Church remain vigilant, we pray: ◆ May leaders receive the grace of humility, we pray: ◆ May those who work in the hospitality and service industry be granted fair wages and a safe environment, we pray: ◆ May those who have died be welcomed at the eternal banquet, we pray: ◆

Our Father . . .

O God,
you invite your children to wait.
Give us strength
to accept the invitation
with a grateful heart
that anticipates the joy
that is to come in your Kingdom.
Through Christ our Lord.
Amen.

✝ Be vigilant at all times and pray.

✝ Stay awake! For you do not know on which day your Lord will come.

Psalm 27 *page 405*

Reading *Luke 12:48*

[Jesus said:] "Much will be required of the person entrusted with much, and still more will be demanded of the person entrusted with more."

Reflection

We are richly blessed by God's grace. Jesus is reminding us that discipleship demands something more of us. When we have knowledge of God's mercy and love, when we are aware of God's abundant blessings, then we have a responsibility to use those blessings to build the Kingdom of God. The Church has been entrusted with the Gospel and the mission of sharing this Good News. Consider how you and your parish respond to these blessings.

Prayers *others may be added*

Loving God, we pray:

♦ Lord, hear our prayer.

That the Church respond to God's will in faith, we pray: ♦ That world leaders respond to crises with wisdom, we pray: ♦ That those abused and neglected receive healing and comfort, we pray: ♦ That the parish community lovingly respond to God's invitation to serve, we pray: ♦

Our Father . . .

Loving Father,
you have entrusted us with the care
 of your children.
Give us a sober mind
so that we may be good stewards
 of the resources
you have blessed us with.
Through Christ our Lord.
Amen.

✝ Stay awake! For you do not know on which day your Lord will come.

✞ The earth is full of the goodness of the Lord.

Psalm 63   *page 411*

Reading   *Luke 12:49–53*

Jesus said to his disciples: "I have come to set the earth on fire, and how I wish it were already blazing! There is a baptism with which I must be baptized, and how great is my anguish until it is accomplished! Do you think that I have come to establish peace on the earth? No, I tell you, but rather division. From now on a household of five will be divided, three against two and two against three; a father will be divided against his son and a son against his father, a mother against her daughter and a daughter against her mother, a mother-in-law against her daughter-in-law and a daughter-in-law against her mother-in-law."

Reflection

A campfire has essential elements; pine needles and twigs make up the tinder, followed by larger kindling and logs. These elements require a spark in the right place at the right time to burn. Once the tinder is ignited, the flames will build and the larger elements can be added to the growing fire. Once Christ ignites our spirit, we have to share the flame entrusted to us. When we do this, his flame spreads. If we do not burn, nothing changes. Christ's passion requires us to share passionately his fire, and when we do, the world is set ablaze.

Prayers   *others may be added*

Divine Fire, we turn to you as we say:

◆ Lord, hear our prayer.

For your divided church, that the Holy Spirit light a fire to mend all divisions, we pray: ◆ For the divided world, that the spirit of truth and understanding transform our relationships, we pray: ◆ For divided households, that the peace of the Lord break down the walls of separation, we pray: ◆ For preachers and missionaries, that the light of your Holy Spirit continue to burn within them, we pray: ◆

Our Father . . .

Good and gracious God,
we come to you with hearts
    that long to know your will.
Set our lives on fire
so that we may work to heal divisions
and forever give you glory.
Through Christ our Lord.
Amen.

✞ The earth is full of the goodness of the Lord.

✝ Lord, this is the people that longs to see your face.

Psalm 25   *page 403*

Reading   *Luke 12:54–59*

Jesus said to the crowds, "When you see a cloud rising in the west you say immediately that it is going to rain—and so it does; and when you notice that the wind is blowing from the south you say that it is going to be hot—and so it is. You hypocrites! You know how to interpret the appearance of the earth and the sky; why do you not know how to interpret the present time?

"Why do you not judge for yourselves what is right? If you are to go with your opponent before a magistrate, make an effort to settle the matter on the way; otherwise your opponent will turn you over to the judge, and the judge hand you over to the constable, and the constable throw you into prison. I say to you, you will not be released until you have paid the last penny."

Reflection

The Jews of Jesus' day were awaiting the Messiah. Signs would announce his coming: the blind will see, the lame will walk, and liberty will be given to captives. This is what Jesus does, but they refuse to see him as the Messiah. They accept the signs of the natural world, but they reject Jesus. We, too, await the Messiah's return, but often we reject all the ways he comes into our lives in the present: prayer, sacraments, Church teaching, and the lives of the saints. Consider how you recognize Christ each day.

Prayers   *others may be added*

With contrite hearts, we pray:

◆ Lord, hear our prayer.

That justice and peace reign over the earth, we pray: ◆ That eyes be opened to the glory of God, we pray: ◆ That justice and mercy guide the imprisoned and persecuted, we pray: ◆ That prudence and fortitude fill those in transition, we pray: ◆

Our Father . . .

Wonder Counselor,
we come to you
    confused by the many signs
and distractions of our world.
Help us to see your signs
and be moved to change our lives,
so we may be ready for your
    coming glory.
Through Christ our Lord.
Amen.

✝ Lord, this is the people that longs to see your face.

✝ Let us go rejoicing to the house of the Lord.

Psalm 51   *page 409*

Reading   *Luke 13:6–9*

[Jesus] told them this parable: "There once was a person who had a fig tree planted in his orchard, and when he came in search of fruit on it but found none, he said to the gardener, 'For three years now I have come in search of fruit on this fig tree but have found none. So cut it down. Why should it exhaust the soil?' He said to him in reply, 'Sir, leave it for this year also, and I shall cultivate the ground around it and fertilize it; it may bear fruit in the future. If not you can cut it down.'"

Reflection

We have a call to repent and to bear fruit, two powerful messages that are connected. We begin with repentance; this puts me in a right relationship with God, mending the damage done by my sinfulness. Once restored, my life can bear fruit. This is an essential element to gain a rich, full life. Jesus' closing carries an ominous tone: give me more time, if the fig does not bear fruit after my attention and effort, cut it down. We are called to thrive under the blessed attention of Christ, may our lives bear an abundant harvest for the Master.

Prayers   *others may be added*

True God, we pray:

◆ Lord hear our prayer.

For the Church, that she continue to feed and nurture the faithful, we pray: ◆ For world leaders, that they continue to provide for those for whom they care, we pray: ◆ For those that are dying on the vine, that God bring healing and life, we pray: ◆ For the dead, that they may receive their eternal reward, we pray: ◆

Our Father . . .

O Divine Master,
you tend the vine
    that is the Church.
Help the vine grow strong;
help it bear abundant fruit;
help it witness your loving care.
Who live and reign with God the Father
in the unity of the Holy Spirit,
one God, for ever and ever.
Amen.

✝ Let us go rejoicing to the house of the Lord.

✝ The Lord has done great things for us; we are filled with joy.

Psalm 34   *page 406*

Reading   *Mark 10:46–52*

As Jesus was leaving Jericho with his disciples and a sizable crowd, Bartimaeus, a blind man, the son of Timaeus, sat by the roadside begging. On hearing that it was Jesus of Nazareth, he began to cry out and say, "Jesus, son of David, have pity on me." Jesus stopped and said, "Call him." So they called the blind man, saying to him, "Take courage; get up, Jesus is calling you." He threw aside his cloak, sprang up, and came to Jesus. Jesus said to him in reply, "What do you want me to do for you?" The blind man replied to him, "Master, I want to see." Jesus told him, "Go your way; your faith has saved you." Immediately he received his sight and followed him on the way.

Reflection

The blind man sees well. He cries out "son of David," a messianic title, he rejects the rebuke of the crowd, and he throws aside his cloak to answer Jesus' call. This man's appeal to Jesus is complete and sacrificial; as a result his sight is restored, and he joins Jesus on his way. Do we have courage to face the hostility of the crowd and call out to our God? Will we leave behind all we have to spend a moment with Jesus?

Prayers   *others may be added*

Son of David, we cry out to you in our blindness and pray:

♦ Hear us, O God.

Grant eyes of compassion to your Church, we pray: ♦ Grant faith to those who seek the living God, we pray: ♦ Refresh the poor and marginalized, we pray: ♦ Strengthen parish communities in the Gospel mission, we pray: ♦

Our Father . . .

Divine Physician,
you healed a disciple
    who called out to you in faith.
Instill within us
the kind of faith that will move us
into your very presence.
Through Christ our Lord.
Amen.

✝ The Lord has done great things for us; we are filled with joy.

✝ Your word, O Lord, is truth;
consecrate us in the truth.

Psalm 24   *page 402*

Reading   *Luke 13:10–13*

Jesus was teaching in a synagogue on the sabbath. And a woman was there who for eighteen years had been crippled by a spirit; she was bent over, completely incapable of standing erect. When Jesus saw her, he called to her and said, "Woman, you are set free of your infirmity." He laid his hands on her, and she at once stood up straight and glorified God.

Reflection

The woman is a captive of her body, making it difficult for her to serve and give glory to God. Jesus sets her free, knowing he will face the hostility of those that do not understand the spirit of the law. We disciples of Christ are called to accompany our neighbors as they confront sin and learn to walk in Christ's footsteps. Like Christ, we might be rejected or chastised in our ministry of accompaniment and healing.

Prayers   *others may be added*

Divine Physician, we come to you and pray:

◆ Hear us, O Christ.

Heal the Church of her sins, we pray: ◆ Heal the world from war and violence, we pray: ◆ Heal the sick and suffering, we pray: ◆ Heal the divisions within our community, we pray: ◆ Heal the brokenhearted, we pray: ◆

Our Father . . .

Master of the Sabbath,
we come to you wounded and weary.
Grant us your mercy
and your healing touch;
so that, strengthened by your grace,
we may offer you praise.
Through Christ our Lord.
Amen.

✝ Your word, O Lord, is truth;
consecrate us in the truth.

Tuesday, October 26, 2021
Weekday

✝ Blessed are those that fear the Lord.

Psalm 23 *page 402*

Reading *Luke 13:18–21*

Jesus said, "What is the Kingdom of God like? To what can I compare it? It is like a mustard seed that a man took and planted in the garden. When it was fully grown, it became a large bush and the birds of the sky dwelt in its branches."

Again he said, "To what shall I compare the Kingdom of God? It is like yeast that a woman took and mixed in with three measures of wheat flour until the whole batch of dough was leavened."

Reflection

Today's Gospel provides two strong images. First, the small mustard seed that grows into a tree in which birds rest. Second, the leaven hidden in the flour. In the latter, the leaven, which was seen as corruption or evil in ancient Israel, represents the Kingdom of God, which may be hidden from those who themselves are unclean or unwilling to see. In the first image, the birds represent the diversity of those who find refuge in God and God's Kingdom. These stories challenge the status quo as Jesus works to usher in a new era, a new understanding of God's plan. Ultimately, it is God's love that will bring about the Kingdom and all are welcome to partake in what God shares.

Prayers *others may be added*

Loving God, we pray:

◆ Lord, hear our prayer.

That the Church be a place of refuge, we pray: ◆ That kingdoms and nations recognize the reign of God, we pray: ◆ That the hearts and minds of the poor be leavened by God's Word, we pray: ◆ That this local community be leaven for a hurting world, we pray: ◆

Our Father . . .

Holy God,
you can use the grandest of gestures
and the simplest of plants
to reveal yourself to the nations.
Plant your Word deep within us
and teach us how to follow you.
Through Christ our Lord.
Amen.

✝ Blessed are those that fear the Lord.

✝ Blessed are those that fear the Lord.

Psalm 23
page 402

Reading
Luke 13:23–25, 29

Someone asked him, "Lord, will only a few people be saved?" He answered them, "Strive to enter through the narrow gate, for many, I tell you, will attempt to enter but will not be strong enough. After the master of the house has arisen and locked the door, then will you stand outside knocking and saying, 'Lord, open the door for us.' He will say to you in reply, 'I do not know where you are from.' . . . And people will come from the east and the west and from the north and the south and will recline at table in the Kingdom of God."

Reflection

Jesus makes it clear that attempts at deciding who will be saved and who will not are misguided. Our assessments of self and others are too often way off the mark. Such judgments are reserved to the One who alone can see into the heart and the actions of each person. Whether or not we understand God's inscrutable criteria is beside the point. Our responsibility is to strive to enter through the narrow gate while being alert that others are also trying to do the same. Our pilgrim journey is not an isolated affair but one we share. Will we help or hinder our companions today?

Sr. Mary Frances Fleischaker, OP
(Daily Prayer 2016)

Prayers
others may be added

Merciful God, we come to you and pray:

♦ Lord, hear us.

For the Church in times of distress, we pray: ♦ For countries affected by war and violence, we pray: ♦ For the brokenhearted and disengaged, we pray: ♦ For this community, we pray: ♦

Our Father . . .

Holy God,
you have saved us in the passion,
    death, and resurrection
    of Jesus, your Son.
Show us the path of life
and grant us the grace
to pursue this path with courage.
Through Christ our Lord.
Amen.

✝ Blessed are those that fear the Lord.

Thursday, October 28, 2021
Feast of Sts. Simon and Jude, Apostles

✝ Their message goes out through all the earth.

Psalm 25 *page 403*

Reading *Luke 6:12–16*

Jesus went up to the mountain to pray, and he spent the night in prayer to God. When day came, he called his disciples to himself, and from them he chose Twelve, whom he also named Apostles: Simon, whom he named Peter, and his brother Andrew, James, John, Philip, Bartholomew, Matthew, Thomas, James the son of Alphaeus, Simon who was called a Zealot, and Judas the son of James, and Judas Iscariot, who became a traitor.

Reflection

This may seem like a short list of disciples, but surely we know the familiar names. Jesus spends the night in prayer, discerning those whom he will call to carry on the Gospel mission once his earthly mission is completed. This may seem extraordinary, but this action is a reminder to each of us to spend time with God in prayer when we are discerning movements in our lives. Take time today to ask Jesus, Why have you called me? What is my mission to share the Gospel?

Prayers *others may be added*

With love, we look to you, Lord, and pray:

♦ Lord, hear our prayer.

That the Church remain faithful to the will of God, we pray: ♦ That world leaders remain fervent in their service to the poor, we pray: ♦ That the lost and forsaken come to know God's love, we pray: ♦ That those discerning life decisions be granted God's wisdom, we pray: ♦

Our Father . . .

Holy Wisdom,
you teach us the path of life.
Open our hearts to your Word
and strengthen our resolve
to follow when you call,
so that, with fervent heart,
we may forever offer you praise.
Who live and reign with God
    the Father
in the unity of the Holy Spirit,
one God, for ever and ever.
Amen.

✝ Their message goes out through all the earth.

Friday, October 29, 2021
Weekday

✝ How great are the works of the Lord!

Psalm 23
page 402

Reading
Luke 14:1–6

On a sabbath Jesus went to dine at the home of one of the leading Pharisees, and the people there were observing him carefully. In front of him there was a man suffering from dropsy. Jesus spoke to the scholars of the law and Pharisees in reply, asking, "Is it lawful to cure on the sabbath or not?" But they kept silent; so he took the man and, after he had healed him, dismissed him. Then he said to them, "Who among you, if your son or ox falls into a cistern, would not immediately pull him out on the sabbath day?" But they were unable to answer his question.

Reflection

The question Jesus poses is complex. Curing was the work of God; sickness was a sign of sinfulness and separation from the community. Healing on the Sabbath was considered work, and therefore not permitted by the Law. Was the Pharisees' initial silence ignorance, confusion, or a passive aggressive stance to "catch" Jesus disobeying the Law? Jesus knows their game and, through this healing, teaches them that God's mercy is above strict application of the Law, especially since they would rescue the oxen, the source of livelihood if it was in harm. God will always rescue us. God's love never takes a day off. Yes, we do rest and keep Sunday holy, but that does not forbid us from caring for our neighbor.

Prayers
others may be added

God of life, we pray:

◆ O God, hear us.

Help your people delight and rest in your countenance, we pray: ◆ Renew your people who suffer in conflict, we pray: ◆ Transform stubborn hearts, we pray: ◆ Heal the sick and comfort the dying, we pray: ◆

Our Father . . .

To the Creator of our Sabbath rest,
you take our confusion and ignorance
as opportunities to teach us
    of your holy will.
Grant us a spirit of rest
and a desire to care for our neighbor.
Through Christ our Lord.
Amen.

✝ How great are the works of the Lord!

Saturday, October 30, 2021
Weekday

✝ How great are the works of the Lord!

Psalm 23 page 402

Reading Luke 14:7–11

[Jesus] told a parable to those who had been invited [to the Sabbath], noticing how they were choosing the places of honor at the table. "When you are invited by someone to a wedding banquet, do not recline at table in the place of honor. A more distinguished guest than you may have been invited by him, and the host who invited both of you may approach you and say, 'Give your place to this man,' and then you would proceed with embarrassment to take the lowest place. Rather, when you are invited, go and take the lowest place so that when the host comes to you he may say, 'My friend, move up to a higher position.' Then you will enjoy the esteem of your companions at the table. For everyone who exalts himself will be humbled, but the one who humbles himself will be exalted."

Reflection

We all know self-important people. Perhaps we find that in response to their pride, we secretly hope that they fall so they will learn humility. Or, maybe we react by reciting a list of our own accomplishments. The fact is, we will always have those among us who are arrogant, but we do not have to let their pride get the better of us. We can acknowledge that their conceit is really an attempt to feel acknowledged and loved by others. Once we acknowledge this, we are free to reach out to them as neighbor, in love and prayer, hoping they will see that their dignity lies not in their accomplishments, but in having been created by God.

—Latissee Heerwig (Daily Prayer 2009)

Prayers others may be added

God of healing, we come to you in prayer as we say:

◆ Lord, hear our prayer.

For persecuted Christians, we pray: ◆ For nations affected by famine, we pray: ◆ For disheartened and disaffected believers, we pray: ◆ For this local Church, we pray: ◆

Our Father . . .

Loving Father,
you are goodness and mercy.
As your adopted sons and daughters,
help us to be conscious of our
inherent dignity,
as created in your image and likeness.
Through Christ our Lord.
Amen.

✝ How great are the works of the Lord!

✝ I love you, Lord, my strength.

Psalm 31   *page 405*

Reading   *Mark 12:28b–33*

One of the scribes came to Jesus and asked him, "Which is the first of all the commandments?" Jesus replied, "The first is this: *Hear, O Israel! The Lord our God is Lord alone! You shall love the Lord your God with all your heart, with all your soul, with all your mind, and with all your strength.* The second is this: *You shall love your neighbor as yourself.* There is no other commandment greater than these." The scribe said to him, "Well said, teacher. You are right in saying, 'He is One and there is no other than he.' And 'to love him with all your heart, with all your understanding, with all your strength, and to love your neighbor as yourself' is worth more than all burnt offerings and sacrifices." And when Jesus saw that he answered with understanding, he said to him, "You are not far from the kingdom of God." And no one dared to ask him any more questions.

Reflection

"You shall love." What if this three-word phrase was the response we gave to challenging questions? In love, we worship a Savior who loves us. God's love is transformative and so we can ask: What if we governed with a holy love? What does it look like to live a life filled with love for neighbor? The scribe responds with understanding, and Jesus tells him he is close to the Kingdom. They respond with silence because when the fullness of the truth reveals itself, the only appropriate response is wonder and awe. Have we chosen to love God and neighbor with all that we are?

Prayers   *others may be added*

Loving God, we pray:

◆ Lord, hear our prayer.

That the Church be filled with the Holy Spirit, we pray: ◆ That war-torn nations be overcome with the peace of Christ, we pray: ◆ That those trapped in unjust systems be restored to the fullness of life, we pray: ◆ That this community of faith be strengthened by God's grace, we pray: ◆

Our Father . . .

O God,
you generously share your wisdom
    with a hungry people.
May the Word set your people free
and satisfy our desire for righteousness.
Through Christ our Lord.
Amen.

✝ I love you, Lord, my strength.

✝ Come to me, all you who labor and are burdened, and I will give you rest, says the Lord.

Psalm 25 *page 403*

Reading *Matthew 5:1–12a*

When Jesus saw the crowds, he went up the mountain, and after he had sat down, his disciples came to him. He began to teach them, saying: / "Blessed are the poor in spirit, / for theirs is the Kingdom of heaven. / Blessed are they who mourn, / for they will be comforted. / Blessed are the meek, / for they will inherit the land. / Blessed are they who hunger and thirst for righteousness, / for they will be satisfied. / Blessed are the merciful, / for they will be shown mercy. / Blessed are the clean of heart, / for they will see God. / Blessed are the peacemakers, / for they will be called children of God. / Blessed are they who are persecuted for the sake of righteousness, / for theirs is the Kingdom of heaven. / Blessed are you when they insult you and persecute you and utter every kind of evil against you falsely because of me. Rejoice and be glad, for your reward will be great in heaven."

Reflection

The purpose of the Beatitudes is to get us home to heaven. The first beatitude names the goal of heaven and then Jesus tells us how to achieve that goal. The last beatitude does the same, but includes a bonus of heavenly rewards. Most people long for heaven, but do not know how to realize it. The Beatitudes offer us curious challenges that we are inspired to realize in our lives. When we act on these challenges, we grow in our relationship with God and others, and that realizes our salvation.

Prayers *others may be added*

To our God, who has prepared a place for us with him, we pray:

♦ Lord, hear our prayer.

For the Church, that she may be steeped in grace, we pray: ♦ For leaders, that they uphold the dignity of life, we pray: ♦ For the hungry, that they be satisfied, we pray: ♦ For our community, that it be strengthened by the Holy Spirit, we pray: ♦

Our Father . . .

Mighty God,
as we celebrate the feast of All Saints,
we pray that our lives and our love
will lead us to our final place
   of peace, mercy, and love
around the eternal banquet.
Through Christ our Lord.
Amen.

✝ Come to me, all you who labor and are burdened, and I will give you rest, says the Lord.

✝ Come, you who are blessed by my Father; inherit the kingdom prepared for you from the foundation of the world.

Psalm 26   *page 404*

Reading   *John 6:37–40*

Jesus said to the crowds: "Everything that the Father gives me will come to me, and I will not reject anyone who comes to me, because I came down from heaven not to do my own will but the will of the one who sent me. And this is the will of the one who sent me, that I should not lose anything of what he gave me, but that I should raise it on the last day. For this is the will of my Father, that everyone who sees the Son and believes in him may have eternal life, and I shall raise him on the last day."

Reflection

These words of Jesus bring us comfort and hope for our salvation. But what if we read it again and place ourselves in the role of Jesus, as a living witness of faith in our troubled world? It presents a grand challenge. The Holy Spirit helps us welcome all, helps us do the Father's will, and helps us accompany those we encounter. Jesus will always be the one to grant salvation, but what if our relationships with others helps them realize their salvation? That would be a well-lived life.

Prayers   *others may be added*

Standing in awe of God's mercy, we pray:

◆ Lord, hear our prayer.

That the Church be strengthened in God's grace, we pray: ◆ That leaders be strengthened by God's compassion, we pray: ◆ That mourners be strengthened by God's mercy, we pray: ◆ That the souls of all the faithful departed rest in peace, we pray: ◆

Our Father . . .

God of compassion,
you promise eternal life to those
    who follow you.
Raise the dead to life in you
and keep the faithful ever in your care.
Through Christ our Lord.
Amen.

✝ Come, you who are blessed by my Father; inherit the kingdom prepared for you from the foundation of the world.

Wednesday, November 3, 2021
Weekday

✝ If you are insulted for the name of Christ, blessed are you, for the Spirit of God rests upon you.

Psalm 31
page 405

Reading
Luke 14:25–27

Great crowds were traveling with Jesus, and he turned and addressed them, "If anyone comes to me without hating his father and mother, wife and children, brothers and sisters, and even his own life, he cannot be my disciple. Whoever does not carry his own cross and come after me cannot be my disciple."

Reflection

Being a disciple is not an easy task. It requires that we make our relationship with Jesus our first priority and that we offer the sacrifice of our whole self. The task is daunting, but we know we have the Holy Spirit as a companion on the journey. The gifts of the Spirit provide the tools we need to set aside all that hinders us from following Christ. These gifts are necessary as we pick up the cross of discipleship.

Prayers
others may be added

With fervent hearts, we pray:

◆ Come, Holy Spirit, renew us.

For the baptized, we pray: ◆ For civil leaders, we pray: ◆ For those struggling in faith, we pray: ◆ For the sick and suffering, we pray: ◆ For missionaries, we pray: ◆ For those overwhelmed by the burden of their cross, we pray: ◆

Our Father . . .

Giver of all good gifts,
you know the incredible blessing
    of a compassionate hand
during moments of struggle.
We ask for your hand and your mercy
as we strive to be disciples
of our Lord and Savior.
Through Christ our Lord.
Amen.

✝ If you are insulted for the name of Christ, blessed are you, for the Spirit of God rests upon you.

✝ Come to me, all you who labor and are burdened, and I will give you rest, says the Lord.

Psalm 36   *page 408*

Reading   *Luke 15:3–7*

[Jesus said:] "What man among you having a hundred sheep and losing one of them would not leave the ninety-nine in the desert and go after the lost one until he finds it? And when he does find it, he sets it on his shoulders with great joy and, upon his arrival home, he calls together his friends and neighbors and says to them, 'Rejoice with me because I have found my lost sheep.' I tell you, in just the same way there will be more joy in heaven over one sinner who repents than over ninety-nine righteous people who have no need of repentance."

Reflection

Consider the shepherd's actions when he finds the lost sheep. The shepherd places the lost sheep upon his shoulders and carries it home. The sheep is exhausted, scared, and unable to make its way home. The shepherd does all the work; all the sheep has to do is cooperate. What does it look like if Jesus were to care for you in this way? Let us challenge ourselves to be those close to Jesus, and if we discover we are lost, to call out to the shepherd and let him return us to the flock.

Prayers   *others may be added*

To the Good Shepherd, may your love carry us home, we pray:

◆ Lord, hear our prayer.

May bishops develop a deep love for their flock, we pray: ◆ May elected officials care for those in their care, we pray: ◆ May the sick, the poor, and those suffering rest in the comfort of the Good Shepherd, we pray: ◆ May our community of faith continue to stay close to the Good Shepherd, we pray: ◆

Our Father . . .

Good Shepherd, walk before us,
leading us to those places
that will bring us abundant life.
Inspire us to follow you
and avoid those things and places
that cause us to stray.
Who live and reign with God the Father
in the unity of the Holy Spirit,
one God, for ever and ever.
Amen.

✝ Come to me, all you who labor and are burdened, and I will give you rest, says the Lord.

☩ Whoever keeps the word of Christ, the love of God is truly perfected in him.

Psalm 51   *page 409*

Reading   *Luke 16:1–8a*

Jesus said to his disciples, "A rich man had a steward who was reported to him for squandering his property. He summoned him and said, 'What is this I hear about you? Prepare a full account of your stewardship, because you can no longer be my steward.' The steward said to himself, 'What shall I do, now that my master is taking the position of steward away from me? I am not strong enough to dig and I am ashamed to beg. I know what I shall do so that, when I am removed from the stewardship, they may welcome me into their homes.' He called in his master's debtors one by one. To the first he said, 'How much do you owe my master?' He replied, 'One hundred measures of olive oil.' He said to him, 'Here is your promissory note. Sit down and quickly write one for fifty.' Then to another he said, 'And you, how much do you owe?' He replied, 'One hundred measures of wheat.' He said to him, 'Here is your promissory note; write one for eighty.' And the master commended that dishonest steward for acting prudently."

Reflection

He squanders and then is complimented, how is this possible? The steward's wages were a part of each deal he made on behalf of his master. As he renegotiates each deal, he is giving away his wages. He makes the master look generous, the people are thrilled by the new deal, and the steward looks great because he made it possible. His sacrifice wins the hearts of all. In a world of selfishness and greed, who will be transformed by our actions of sacrifice, love, mercy, and forgiveness? The simple answer is all of us.

Prayers   *others may be added*

With humble hearts, we pray:

◆ Lord, hear our prayer.

That your wounded Church be transformed by your holy sacrifice, we pray: ◆ That community leaders understand the prudent use of the master's generous gifts, we pray: ◆ That the poor may encounter generous people willing to share, we pray: ◆ That the hearts of all be inspired to selfless acts of sacrifice, we pray: ◆

Our Father . . .

Just Master,
bless us with a generous heart
during times of great hardship,
so that we might catch a glimpse
of your great loving sacrifice
and understand it's worth.
Through Christ our Lord.
Amen.

☩ Whoever keeps the word of Christ, the love of God is truly perfected in him.

✝ Jesus Christ became poor although he was rich, so that by his poverty you might become rich.

Psalm 116 — page 416

Reading — Luke 16:9–13

Jesus said to his disciples: "I tell you, make friends for yourselves with dishonest wealth, so that when it fails, you will be welcomed into eternal dwellings. The person who is trustworthy in very small matters is also trustworthy in great ones; and the person who is dishonest in very small matters is also dishonest in great ones. If, therefore, you are not trustworthy with dishonest wealth, who will trust you with true wealth? If you are not trustworthy with what belongs to another, who will give you what is yours? No servant can serve two masters. He will either hate one and love the other, or be devoted to one and despise the other. You cannot serve God and mammon."

Reflection

Some of us have heard that "No servant can serve two masters" (Matthew 6:24). It prompts the following questions: Who are our "masters" today? Do we bow down to our jobs, to the popularity of others or our own? Do we worship at the altar of our passions and desires? Toward what do we devote our energy, attention, and efforts? Jesus invites us to focus our whole self on our love for God and, secondarily, on our relationships with others. If we do this, we will find a peace that will never be discovered in the world with its divided hearts.

Prayers — others may be added

With confidence, we pray:

◆ Lord, hear our prayer.

For the pilgrim Church that strives to find its way home, we pray: ◆ For world leaders that are consumed by pride and greed, we pray: ◆ For those with divided hearts that yearn to rest in God, we pray: ◆ For this faith community that works to embody Christ's love, we pray: ◆

Our Father . . .

Holy God,
in a world of many masters
and even more distractions,
we ask you to give us clarity
to worship your Son, Jesus Christ.
Who lives and reigns with you
in the unity of the Holy Spirit,
one God, for ever and ever.
Amen.

✝ Jesus Christ became poor although he was rich, so that by his poverty you might become rich.

Sunday, November 7, 2021
Thirty-Second Sunday in Ordinary Time

✝ Blessed are the poor in spirit, for theirs is the kingdom of heaven.

Psalm 72
page 412

Reading
Mark 12:41–44

Jesus sat down opposite the treasury and observed how the crowd put money into the treasury. Many rich people put in large sums. A poor widow also came and put in two small coins worth a few cents. Calling his disciples to himself, he said to them, "Amen, I say to you, this poor widow put in more than all the other contributions to the treasury. For they have all contributed from their surplus wealth, but she, from her poverty, has contributed all she had, her whole livelihood."

Reflection

The story of the widow's mite invites us to reflect on what we offer to God. The widow gives from her poverty while the wealthy from their surplus. Jesus tells the disciples that the widow's is the greatest or the "mightiest" of the gifts offered. Its greatness comes from her own sacrifice: the gift cost her everything. The sacrifice then leads her to a total dependence upon God to satisfy all her needs. Both the sacrifice and the dependence demonstrate a relationship with God that he desires and considers mighty indeed.

Prayers
others may be added

Trusting in you, O God, we pray:

♦ Lord, hear our prayer.

That the Church graciously share from its bounty, we pray: ♦ That leaders prudently share their resources, we pray: ♦ That widows and orphans might benefit from the gifts of others, we pray: ♦ That this community be strengthened in it ministry to the poor, we pray: ♦

Our Father . . .

O God of all creation,
you want for nothing,
please accept the humble gifts
   we offer your Church.
Help us to give of ourselves;
bless us, grace us,
and allow our gifts to bear great fruit.
Through Christ our Lord.
Amen.

✝ Blessed are the poor in spirit, for theirs is the kingdom of heaven.

✝ Shine like lights in the world, as you hold on to the word of life.

Psalm 103   *page 414*

Reading   *Luke 17:1–6*

Jesus said to his disciples, "Things that cause sin will inevitably occur, but woe to the one through whom they occur. It would be better for him if a millstone were put around his neck and he be thrown into the sea than for him to cause one of these little ones to sin. Be on your guard! If your brother sins, rebuke him; and if he repents, forgive him. And if he wrongs you seven times in one day and returns to you seven times saying, 'I am sorry,' you should forgive him."

And the Apostles said to the Lord, "Increase our faith." The Lord replied, "If you have faith the size of a mustard seed, you would say to this mulberry tree, 'Be uprooted and planted in the sea,' and it would obey you."

Reflection

Sin will happen in the world, but Jesus warns us not to be the cause of sin. He gives us a simple strategy regarding how we deal with sin. It actually starts before the rebuke. We must know when an action is sinful, we must know right from wrong, good from bad, righteous behavior from sinful. Once we know this, we must be willing to confront or rebuke sinfulness when it rises up. But, once rebuked, we must be ready to generously forgive the other. This action of forgiveness is prominent in Jesus ministry.

Prayers   *others may be added*

Merciful God, who knows our weakness, we pray:

◆ Lord, hear our prayer.

For the wounded Church, who needs your healing touch, we pray: ◆ For war-torn nations, who need your gifts of peace and mercy, we pray: ◆ For the weak and the vulnerable, who long for your protection, we pray: ◆ For divided families, who long for reconciliation, we pray: ◆

Our Father . . .

God of mercy, Jesus, your Son,
has shown us the way to forgiveness.
Grant us pardon for our sins
and strengthen us in virtue
so that we may one day
share in eternal life.
Through Christ our Lord.
Amen.

✝ Shine like lights in the world, as you hold on to the word of life.

Tuesday, November 9, 2021
Feast of the Dedication of the Lateran Basilica

† I have chosen and consecrated this house, says the Lord, that my name may be there forever.

Psalm 31 *page 405*

Reading *John 2:13–17*

Since the Passover of the Jews was near, Jesus went up to Jerusalem. He found in the temple area those who sold oxen, sheep, and doves, as well as the money changers seated there. He made a whip out of cords and drove them all out of the temple area, with the sheep and oxen, and spilled the coins of the money changers and overturned their tables, and to those who sold doves he said, "Take these out of here, and stop making my Father's house a marketplace." His disciples recalled the words of Scripture, *Zeal for your house will consume me.*

Reflection

Talk about cleaning house. The trading of goods and the exchange of money were necessary for temple sacrifice, but they had crept into the temple and desecrated it. Sin creeps into our lives, and if we do not remove it regularly through the Sacrament of Penance, the desecration grows. Let us resolve to clean our house and purify the temple of our life, so Christ feels welcome.

Prayers *others may be added*

With contrite hearts, we come to you and pray:

♦ Lord, hear our prayer.

For the Church, that she remain vigilant in showing mercy, we pray: ♦ For leaders, that they strive to follow the path of righteousness and holiness, we pray: ♦ For those neglected and abused, that they may be healed in Christ, we pray: ♦ For the marginalized, that they find welcome in this local church, we pray: ♦

Our Father . . .

Holy and Righteous One,
you cleansed your temple
by removing the very things
that desecrated it.
Give us fortitude and perseverance
to cleanse the temple
that you entrusted to us.
Who live and reign with God the Father
in the unity of the Holy Spirit,
one God, for ever and ever.
Amen.

† I have chosen and consecrated this house, says the Lord, that my name may be there forever.

✝ In all circumstances, give thanks, for this is the will of God for you in Christ Jesus.

Psalm 25   *page 403*

Reading   *Luke 17:11–19*

As Jesus continued his journey to Jerusalem, he traveled through Samaria and Galilee. As he was entering a village, ten lepers met him. They stood at a distance from him and raised their voice, saying, "Jesus, Master! Have pity on us!" And when he saw them, he said, "Go show yourselves to the priests." As they were going they were cleansed. And one of them, realizing he had been healed, returned, glorifying God in a loud voice; and he fell at the feet of Jesus and thanked him. He was a Samaritan. Jesus said in reply, "Ten were cleansed, were they not? Where are the other nine? Has none but this foreigner returned to give thanks to God?" Then he said to him, "Stand up and go; your faith has saved you."

Reflection

We see Jesus perform two actions, both inspired by the lepers. The first is inspired by the request to be healed; Jesus in his mercy grants the healing. The second is inspired by the gratitude of the leper who returned. This gratitude moved Jesus to give an even greater gift, the gift of salvation. All are healed, but it is the action of a grateful heart that brings a richer blessing. Help us always to be grateful people, saved by his divine mercy.

Prayers   *others may be added*

Savior of the world, we pray:

◆ Lord, hear our prayer.

That the Church may be filled with a spirit of thanksgiving, we pray: ◆ That leaders work to bring healing to the workplace and restore hope, we pray: ◆ That the sick may know the healing touch of God, we pray: ◆ That priests, nurses, physicians, and all who provide care may be filled with a spirit of compassion, we pray: ◆

Our Father . . .

Divine Physician,
your healing hands restored the lepers
and saved those that responded
    with gratitude.
Grant us grateful hearts
    for the many ways
you have transformed our lives.
Who live and reign with God the Father
in the unity of the Holy Spirit,
one God, for ever and ever.
Amen.

✝ In all circumstances, give thanks, for this is the will of God for you in Christ Jesus.

✝ I am the vine, you are the branches, says the Lord: whoever remains in me and I in him will bear much fruit.

Psalm 80   *page 412*

Reading   *Luke 17:20–25*

Asked by the Pharisees when the Kingdom of God would come, Jesus said in reply, "The coming of the Kingdom of God cannot be observed, and no one will announce, 'Look, here it is,' or, 'There it is.' For behold, the Kingdom of God is among you."

Then he said to his disciples, "The days will come when you will long to see one of the days of the Son of Man, but you will not see it. There will be those who will say to you, 'Look, there he is,' or 'Look, here he is.' Do not go off, do not run in pursuit. For just as lightning flashes and lights up the sky from one side to the other, so will the Son of Man be in his day. But first he must suffer greatly and be rejected by this generation."

Reflection

Jesus warns us not to chase after him. The Kingdom of God is going to come; that is his promise to us. The only import question to consider is, What will he find me doing when he returns? If we begin each day, resolved to build his Kingdom and live our lives witnessing the love of God in a world that does not know him, then when our day comes he will find us busy doing his will. It will be our witness and his loving sacrifice that will let us see his glorious Kingdom.

Prayers   *others may be added*

Abba Father, you will not hide from your children or turn a deaf ear to our prayers, so we pray:

◆ **Lord, hear our prayer.**

For Church leaders, we pray: ◆ For world leaders, we pray: ◆ For nonbelievers, we pray: ◆ For the sick and suffering, we pray: ◆ For families, we pray: ◆ For the dead, we pray: ◆

Our Father . . .

Blessed Father,
we long for your Son's return,
give us the strength
to build your Kingdom here on earth
as we wait for your Son's return.
Through Christ our Lord.
Amen.

✝ I am the vine, you are the branches, says the Lord: whoever remains in me and I in him will bear much fruit.

✝ Stand erect and raise your heads because your redemption is at hand.

Psalm 35 — page 407

Reading — Luke 17:26–30, 32-33

Jesus said to his disciples: "As it was in the days of Noah, so it will be in the days of the Son of Man; they were eating and drinking, marrying and giving in marriage up to the day that Noah entered the ark, and the flood came and destroyed them all. Similarly, as it was in the days of Lot: they were eating, drinking, buying, selling, planting, building; on the day when Lot left Sodom, fire and brimstone rained from the sky to destroy them all. So it will be on the day the Son of Man is revealed. . . . Remember the wife of Lot. Whoever seeks to preserve his life will lose it, but whoever loses it will save it."

Reflection

Why does Lot's wife look back? She longed for the wickedness of her past and it destroys her future. We are all aware of the sins of our past. The pain, failures, and regrets for the actions of our past all linger in the shadows of our lives. If we focus on the light before us, those shadows can do us no harm. But, if we look back and focus on the darkness of our past, we will not be able to see the light of our future. We are invited to live in light of salvation that Christ offers.

Prayers — *others may be added*

Light of the world, we turn to you in prayer and say:

◆ Hear us, O Christ.

Grant Church leaders a spirit of compassion, we pray: ◆ Grant wisdom to government leaders, we pray: ◆ Grant relief and healing to those who suffer, we pray: ◆ Grant freedom to those trapped by sin, we pray: ◆

Our Father:

Divine Light,
our past is filled with mistakes
    and disappointments.
Illuminate our future
and give us the grace
to leave our darkness behind.
We ask this through Christ,
the light of our salvation.
Amen.

✝ Stand erect and raise your heads because your redemption is at hand.

Saturday, November 13, 2021
Memorial of St. Frances Xavier Cabrini, Virgin

✝ God has called us through the Gospel, to possess the glory of our Lord Jesus Christ.

Psalm 16   *page 400*

Reading   *Luke 18:1–8*

Jesus told his disciples a parable about the necessity for them to pray always without becoming weary. He said, "There was a judge in a certain town who neither feared God nor respected any human being. And a widow in that town used to come to him and say, 'Render a just decision for me against my adversary.' For a long time the judge was unwilling, but eventually he thought, 'While it is true that I neither fear God nor respect any human being, because this widow keeps bothering me I shall deliver a just decision for her lest she finally come and strike me.'" The Lord said, "Pay attention to what the dishonest judge says. Will not God then secure the rights of his chosen ones who call out to him day and night? Will he be slow to answer them? I tell you, he will see to it that justice is done speedily. But when the Son of Man comes, will he find faith on earth?"

Reflection

How persistent are we in our prayer life? Is prayer a regular part of our daily rituals? Do we share our hopes, dreams, and failures with our God? Have we cried out to him in our need? God longs to be a constant presence in our lives. God desires a relationship with us. We must be persistent in our prayer; it is through our persistence that our relationship grows.

Prayers   *others may be added*

Loving God, we pray:

◆ O God, hear us.

Open the Church to the gifts of healing and reconciliation, we pray: ◆ Open our hearts and minds to the gift of prayer, we pray: ◆ Protect the persecuted, we pray: ◆ Renew us with your Holy Spirit, we pray: ◆ Raise up the dead to eternal life, we pray: ◆

Our Father . . .

Counselor,
you know our hopes and our dreams,
our successes and our failures.
Open our hearts to your divine will
and guide our hearts as we pray
to Jesus, your Son,
who lives and reigns with you
in the unity of the Holy Spirit,
one God, for ever and ever.
Amen.

✝ God has called us through the Gospel, to possess the glory of our Lord Jesus Christ.

✝ Be vigilant at all times and pray that you have the strength to stand before the Son of Man.

Psalm 80   page 412

Reading   Mark 13:24–32

[Jesus said to his disciples:] "Learn a lesson from the fig tree. When its branch becomes tender and sprouts leaves, you know that summer is near. In the same way, when you see these things happening, know that he is near, at the gates. Amen, I say to you, this generation will not pass away until all these things have taken place. Heaven and earth will pass away, but my words will not pass away.

"But of that day or hour, no one knows, neither the angels in heaven, nor the Son, but only the Father."

Reflection

Can we read the signs of the times? Most of us are not meteorologists, but if we are attentive to the world around us, we may be able to predict what weather will affect us. The same holds true for our spiritual lives. If we are attentive, we can see what is coming. The liturgical seasons nurture our growth and inspire us to live the faith in a manner that transforms our lives and inspires others to do the same. As we grow, we ready ourselves for Jesus' coming.

Prayers   *others may be added*

God of the wind and the rain, may we understand your plans for us today, we pray:

◆ Lord, hear our prayer.

Help the Church read the signs of the times and act on your will, we pray: ◆ Guide elected officials in creating a just world, we pray: ◆ Awaken your healing mercy in those trapped in addiction, we pray: ◆ Renew the hearts of your faithful, we pray: ◆

Our Father . . .

God of majesty and wonder:
we long to see what you see,
to imagine the world in its perfection.
Give us eyes to see your goodness
and work toward its realization.
Through Christ our Lord.
Amen.

✝ Be vigilant at all times and pray that you have the strength to stand before the Son of Man.

✝ I am the light of the world, says the Lord; whoever follows me will have the light of life.

Psalm 72   *page 412*

Reading   *Luke 18:35–43*

As Jesus approached Jericho a blind man was sitting by the roadside begging, and hearing a crowd going by, he inquired what was happening. They told him, "Jesus of Nazareth is passing by." He shouted, "Jesus, Son of David, have pity on me!" The people walking in front rebuked him, telling him to be silent, but he kept calling out all the more, "Son of David, have pity on me!" Then Jesus stopped and ordered that he be brought to him; and when he came near, Jesus asked him, "What do you want me to do for you?" He replied, "Lord, please let me see." Jesus told him, "Have sight; your faith has saved you." He immediately received his sight and followed him, giving glory to God. When they saw this, all the people gave praise to God.

Reflection

The blind survive on the generosity of the crowd of passersby. Anger the crowd, and you may starve. This blind man is willing to risk the rebuke of the crowd to get closer to Jesus. This is a bold leap of faith. His faith not only heals him but also saves him and puts him on the path with Jesus. Today, we face the same rebukes as our world walks by. This should not deter us but rather, inspire us to risk everything to meet him.

Prayers   *others may be added*

Son of David, you heard the blind man calling out to you in faith, hear our call as we pray:

◆ Hear us, O Christ.

May sight be restored to the blind spots within the Church, we pray: ◆ May the Lord send leaders that will walk in the path of light, we pray: ◆ May healing be granted to the sick and suffering, we pray: ◆ May this community be granted a spirit of welcome, we pray: ◆

Our Father . . .

God of mercy,
you sent your Son to give sight
    to the blind.
Give us a faith
that opens our eyes
to see the son of David in his glory.
We ask this through Christ our King.
Amen

✝ I am the light of the world, says the Lord; whoever follows me will have the light of life.

✝ God loved us, and sent his Son as expiation for our sins.

Psalm 96
page 413

Reading
Luke 19:2–6

Now a man there named Zacchaeus, who was a chief tax collector and also a wealthy man, was seeking to see who Jesus was; but he could not see him because of the crowd, for he was short in stature. So he ran ahead and climbed a sycamore tree in order to see Jesus, who was about to pass that way. When he reached the place, Jesus looked up and said, "Zacchaeus, come down quickly, for today I must stay at your house." And he came down quickly and received him with joy.

Reflection

Can you imagine what it looked like for Zacchaeus, the chief tax collector, to be perched halfway up a tree? He willingly plays the fool to catch a glimpse of Jesus. Are we willing to be seen as foolish in the eyes of the world in order to have our moment with Jesus? The encounter changes Zacchaeus. He generously gives his wealth to others and restores all he may have harmed according to the prescriptions of the Jewish law. Jesus changes everything if we take a chance and welcome him into our home.

Prayers
others may be added

With longing hearts, we pray:

♦ Lord, hear our prayer.

For the Church who accompanies sinners, we pray: ♦ For leaders who seek the common good, we pray: ♦ For the unjustly judged who seek reparation, we pray: ♦ For strangers among us who seek welcome, we pray: ♦

Our Father . . .

Almighty and ever-living God,
we stand before you as a sinful people
despised by the world.
We long to see your Son pass by
and we hope for the moment
to invite him into our homes.
Do not delay,
but send your Holy Spirit
into our homes and our hearts.
Through Christ our Lord.
Amen.

✝ God loved us, and sent his Son as expiation for our sins.

✝ Holy, holy, holy Lord, mighty God!

Psalm 51   page 409

Reading
Luke 19:12–13, 15–20, 22ac, 23–24a, 26

[Jesus] said, "A nobleman went off to a distant country to obtain the kingship for himself and then to return. He called ten of his servants and gave them ten gold coins and told them, 'Engage in trade with these until I return.' . . . But when he returned after obtaining the kingship, he had the servants called . . . to learn what they had gained by trading. The first came forward and said, 'Sir, your gold coin has earned ten additional ones.' He replied, 'Well done, good servant! . . . Take charge of ten cities.' Then the second came and reported, 'Your gold coin, sir, has earned five more.' And to this servant too he said, 'You, take charge of five cities.' Then the other servant came and said, 'Sir, here is your gold coin; I kept it stored away in a handkerchief. . . .' He said to him . . . 'You knew I was a demanding man. . . . Why did you not put my money in a bank? Then on my return I would have collected it with interest.' And to those standing by he said . . . 'I tell you, to everyone who has, more will be given, but from the one who has not, even what he has will be taken away.'"

Reflection

"Well done, good servant." Isn't that what we all long to hear from our King? We have been given various gifts. We are expected to use the gifts entrusted to us. When we allow God to bless our efforts with abundance, we cooperate with God's grace. It is a simple plan; we respond and God blesses us. If we reject his plan we are condemned, and that choice is ours to make or reject.

Prayers   others may be added

We come before the Lord and pray:

◆ Lord, hear our prayer.

Bless the leaders of the Church, we pray: ◆ Strengthen the gifts you have bestowed upon us, we pray: ◆ Enlighten those searching for meaning, we pray: ◆ Show us the path of life, we pray: ◆

Our Father . . .

Good and gracious God,
you have entrusted us
    with various abilities and talents.
Bless our efforts
as we use them for your glory,
and empower us with the Holy Spirit.
Through Christ our Lord.
Amen.

✝ Holy, holy, holy Lord, mighty God!

✝ If today you hear his voice, harden not your hearts.

Psalm 51 *page 409*

Reading *Luke 19:41–44*

As Jesus drew near Jerusalem, he saw the city and wept over it, saying, "If this day you only knew what makes for peace—but now it is hidden from your eyes. For the days are coming upon you when your enemies will raise a palisade against you; they will encircle you and hem you in on all sides. They will smash you to the ground and your children within you, and they will not leave one stone upon another within you because you did not recognize the time of your visitation."

Reflection

With a simple search, today's technology allows us to know what is happening anywhere in the world. We can watch trending videos or news with no effort at all. Our phones carry limitless activities and multiple forms of communication. We can say we are a little distracted. How sad would it be for us today, if we did not recognize the moment of our visitation? We are called to share our lives with God and others. We must be ready to protect, nurture and develop our relationships and build his Kingdom for his peace to reign.

Prayers *others may be added*

Holy God, we come to you and pray:

♦ O God, hear us.

That the Church be a beacon of hope, we pray: ♦ That civic leaders be a source of justice, we pray: ♦ That the lonely and addicted be refreshed in body and mind, we pray: ♦ That the parish family be strengthened in its mission, we pray: ♦

Our Father . . .

Creator of all,
you have blessed us
    with the goodness of creation.
Grant us eyes to see that goodness
and heal us from any addiction
or selfish ambition
as we seek to serve you.
Through Christ our Lord.
Amen.

✝ If today you hear his voice, harden not your hearts.

✝ My sheep hear my voice, says
the Lord; I know them, and they
follow me.

Psalm 51   *page 409*

Reading   *Luke 19:45–48*

Jesus entered the temple area and pro-
ceeded to drive out those who were selling things, saying to them, "It is written,
*My house shall be a house of prayer,
but you have made it a den of thieves.*"
And every day he was teaching in the
temple area. The chief priests, the scribes,
and the leaders of the people, meanwhile, were seeking to put him to death,
but they could find no way to accomplish their purpose because all the people were hanging on his words.

Reflection

Why does the gathered assembly hang
on Jesus' every word? Certainly, Jesus'
daily teaching would have been challenging, inspiring, and filled with truth.
Each of these attributes was attractive
to those who listened and of course their
hearts were open to hear God's truth.
In contrast, the leaders were plotting to
put him to death. Imagine our world,
filled with hungry people who yearn for
God's Word. Those who hear God's
Word have no choice but to respond, to
build up the Kingdom. If the Church
goes forth proclaiming God's justice
then no harm shall befall the nations.

Prayers   *others may be added*

To our God, who shares his truth and
allows that same truth to protect us,
we pray:

◆ Lord, hear our prayer.

For bishops, priests, deacons,
and lay ministers who preach the
Gospel, we pray: ◆ For the leaders of
the world, we pray: ◆ For those who
lack faith, we pray: ◆ For teachers
and catechists, we pray: ◆ For those
who have died, we pray: ◆

Our Father . . .

Author of truth,
we thank you for your presence
   in the world.
Grant us wisdom to seek your truth
and fill us with a desire for your Word.
Through Christ our Lord.
Amen.

✝ My sheep hear my voice, says
the Lord; I know them, and they
follow me.

✝ Our Savior Jesus Christ has destroyed death and brought life to light through the Gospel.

Psalm 70 *page 411*

Reading *Luke 20:27–36*

Some Sadducees, those who deny that there is a resurrection, came forward and put this question to Jesus, saying, "Teacher, Moses wrote for us, *If someone's brother dies leaving a wife but no child, his brother must take the wife and raise up descendants for his brother.* Now there were seven brothers; the first married a woman but died childless. Then the second and the third married her, and likewise all the seven died childless. Finally the woman also died. Now at the resurrection whose wife will that woman be? For all seven had been married to her." Jesus said to them, "The children of this age marry and remarry; but those who are deemed worthy to attain to the coming age and to the resurrection of the dead neither marry nor are given in marriage. They can no longer die, for they are like angels; and they are the children of God because they are the ones who will rise."

Reflection

The leaders are trying to set a trap for Jesus, but he reveals a profound insight into what awaits us after this life. So what would happen if we lived our lives, with this vision of the life to come, as our motivation? We would live passionately in love with God and neighbor. We would forgive all and mend damaged relationships. We would live sacrificially, knowing that the things of this world will be left in this world.

Prayers *others may be added*

With humble hearts, we pray:

◆ Lord, hear our prayer.

For the baptized, that they be strengthened in love, we pray: ◆ For those who are persecuted, that they find refuge in God, we pray: ◆ For the poor and suffering, that they be restored to the fullness of life, we pray: ◆ For couples, that they be nurtured by the Spirit, we pray: ◆

Our Father:

Author of truth,
you reveal to use the path of life.
Give us wisdom as we learn
    to follow you.
Help us to witness your glory
so that from age to age,
we may offer you praise.
Through Christ our Lord.
Amen.

✝ Our Savior Jesus Christ has destroyed death and brought life to light through the Gospel.

✝ Blessed is he who comes in the name of the Lord! Blessed is the kingdom of our father David that is to come!

Psalm 96 *page 413*

Reading *John 18:33b–37*

Pilate said to Jesus, "Are you the King of the Jews?" Jesus answered, "Do you say this on your own or have others told you about me?" Pilate answered, "I am not a Jew, am I? Your own nation and the chief priests handed you over to me. What have you done?" Jesus answered, "My kingdom does not belong to this world. If my kingdom did belong to this world, my attendants would be fighting to keep me from being handed over to the Jews. But as it is, my kingdom is not here." So Pilate said to him, "Then you are a king?" Jesus answered, "You say I am a king. For this I was born and for this I came into the world, to testify to the truth. Everyone who belongs to the truth listens to my voice."

Reflection

The kingdom of God, in the words of our Lord and Savior, *does not come for all to see; nor shall they say: Behold, here it is, or behold, there it is; but the kingdom of God is within us, for the word of God is very near, in our mouth and in our heart.* Thus it is clear that he who prays for the coming of God's kingdom prays rightly to have it within himself, that there it may grow and bear fruit and become perfect. For God reigns in each of his holy ones. Anyone who is holy obeys the spiritual laws of God, who dwells in him as in a well-ordered city.

From a notebook on prayer by Origen, priest (Office of Readings, Christ the King)

Prayers *others may be added*

Lord of Hosts, we come to you and pray:

◆ Lord, hear our prayer.

For the leaders of our Church, may they set an example of generous love in a hungry world, we pray: ◆ For civic leaders, may they strive to satisfy the basic needs of the most vulnerable in their communities, we pray: ◆ For the hungry, naked, homeless, and sick, may they receive needed assistance, we pray: ◆ For the imprisoned, may they find healing and reconciliation, and forgiveness, we pray: ◆

Our Father . . .

Mighty God,
you are the source of all life.
Watch over us as we strive
    to proclaim your Word,
and help us as we use our gifts
    to build up your Kingdom.
Through Christ our Lord.
Amen.

✝ Blessed is he who comes in the name of the Lord! Blessed is the kingdom of our father David that is to come!

Monday, November 22, 2021
Memorial of St. Cecilia, Virgin and Martyr

✝ Stay awake! For you do not know when the Son of Man will come.

Psalm 72
page 412

Reading
Luke 21:1–4

When Jesus looked up he saw some wealthy people putting their offerings into the treasury and he noticed a poor widow putting in two small coins. He said, "I tell you truly, this poor widow put in more than all the rest; for those others have all made offerings from their surplus wealth, but she, from her poverty, has offered her whole livelihood."

Reflection

What, in our poverty, can we offer God? The answer is the gift of self. We give our stories, our passions, our memories, our time spent with the beloved. This is the only gift we can call our own. The stuff we accumulate is already his, we have simply been entrusted with it for a time. Our experiences, and our use of the precious gift of life, are uniquely ours. It is a gift that will not be taken from us, but must be surrendered to his love. Like the widow, let us surrender it all and rest in God's mercy.

Prayers
others may be added

To our Lord, who sees the gifts and sacrifices we offer, we pray:

♦ Lord, hear our prayer.

That the Church use her gifts to build up the Body of Christ, we pray: ♦
That leaders look on the sacrifices of the vulnerable and seek ways to alleviate their suffering, we pray: ♦
That widows in our midst rest in the generous hearts and compassionate spirits of the community, we pray: ♦
That the faithful have the courage to offer all that they are, we pray: ♦

Our Father . . .

Loving God,
you know what we have to offer.
Give us the courage to approach you and
　your Church
　with a pleasing sacrifice
that honors your generous nature.
Through Christ our Lord.
Amen.

✝ Stay awake! For you do not know when the Son of Man will come.

✝ Remain faithful until death, and
I will give you the crown of life.

Psalm 23   *page 402*

Reading   *Luke 21:5–9*

While some people were speaking about how the temple was adorned with costly stones and votive offerings, Jesus said, "All that you see here—the days will come when there will not be left a stone upon another stone that will not be thrown down."

Then they asked him, "Teacher, when will this happen? And what sign will there be when all these things are about to happen?" He answered, "See that you not be deceived, for many will come in my name, saying, 'I am he,' and 'The time has come.' Do not follow them! When you hear of wars and insurrections, do not be terrified; for such things must happen first, but it will not immediately be the end."

Reflection

Jesus tells us the signs to look for, but then says it will not immediately be the end. Why is he specific and vague in the same moment? The problem is in the question. Rather than ask what we should look for, what if we changed the question to ask, How should I prepare for the end? If I focus on getting ready to meet God each day, that day will eventually arrive and God will find me ready. The guidance also prevents me from wasting time in empty pursuits.

Prayers   *others may be added*

To the Lord, who hears our prayers and answers, we pray:

◆ Lord, hear our prayer.

For the Church, we pray: ◆ For world leaders, we pray: ◆ For the fear-filled and skeptical, we pray: ◆ For procrastinators, we pray: ◆ For the parish family, we pray: ◆ For the dying, we pray: ◆

Our Father . . .

Loving God,
source of life and all good things,
in your mercy, inspire us to live each day
as though it were our last,
so our lives may be lived to their fullest,
inspired by your Holy Spirit
and blessed by your Son, Jesus Christ.
Who lives and reigns with you
in the unity of the Holy Spirit,
one God, for ever and ever.
Amen.

✝ Remain faithful until death, and
I will give you the crown of life.

✝ Remain faithful until death, and
I will give you the crown of life.

Psalm 22 *page 401*

Reading *Luke 21:12–19*

Jesus said to the crowd: "They will seize
and persecute you, they will hand you
over to the synagogues and to prisons,
and they will have you led before kings
and governors because of my name. It
will lead to your giving testimony.
Remember, you are not to prepare your
defense beforehand, for I myself shall
give you a wisdom in speaking that all
your adversaries will be powerless to
resist or refute. You will even be handed
over by parents, brothers, relatives, and
friends, and they will put some of you
to death. You will be hated by all
because of my name, but not a hair on
your head will be destroyed. By your
perseverance you will secure your lives."

Reflection

What Jesus says in the Gospel was certainly true for St. Andrew Dũng-Lạc
and his companions. One hundred and
seventeen Vietnamese martyrs endured
persecution, imprisonment, and eventually death, all because they shared the
message of Jesus Christ. Still, in the
twenty-first century, Christians around
the world endure persecution for their
faith. Each Sunday, when we profess the
Creed and receive Communion, we
reaffirm our commitment to living the
Gospel no matter the costs. Maybe it is
hard to imagine being hated in our
towns or neighborhoods because of our
love for Christ, but what would it look
like for you to risk everything to share
the Gospel?

Timothy A. Johnston

Prayers *others may be added*

To the Suffering Servant, who knows
what awaits us, we pray:

◆ Lord, hear our prayer.

For persecuted Christians, we pray: ◆
For government leaders who ensure
liberty and justice, we pray: ◆ For those
that are abandoned by family and friends,
we pray: ◆ For refugees and immigrants,
we pray: ◆

Our Father . . .

Merciful God,
you know the price we pay
    for being your disciples.
Through the intercession of
    St. Andrew Dũng-Lạc
    and his companions,
strengthen us for the mission
of sharing the Gospel
and help us become ministers of peace.
Through Christ our Lord.
Amen.

✝ Remain faithful until death, and
I will give you the crown of life.

✝ Stand erect and raise your heads
because your redemption is at hand.

Psalm 104   *page 415*

Reading   *Luke 21:25–28*

[Jesus said to his disciples:] "There will be signs in the sun, the moon, and the stars, and on earth nations will be in dismay, perplexed by the roaring of the sea and the waves. People will die of fright in anticipation of what is coming upon the world, for the powers of the heavens will be shaken. And then they will see the Son of Man coming in a cloud with power and great glory. But when these signs begin to happen, stand erect and raise your heads because your redemption is at hand."

Reflection

The prophetic nature of what is to come is filled with destruction, suffering, and fear. But the ultimate end is realized in the glory of the Lord. We are invited to raise our heads in preparation for our redemption. So often in the world we bow our heads in our weakness and our shame. However, Jesus calls us to look up because the mercy and sacrifice of Christ has redeemed us. As redeemed children of a triumphant God, this is our time to celebrate Jesus' homecoming.

Prayers   *others may be added*

To our Lord, who inspires us in our final days, we pray:

◆ Lord, hear our prayer.

For the Church, may her love for the Lord inspire those who seek God, we pray: ◆ For leaders, may they work for peace and justice, we pray: ◆ For the downtrodden, may they be filled with hope, we pray: ◆ For the baptized, may they remain fervent in faith, we pray: ◆

Our Father . . .

Mighty One,
we live in a world that bows down
    to everyone and everything.
Give us courage to stand before
principalities and dominions
    with heads held up
and give you glory,
in our Lord, Jesus Christ, your Son,
who lives and reigns with you
in the unity of the Holy Spirit,
one God, forever and ever.
Amen.

✝ Stand erect and raise your heads
because your redemption is at hand.

✝ Stand erect and raise your heads because your redemption is at hand.

Psalm 35   *page 407*

Reading   *Luke 21:29–33*

Jesus told his disciples a parable. "Consider the fig tree and all the other trees. When their buds burst open, you see for yourselves and know that summer is now near; in the same way, when you see these things happening, know that the Kingdom of God is near. Amen, I say to you, this generation will not pass away until all these things have taken place. Heaven and earth will pass away, but my words will not pass away."

Reflection

"My words will not pass away." What a profound statement. Jesus' words are true and invite us to consider all that will pass away and what is of true value. The truth carries a light that cannot be quenched by lies and deception. As children of the light, we are called to seek the truth and proclaim it to others. We become a beacon in the darkness that will not be diminished. We must ask ourselves, Do we witness to his truth and light, or hide in the darkness?

Prayers   *others may be added*

Turning to you, we pray:

◆ Lord, hear our prayer.

For bishops, may they be filled with the light of truth, we pray: ◆ For world leaders, may they be guided by truth and wisdom, we pray: ◆ For victims of abuse, may they receive God's healing grace, we pray: ◆ For the parish family, may they be enlightened by the Holy Spirit, we pray: ◆

Our Father . . .

God Most High,
the world can be filled with darkness.
Shower us with your grace,
so that we may radiate your light
and scatter the darkness
that surrounds us.
Through Christ our Lord.
Amen.

✝ Stand erect and raise your heads because your redemption is at hand.

✝ Be vigilant at all times and pray that you may have the strength to stand before the Son of Man.

Psalm 70 *page 411*

Reading *Luke 21:34–36*

Jesus said to his disciples: "Beware that your hearts do not become drowsy from carousing and drunkenness and the anxieties of daily life, and that day catch you by surprise like a trap. For that day will assault everyone who lives on the face of the earth. Be vigilant at all times and pray that you have the strength to escape the tribulations that are imminent and to stand before the Son of Man."

Reflection

If you talk to any athlete or performer, they will tell you of the importance of regular practice if you wish to be successful. The Christian virtues help us practice faith regularly, which ensures the stamina to remain steadfast and ultimately successful in the Christian life. As we grow in strength and faith, we develop the fortitude that is needed to stand before our friends and avoid the trials that will come. This practice of the Christian way of life helps us remain vigilant as we await Christ's return.

Prayers *others may be added*

To our Lord and God, who calls us to practice our faith, we pray:

♦ Lord, hear our prayer.

Grant Christians the stamina needed to remain vigilant, we pray: ♦ Inspire leaders to ensure equity and opportunity among their people, we pray: ♦ Enrich the lives of those who lack faith, we pray: ♦ Nurture the faith of your chosen people, we pray: ♦

Our Father . . .

Ever-living God,
keep us vigilant as we await your return.
Help us practice virtue
and keep us from all distractions.
Though Christ our Lord.
Amen.

✝ Be vigilant at all times and pray that you may have the strength to stand before the Son of Man.

✝ Show us, Lord, your love; and grant us your salvation.

Psalm 33   *page 406*

Reading   *Luke 21:25–28, 34–36*

Jesus said to his disciples: "There will be signs in the sun, the moon, and the stars, and on earth nations will be in dismay, perplexed by the roaring of the sea and the waves. People will die of fright in anticipation of what is coming upon the world, for the powers of the heavens will be shaken. And then they will see the Son of Man coming in a cloud with power and great glory. But when these signs begin to happen, stand erect and raise your heads because your redemption is at hand.

"Beware that your hearts do not become drowsy from carousing and drunkenness and the anxieties of daily life, and that day catch you by surprise like a trap. For that day will assault everyone who lives on the face of the earth. Be vigilant at all times and pray that you have the strength to escape the tribulations that are imminent and to stand before the Son of Man."

Reflection

This Gospel tells us two things. First, the Son of Man will return; second, there will be people who will not be prepared. Jesus suggests a simple solution: stay awake. We spend a great deal of time living in a state of sleep deprivation, running from one task to another, distracted, and often off balance. Jesus longs for us to narrow our focus to our relationship God. This attention and focus will ground us and prepare us for Jesus' return, so that we can become a sober people actively building his Kingdom nurtured by their faithful relationship with Christ.

Prayers   *others may be added*

To our loving Father, who gently calls us to stay awake, we pray:

◆ Lord, hear our prayer.

For the Church as she awaits Christ's return, we pray: ◆ For political leaders as they work for the common good, we pray: ◆ For the poor as they await justice, we pray: ◆ For the weary of heart in their longing for renewal, we pray: ◆

Our Father . . .

O God, source of wisdom,
we are worn and tired by the pressures
    of our world.
Grant us wisdom and a fresh vision
that will allow us to focus
on our relationship with you.
Through Christ our Lord.
Amen.

✝ Show us, Lord, your love; and grant us your salvation.

✝ O house of Jacob, come, let us walk in the light of the LORD!

Psalm 144   *page 419*

Reading   *Matthew 8:5–11*

When Jesus entered Capernaum, a centurion approached him and appealed to him, saying, "Lord, my servant is lying at home paralyzed, suffering dreadfully." He said to him, "I will come and cure him." The centurion said in reply, "Lord, I am not worthy to have you enter under my roof; only say the word and my servant will be healed. For I too am a man subject to authority, with soldiers subject to me. And I say to one, 'Go,' and he goes; and to another, 'Come here,' and he comes; and to my slave, 'Do this,' and he does it." When Jesus heard this, he was amazed and said to those following him, "Amen, I say to you, in no one in Israel have I found such faith. I say to you, many will come from the east and the west, and will recline with Abraham, Isaac, and Jacob at the banquet in the Kingdom of heaven."

Reflection

The centurion is a man that understands how power and authority work. He makes a selfless request on behalf of a servant, and Christ lifts him up. His humility is realized when he sends servants with his request so his status as a Gentile does not defile or humiliate Jesus. He does not expect Jesus to defile himself by entering a Gentile's home. This demonstration of humility, faith, and authority are remembered at every Mass, prior to receiving the Body of Christ, as a model for us to follow.

Prayers   *others may be added*

To the Divine Master, who exercises true power and authority, we pray:

♦ Lord, hear our prayer.

That our Church leaders may exercise benevolent authority, we pray: ♦
That community leaders may justly use their power and authority, we pray: ♦
That those who suffered abuse may find healing and peace, we pray: ♦ That this community of faith may remain awake in this Advent season, we pray: ♦

Our Father . . .

O God,
you inspired the centurion
to call upon your Son.
May his example continue to
    inspire others
to place their faith and trust in your
    beloved Son,
who lives and reigns with God the Father
in the unity of the Holy Spirit,
one God, for ever and ever.
Amen.

✝ O house of Jacob, come, let us walk in the light of the LORD!

✝ Come after me, says the Lord, and I will make you fishers of men.

Psalm 80   *page 412*

Reading   *Matthew 4:18–22*

As Jesus was walking by the Sea of Galilee, he saw two brothers, Simon who is called Peter, and his brother Andrew, casting a net into the sea; they were fishermen. He said to them, "Come after me, and I will make you fishers of men." At once they left their nets and followed him. He walked along from there and saw two other brothers, James, the son of Zebedee, and his brother John. They were in a boat, with their father Zebedee, mending their nets. He called them, and immediately they left their boat and their father and followed him.

Reflection

Today's Gospel invites us to reflect on the call of the first disciples. Jesus extends the same invitation to us even today. Take a moment to imagine your response if you heard Jesus calling you to join his crew. Now, consider those moments in your life when you have said yes to Jesus' invitation. Where did it lead you? How did you grow? Every time we say *yes* to God and deny ourselves, we put his will before our own. Let us always have the courage to follow Jesus wherever he might lead us.

Prayers   *others may be added*

To the Prince of Peace, who walks before us, we pray:

◆ Lord, hear our prayer.

For those called to lead the Church, we pray: ◆ For those called to serve their community as an elected official, we pray: ◆ For those who have lost their way, we pray: ◆ For those discerning their vocation, we pray: ◆ For those who may struggle during this season of hope, we pray: ◆

Our Father . . .

Mighty God,
you called St. Andrew
and the other disciples
to be "fishers of men."
May your Holy Spirit fill us with courage
and strengthen us to follow you
as we go forth sharing the Good News.
Through Christ our Lord.
Amen.

✝ Come after me, says the Lord, and I will make you fishers of men.

Wednesday, December 1, 2021
Advent Weekday

✝ Behold, the Lord comes to save his people; blessed are those prepared to meet him.

Psalm 116   *page 416*

Reading   *Matthew 15:29–37*

At that time: Jesus walked by the Sea of Galilee, went up the mountain, and sat down there. Great crowds came to him, having with them the lame, the blind, the deformed, the mute, and many others. They placed them at his feet, and he cured them. The crowds were amazed when they saw the mute speaking, the deformed made whole, the lame walking, and the blind able to see, and they glorified the God of Israel.

Jesus summoned his disciples and said, "My heart is moved with pity for the crowd, for they have been with me now for three days and have nothing to eat. I do not want to send them away hungry, for fear they may collapse along the way." The disciples said to him, "Where could we ever get enough bread in this deserted place to satisfy such a crowd?" Jesus said to them, "How many loaves do you have?" "Seven," they replied, "and a few fish." He ordered the crowd to sit down on the ground. Then he took the seven loaves and the fish, gave thanks, broke the loaves, and gave them to the disciples, who in turn gave them to the crowds. They all ate and were satisfied. They picked up the fragments left over—seven baskets full.

Reflection

The miracle stories reveal two components: first, a demonstration of faith; second, an offering by the person involved. Jesus takes these small offerings, these small demonstrations of faith, and transforms them into something greater. The individual gives up something in sacrifice so that Jesus, who does the heavy lifting, can transform it into something wonderful. As I look at my day, what act of faith is God asking me to make, what gift is he inviting me to share?

Prayers   *others may be added*

To our God, who invites us to share, we pray:

◆ Lord, hear our prayer.

That the baptized grow in charity, we pray: ◆ That leaders work to care for the poor, we pray: ◆ That the hungry be filled, we pray: ◆ That the despairing be filled with hope, we pray: ◆

Our Father . . .

Giver of great gifts,
you invite us to share what we have
with a desperate and wanting world.
We ask that you bless our simple offering
and transform the world.
Through Christ our Lord.
Amen.

✝ Behold, the Lord comes to save his people; blessed are those prepared to meet him.

✝ Seek the LORD while he may be found; call him while he is near.

Psalm 47 *page 409*

Reading *Matthew 7:21, 24–27*

Jesus said to his disciples: "Not everyone who says to me, 'Lord, Lord,' will enter the Kingdom of heaven, but only the one who does the will of my Father in heaven.

"Everyone who listens to these words of mine and acts on them will be like a wise man who built his house on rock. The rain fell, the floods came, and the winds blew and buffeted the house. But it did not collapse; it had been set solidly on rock. And everyone who listens to these words of mine but does not act on them will be like a fool who built his house on sand. The rains fell, the floods came, and the winds blew and buffeted the house. And it collapsed and was completely ruined."

Reflection

It is not enough to know about Jesus, we must have a relationship with him. In both scenarios, the storm brings its fury; nobody can escape the trials of life. When trials come, our relationship with Jesus will help weather them. The forecast is calling for a storm. What are you doing to prepare for it? Being attentive to Jesus and listening for the Father's will is a good place to begin.

Prayers *others may be added*

God of compassion, we pray:

◆ Lord, hear our prayer.

For the pope, bishops, and pastors, grant them wisdom to know your will, we pray: ◆ For civil leaders, grant them prudence in their decision-making, we pray: ◆ For those who hunger for justice, grant them fortitude in their advocacy, we pray: ◆ For caregivers, grant them strength and courage in Christ, we pray: ◆

Our Father . . .

O God, you are our refuge and strength.
You know the power of the storm
that lies before us.
Come, be our strong shelter
and protect us on our journey
as we forever proclaim your name.
Through Christ our Lord.
Amen.

✝ Seek the LORD while he may be found; call him while he is near.

Friday, December 3, 2021
Memorial of St. Francis Xavier, Priest

✝ Behold, our Lord shall come with power; he will enlighten the eyes of his servants.

Psalm 63 *page 411*

Reading *Matthew 9:27–31*

As Jesus passed by, two blind men followed him, crying out, "Son of David, have pity on us!" When he entered the house, the blind men approached him and Jesus said to them, "Do you believe that I can do this?" "Yes, Lord," they said to him. Then he touched their eyes and said, "Let it be done for you according to your faith." And their eyes were opened. Jesus warned them sternly, "See that no one knows about this." But they went out and spread word of him through all that land.

Reflection

The healing story we hear today once again makes a connection between faith and healing. When we examine our prayer life, what expectations do we carry into the relationship? Do we trust God? Faith grows when we spend time with God in the study of Scripture, prayer, a quiet walk, and through devotions like adoration. Just like every human relationship, we need to nurture our life in Christ. This nurturing leads to a stronger faith in Christ and deeper love for Christ.

Prayers *others may be added*

To our God, who is moved by the faith of his followers, we pray:

♦ O God, hear us.

Heal the blindness within the Church and strengthen her in faith, we pray: ♦ Heal the blindness within our government leaders and inspire them in works of justice, we pray: ♦ Heal the blindness within our teachers and catechists and renew their fervor for the Gospel, we pray: ♦ Heal the blindness within this community and animate it for mission, we pray: ♦

Our Father . . .

Faithful God,
you invite us to put our trust in you.
Nurture our relationships
so that those we meet this day
may come to know you better.
Through Christ our Lord.
Amen.

✝ Behold, our Lord shall come with power; he will enlighten the eyes of his servants.

✝ The Lord is our Judge, our Lawgiver, our King; he it is who will save us.

Psalm 96   *page 413*

Reading   *Matthew 9:35–36; 10:1, 5a, 7*

Jesus went around to all the towns and villages, teaching in their synagogues, proclaiming the Gospel of the Kingdom, and curing every disease and illness. At the sight of the crowds, his heart was moved with pity for them because they were troubled and abandoned, like sheep without a shepherd. . . .

Then he summoned his Twelve disciples and gave them authority over unclean spirits to drive them out and to cure every disease and every illness.

Jesus sent out these twelve after instructing them, "As you go, make this proclamation: 'The Kingdom of heaven is at hand.'"

Reflection

Matthew's description of the crowd as "troubled and abandoned" can describe today's world. Today, Jesus sends out the faithful with the same message of hope. He empowers us to reach out to our neighbors and accompany them in their times of struggle and in their times of joy. God will use our sensitive hearts and simple actions to bring about his change in the world. He empowers us, and we are called to share that blessing without reservation or doubt.

Prayers   *others may be added*

To our God, who understands our woundedness, we pray:

◆ Lord, hear our prayer.

For missionaries throughout the world, we pray: ◆ For civic leaders, we pray: ◆ For those who experience mental illness, we pray: ◆ For those who promote care and compassion within their neighborhoods, we pray: ◆

Our Father . . .

Divine Physician,
Jesus, your Son, went about healing and teaching about the Kingdom.
Hear our plea for healing,
and send your Holy Spirit
to bind our wounds and refresh the soul.
Through Christ our Lord.
Amen.

✝ The Lord is our Judge, our Lawgiver, our King; he it is who will save us.

✝ Prepare the way of the Lord, make straight his paths: all flesh shall see the salvation of God.

Psalm 23 *page 402*

Reading *Luke 3:1–6*

In the fifteenth year of the reign of Tiberius Caesar, when Pontius Pilate was governor of Judea, and Herod was tetrarch of Galilee, and his brother Philip tetrarch of the region of Ituraea and Trachonitis . . . the word of God came to John in the desert. John went throughout the whole region of the Jordan, proclaiming a baptism of repentance for the forgiveness of sins, as it is written in the book of the words of the prophet Isaiah: / *A voice of one crying out in the desert: / "Prepare the way of the Lord, / make straight his paths. / Every valley shall be filled / and every mountain and hill shall be made low. / The winding roads shall be made straight, / and the rough ways made smooth, / and all flesh shall see the salvation of God."*

Reflection

If we were truly expecting Christ's return wouldn't we behave differently? If we truly expected Christ to come again, wouldn't we put more energy into how we act, into what we say, into what we think? That Christ has not yet returned may be in itself reflective of how much he loves us. God is patient with us. He has withheld his judgment, hoping that we will finally come around. He has come to us in word and sacrament. He has fed us his body and blood and given us his spirit to dwell in us. In all of this, we might finally understand and say yes to him. And the way to do that is to follow the words of the Baptist: "Prepare the way of the Lord" (Matthew 3:3). We have been given some time; let us not waste a moment more.

Rev. Michael J. K. Fuller (Daily Prayer 2008)

Prayers *others may be added*

To our God, who has prepared a place for us with him, we pray:

◆ Lord, hear our prayer.

That the baptized grow in grace and love, we pray: ◆ That leaders bear witness to acts of unity and harmony, we pray: ◆ That families grow in love and harmony, we pray: ◆ That this faith community be filled with the Holy Spirit, we pray: ◆

Our Father . . .

God of glory, source of all joy,
help us to overcome fear and anxiety,
and to trust you in all things.
Through Christ our Lord.
Amen.

✝ Prepare the way of the Lord, make straight his paths: all flesh shall see the salvation of God.

✝ Behold the king will come, the Lord of the earth, and he himself will lift the yoke of our captivity.

Psalm 119   page 418

Reading   Luke 5:17–24

And some men brought on a stretcher a man who was paralyzed; they were trying to bring him in and set him in his presence. But not finding a way to bring him in because of the crowd, they went up on the roof and lowered him on the stretcher through the tiles into the middle in front of Jesus. When Jesus saw their faith, he said, "As for you, your sins are forgiven."

Then the scribes and Pharisees began to ask themselves, "Who is this who speaks blasphemies? Who but God alone can forgive sins?" Jesus knew their thoughts and said to them in reply, "What are you thinking in your hearts? Which is easier, to say, 'Your sins are forgiven,' or to say, 'Rise and walk'? But that you may know that the Son of Man has authority on earth to forgive sins'' — he said to the man who was paralyzed, "I say to you, rise, pick up your stretcher, and go home."

Reflection

Incredible acts are described in today's Gospel; they reveal the mighty work of God. How are they accomplished? It is the faith of the four friends who will not stop until their friend is in the presence of Jesus. This perseverance moves Jesus to not only heal the man but also forgive his sins. This dedication, desire, and faith allow Jesus to do the miraculous. Do I surround myself with friends like this or do my friends lead me astray. Does my friendship lead others to Christ?

Prayers   others may be added

To our God, who has prepared a place for us with him, we pray:

◆ O God, hear us.

For the Church, we pray: ◆ For world leaders, we pray: ◆ For children, we pray: ◆ For the poor and hungry, we pray: ◆ For this parish family, we pray: ◆ For friends and benefactors, we pray: ◆ For the dead, we pray: ◆

Our Father . . .

God of abundant life,
through your servant, Nicholas,
you show us true compassion and service.
Grant us compassionate hearts
so that we might go forth doing good,
and leading others into your presence.
Through Christ our Lord.
Amen.

✝ Behold the king will come, the Lord of the earth, and he himself will lift the yoke of our captivity.

Tuesday, December 7, 2021
Memorial of St. Ambrose, Bishop and Doctor of the Church

✝ The day of the Lord is near: Behold, he comes to save us.

Psalm 25 *page 403*

Reading *Matthew 18:12–14*

Jesus said to his disciples: "What is your opinion? If a man has a hundred sheep and one of them goes astray, will he not leave the ninety-nine in the hills and go in search of the stray? And if he finds it, amen, I say to you, he rejoices more over it than over the ninety-nine that did not stray. In just the same way, it is not the will of your heavenly Father that one of these little ones be lost."

Reflection

We all find ourselves lost at times. As children, we were instructed to approach a trustworthy adult and ask for help. As adults, who may be lost or distracted, we are still called to approach a trustworthy person. This Gospel is a sure reminder that Jesus, the Good Shepherd, will always find us, protect us, and accompany us. The fear and loneliness of being lost is dispelled when we experience God's joy, mercy, and strong hand as he brings us back.

Prayers *others may be added*

To our God, who has prepared a place for us with him, we pray:

◆ Lord, hear our prayer.

For those who feel abandoned by the Church, we pray: ◆ For those who are misled by divination, superstition, and idolatry, we pray: ◆ For those who feel alone and lost, we pray: ◆ For those who seek reconciliation and wholeness, we pray: ◆

Our Father . . .

Good Shepherd, who constantly seeks his lost sheep,
keep vigilant watch over us
as we strive to make our way home to you.
Through Christ our Lord.
Amen.

✝ The day of the Lord is near: Behold, he comes to save us.

✝ Hail, Mary, full of grace, the Lord is with you; blessed are you among women.

Canticle of Mary   *page 421*

Reading   *Luke 1:26–30a, 35b–38*

The angel Gabriel was sent from God to a town of Galilee called Nazareth, to a virgin betrothed to a man named Joseph, of the house of David, and the virgin's name was Mary. And coming to her, he said, "Hail, full of grace! The Lord is with you." But she was greatly troubled at what was said and pondered what sort of greeting this might be. Then the angel said to her, "Do not be afraid, Mary . . . the Holy Spirit will come upon you, and the power of the Most High will overshadow you. Therefore the child to be born will be called holy, the Son of God. And behold, Elizabeth, your relative, has also conceived a son in her old age, and this is the sixth month for her who was called barren; for nothing will be impossible for God." Mary said, "Behold, I am the handmaid of the Lord. May it be done to me according to your word."

Reflection

Today, the Church celebrates the mystery of Mary's Immaculate Conception. While the Gospel speaks of Jesus' conception, it invites us to look back at how Mary arrived at this moment in history. From time immemorial, God protected Mary from sin so that she, if she said yes, could carry the Messiah within her womb. Along the way, Mary's life is full of blessings and challenges, but her *fiat* brought forth the salvation of the world. Like Mary, are we willing to say *yes* to God's invitation to bear witness to Christ?

Prayers   *others may be added*

To our God, who asks Mary to cooperate with his plan of salvation, we pray:

◆ Send your Holy Spirit.

Upon the Church: ◆ Upon expectant mothers and fathers: ◆ Upon those filled with fear and anxiety: ◆ Upon those facing infertility: ◆ Upon the poor and marginalized: ◆ Upon this local church: ◆

Our Father . . .

Gracious God,
you humbly asked Mary,
    your servant,
to share in the salvation of humanity.
Give us the strength to say yes
to your plan for our lives.
Through Christ our Lord.
Amen.

✝ Hail, Mary, full of grace, the Lord is with you; blessed are you among women.

✝ Let the clouds rain down the Just One, and the earth bring forth a Savior.

Psalm 103 *page 414*

Reading *Matthew 11:11–15*

Jesus said to the crowds: "Amen, I say to you, among those born of women there has been none greater than John the Baptist; yet the least in the Kingdom of heaven is greater than he. From the days of John the Baptist until now, the Kingdom of heaven suffers violence, and the violent are taking it by force. All the prophets and the law prophesied up to the time of John. And if you are willing to accept it, he is Elijah, the one who is to come. Whoever has ears ought to hear."

Reflection

John the Baptist is the messenger sent to pave the way for Christ's coming. As a prophet, one who calls the community back to right relationship with God, he helped us see the Messiah; he helped us come to know the Messiah. Jesus' words to the crowd remind us of the important role John played in the salvation of the world. He worked diligently to open the hearts and eyes of the people. He always pointed to his cousin, Jesus. Even today, we can heed John's call to repentance and prepare ourselves for the Second Coming of Christ.

Prayers *others may be added*

Merciful God, we pray:

◆ Lord, hear our prayer.

For members of the Church, may they grow in faith, we pray: ◆ For leaders, may they foster peace and justice, we pray: ◆ For those struggling to hear God's Word, may their ears be opened, we pray: ◆ For the poor and outcast, may they find a home in this community, we pray: ◆

Our Father . . .

O God,
your servant John prepared the way for your Son.
Send your Holy Spirit
to strengthen us in our mission
of sharing the Good News.
Through Christ our Lord.
Amen.

✝ Let the clouds rain down the Just One, and the earth bring forth a Savior.

✝ The Lord will come; go out to meet him! He is the prince of peace.

Psalm 70 *page 411*

Reading *Matthew 11:16–19*

Jesus said to the crowds: "To what shall I compare this generation? It is like children who sit in marketplaces and call to one another, 'We played the flute for you, but you did not dance, we sang a dirge but you did not mourn.' For John came neither eating nor drinking, and they said, 'He is possessed by a demon.' The Son of Man came eating and drinking and they said, 'Look, he is a glutton and a drunkard, a friend of tax collectors and sinners.' But wisdom is vindicated by her works."

Reflection

John's mission is to prepare the world for the Messiah. Some listened to his call, while others mocked and ignored him. Jesus' ministry is one of healing, forgiving, and transforming; he reveals God's love and care for the chosen people. We live in a world that has rejected God's mercy and love. Like John, we are called to prepare the world for Jesus' return.

Prayers *others may be added*

To our God, who reaches out to us in many ways, we pray:

◆ Lord, hear our prayer.

For prophets who herald the coming of the Messiah, we pray: ◆ For world leaders who act justly and walk humbly, we pray: ◆ For those of advanced age who show us the path to wisdom, we pray: ◆ For those who hear the cries of the hungry, the thirsty, and the broken and respond to their needs, we pray: ◆

Our Father . . .

Beloved Father,
you reach out to us
and call us to grow in a loving,
    fruitful relationship with you.
Give us ears to hear your voice
and the courage to follow it.
Through Christ our Lord.
Amen.

✝ The Lord will come; go out to meet him! He is the prince of peace.

✟ Prepare the way of the Lord, make straight his paths: All flesh shall see the salvation of God.

Psalm 27   *page 405*

Reading   *Matthew 17:9a, 10–13*

As they were coming down from the mountain, the disciples asked Jesus, "Why do the scribes say that Elijah must come first?" He said in reply, "Elijah will indeed come and restore all things; but I tell you that Elijah has already come, and they did not recognize him but did to him whatever they pleased. So also will the Son of Man suffer at their hands." Then the disciples understood that he was speaking to them of John the Baptist.

Reflection

In the last lines of the Old Testament, it says that Elijah will return before the day the Lord comes in order to turn the hearts of the people back to the Lord (Malachi 3:23–24). The disciples are beginning to see how this has come true in John the Baptist, one of the two great figures of Advent. The other, of course, is Mary. Both John and Mary point to the singular event of the incarnation. It is the dawn of a new age; it is the Kingdom of God at hand. And so we should follow John's lead, and turn our hearts to the coming of the Lord.

Rev. Michael J. K. Fuller (Daily Prayer 2008)

Prayers   *others may be added*

Wonder Counselor, we turn to you and pray:

◆ Lord, hear our prayer.

For those in the Church who preach and bear the message of the Kingdom of God, we pray: ◆ For those who cannot distinguish the voice of God from the noise and chaos of our culture, we pray: ◆ For the elderly in our community, we pray: ◆ For those who have difficulty recognizing Jesus' presence in their daily life, we pray: ◆

Our Father . . .

O God,
you call us to yourself
through Jesus, your Son.
Help us know the power
    and strength of your Word
and be inspired by your Holy Spirit
to share the Good News.
Through Christ our Lord.
Amen.

✟ Prepare the way of the Lord, make straight his paths: All flesh shall see the salvation of God.

✝ The Spirit of the Lord is upon me, because he has anointed me to bring glad tidings to the poor.

Psalm 25 *page 403*

Reading *Luke 3:15–17*

The people were filled with expectation, and all were asking in their hearts whether John might be the Christ. John answered them all, saying, "I am baptizing you with water, but one mightier than I is coming. I am not worthy to loosen the thongs of his sandals. He will baptize you with the Holy Spirit and fire. His winnowing fan is in his hand to clear his threshing floor and to gather the wheat into his barn, but the chaff he will burn with unquenchable fire."

Reflection

The wheat and chaff are both part of the same plant, but each faces a different fate. The people seek advice regarding how to live holy lives in their day-to-day living. The desire and pursuit of holiness builds the Kingdom. The useful and the holy will be gathered into the barn that is the eternal gift of heaven. Those remaining, the chaff, do not seek holiness or desire to be useful. They live lives of self-centeredness and selfishness. They will not inherit God's Kingdom on that final day.

Prayers *others may be added*

To the Author of Life, who invites us to bear fruit, we pray:

♦ Lord, hear our prayer.

For the Church, that she preach the truth without fear, we pray: ♦ For divided families and immigrants, that they seek common ground, we pray: ♦ For the poor and vulnerable, that they be restored to the fullness of life, we pray: ♦ For the parish, that it be a place of hospitality, we pray: ♦

Our Father . . .

Master of the harvest,
you call us to bear fruit
and become a blessing
to the world around us.
May our life benefit those that hunger.
Through Christ our Lord.
Amen.

✝ The Spirit of the Lord is upon me, because he has anointed me to bring glad tidings to the poor.

Monday, December 13, 2021
Memorial of St. Lucy, Virgin and Martyr

✝ Show us, Lord, your love, and grant us your salvation.

Psalm 119 *page 418*

Reading *Matthew 21:23–27*

When Jesus had come into the temple area, the chief priests and the elders of the people approached him as he was teaching and said, "By what authority are you doing these things? And who gave you this authority?" Jesus said to them in reply, "I shall ask you one question, and if you answer it for me, then I shall tell you by what authority I do these things. Where was John's baptism from? Was it of heavenly or of human origin?" They discussed this among themselves and said, "If we say 'Of heavenly origin,' he will say to us, 'Then why did you not believe him?' But if we say, 'Of human origin,' we fear the crowd, for they all regard John as a prophet." So they said to Jesus in reply, "We do not know." He himself said to them, "Neither shall I tell you by what authority I do these things."

Reflection

We all want to know who is in charge. Those who exercised authority in the temple had forgotten the true authority in the temple was God. Jesus' simple question about John presents a conundrum. Eventually, they admitted they didn't know the origin of John's power. Power and authority can also seduce us, but that temptation is easily corrected when we surrender to the true authority that is our God and follow his Son, Jesus Christ.

Prayers *others may be added*

To the King of Kings, whose authority surrounds us, we pray:

◆ Lord, hear our prayer.

For those who lead the Church and the parish community in various ministries, we pray: ◆ For those leaders who use their authority to serve the common good, we pray: ◆ For those who lead others to resolve conflicts, we pray: ◆ For the sick and dying who long for Christ's mercy, we pray: ◆

Our Father . . .

Saving God,
Jesus teaches us the way to eternal life
and his authority is a rich blessing.
Send your Holy Spirit upon us
to enlighten our path
as we seek to follow you
in word and deed.
Through Christ our Lord.
Amen.

✝ Show us, Lord, your love, and grant us your salvation.

Tuesday, December 14, 2021
Memorial of St. John of the Cross,
Priest and Doctor of the Church

† Come, O Lord, do not delay; forgive the sins of your people.

Psalm 100 *page 414*

Reading *Matthew 21:28–31*

Jesus said to the chief priests and elders of the people: "What is your opinion? A man had two sons. He came to the first and said, 'Son, go out and work in the vineyard today.' He said in reply, 'I will not,' but afterwards changed his mind and went. The man came to the other son and gave the same order. He said in reply, 'Yes, sir,' but did not go. Which of the two did his father's will?" They answered, "The first." Jesus said to them, "Amen, I say to you, tax collectors and prostitutes are entering the kingdom of God before you."

Reflection

Who does the will of the Father? Jesus' answer probably shocked his audience. We have probably encountered someone who is obstinate at first, but upon reflection chooses a different path. Is that what happens with the first son? Ultimately, Jesus is teaching that no matter how religious or scrupulous we may claim to be, it is really about the heart. Does the Word of God change the heart to the point of action and transformation? Those who believe and allow God to change them will inherit the Kingdom.

Prayers *others may be added*

To our God, who moves hearts and minds to action, we pray:

◆ Lord, hear our prayer.

For Carmelites and anyone inspired by John of the Cross, we pray: ◆ For those incarcerated and abused, we pray: ◆ For those persecuted because of faith, we pray: ◆ For those who hunger for physical and spiritual food, we pray: ◆

Our Father . . .

Loving Father,
you invite us to serve one another.
Like St. John, strengthen us
in the mission to build up the Kingdom.
Through Christ our Lord.
Amen.

† Come, O Lord, do not delay; forgive the sins of your people.

Wednesday, December 15, 2021
Advent Weekday

✝ Raise your voice and tell the Good News: Behold, the Lord God comes with power.

Psalm 22   *page 401*

Reading   *Luke 7:18b–23*

At that time, John summoned two of his disciples and sent them to the Lord to ask, "Are you the one who is to come, or should we look for another?" When the men came to the Lord, they said, "John the Baptist has sent us to you to ask, 'Are you the one who is to come, or should we look for another?'" At that time Jesus cured many of their diseases, sufferings, and evil spirits; he also granted sight to many who were blind. And Jesus said to them in reply, "Go and tell John what you have seen and heard: the blind regain their sight, the lame walk, lepers are cleansed, the deaf hear, the dead are raised, the poor have the good news proclaimed to them. And blessed is the one who takes no offense at me."

Reflection

As Jesus' ministry unfolds, word spreads to John the Baptist and his disciples about the wonders he performs. These miracles are a sign of the Messiah and a sign of greater miracles to come. John certainly recognized this and directed his disciples to follow Jesus. What signs do we see today that direct us to follow Christ? Today, spend time contemplating the face of Christ and our mission to proclaim his salvation.

Prayers   *others may be added*

To our God, who has planned all things well, we pray:

◆ Lord, hear our prayer.

For prophets in our midst who point us to Christ, we pray: ◆ For those who suffer religious persecution, we pray: ◆ For those who lack faith, we pray: ◆ For the poor, sick, and suffering, we pray: ◆ For those who preach the Gospel, we pray: ◆

Our Father . . .

Holy One of Israel,
you sent Jesus, your Son,
to reveal your love and mercy.
Open our eyes
so that we may see your glory;
open our ears so that we may
     hear your voice;
grant us the grace to share the Gospel.
Through Christ our Lord.
Amen.

✝ Raise your voice and tell the Good News: Behold, the Lord God comes with power.

Thursday, December 16, 2021
Advent Weekday

✝ Prepare the way of the Lord, make straight his paths: All flesh shall see the salvation of God.

Psalm 51   *page 409*

Reading   *Luke 7:24–27*

When the messengers of John the Baptist had left, Jesus began to speak to the crowds about John. "What did you go out to the desert to see—a reed swayed by the wind? Then what did you go out to see? Someone dressed in fine garments? Those who dress luxuriously and live sumptuously are found in royal palaces. Then what did you go out to see? A prophet? Yes, I tell you, and more than a prophet. This is the one about whom Scripture says: / *Behold, I am sending my messenger ahead of you, / he will prepare your way before you.*"

Reflection

All great things require preparation, and so it is no surprise that we need to prepare our hearts for Christ's coming. John prepared the way for those who would listen, and today, the Advent season provides us the space and rhythm to prepare ourselves for his coming both at his birth and at the end of time. How do you prepare for Christ's coming during this season of joyful hope?

Prayers   *others may be added*

To our Holy God, who speaks to his repentant people, we pray:

♦ Lord, hear our prayer.

That the Church receive the grace to live in this season of preparation and waiting, we pray: ♦ That world leaders carefully discern decisions that impact their communities, we pray: ♦ That the poor and suffering be granted reprieve from their burdens, we pray: ♦ That our faith community be granted wisdom for the Gospel mission, we pray: ♦

Our Father . . .

God of grace,
we have prepared for many earthly
    journeys.
Help us remain focused on you
and your coming in glory
so that on that final day,
we may find ourselves in your presence.
Through Christ our Lord.
Amen.

✝ Prepare the way of the Lord, make straight his paths: All flesh shall see the salvation of God.

Friday, December 17, 2021
Advent Weekday

✝ O Wisdom of our God Most High, guiding creation with power and love: come to teach us the path of knowledge!

Psalm 33 *page 406*

Reading *Matthew 1:17*

Thus the total number of generations from Abraham to David is fourteen generations; from David to the Babylonian exile, fourteen generations; from the Babylonian exile to the Christ, fourteen generations.

Reflection

In recounting the genealogy of Jesus, we are reminded of the Father's plan from the beginning of creation to send his Son. At the same time, we see more clearly than normal the reality of the incarnation in time, some two thousand years ago. With this knowledge, we now look to the coming of Christ in glory at the end of time. May he come quickly and not delay!

Rev. Daren J. Zehnle (Daily Prayer 2009)

Prayers *others may be added*

In hope, we pray:

◆ Lord, hear our prayer.

For the Church, may it be a herald of Good News, we pray: ◆ For those walking in darkness, may they come to know the Light of the World, we pray: ◆ For families, may they be graced with health and wholeness, we pray: ◆ For those who experience loneliness and loss, may they be filled with the Holy Spirit, we pray: ◆

Our Father . . .

Lord Jesus Christ,
hasten to come to us.
We sit in darkness,
waiting for the radiance of your light.
Cast your light upon us now,
that we may recognize you
    when you come in glory,
for you live and reign with the Father
in the unity of the Holy Spirit,
one God, forever and ever.
Amen.

✝ O Wisdom of our God Most High, guiding creation with power and love: come to teach us the path of knowledge!

✝ O Leader of the House of Israel, giver of the Law to Moses on Sinai: Come to rescue us with your mighty power!

Canticle of Mary
page 421

Reading
Matthew 1:18–21

This is how the birth of Jesus Christ came about. When his mother Mary was betrothed to Joseph, but before they lived together, she was found with child through the Holy Spirit. Joseph her husband, since he was a righteous man, yet unwilling to expose her to shame, decided to divorce her quietly. Such was his intention when, behold, the angel of the Lord appeared to him in a dream and said, "Joseph, son of David, do not be afraid to take Mary your wife into your home. For it is through the Holy Spirit that this child has been conceived in her. She will bear a son and you are to name him Jesus, because he will save his people from their sins."

Reflection

If we only knew part of today's story, it could easily be read as a scandalous scenario. However, we know from the passage that Joseph is a righteous man. An angel helps him comprehend what has unfolded with Mary. Once he has the full story, Joseph protects Mary and trusts God's will. Joseph is a man of bold action who does not hesitate to do good deeds. He is a model for us all as we seek to serve God.

Prayers
others may be added

To our loving Father, who cares for his children, we pray:

◆ Lord, hear our prayer.

For the Church who calls its members into the mystery of the incarnation, we pray: ◆ For leaders who call us to justice, we pray: ◆ For expectant parents who reveal God's goodness, we pray: ◆ For those dealing with chronic illness and pain who reveal God's compassion, we pray: ◆

Our Father . . .

God of life,
you entrusted your Son
    to a righteous man
who acted with reckless abandon
to protect your Son and his mother.
Inspire us to act
when your Holy Spirit calls us.
Through Christ our Lord.
Amen.

✝ O Leader of the House of Israel, giver of the Law to Moses on Sinai: Come to rescue us with your mighty power!

✝ O Root of Jesse's stem, sign of God's love for all his people: come to save us without delay!

Psalm 31   *page 405*

Reading   *Luke 1:39–45*

Mary set out and traveled to the hill country in haste to a town of Judah, where she entered the house of Zechariah and greeted Elizabeth. When Elizabeth heard Mary's greeting, the infant leaped in her womb, and Elizabeth, filled with the Holy Spirit, cried out in a loud voice and said, "Blessed are you among women, and blessed is the fruit of your womb. And how does this happen to me, that the mother of my Lord should come to me? For at that moment the sound of your greeting reached my ears, the infant in my womb leaped for joy. Blessed are you who believed that what was spoken to you by the Lord would be fulfilled."

Reflection

Mary receives the message of the angel, and, unlike Zechariah, she cannot be silent: she must share her joy. When she greets Elizabeth, several things happen at once. Elizabeth is filled with the Holy Spirit, and suddenly and mysteriously, she understands who Mary is, "blessed . . . among women." At the same time, the infant John the Baptist leaps in her womb, and Elizabeth recognizes that, blessed as Mary is, the child in her womb is more blessed still. Mary is blessed not because she carries the Christ in her womb, but because she "believed." We are all called to be like Mary.

Ward Johnson and Corinna Laughlin
(Daily Prayer 2010)

Prayers   *others may be added*

To our Lord, who hears our plea, we pray:

♦ Come, Lord Jesus.

Bless your people, O Lord, we pray: ♦ Raise up just leaders, O Lord, we pray: ♦ Guide parents, O Lord, we pray: ♦ Fill the hungry, O Lord, we pray: ♦ Comfort the sick and dying, O Lord, we pray: ♦

Our Father . . .

Just and compassionate God,
show us your will for our lives
and open our hearts to receive the
    Christ child.
Through Christ our Lord.
Amen.

✝ O Root of Jesse's stem, sign of God's love for all his people: come to save us without delay!

Monday, December 20, 2021
Advent Weekday

✝ O Key of David, opening the gates of God's eternal Kingdom: come and free the prisoners of darkness!

Psalm 96
page 413

Reading
Luke 1:26–33

The angel Gabriel was sent from God to a town of Galilee called Nazareth, to a virgin betrothed to a man named Joseph, of the house of David, and the virgin's name was Mary. And coming to her, he said, "Hail, full of grace! The Lord is with you." But she was greatly troubled at what was said and pondered what sort of greeting this might be. Then the angel said to her, "Do not be afraid, Mary, for you have found favor with God. Behold, you will conceive in your womb and bear a son, and you shall name him Jesus. He will be great and will be called Son of the Most High, and the Lord God will give him the throne of David his father, and he will rule over the house of Jacob forever, and of his Kingdom there will be no end."

Reflection

Imagine, an angel appearing and calling out, "Hail, favored one!" How might you react? This greeting puzzles Mary. How is she *favored* in God's eyes? Ultimately, Mary humbly accepts God's plan; she trusts God with her whole being. God's will might have been different from Mary's, but she chose to cooperate willingly with God's salvific plan. We, too, are favored in God's eyes and God calls each of us to cooperate within the plan of salvation history.

Prayers
others may be added

To our God, who has prepared a place for us with him, we pray:

◆ Lord, hear our prayer.

That the Church have the courage to follow God's will like Mary, we pray: ◆ That leaders not discount the contributions of the very young and the aged, we pray: ◆ That all disciples trust and cooperate with God's plan, we pray: ◆ That ministers bring comfort and hope to the dying, we pray: ◆

Our Father . . .

God of grace,
your very nature permeates the life
of your servant Mary.
Through her intercession,
transform our hearts to humbly
accept our mission of proclaiming
    the Gospel.
Through Christ our Lord.
Amen.

✝ O Key of David, opening the gates of God's eternal Kingdom: come and free the prisoners of darkness!

Tuesday, December 21, 2021
Advent Weekday

✝ O Radiant Dawn, splendor of eternal light, sun of justice: come and shine on those who dwell in darkness and in the shadow of death.

Canticle of Mary   *page 421*

Reading   *Luke 1:39–45*

Mary set out in those days and traveled to the hill country in haste to a town of Judah, where she entered the house of Zechariah and greeted Elizabeth. When Elizabeth heard Mary's greeting, the infant leaped in her womb, and Elizabeth, filled with the Holy Spirit, cried out in a loud voice and said, "Most blessed are you among women, and blessed is the fruit of your womb. And how does this happen to me, that the mother of my Lord should come to me? For at the moment the sound of your greeting reached my ears, the infant in my womb leaped for joy. Blessed are you who believed that what was spoken to you by the Lord would be fulfilled."

Reflection

Mary embodies the role of a humble servant when she heads out to visit Elizabeth. She knows Elizabeth's age and knows this pregnancy will be difficult for Elizabeth. It will also be an opportunity for Mary to learn from her cousin what awaits her as she carries a child. Mary chooses to focus on another as she realizes the will of God as best she can in her own life. Where does our humble service take us as we try to do the will of God in our life?

Prayers   *others may be added*

To our God, who has prepared a place for us with him, we pray:

◆ Lord, hear our prayer.

For the Church as she advocates for the poor, we pray: ◆ For world leaders in their pursuit of justice and peace, we pray: ◆ For parents, catechists, and teachers who guide young hearts and minds, we pray: ◆ For expectant parents as they prepare to welcome a child, we pray: ◆

Our Father . . .

O God,
like Mary, make us humble of heart
and fill us with your Holy Spirit
as we prepare to you receive
the gift of your Son, Jesus.
Who lives and reigns with you
in the unity of the Holy Spirit,
one God, for ever and ever.
Amen.

✝ O Radiant Dawn, splendor of eternal light, sun of justice: come and shine on those who dwell in darkness and in the shadow of death.

✝ O King of all nations and keystone of the Church: come and save man, whom you formed from the dust!

Psalm 108   page 415

Reading   Luke 1:46–55

"My soul proclaims the greatness of the Lord; / my spirit rejoices in God my savior, / for he has looked upon his lowly servant. / From this day all generations will call me blessed: / the Almighty has done great things for me, / and holy is his Name. / He has mercy on those who fear him / in every generation. / He has shown the strength of his arm, / and has scattered the proud in their conceit. / He has cast down the mighty from their thrones / and has lifted up the lowly. / He has filled the hungry with good things, / and the rich he has sent away empty. / He has come to the help of his servant Israel / for he remembered his promise of mercy, / the promise he made to our fathers, / to Abraham and his children for ever."

Reflection

Mary said: My soul proclaims the greatness of the Lord, my spirit rejoices in God my Savior.

The Lord has exalted me by a gift so great, so unheard of, that language is useless to describe it, and the depths of love in my heart can scarcely grasp it. I offer then all the powers of my soul in praise and thanksgiving. As I contemplate his greatness, which knowns no limits, I joyfully surrender my whole life, my senses, my judgment, for my spirit rejoices in the eternal Godhead of that Jesus, that Savior, whom I have conceived in this world of time.

From a commentary on Luke by Venerable Bede (Office of Readings for December 22)

Prayers   others may be added

With joyful hope, we pray:

♦ Hear us, O Christ.

For members of the Church, may they understand and live their mission as a child of God, we pray: ♦ For leaders, may they be filled with courage and hope, we pray: ♦ For those struggling with prayer, may they know God's presence, we pray: ♦ For the elderly, may they be protected from injury, we pray: ♦

Our Father . . .

Almighty and ever-living God,
like Mary, we are filled with joy
at the coming of our Lord.
Open our hearts to your Word
so that, as we share the news of salvation,
we may forever praise your name.
Through Christ our Lord.
Amen.

✝ O King of all nations and keystone of the Church: come and save man, whom you formed from the dust!

✝ O Emmanuel, our King and Giver of Law: come to save us, Lord our God!

Psalm 63   *page 411*

Reading   *Luke 1:57–63*

When the time arrived for Elizabeth to have her child she gave birth to a son. Her neighbors and relatives heard that the Lord had shown his great mercy toward her, and they rejoiced with her. When they came on the eighth day to circumcise the child, they were going to call him Zechariah after his father, but his mother said in reply, "No. He will be called John." But they answered her, "There is no one among your relatives who has this name." So they made signs, asking his father what he wished him to be called. He asked for a tablet and wrote, "John is his name," and all were amazed.

Reflection

There is great power in a name. It connects our past, our families, and it speaks to our hope in the future. John's name means "God is gracious"; it speaks to the gift this child is to his barren mother. It also speaks to his prophetic ministry of preparing "a people fit for the Lord" (Luke 1:17). Zechariah spent nine months in silence contemplating all that has happened, especially the important role his son would play in the history of his people.

Prayers   *others may be added*

To the Incarnate Word, we pray:

◆ Lord, hear our prayer.

For members of the Church, we pray: ◆ For world leaders, we pray: ◆ For the voiceless and powerless, we pray: ◆ For couples hoping to get pregnant, we pray: ◆ For families who adopt, we pray: ◆ For the dying, we pray: ◆

Our Father . . .

Blessed God,
you love and care for us.
shower us with the gifts of the Spirit
so that we may be strengthened
in our mission of sharing the Gospel.
Through Christ our Lord.
Amen.

✝ O Emmanuel, our King and Giver of Law: come to save us, Lord our God!

✝ O Virgin of virgins, how shall this be? For neither before you was any like you, nor shall there be after. Daughters of Jerusalem, why do you marvel at me? The thing which you behold is a Divine Mystery.

Psalm 47   page 409

Reading   Luke 1:67, 73–79

Zechariah his father, filled with the Holy Spirit, prophesied, saying: . . . / "This was the oath he swore to our father Abraham: / to set us free from the hand of our enemies, / free to worship him without fear, / holy and righteous in his sight all the days of our life. / You, my child, shall be called the prophet of the Most High, / for you will go before the Lord to prepare his way, / to give his people knowledge of salvation / by the forgiveness of their sins. / In the tender compassion of our God / the dawn from on high shall break upon us, / to shine on those who dwell in darkness and the shadow of death, / and to guide our feet into the way of peace."

Reflection

Zechariah knows the history of his people. He knows God. They say that the language of God is silence. Zechariah has taken a nine-month crash course in the study of God's language. In that silence, he understood God. With this new vision, he looks at the journey the people have taken and he sees the guiding hand of God leading them to this point. He sees, in his son, the one who will prepare the way for the Messiah. When we spend time in the silence, do we see God's hand or our own hand?

Prayers   others may be added

Son of God, we come to you with joyful hearts, as we pray:

◆ Lord, hear our prayer.

For the Church who proclaims the Good News of salvation, we pray: ◆ For those who faithfully live the covenant relationship with the Lord, we pray: ◆ For those sitting in darkness, awaiting the great Light, we pray: ◆ For those who are forgotten amid the rush of the holidays, we pray: ◆

Our Father . . .

O God of glory,
Zechariah announced your
        marvelous deeds.
Give us the voice
to bear witness
to your gift of salvation.
Through Christ our Lord.
Amen.

✝ O Virgin of virgins, how shall this be? For neither before you was any like you, nor shall there be after. Daughters of Jerusalem, why do you marvel at me? The thing which you behold is a Divine Mystery.

✝ A holy day has dawned upon us. Come, you nations, and adore the Lord. Today a great light has come upon the earth.

Psalm 103   *page 414*

Reading   *Luke 2:8–14*

Now there were shepherds in that region living in the fields and keeping the night watch over their flock. The angel of the Lord appeared to them and the glory of the Lord shone around them, and they were struck with great fear. The angel said to them, "Do not be afraid; for behold, I proclaim to you good news of great joy that will be for all the people. For today in the city of David a savior has been born for you who is Christ and Lord. And this will be a sign for you: you will find an infant wrapped in swaddling clothes and lying in a manger." And suddenly there was a multitude of the heavenly host with the angel, praising God and saying: / "Glory to God in the highest / and on earth peace to those on whom his favor rests." /

Reflection

The shepherds led quiet solitary lives, moving and resting with the rhythms of the world around them. Their vigilance protected the flocks. The sudden appearance of angels would have been shocking and wonderful to behold. There are times in our lives when we should be vigilant, watching and waiting for the wonders God longs to reveal. When he comes in his glory, will he find us alert and waiting, or distracted and fixated on the things of this world?

Prayers   *others may be added*

To our Messiah and Lord, we come with hearts full of joy, as we pray:

♦ Lord, hear our prayer.

May the Church welcome all who come seeking shelter and love, we pray: ♦ May immigrants, refugees, and the homeless be welcomed in our midst, we pray: ♦ May the sick and suffering receive the grace of healing and comfort, we pray: ♦ May this community grow in love for the Christ child, we pray: ♦

Our Father . . .

Word Incarnate,
you stepped into human history
to show us how to live.
Awaken within us a desire to serve
and a love for the Gospel.
Who live and reign with God the Father
in the unity of the Holy Spirit,
one God, for ever and ever.
Amen.

✝ A holy day has dawned upon us. Come, you nations, and adore the Lord. Today a great light has come upon the earth.

Sunday, December 26, 2021
Feast of the Holy Family of Jesus, Mary, and Joseph

✝ May the peace of Christ rule our hearts.

Psalm 103 *page 414*

Reading *Luke 2:46–51*

After three days [Jesus' parents] found him in the temple, sitting in the midst of the teachers, listening to them and asking them questions, and all who heard him were astounded at his understanding and his answers. When his parents saw him, they were astonished, and his mother said to him, "Son, why have you done this to us? Your father and I have been looking for you with great anxiety." And he said to them, "Why were you looking for me? Did you not know that I must be in my Father's house?" But they did not understand what he said to them. He went down with them and came to Nazareth, and was obedient to them; and his mother kept all these things in her heart.

Reflection

Nazareth is a kind of school where we may begin to discover what Christ's life was like and even to understand his Gospel. Here we can observe and ponder the simple appeal of the way God's Son came to be known, profound yet full of hidden meaning. And gradually we may even learn to imitate him.

Pope Paul VI, January 5, 1964 address
(Office of Readings, Holy Family)

Prayers *others may be added*

Light of the nations, hear our prayer:

◆ Lord, hear our prayer.

For the Church who proclaims the mystery of the incarnation, we pray: ◆ For the baptized who give witness of Christ's presence, we pray: ◆ For families who struggle, we pray: ◆ For wisdom figures who lead us, we pray: ◆

Our Father . . .

Blessed Trinity,
you know what it means
   to live in communion;
help us to share our lives
and in the sharing
come to know you better.
Through Christ our Lord.
Amen.

✝ May the peace of Christ rule our hearts.

✝ We praise you, God: we acknowledge you as Lord: your glorious band of apostles extols you.

Psalm 31 *page 405*

Reading *John 20:1a, 2–4, 6–8*

On the first day of the week, Mary Magdalene ran and went to Simon Peter and to the other disciple whom Jesus loved, and told them, "They have taken the Lord from the tomb, and we don't know where they put him." So Peter and the other disciple went out and came to the tomb. . . . When Simon Peter arrived after him, he went into the tomb and saw the burial cloths there, and the cloth that had covered his head, not with the burial cloths but rolled up in a separate place. Then the other disciple also went in, the one who had arrived at the tomb first, and he saw and believed.

Reflection

Today, we hear a description of "the other disciple, the one whom Jesus loved," in a race with Peter. While it is true John and Jesus are very good friends, the description of John includes all believers. The disciple waits for Peter, the head of the Church, and then he enters and believes. We are called to do the same; that is, to follow the lead of Peter and believe. Believe because we have seen the great wonders our God has done in our life and in the lives of others.

Prayers *others may be added*

Filled with joy, we pray:

◆ Lord, hear our prayer.

For members of the Church, we pray: ◆ For world leaders, we pray: ◆ For those who lack faith, we pray: ◆ For the poor and oppressed, we pray: ◆ For the sick and dying, we pray: ◆ For friends and family, we pray: ◆

Our Father . . .

Holy Father,
the apostle John
teaches us the gift of friendship and love.
Grant us the grace of companionship
as we go forth sharing the Good News.
Through Christ our Lord.
Amen.

✝ We praise you, God: we acknowledge you as Lord: your glorious band of apostles extols you.

Tuesday, December 28, 2021
Feast of The Holy Innocents, Martyrs

✝ We praise you, O God, we acclaim you as Lord; the white-robed army of martyrs praise you.

Psalm 33 page 406

Reading *Matthew 2:13–15*

When the magi had departed, behold, the angel of the Lord appeared to Joseph in a dream and said, "Rise, take the child and his mother, flee to Egypt, and stay there until I tell you. Herod is going to search for the child to destroy him." Joseph rose and took the child and his mother by night and departed for Egypt. He stayed there until the death of Herod, that what the Lord had said through the prophet might be fulfilled, / *Out of Egypt I called my son.*

Reflection

Why are you afraid, Herod, when you hear of the birth of a king? . . . You are not restrained by the love of weeping mothers or fathers mourning the death of their sons, nor by the cries and sobs of children. . . . You imagine that if you accomplish your desire you can prolong your own life, though you are seeking to kill Life himself.

The children die for Christ, though they do not know it. The parents mourn for the death of martyrs. . . . See the kind of kingdom that is his, coming as he did in order to be this kind of king. See how the deliverer is already working deliverance, the savior already working salvation.

From a sermon by St. Quodvultdeus
(Office of Readings for Holy Innocents)

Prayers *others may be added*

Protect and save us, Lord, as we pray:

♦ Lord, hear our prayer.

That the members of the Church come to trust in and follow God's Word, we pray: ♦ That we may trust in the providence of God to take care of his people, we pray: ♦ That we may look to Joseph as a model for deep listening and deep faithfulness in God, we pray: ♦ For the vulnerable and those at risk, we pray: ♦

Our Father . . .

Merciful God,
these Innocents unknowingly
    gave their life
so that Christ, King of Kings,
would one day be raised from the dead
and raise each of us to eternal life.
May your grace help us bear witness
    to Christ's love
through the faith we profess.
Through Christ our Lord.
Amen.

✝ We praise you, O God, we acclaim you as Lord; the white-robed army of martyrs praise you.

Wednesday, December 29, 2021

Fifth Day within the Octave of Christmas

✝ The light of revelation to the Gentiles and glory for your people Israel.

Psalm 34 *page 406*

Reading *Luke 2:22ac, 24, 26–32*

When the days were completed for their purification . . . the parents of Jesus took him up to Jerusalem to present him to the Lord . . . and to offer the sacrifice of *a pair of turtledoves or two young pigeons*, in accordance with the dictate in the law of the Lord. . . .

It had been revealed to [Simeon] by the Holy Spirit that he should not see death before he had seen the Christ of the Lord. He came in the Spirit into the temple; and when the parents brought in the child Jesus to perform the custom of the law in regard to him, he took him into his arms and blessed God, saying: / "Lord, now let your servant go in peace; / your word has been fulfilled: / my own eyes have seen the salvation / which you prepared in the sight of every people, / a light to reveal you to the nations / and the glory of your people Israel."

Reflection

How often have we looked at Christ and seen our God, incarnate, healer, and miracle worker who comes to save the world? Today, we glimpse something else, the humble humanity we all share. We see that nobody goes through life alone. We work together to realize the plan of God. Apart from one another, we wither and die, but together we give glory to God. Jesus needs his parents to offer the appropriate sacrifice. When and how do we rely on family, friends, and community to grow in our worship of the Lord?

Prayers *others may be added*

Emmanuel, with joyful hearts, we pray:

◆ Lord, hear our prayer:

For the catechists who reveal the presence of Christ among us, we pray: ◆ For those on unexpected journeys, we pray: ◆ For those who feel unworthy to approach the altar of the Lord, we pray: ◆ For the elderly, the sick, the suffering, and poor, we pray: ◆

Our Father . . .

O Word Incarnate,
you came into the world to reveal God's
    love and mercy.
May we have ears to hear you call us
    and eyes to see your light
as we go forth announcing the Good
    News of salvation.
Who live and reign with God the Father
in the unity of the Holy Spirit,
one God, for ever and ever.
 Amen.

✝ The light of revelation to the Gentiles and glory for your people Israel.

✝ A holy day has dawned upon us. Come, you nations, and adore the Lord. Today a great light has come upon the earth.

Psalm 145 — page 420

Reading — Luke 2:36–38

There was a prophetess, Anna, the daughter of Phanuel, of the tribe of Asher. She was advanced in years, having lived seven years with her husband after her marriage, and then as a widow until she was eighty-four. She never left the temple, but worshiped night and day with fasting and prayer. And coming forward at that very time, she gave thanks to God and spoke about the child to all who were awaiting the redemption of Jerusalem.

Reflection

Anna knows the joys and pains of the world; she has known marriage and the pain of loss. She has chosen to spend her time in praise to God in his holy temple, and that choice has given her life and insight. She is led to the infant. Once she encounters the child, she joyfully sings his praise to all. What is our response when we experience our God in a profound way? Do we keep it to ourselves, or do we tell everyone we know?

Prayers — others may be added

In praise to our God and King, we pray:

◆ O God, hear us.

For those who preach the Gospel, we pray: ◆ For children in their pursuit of wisdom, we pray: ◆ For those who seek to find life in God's house, we pray: ◆ For the poor and marginalized in our midst, we pray: ◆

Our Father . . .

God of blessings,
you promised Anna that she would
   see salvation.
Her response was to praise you.
May we see the promise
and give glory to your Son, Jesus,
who lives and reigns with you
in the unity of the Holy Spirit,
one God for ever and ever.
Amen.

✝ A holy day has dawned upon us. Come, you nations, and adore the Lord. Today a great light has come upon the earth.

✝ The Word of God became flesh and dwelt among us. To those who accepted him he gave power to become the children of God.

Psalm 16   *page 400*

Reading   *John 1:1–5, 14*

In the beginning was the Word, / and the Word was with God, and the Word was God. / He was in the beginning with God. / All things came to be through him, / and without him nothing came to be. / What came to be through him was life, / and this life was the light of the human race; / the light shines in the darkness, / and the darkness has not overcome it. . . .

And the Word became flesh / and made his dwelling among us, / and we saw his glory, / the glory as of the Father's only Son, / full of grace and truth. /

Reflection

Have you been lost in the dark? It can be a fearful and paralyzing experience. In our paralyzing darkness, our God comes to us as light and gives us an opportunity to become his children. Because we are children of his light, we can boldly go out into the darkness of the world and be a light to those who are lost. We share the light because it has been generously given to us. We are simply servants who share the gift of Light.

Prayers   *others may be added*

To the Word who lived before all creation, we pray:

◆ Lord, hear our prayer.

May the light of Christ shine within the Church, we pray: ◆ May the lost, afraid, and alone revel in Christ's light, we pray: ◆ May hardened hearts be softened by God's Word, we pray: ◆ May those searching for truth come to know Christ, we pray: ◆

Our Father . . .

God of light,
you shine in a world of darkness and fear.
May we be drawn to your warmth and
    light;
may we always know your peace
    and consolation.
Through Christ our Lord.
Amen.

✝ The Word of God became flesh and dwelt among us. To those who accepted him he gave power to become the children of God.

Psalter

Psalm 8:4–5, 6–7, 8–9

When I behold your heavens, the work of your fingers,
    the moon and the stars which you set in place —
What is man that you should be mindful of him,
    or the son of man that you should care for him?

You have made him little less than the angels,
    and crowned him with glory and honor.
You have given him rule over the works of your hands,
    putting all things under his feet.

All sheep and oxen,
    yes, and the beasts of the field,
The birds of the air, the fishes of the sea,
    and whatever swims the paths of the sea.

Psalm 16:1–2, 5, 7–8, 9–10, 11

Keep me, O God, for in you I take refuge;
    I say to the LORD, "My Lord are you."
O LORD, my allotted portion and my cup,
    you it is who hold fast my lot.

I bless the LORD who counsels me;
    even in the night my heart exhorts me.
I set the LORD ever before me;
    with him at my right hand I shall not be disturbed.

Therefore my heart is glad and my soul rejoices,
    my body, too, abides in confidence;
because you will not abandon my soul to the netherworld,
    nor will you suffer your faithful one to undergo corruption.

You will show me the path to life,
    fullness of joys in your presence,
    the delights at your right hand forever.

Psalm 22:8–9, 17–18a, 19–20, 23–24

All who see me scoff at me;
   they mock me with parted lips, they wag their heads:
"He relied on the LORD; let him deliver him,
   let him rescue him, if he loves him."

Indeed, many dogs surround me,
   a pack of evildoers closes in upon me;
They have pierced my hands and my feet;
   I can count all my bones.

They divide my garments among them,
   and for my vesture they cast lots.
But you, O LORD, be not far from me;
   O my help, hasten to aid me.

I will proclaim your name to my brethren;
   in the midst of the assembly I will praise you:
"You who fear the LORD, praise him;
   all you descendants of Jacob, give glory to him;
   revere him, all you descendants of Israel!"

Psalm 23:1–3a, 3b–4, 5, 6

The LORD is my shepherd; I shall not want.
  In verdant pastures he gives me repose;
Beside restful waters he leads me;
  he refreshes my soul.

He guides me in right paths
  for his name's sake.
Even though I walk in the dark valley
  I fear no evil; for you are at my side
With your rod and your staff
  that give me courage.

You spread the table before me
  in the sight of my foes;
You anoint my head with oil;
  my cup overflows.

Only goodness and kindness follow me
  all the days of my life;
And I shall dwell in the house of the LORD
  for years to come.

Psalm 24:1–2, 3–4, 5–6, 7–10

The LORD's are the earth and its fullness;
  the world and those who dwell in it.
For he founded it upon the seas
  and established it upon the rivers.

Who can ascend the mountain of the LORD?
  Or who may stand in his holy place?
One whose hands are sinless, whose heart is clean,
  who desires not what is vain.

He shall receive a blessing from the LORD,
  a reward from God his savior.
Such is the race that seeks for him,
  that seeks the face of the God of Jacob.

Lift up, O gates, your lintels;
    reach up, you ancient portals,
    that the king of glory may come in!

Who is this king of glory?
    The LORD, strong and mighty,
    the LORD, mighty in battle.

Lift up, O gates, your lintels;
    reach up, you ancient portals,
    that the king of glory may come in!

Who is this king of glory?
    The LORD of hosts; he is the king of glory.

Psalm 25:2–3, 4–5ab, 6 and 7bc

In you I trust; let me not be put to shame,
    let not my enemies exult over me.
No one who waits for you shall be put to shame;
    those shall be put to shame who heedlessly break faith.

Your ways, O LORD, make known to me;
    teach me your paths,
Guide me in your truth and teach me,
    for you are God my savior.

Remember that your compassion, O LORD,
    and your kindness are from of old.
In your kindness remember me,
    because of your goodness, O LORD.

Psalm 26

Judge me, LORD!
    For I have walked in my integrity.
In the LORD I trust;
    I do not falter.
Examine me, Lord, and test me;
    search my heart and mind.
Your mercy is before my eyes;
    I walk guided by your faithfulness.

I do not sit with worthless men,
    nor with hypocrites do I mingle.
I hate an evil assembly;
    with the wicked I do not sit.
I will wash my hands in innocence
    so that I may process around your altar, Lord,
To hear the sound of thanksgiving,
    and recount all your wondrous deeds.
Lord, I love the refuge of your house,
    the site of the dwelling-place of your glory.

Do not take me away with sinners,
    nor my life with the men of blood,
In whose hands there is a plot,
    their right hands full of bribery.
But I walk in my integrity;
    redeem me, be gracious to me!
My foot stands on level ground;
    in assemblies I will bless the LORD.

Psalm 27:7–8a, 8b–9abc, 13–14

Hear, O LORD, the sound of my call;
   have pity on me, and answer me.
Of you my heart speaks; you my glance seeks.

Your presence, O LORD, I seek.
Hide not your face from me;
   do not in anger repel your servant.
You are my helper; cast me not off.

I believe that I shall see the bounty of the LORD
   in the land of the living.
Wait for the LORD with courage;
   be stouthearted, and wait for the LORD.

Psalm 31:2, 6, 12–13, 15–16, 17, 25

In you, O LORD, I take refuge;
   let me never be put to shame.
In your justice rescue me.
Into your hands I commend my spirit;
   you will redeem me, O LORD, O faithful God.

For all my foes I am an object of reproach,
   a laughingstock to my neighbors, and a dread to my friends;
   they who see me abroad flee from me.
I am forgotten like the unremembered dead;
   I am like a dish that is broken.

But my trust is in you, O LORD;
   I say, "You are my God.
In your hands is my destiny; rescue me
   from the clutches of my enemies and my persecutors."

Let your face shine upon your servant;
   save me in your kindness.
Take courage and be stouthearted,
   all you who hope in the LORD.

Psalm 33:4–5, 18–19, 20, 22

Upright is the word of the LORD,
    and all his works are trustworthy.
He loves justice and right;
    of the kindness of the LORD the earth is full.

See, the eyes of the LORD are upon those who fear him,
    upon those who hope for his kindness,
To deliver them from death
    and preserve them in spite of famine.

Our soul waits for the LORD,
    who is our help and our shield.
May your kindness, O LORD, be upon us
    who have put our hope in you.

Psalm 34:2–3, 4–5, 6–7

I will bless the LORD at all times;
    his praise shall be ever in my mouth.
Let my soul glory in the LORD;
    the lowly will hear me and be glad.

Glorify the LORD with me,
    let us together extol his name.
I sought the LORD, and he answered me
    and delivered me from all my fears.

Look to him that you may be radiant with joy,
    and your faces may not blush with shame.
When the afflicted man called out, the LORD heard,
    and from all his distress he saved him.

Psalm 35:1–2, 3–4, 5–6, 7–8, 9–10

Oppose, O Lord, those who oppose me;
　war upon those who make war upon me.
Take up the shield and buckler;
　rise up in my defense.

Brandish lance and battle-ax
　against my pursuers.
Say to my soul,
　"I am your salvation."
Let those who seek my life
　be put to shame and disgrace.
Let those who plot evil against me
　be turned back and confounded.

Make them like chaff before the wind,
　with the angel of the LORD driving them on.
Make their way slippery and dark,
　with the angel of the LORD pursuing them.

Without cause they set their snare for me;
　without cause they dug a pit for me.
Let ruin overtake them unawares;
　let the snare they have set catch them;
　let them fall into the pit they have dug.

Then I will rejoice in the LORD,
　exult in God's salvation.
My very bones shall say,
　"O LORD, who is like you,
Who rescue the afflicted from the powerful,
　the afflicted and needy from the despoiler?"

Psalm 36:6–7, 8–9, 10–11

O LORD, your kindness reaches to heaven;
    your faithfulness to the clouds.
Your justice is like the mountains of God;
    your judgments like the mighty deep.

How precious is your kindness, O God!
    The children of men take refuge in the shadow of your wings.
They have their fill of the prime gifts of your house;
    from your delightful stream you give them to drink.

For with you is the fountain of life,
    and in your light we see light.
Keep up your kindness toward your friends,
    your just defense of the upright heart.

Psalm 42:2–3, 4–5, 6, 9

As the deer longs for streams of water,
    so my soul longs for you, O God.
My soul thirsts for God, the living God.
    When can I enter and see the face of God?

My tears have been my bread day and night,
    as they ask me every day, "Where is your God?"
Those times I recall
    as I pour out my soul,
When I would cross over to the shrine of the Mighty One,
    to the house of God,
Amid loud cries of thanksgiving,
    with the multitude keeping festival.

Why are you downcast, my soul;
    why do you groan within me?
Wait for God, for I shall again praise him,
    my savior and my God.

By day may the LORD send his mercy,
    and by night may his righteousness be with me!
    I will pray to the God of my life.

Psalm 47:2–3, 6–7, 8–9

All you peoples, clap your hands,
    shout to God with cries of gladness.
For the Lord, the Most High, the awesome,
    is the great king over all the earth.

God mounts his throne amid shouts of joy;
    the Lord, amid trumpet blasts.
Sing praise to God, sing praise;
    sing praise to our king, sing praise.

For king of all the earth is God;
    sing hymns of praise.
God reigns over the nations,
    God sits upon his holy throne.

Psalm 51:3–6a, 12–13, 17

Have mercy on me, God, in accord with your merciful love;
    in your abundant compassion blot out my transgressions.
Thoroughly wash away my guilt;
    and from my sin cleanse me.

For I know my transgressions;
    my sin is always before me.
Against you, you alone have I sinned;
    I have done what is evil in your eyes
So that you are just in your word,
    and without reproach in your judgment.

A clean heart create for me, God;
    renew within me a steadfast spirit.
Do not drive me from before your face,
    nor take from me your holy spirit.

Lord, you will open my lips;
    and my mouth will proclaim your praise.

Psalm 60:3–4, 5–6, 7, 8–10, 11–14

O God, you rejected us, broke our defenses;
    you were angry but now revive us.
You rocked the earth, split it open;
    repair the cracks for it totters.
You made your people go through hardship,
    made us stagger from the wine you gave us.
Raise up a banner for those who revere you,
    a refuge for them out of bow shot.

Help with your right hand and answer us
    that your loved ones may escape.

In the sanctuary God promised:
    "I will exult, will apportion Shechem;
    the valley of Succoth I will measure out.
Gilead is mine, mine is Manasseh;
    Ephraim is the helmet for my head,
    Judah, my own scepter.
Moab is my washbowl;
    upon Edom I cast my sandal.
    I will triumph over Philistia."

Who will bring me to the fortified city?
    Who will lead me into Edom?
Was it not you who rejected us, God?
    Do you no longer march with our armies?
Give us aid against the foe;
    worthless is human help.
We will triumph with the help of God,
    who will trample down our foes.

Psalm 63:2, 3–4, 5–6, 8–9

O God, you are my God, whom I seek;
    for you my flesh pines and my soul thirsts.

Thus have I gazed toward you in the sanctuary
    to see your power and your glory,
For your kindness is a greater good than life;
    my lips shall glorify you.

Thus I will bless you as I live;
    lifting up my hands, I will call upon your name.
As with the riches of the banquet shall my soul be satisfied,
    and with exultant lips my mouth shall praise you.

You are my help,
    and in the shadow of your wings I shout for joy.
My soul clings fast to you;
    your right hand upholds me.

Psalm 70:2–6

Graciously rescue me, God!
    Come quickly to help me, LORD!
Let those who seek my life
    be confused and put to shame.
Let those who desire my ruin
    turn back in disgrace.
Let those who say "Aha!"
    turn back in their shame.

But may all who seek you
    rejoice and be glad in you,
Those who long for your help
    always say, "God be glorified!"
I am miserable and poor.
    God, come to me quickly!
You are my help and deliverer.
    LORD, do not delay.

Psalm 72:1–2, 7–8, 12–13, 17

O God, with your judgment endow the king,
    and with your justice, the king's son;
He shall govern your people with justice
    and your afflicted ones with judgment.

Justice shall flower in his days,
    and profound peace, till the moon be no more.
May he rule from sea to sea,
    and from the River to the ends of the earth.

He shall rescue the poor man when he cries out,
    and the afflicted when he has no one to help him.
He shall have pity for the lowly and the poor;
    the lives of the poor he shall save.

May his name be blessed forever;
    as long as the sun his name shall remain.
In him shall all the tribes of the earth be blessed;
    all the nations shall proclaim his happiness.

Psalm 80:2, 15–16, 18–19

O shepherd of Israel, hearken,
From your throne upon the cherubim, shine forth.
Rouse your power.
    and come to save us.

Once again, O Lord of hosts,
    look down from heaven, and see;
Take care of this vine,
    and protect what your right hand has planted
    [the son of man whom you yourself made strong].

May your help be with the man of your right hand,
    with the son of man whom you yourself made strong.
Then we will no more withdraw from you;
    give us new life, and we will call upon your name.

Psalm 85:8 and 10, 11–12, 13–14

Show us, O Lord, your mercy,
    and grant us your salvation.
Near indeed is his salvation to those who fear him,
    glory dwelling in our land.

Kindness and truth shall meet;
    justice and peace shall kiss.
Truth shall spring out of the earth,
    and justice shall look down from heaven.

The Lord himself will give his benefits;
    our land shall yield its increase.
Justice shall walk before him,
    and salvation, along the way of his steps.

Psalm 96:1–2, 2–3, 11–12, 13

Sing to the Lord a new song;
    sing to the Lord, all you lands.
Sing to the Lord; bless his name.

Announce his salvation, day after day.
Tell his glory among the nations;
    among all peoples, his wondrous deeds.

Let the heavens be glad and the earth rejoice;
    let the sea and what fills it resound;
    let the plains be joyful and all that is in them!
Then shall all the trees of the forest exult.

They shall exult before the Lord, for he comes;
    for he comes to rule the earth.
He shall rule the world with justice
    and the peoples with his constancy.

Psalm 100:2, 3, 4

Sing joyfully to the LORD, all you lands;
 serve the LORD with gladness;
 come before him with joyful song.

Know that the LORD is God;
 he made us, his we are;
 his people, the flock he tends.

Enter his gates with thanksgiving,
 his courts with praise;
Give thanks to him; bless his name.

Psalm 103:1–2, 3–4, 9–10, 11–12

Bless the LORD, O my soul;
 and all my being, bless his holy name.
Bless the LORD, O my soul,
 and forget not all his benefits.

He pardons all your iniquities,
 he heals all your ills.
He redeems your life from destruction,
 he crowns you with kindness and compassion.

He will not always chide,
 nor does he keep his wrath forever.
Not according to our sins does he deal with us,
 nor does he requite us according to our crimes.

For as the heavens are high above the earth,
 so surpassing is his kindness toward those who fear him.
As far as the east is from the west,
 so far has he put our transgressions from us.

Psalm 104:1, 24ac, 29–30, 31, 34

Bless the LORD, O my soul!
    O LORD, my God, you are great indeed!
How manifold are your works, O LORD!
    The earth is full of your creatures.

If you take away their breath, they perish
    and return to their dust.
When you send forth your spirit, they are created,
    and you renew the face of the earth.

May the glory of the LORD endure forever;
    may the LORD be glad in his works!
Pleasing to him be my theme;
    I will be glad in the LORD.

Psalm 108:2–7

My heart is steadfast, God;
    my heart is steadfast.
    Let me sing and chant praise.
Awake, lyre and harp!
    I will wake the dawn.
I will praise you among the peoples, LORD;
    I will chant your praise among the nations.
For your mercy is greater than the heavens;
    your faithfulness, to the skies.
Appear on high over the heavens, God;
    your glory above all the earth.
Help with your right hand and answer us
    that your loved ones may escape.

Psalm 116:12–13, 15–16bc, 17–18

How shall I make a return to the LORD
    for all the good he has done for me?
The cup of salvation I will take up,
    and I will call upon the name of the LORD.

Precious in the eyes of the LORD
    is the death of his faithful ones,
I am your servant, the son of your handmaid;
    you have loosed my bonds.

To you will I offer sacrifice of thanksgiving,
    and I will call upon the name of the LORD.
My vows to the LORD I will pay
    in the presence of all his people.

Psalm 118:1–4, 5, 19–25, 28–29

Give thanks to the LORD, for he is good,
    his mercy endures forever.
Let Israel say:
    his mercy endures forever.
Let the house of Aaron say,
    his mercy endures forever.
Let those who fear the LORD say,
    his mercy endures forever.

In danger I called on the LORD;
    the LORD answered me and set me free.

Open the gates of righteousness;
    I will enter and thank the LORD.
This is the LORD's own gate,
    through it the righteous enter.
I thank you for you answered me;
    you have been my savior.
The stone the builders rejected
    has become the cornerstone.
By the LORD has this been done;
    it is wonderful in our eyes.
This is the day the LORD has made;
    let us rejoice in it and be glad.
LORD, grant salvation!
    LORD, grant good fortune!

You are my God, I give you thanks;
    my God, I offer you praise.
Give thanks to the LORD, for he is good,
    his mercy endures forever.

Psalm 119:1–2, 4–5, 17–18, 33–34

Blessed are they whose way is blameless,
    who walk in the law of the LORD
Blessed are they who observe his decrees,
    who seek him with all their heart.

You have commanded that your precepts
    be diligently kept.
Oh, that I might be firm in the ways
    of keeping your statutes!

Be good to your servant, that I may live
    and keep your words.
Open my eyes, that I may consider
    the wonders of your law.

Instruct me, O LORD, in the way of your statutes,
    that I may exactly observe them.
Give me discernment, that I may observe your law
    and keep it with all my heart.

Psalm 127:1b–5

Unless the LORD build the house,
    they labor in vain who build.
Unless the LORD guard the city,
    in vain does the guard keep watch.

It is vain for you to rise early
    and put off your rest at night,
To eat bread earned by hard toil—
    all this God gives to his beloved in sleep.

Certainly sons are a gift from the LORD,
    the fruit of the womb, a reward.
Like arrows in the hand of a warrior
    are the sons born in one's youth.

Blessed is the man who has filled his quiver with them.
He will never be shamed
    for he will destroy his foes at the gate.

Psalm 144:1–2, 6–7, 9–10a, 15

Blessed be the Lord, my rock,
    who trains my hands for battle,
    my fingers for war;
My safeguard and my fortress,
    my stronghold, my deliverer,
My shield, in whom I take refuge,
    who subdues peoples under me.

Flash forth lightning and scatter my foes;
    shoot your arrows and rout them.
Reach out your hand from on high;
    deliver me from the many waters;
    rescue me from the hands of foreign foes.

O God, a new song I will sing to you;
    on a ten-stringed lyre I will play for you.
You give victory to kings;
    you delivered David your servant.

Blessed the people so fortunate;
    blessed the people whose God is the Lord.

Psalm 145:1–2, 8–9, 10–11, 13b–14

I will extol you, O my God and King,
    and I will bless your name for ever and ever.
Every day will I bless you,
    and I will praise your name for ever and ever.

The LORD is gracious and merciful,
    slow to anger and of great kindness.
The LORD is good to all
    and compassionate toward all his works.

Let all your works give you thanks, O LORD,
    and let your faithful ones bless you.
Let them discourse of the glory of your kingdom
    and speak of your might.

The LORD is faithful in all his words
    and holy in all his works.
The LORD lifts up all who are falling
    and raises up all who are bowed down.

Canticle of Mary (Luke 1:46–55)

My soul proclaims the greatness of the Lord,
my spirit rejoices in God my savior
for he has looked with favor on his lowly servant.

From this day all generations will call me blessed:
the Almighty has done great things for me,
and holy is his Name.

He has mercy on those who fear him
in every generation.
He has shown the strength of his arm,
he has scattered the proud in their conceit.

He has cast down the mighty from their thrones,
and has lifted up the lowly.
He has filled the hungry with good things,
and the rich he has sent away empty.

He has come to the help of his servant Israel
for he has remembered his promise of mercy,
the promise he made to our fathers,
to Abraham and his children for ever.

Canticle of Zechariah (Luke 1:67–79)

Blessed be the Lord, the God of Israel;
for he has come to his people and set them free.

He has raised up for us a mighty savior,
born of the house of his servant David.

Through his prophets he promised of old
   that he would save us from our enemies,
   from the hands of all who hate us.

He promised to show mercy to our fathers
and to remember his holy covenant.

This was the oath he swore to our father Abraham:
To set us free from the hand of our enemies,
free to worship him without fear,
holy and righteous in his sight
   all the days of our life.

You, my child, shall be called the prophet of the Most High,
for you will go before the Lord to prepare his way,
to give his people knowledge of salvation
by the forgiveness of their sins.

In the tender compassion of our God
the dawn from on high shall break upon us,
to shine on those who dwell in the darkness and the shadow
      of death,
and to guide our feet into the way of peace.